NOTICES

OF

MINING MACHINERY

AND

VARIOUS MECHANICAL APPLIANCES IN USE

CHIEFLY IN THE

PACIFIC STATES AND TERRITORIES

FOR

MINING, RAISING AND WORKING ORES

WITH

COMPARATIVE NOTICES OF FOREIGN APPARATUS FOR SIMILAR PURPOSES.

BY

WILLIAM P. BLAKE.

NEW HAVEN, CONN.
CHRALES C. CHATFIELD & Co
1871.

PREFACE.

The letter of instructions from the Secretary of the Treasury, in 1868, to the Commissioner of Mining Statistics, indicated as one of the most important subjects for inquiry, "the relative merits of the various inventions, machines, and mechanical contrivances in use or projected for the reduction of the precious metals, and for all other purposes connected with the business of mining and metallurgy."

At the request of Commissioner Raymond, the writer undertook the preparation of a report upon the subject, and notices of the principal mechanical appliances in use were submitted, and printed as Part IV of the Commissioner's report to Congress for the year 1870. The present volume is a reprint of that part, with some modifications. Under the circumstances, it was not possible to prepare a systematic and comprehensive treatise upon the machines used in mining, and this was not attempted. The time and means were limited, and only the intervals between other daily duties could be devoted to the work.

The notices were written in the winter of 1869–'70, and since the delivery of the manuscript there have been notable advances in the construction and use of mining machinery. The activity and enterprise of the miners of the Pacific slope is shown in the rapid succession of improvements. It is not possible in the ordinary course of publication of reports of this kind to keep pace with the march of improvement and discovery. However fresh and recent a description may be, before it can be published some new advance needs to be chronicled. For example, the diamond drill, described and commended to the attention of miners in these pages, has since been put into successful operation by prospecting in advance some of the gold mines of California. There has also been a fine example of subaqueous mining and blasting in the removal of Blossom Rock, one of the obstructions to the navigation of the harbor of San Francisco. Other blasting operations upon a large scale have been carried on at the Blue Point Tunnel, at Smartsville, California. Hydraulic nozzles, so constructed as to be readily adjustible to any angle, and under easy control, have been introduced. The new Stephens and Rawlings buddle is reported as being used with great success in concentrating the battery sands at Grass Valley. A 60-stamp mill, remarkable for its completeness and admirable arrangement, has recently been built by the Union Iron Works, of San Francisco, for the Eberhardt and Aurora Mining Company, at White Pine. The sixty stamps are grouped in six double batteries. There are twenty-two grinding and amalgamating pans, eleven settlers, and three agitators.

It is built upon a hill-side, so that the ore descends by its gravity from one machine to another, and is not handled at any stage of the treatment. The stamps are fed automatically, and even the quicksilver, strained from the amalgam, is returned by mechanism to its reservoir above the amalgamators. Automatic operation of machines is of great importance where labor is so scarce and high. Increased attention has of late been given to improvements in this respect.

WILLIAM P. BLAKE.

NEW HAVEN, CONN., *November*, 1870.

CONTENTS.

INTRODUCTORY.

SECTION I.

BREAKING DOWN ROCKS AND ORES.

SECTION II.

BORING AND EXCAVATING BY MACHINERY.

SECTION III.

TRANSPORTATION, VENTILATION, ETC.

SECTION IV.

BREAKING, CRUSHING AND GRINDING ORES.

SECTION V.

SEPARATION AND CONCENTRATION.

INTRODUCTORY.

THE MANUFACTURE OF MINING MACHINERY IN CALIFORNIA.

The great demand for mining implements of all kinds which attended the sudden development of gold mining in California was at first supplied from the Atlantic States and from Europe. Some of the first quartz mills erected in the State were imported from England. Relics of them may still be found in Grass Valley and on the Mariposa Estate. But this dependence upon eastern and foreign workshops did not long continue; founderies and machine-shops were started in San Francisco, and their extent and number has been increased to keep pace with the rapid enlargement of the mining field of the Pacific slope. With the constantly increasing discoveries of new districts, and the opening of new sources of gold, silver, and copper, the demand for machinery has been enormous and peremptory. But it has been most succesfully met by the mechanical engineers of the Pacific slope. Their work is characterized by great boldness, independence of precedent, ingenuity and originality; and they to-day furnish some of the best machinery in the world for certain departments of the art of mining.

The directions in which the greatest advance has been made are: 1. The improvements in breakers, stamp-batteries, &c., and the substitution of iron for wood in stamps and ore-dressing and concentrating machines. 2. The manufacture of pans for grinding and amalgamating. 3. The introduction of silvered and amalgamated copper-plates for saving gold and quicksilver. 4. The art of placer mining has been revolutionized; cumbrous and slow working hand machines have given way to gigantic operations which in their extent and effect approach those of Nature. The under current sluice is but one of the improvements to which the development of this art has led.

The effects of the discoveries, and of the improvements following them, have been wide-spread. Invention and production have everywhere been stimulated. Attention has been steadily directed to the invention of machines to be substituted for hand labor, especially in rock-drilling, and to the improvement of explosives, all tending to diminish the cost of moving rock and extracting the precious ore. Rock-drilling machines have passed through a great variety of modifications in the United States, and the Leschot diamond drill, which originated in France, here finds its greatest development and its most general and successful practical application.

The iron founderies and machine-shops of San Francisco have been sustained chiefly by the demand for mining machinery, and were most numerous and successful in 1865 and 1866, during the period of greatest expansion in prospecting and mining, and the formation of companies to develop claims and mining ground in all directions. The value of the castings produced at these founderies in the year 1866 is estimated at little less than two millions of dollars, the greater portion being for quartz mills and mining machinery. There were then thirteen establishments in full operation, employing about 1,000 men. The number of large establishments now in operation is somewhat less. In addition to the works in San Francisco, there are founderies in the other large cities, as Sacramento, Stockton and Marysville, Nevada City, and at nearly all the chief mining centers, where mills are built, shoes and dies cast, and repairs made.

The principal establishments in San Francisco at which mining machinery is manufactured are the Union Iron Works, the Pacific Iron Works, the Vulcan Iron Works, the Miners' Foundery, and the Golden State Iron Works.

The first named is the pioneer establishment, having been founded in the year 1849, by the Messrs. Donahue Brothers, upon a very limited scale, from which it has grown to be the largest and best appointed on the coast. At the commencement, the blast for melting was produced by a blacksmith's bellows, and the tools and materials were few and imperfect. At present, there are in the machine-shop twenty-five lathes, eight planers, and much powerful drilling, cutting, gearing, and shaping machinery. One of the planers is the largest in the State. The smithery is provided with a fifteen-ton steam hammer for forging large work, and the boiler department has automatic punching and riveting machines. The main building is of brick, three stories high, with a frontage of 187½ feet, and a depth of 120 feet. About 300 men are employed.

The Pacific Works were started in 1850. In 1867 they worked up 700 tons of pig iron, 350 tons of bar and plate iron, with 700 tons of coal; and the value of the product was $300,000.

The Vulcan, in 1867, worked up 1,200 tons of pig iron and 200 tons of bar and round iron.

This brief mention of some of the more important of the machine making establishments will serve to give a general idea of the capacity of the coast for the production of mining machinery.

California not only manufactures mills and machinery for the Pacific slope, for Nevada, Idaho, Oregon, Washington, and Arizona, but exports to British Columbia, Mexico, Central America, South America, Colorado, North Carolina, and, to some extent, to Australia. Its stamp-mills for gold quartz crushing are superior to any other, and are regarded as models to be followed. There is no country where so much money and effort has been expended in so short a time in experimenting with, and perfecting, the various machines used in mining; and although it may be said that there has been a great waste of material and money in the headlong, blundering way in which the progress has been made, it must be admitted that the result on the whole is more satisfactory than it would probably have been by this time, if every problem had been the subject of slow and careful deliberation. The great value of time and labor in these new and rapidly expanding metalliferous regions is to be considered, and likewise the enormous rates of interest, ranging from twelve to thirty-six per cent. per annum; the great cost of transportation, ranging from five to twenty-five cents per pound; and other conditions very different from those in older mining regions, so that it is not possible to make any just comparison between the one and the other without giving a fair consideration to these peculiar and difficult circumstances under which the development has been made.

In the following notices of the mechanical appliances of mining the attempt has not been made to give a complete description of them all. Neither time nor the space allowed permitted this; but it has been the endeavor as far as possible to describe the machinery and apparatus of mining now in use on the Pacific slope, and to add such notices of machines used abroad for similar purposes, and to make such comparisons as would be likely to interest and instruct those engaged in mining, and to furnish the data for a general reply to the natural inquiry, what is the position of the United States in this respect, compared with that of European countries.

The writer desires to make special acknowledgment to the Union Iron Works of San Francisco for drawings of stamp-mills, hoisting works, and other machinery, from which many of the illustrations have been reduced for these pages. He is also indebted, for valuable information, to Mr. Irving M. Scott, to Mr. Moore, of the Vulcan Foundery, and A. S. Hallidie, esq., president of the Mechanics' Institute.

For information concerning the machinery now in use abroad, he has consulted his own notes upon the machinery at the Paris Exposition, and elsewhere, and the works of Burat upon the machinery of the Belgian and French collieries. Having recently, in part, rewritten the report upon mining* in the series of reports upon the Paris Exposition, he has felt at liberty to make free use of those pages and of many of the illustrations, electrotyped copies of which had been secured for the purpose.

* Report on mining and the mechanical preparation of ores, by Henry F. Q. D'Aligny, and Alfred Huet, F. Geyler, and C. Lepainteur. Washington: Government Printing Office. 1870.

SECTION I.—AGENCIES AND INSTRUMENTS OF BREAKING DOWN ROCKS AND ORES.

CHAPTER I.

WATER—HYDRAULIC MINING.

The placer miner avails himself of the results of forces which have been acting for unnumbered ages. Frost, ice, and mountain torrents, aided by the decay of rocks, have broken down the veins and liberated the gold, leaving it distributed under the gravel and sand in the beds of ancient and existing streams. The force required for breaking up the rocks and veins has been expended and the work of the placer miner is rather to clean up, or harvest, what nature has already mined for him. But the operations of nature have been so vast, and so gigantic have been the deposits made by rivers and floods, that the pick, shovel, and pan are inadequate for the profitable collection of the gold, and other mechanical appliances are brought to bear. Powder and nitro-glycerine are used to blow up and disintegrate the deep and consolidated deposits; water under pressure is made to undermine and wash away high banks of gravel; powerful cranes and hoisting apparatus, and for some of the harder cemented gravels massive stamp-mills, are required.

As water was Nature's principal instrument in preparing these earth deposits, so, also, is water the surface miner's great agent for breaking down and reassorting them. It is brought to bear directly upon the materials, either with the momentum it acquires in falling from a considerable elevation, or with the gentler force of a shorter fall as it runs down a sloping channel. The first is the *hydraulic process*, and the second is *sluicing*. The operation of the first is to break and disintegrate, and of the second to separate, assort, and concentrate. In hydraulic mining, the two are necessarily connected and form one continuous operation. Water falling through pipes from a height of from 100 to 200 feet is delivered through nozzles in continuous streams against the base of a bank of earth. It undermines the bank; the overhanging masses fall to the base and are broken apart and loosened; the water penetrates every crack and pore; large boulders are thrown aside like pebbles; the whole mass is stirred and mingled, while the accumulated waters flow away down the slope thick with sand and earth, leaving the larger boulders and the gold resting clean-washed upon the surface of the bed-rock.

This process is applicable wherever deposits have accumulated to such a depth upon the lower stratum holding the gold that they cannot be economically removed by digging. For its successful operation there are two essential conditions: first, sufficient head or height and quantity of water; second, a rapid fall or slope from the base of the bank, so that the water will flow swiftly away and carry the loosened gravel, sand, and earth with it. In California there is comparatively little difficulty in attaining these conditions by an adequate expenditure of money. The high mountains give numerous streams flowing toward and across the gold region, and the deep valleys and ravines permit of ample fall and drainage. But the streams have to be diverted from their courses and carried in ditches and flumes for many miles along the hillsides, while in most cases the best gold deposits are in trough-like or basin-shaped depressions, hemmed in by rocky walls, through which artificial outlets must be cut, so as to give the requisite drainage.

Thus, when the position, depth, and richness of a deposit are ascertained, and it is decided to work it by the hydraulic method, the first operation is to provide an outlet for the water. This is done by cutting a tunnel through the rim-rock from an adjoining ravine or valley, so as to tap the lowest part of the basin, and, if possible, to secure a vertical fall of fifty to one hundred feet from the base of the deposit. Such tunnels are usually costly and laborious undertakings; they require great engineering skill for their proper projection, and often many years of time. In driving some of the longer tunnels, from five to seven years have been consumed and an expenditure of from $10 to $60 per linear foot incurred. They vary in length from a few hundred feet to a mile, and are usually from six to eight feet in width by seven in height.

MINING DITCHES IN CALIFORNIA.

In the year 1867 there were 5,328 miles of artificial water-courses for mining purposes in the State of California, besides the subsidiary branches, estimated at over 800 miles more. These water-courses are ditches cut, wherever possible, into the earth of the hillsides, and crossing rocky points and deep valleys by means of flumes, or, better, in iron pipes. The ditches are usually about eight feet wide at the top, six at the bottom, and three feet deep. The grade varies from twelve to eighteen feet to the mile. Formerly flumes were constructed on a large scale and at great cost; but now large sheet-iron pipes are substituted with great advantage in durability and economy. Some of the flumes were of great length and height; one near Big Oak Flat, in Tuolumne County, being 1,300 feet long and a part of it 256 feet above the surface and supported upon wooden towers. Upon the Truckee ditch there were, at one time, 13 miles of flume, eight feet wide and four feet deep, hung upon the side of a deep cañon. Upon the Pilot Creek ditch there was one piece of flume 300 feet long and 95 feet high.

The boards used for making flumes are usually from one and a quarter to one and a half inch thick. They are laid down rough and then battened. Sills are placed at intervals of two and a half feet, with posts and a cap for the support of the flume-box. The sills are four inches square, the posts three by four, and the caps one and a half by four inches. In addition to the first cost of a flume, it is expensive to keep in repair, and is liable to a great many accidents. It may be burned or blown down, and if it is left dry for several months, all the boards curl up and split so that they cannot be used again. It is said that the repairs of a flume cost 90 per cent. more than those of a ditch. For all these reasons, flumes are not now constructed where they can possibly be avoided, and iron pipes are substituted. These pipes are made of stout sheet-iron or boiler-iron, and vary in size from 10 to 40 inches in diameter, according to the quantity of water to be carried. From 7 to 11 inches is a common diameter for the smaller pipes, and these are made of No. 20 iron. A sheet two feet wide and six feet long will make two joints of 11-inch pipe. These joints are put together to form sections 20 feet long, and these sections are united upon the ground and secured by means of strong wire wound around two projecting ears or hooks of iron, one upon each section. The whole pipe is also firmly fastened to the surface by posts securely set in the ground, to prevent its weight from carrying it down the steep slopes. The examples of the successful use of pipes for carrying water across depressions and ravines are numerous. Upon the South Fork Canal, in Eldorado County, a pipe is used to carry 50 inches of water across a valley 1,600 feet wide and 190 feet deep. This pipe is 10 inches in diameter, the iron about one-sixteenth of an inch thick, and the supply end is ninety feet higher than the delivery. On the Excelsior Company's ditch, near Smartsville, there are five miles of low flume, 6,000 feet of 40-inch pipe, 3,000 feet of 20-inch pipe, and half a mile of 38-inch pipe. The 40-inch pipe crosses a depression 150 feet deep, and with a head of thirty-two feet carries 2,500 inches of water. Upon the Dutch Flat ditch there are 3,500 feet of 31-inch iron pipe and 837 feet of 32-inch pipe.

The aggregate cost of the ditches in California for the supply of water is reported as $15,575,400.* They are generally built by companies and owned distinct from the mining companies; and the water is sold to the miners at so much per inch per day of ten hours.

THE MINER'S INCH OF WATER.

The miner's inch of water is not a very definite and fixed quantity, for the methods of delivering it differ in different places. It varies according to the pressure or head and the height of the aperture. Usually the pressure is six inches, and the aperture is a horizontal slit one inch high and about twenty-four inches long, which can be closed to any desired degree so as to leave an opening one inch long, giving one inch of water, or ten or twelve inches long, giving corresponding numbers of inches of water. It is thus usual to consider the miner's inch as that quantity which will pass through an opening of one square inch area under a mean pressure or head of six inches. The quantity discharged from such an opening (one miner's inch) in twenty-four hours is equal to 2,274 cubic feet. A cubic foot is equal to 7.49 United States gallons, or thirty-eight miner's inches.

The Eureka Lake and Canal Company deliver water through an aperture two inches high and under a pressure of six inches. The amount delivered by them through an aperture twenty inches long and two inches high is considered to be forty inches. Upon the Excelsior ditch, and also upon the Sear's ditch, water is delivered under a pressure of ten inches, measured from the center of the orifice. Upon the Mokelumne Hill and Campo Seco ditch, water is delivered under a pressure of four inches. The Phœnix ditch Company deliver it through an orifice three inches high and under a pressure of four inches over the orifice. Upon the Gold Hill ditch, El Dorado County, a miner's inch has been measured out through an orifice two inches high and an inch wide under a four-inch pressure. Another ditch in El Dorado County has sold for an inch of water the amount that escapes through an orifice three inches high and an inch wide without pressure.

At Smartsville water is sold with a head of nine inches with a four-inch opening 125 inches long, giving 11.8 per cent. for an "inch" more than is usually given. The quantity discharged through an opening four inches deep, with a nine-inch head over the middle of the opening with the coefficient of discharge =.0615 is 106.6 cubic feet per hour, or 1.7767 cubic feet per minute.

A "head of water" is 500 inches daily for ten hours, and is the quantity required for a first-class hydraulic operation.

* Langley's Directory, 1867.

The distribution of the water to the hose-pipes is generally by a side iron pipe leading from the main pipe or reservoir, and connecting at the bottom with a strong cast-iron box. This box is provided with openings in different directions, to which the smaller pipes are fitted; and these again connect with flexible canvas hose, strongly made and covered with netting and bound at intervals with iron. They terminate in brass nozzles with orifices from two to three inches in diameter.

ECONOMY OF THE HYDRAULIC PROCESS.

It is not easy to estimate the average cost of washing by the hydraulic process. It requires not only very careful measurements of the bulk of the materials removed, and of the amount and pressure of the water used, but the nature of the material must be taken into the account, whether hard or soft, cemented or loose gravel, sand or stiff clay; for the rate of progress will vary greatly according to the resistance of the materials to the disintegrating or moving action of the water. The following, from a report made by the writer in 1859, may here be cited as showing the estimate at that time of the value of the hydraulic method compared with hand labor:

As a labor-saving process the results of this method compare favorably with those attained by machinery in the various departments of human industry where manual labor has been superseded. With one pipe of an inch and a half or two inches aperture and a pressure or head of ninety feet, a boy can excavate and wash as much auriferous earth in one day as could ten or fifteen men without its aid. It is common to estimate the work of a pipe as equal to the labor of ten men; in some locations a pipe of the size mentioned might effect more than twenty men in the same time. The water is ever active and untiring, and works as rapidly in inaccessible places as upon an exposed bank. The quantity of earth moved will, of course, vary greatly at different places, depending chiefly upon its character; whether sandy, a mixture of clay and sand, or clay alone. The amount of gravel and boulders also varies greatly in all gold placers. From measurements made last year in North Carolina, where a pipe of medium size had been in use at the Wilkerson placer, I estimated that with a head of sixty feet, and a pipe of one and a half or two inches in diameter, over a thousand bushels of earth could be moved and washed in a day. If this estimate is correct, earth which contains only the twenty-fifth part of a grain of gold, or about two mills' worth in a bushel, will pay about two dollars a day to a pipe. In washing by this process it is essential that the fall or descent of the bed-rock from the point being washed should be sufficiently rapid to insure a swift current in the waste water, so that it will carry the loosened sand and clay away in suspension or force it along the sluice boxes.*

In California, at Gold Run, upon the railroad divide between Bear River and the North Fork of the American, the gravel is very soft and deep; there is abundance of water under great pressure, and all the conditions are extremely favorable for the hydraulic process. It is not necessary to spend time in blasting the hard cemented gravel, as at Smartsville, or to puddle, as at La Porte or at Dutch Flat, to remove large boulders; the washing continues without interruption. Two men can do all the work in a claim that uses 300 inches of water. It is estimated there that one pipe will break down as much gravel as the water from three pipes can wash away; while at Dutch Flat three pipes are required to break down as much gravel as the water of one pipe can wash away. Estimating, as is there done, an inch of water to be equivalent to a supply of 145 pounds per minute, or 8,700 pounds per hour, it follows that 300 inches supplies 15,000 tons in a day of twelve hours. Estimating the quantity carried away by this water as equal to one-tenth of its weight (although one-fifth is generally allowed) it follows that 1,500 tons are moved, or 750 tons per day to each of the two men. It is not

* The gold placers of the vicinity of Dahlonega, Georgia.

supposed that this result is uniformly attained, but that it has been attained under favorable circumstances.

Mr. Laur, during his visit to California, in the service of the French government, estimated that with miners' wages at the uniform rate of twenty francs per day, the expense of the manual labor necessary for working one cubic metre of gravel by the several methods usually employed was :*

	Francs.	Centimes.
By the pan (about)	75	00
By the rocker (about)	20	00
By the long tom (about)	5	00
By the sluice (about)	1	71
By the hydraulic washing (about)	0	28

Being twenty-eight centimes, or about six cents per cubic yard for mining gravel by the hydraulic method. And this appears to include the cost of the water, for he states that during ten days 28,080 cubic metres of gravel were worked over with an expense for :*

	Francs.
Water	5,000
Manual labor	864
Sundries (about)	500
Total	6,764

From examinations made by Professor Silliman of the quantity of water used and of gravel washed upon the Blue Gravel Company's claim near Smartsville, it appears that 17,074,758.15 cubic yards of water were used to wash 989,165 cubic yards of gravel; hence, one cubic yard required 17.2618 cubic yards of water, equal to 3,486 gallons. † The whole amount paid out for water during 43 months was $57,261, at the rate of fifteen cents per miner's inch. The cost of water per cubic yard of gravel moved is five cents and seven-tenths, deduced from the foregoing; and it is stated by Black that in the Middle Yuba district, with the cost of water twenty cents an inch, the cost of mining a cubic yard of gravel is seven and a half cents.

TAIL SLUICING.

As an example of tail sluicing upon a large scale, the Teaff sluice, Dutch Flat, probably the largest in California, may be cited. The total length of this sluice is 5,500 feet; of this, 2,500 feet are 5½ feet wide and 26 inches deep, in a tunnel; and 3,000 feet of its length is six feet wide. It cost $55,000, and was four years building. Several companies deliver their tailings into it, with an aggregate of 1,550 inches of water. The bottom is paved with boulders, 14 inches deep, and the grade is ten inches in twelve feet; but it is believed that eight inches would have been better. The descent is broken at intervals of 120 feet by drops, or dumps, two and a half feet high in the tunnel and five feet outside. These serve to break up the masses of cemented pebbles, and thus liberate the gold. The force of the current in this sluice is such that boulders of rock ten and fifteen inches, and even twenty inches in diameter, are swept along at the rate of nearly ten miles an hour. This

* De la Production des Métaux Précieux en Californie, &c.
† Report upon the Blue Gravel Gold Mining and Water Company. Inedited.

constant pounding and attrition of the paved bottom of the sluice by the rolling rocks and gravel wear it rapidly away, this wear being as great as two inches of depth in three months; and half of the paving stones become broken, so as to be unfit for use.

From fifteen to twenty pounds of quicksilver are put into the sluice daily, in the evening; but as the sluice continually catches quicksilver, swept from the claims above, the owner is never obliged to buy any. He takes out more than he puts in.

Rock suitable for paving is selected from the round boulders swept down the sluice. They are stopped by means of a strong iron grating placed across the sluice in an inclined position. The spaces between the bars measure eight inches, so that only the larger boulders are arrested. A Chinaman, standing by the grate, examines every boulder that stops, and saves those suitable for the pavement.

Among other notable sluicing operations, the following may be mentioned: Hoskins's tail-sluice, at Indiana Hill ravine, in sections, the longest twenty-four feet in length, with intermediate abrupt pitches over rocks. There are fifteen boxes, six or eight feet wide and two or two and a half feet deep, with a grade of eight inches in twelve feet. Moody's tail-sluice, in Cañon Creek, double, two thousand feet long, each eight feet wide and about four feet deep. Kinder and White's tail-sluice, in the same cañon, has two sluices, eight feet wide and seven hundred feet long, grade three inches in twelve feet.

CHAPTER II.

HAND TOOLS.

It may at first, to many, seem trivial to devote much space to the form and peculiarities of tools used daily by miners; but this view will not be held when we reflect upon the importance, in the aggregate, of the proper construction of even the simplest and most common implement. With light, strong, and well-proportioned tools, the skillful miner can accomplish much more work in the same time than he possibly could with clumsily and roughly made ones. The American shovel and the American axe may be taken as familiar examples. No one who has sufficient manual dexterity to use them properly can fail to appreciate how far superior they are to other forms for the same purposes.

MINING PICKS.

There are three principal types of picks in use among the miners of the Pacific slope, the "surface pick" or ordinary excavating pick; the "drifting" or "quartz pick," and the "poll pick," and a pick for coal-mining. Of each of these forms there are several sizes and different weights, there being not less than 31 in all manufactured by John Wright, of San Francisco, who has made many improvements in the form and quality. I have received from him the following table showing the weight of each size from No. 1 to No. 31:

Picks manufactured in California.

Number.	Description.	Pounds.	Number.	Description.	Pounds.
1	Round-eye surface	4	17	Drifting	4½
2	......do	4½	18	....do	5
3	......do	5	19	....do	5½
4	......do	5½	20	....do	6
5	......do	6	21	Poll	4
6	......do	6½	22	....do	4½
7	......do	7	23	....do	5
8	Flat-eye surface	4	24	....do	5½
9	......do	4½	25	....do	6
10	......do	5	26	....do	6½
11	......do	5½	27	....do	7
12	......do	6	28	Coal	2
13	......do	6½	29	....do	2½
14	......do	7	30	....do	3
15	Drifting	3½	31	....do	3½
16	......do	4			

Surface pick.—Of the surface pick there are two different styles, the round eye and the flat eye. The first is the common round-eyed excavating pick, Nos. 1 to 7, weighing from 4 to 7 pounds, each succeeding number being half a pound heavier than the preceding. The 5-pound pick, No. 3, is about the medium and usual size, and is 27 inches long; No. 4 pick is 27½ inches long; No. 5 pick is 28 inches, and so on. The next numbers, from No. 8 to No. 14, are made with flat eyes, 3 inches by 1 inch, while the round eye are 2 inches by 3 inches for the medium size, varying a trifle with the size and weight of the pick. The lengths are about the same in both styles of eye. The round-eyed pick is generally used in surface or placer mining, and is probably the most convenient and serviceable pick for that work. The eye being large, it is easy to fit a handle, and it is less liable to break. The eye, as made by Mr. Wright, being lengthened or raised upon the handle from 2½ to 3 inches, gives a firm bearing to the handle, and is a great improvement upon the old style, which merely has a lip on each side of the eye. The flat-eyed picks have the same advantage; and they avoid all necessity for strapping the handle. This style is preferred for sluicing, as they do not spatter the water so much as those with the round and thicker eye. The heavier picks of these styles are used chiefly in grading and heavy digging in bed-rock.

Surface Pick.

The form of the surface pick is indicated by the figure, giving a side view of the medium-sized pick, drawn to a scale of one-eighth.

Drifting or quartz pick.—The five numbers, from No. 15 to No. 20, comprise the different weights of the "drifting" or "quartz pick" made sharp at each end. The medium size (No. 17) is 24 inches long with an eye 3 inches by 1 inch. The form is shown by the wood-cut.

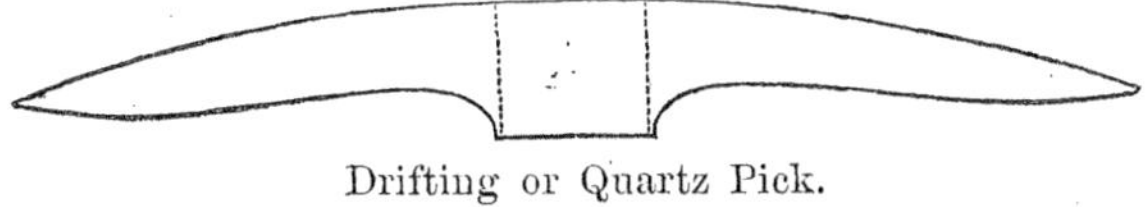

Drifting or Quartz Pick.

The weight of this form of pick ranges from 3½ to 6 pounds. The smallest size (No. 15) is used chiefly in contracted, narrow drifts, where there is not much room to swing the tools, and also in working out the gouge or selvage from quartz veins. The sizes 16, 17, and 18 are mostly used in drifts where there is plenty of room, and in pulling down rock. These picks also have the raised eye, and are a great improvement upon the old style. The latter are raised at each side, and have a bearing of only 1¼ to 1½ inch; while in this construction the eye is lengthened from 2½ to 3 inches, and thus gives a firm support to the handle. This is very important for the drifting picks, since they are much used in prying, and in the ordinary construction the handle is apt to become loose.

The poll pick.—The "poll pick" is a favorite form with miners, since it combines the long, sharp point for drifting and a hammer-head for striking and breaking the rock or driving gads. It is a pick and hammer combined. The form, with the raised or socket eye, as manufactured by Mr. Wright, is shown in the figure.

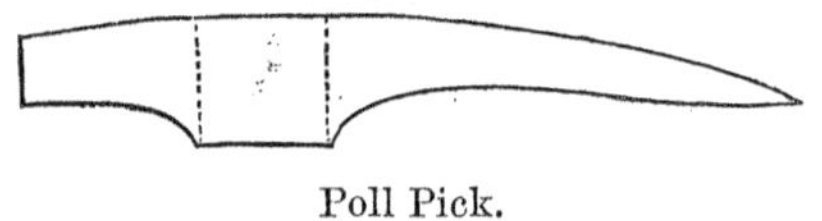

Poll Pick.

The medium size, (No. 23,) weighing 5 pounds, and about 16½ inches long, is most in use; but the weight varies from 4 to 7 pounds, some miners preferring the largest size. It is a form common in most quartz mines, and especially liked by Cornishmen. Such picks are made stout and strong. The hammer end or head in the medium size is 3½ inches long and the point about 10 inches, the eye being 3 by 1 inches.

These various styles of picks are made of the best quality of iron and steel, and for excellence and beauty of finish are unsurpassed. The handles are made of white hickory, are usually 36 inches long for the surface picks, and 34 inches for the drifting and poll-picks.

The poll-pick is evidently made upon the Cornish pattern. In Cornwall the head is usually about 15 inches long, and the handle from 24 to 26 inches. It varies in weight according to the ground to be worked; but 3 or 4 pounds are the most common weights—occasionally 5 pounds. For working downwards a 10-pound head is often used. The poll-pick is the most approved form for working in vein-mines throughout Cornwall, Derbyshire, and the north of England. The double-pointed pick is more used in collieries. Those used for under-cutting coal, called the "holing pick," have handles from 27 to 30 inches long, and in South Wales 34 inches. Picks with handles of unusual length are used in England at the Box Tunnel stone quarries, where the stone is soft and can be cut like coal, and has to be cut out in great blocks. The handles are from five to six feet long. When the men have struck the blow they drop the pick and then draw it out. In the extreme west of Cornwall, where the lodes are very narrow, only 3 or 4 inches wide, the miners use what is known among them as a "packer" or "poker." It is nothing more than a long wedge, and is common at St. Ives and at St. Just, and the peninsula of Land's End.

For purposes of comparison, the following table will be useful. It is compiled partly from the measurements of mining tools exhibited in the Museum of Practical Geology, attached to the Royal School of Mines, in London, as enumerated in the descriptive catalogue of that institution:

Dimensions of mining picks of several countries.

Number.	Length of handle.	Length of head.	Weight.		Description.
	Inches.	*Inches.*	*lbs.*	*oz.*	
1	26.0	17.7	4	8	Cornish poll-pick for hard ground: Length over eye, 2.2 inches; of poll-end, 3 inches; of pick-end, 12.5 inches; thickness (depth) at poll-end, 1.2 inch; at pick-end, 1.1 inch; width over eye, 3.1 inches; at poll-end, 1.2 inch; at pick-end, 1.1 inch; poll-end 8-sided; point set at 85° to handle.
2	26.5	22.6	2	10	Cornish poll-pick for soft ground: Length over eye, 2.1 inches; of poll-end, 3 inches; of pick-end, 17.5 inches; thickness at poll-end, 0.8 inch; at pick-end, 0.9 inch; width over eye, 1 inch; at poll-end, 0.8 inch; at pick-end, 0.8 inch; point set at 83° to handle.
3	29.0	15.4	4	6	Derbyshire double pick, used in rock or vein, with short points.
4	29.0	15.7	3	10	Derbyshire "slitter," double, one side pointed, the other horizontal edge, 0.4 inch wide.
5	28.0	10.7	4	6	Derbyshire poll-pick, (mandrel,) short, bluff point; for hard veins and rock, where "slitter" is too slight.
6	25.0	18.9	4	6	Northumberland, double, straight-armed; arms thickened in the middle, like two gads.
7	29.0	15.2	5	2	Flintshire, single-pointed, with short 8-sided poll.
8	29.0	21.0	5	14	Flintshire, double; one wedge-point arm, the other with horizontal, chisel edge, 0.1 inch wide.
9	19.1	17.0	2	12	Monmouthshire (coal) cutting mandrels; straight, taper directly from center to points.
10	20.4	17.0	2	14	
11	33.3	19.0	3	5	Monmouthshire holing mandrel, stronger and bluffer.
12	33.8	19.0	3	5	
13	33.3	18.0	3	8	
14	30.0	22.3	6	6	Monmouthshire bottom mandrel; curved, double-pointed.
15	30.5	21.3	7	3	Monmouthshire bottom mandrel; curved, 2 chisel arms—1 horizontal, 1 vertical.
16	30.7	24.0	9	5	Monmouthshire rock mandrel; curved, 8-sided arms—1 wedge-pointed, 1 chisel end.
17	27.6	17.2	3	10	Flintshire (coal) metal-driving pick; tapered V cheek-pieces.
18	28.3	18.0	2	10	Flintshire (coal) holing pick; tapered V cheek-pieces; chisel-edged arms, 0.1 inch wide, with strongly curved top surface.
19	27.5	16.3	3	0	Flintshire (coal) heading pick; tapered V cheek-pieces; slightly curved; arms taper regularly.
20	32.0	17.8	4	5	North of England, (coal;) lower edge horizontal; top, 2 inclined planes; in plan, a lozenge, diminishing from center.
21	32.0	18.0	4	5	North of England; like the foregoing, except that the arms are bent or anchored, meeting at 155°.
22	30.0	19.7	7	0	North of England stone pick; slightly anchored; tapering V cheek-pieces; arms beveled to 8-sided sections, with 4-sided pyramid at points.
23	30.0	23.0	8	0	North of England stone pick; like the foregoing, but stronger and more anchored.
24	27.7	13.6	5	6	Saxon pick; single armed; tapered octagonal section; no poll; greatest thickness, 1.5 inch; breadth over eye, 2.12 inches; head set at 85° to handle.
25	20.5	15.4	4	3	Russian poll-pick; slender curved arm; length of pick-end, 12.8 inches; greatest diameter, 0.7 inch; eye circular.
26	20.5	12.5	3	6	Russian gravel pick; single curved arm; blade broadens to a spoonbill near the point.

It is curious to notice how great are the variations in this apparently trivial tool among different nations. Yet the proper form of a pick is not unimportant. If it only affected by a small fraction (and it does more than that) the amount of work which a laborer can perform daily, its aggregate importance to the effective daily labor of the world could scarcely be estimated in money. Our American patterns are so excellent, that there is little excuse for those who do not select the tool best suited to the work.

The Saxon gad resembles a long slender hammer. It is furnished with a narrow rectangular eye. When in use, it is held by a handle inserted into this eye, and is driven by striking the poll-end. A common size is, length of the iron, 6.2; of the eye, 0.86; of the handle, 14.0; breadth across the eye, 0.95; greatest depth, 0.7—all in inches. The point is formed by a small bluff pyramid, and the poll-end also contracts suddenly. Weight, 10 ounces. As the Saxon miners are enabled, from the fissured character of the rock, to make considerable use of these gads, they carry them under-ground in sets of a dozen or fifteen, strung by the eyes upon iron stays, with a joint or yoke in the middle, so that the whole may be slung over the shoulder, the gads being equally distributed before and behind. The gad passes over, as it were, by degrees into the pick. Thus the *fimmel* is a large hammer-like gad, weighing, with handle, 2 pounds, 8 ounces, and having a head 10.2 inches and a handle 12.6 inches long. The small heavy poll-pick, weighing 7 pounds, 12 ounces, is very similar in form, but has a head 13.5 inches, and a handle 19 inches long. The ordinary German gads, and those of Hungary, are stronger and more hammer-like than those of Saxony. The Hungarian steel gads weigh 13 or 14 ounces, and the common gad 2 pounds 6 ounces.

HAND-DRILLS.

The hand-drills in California are made of English octagon steel, generally one inch in diameter for ordinary powder; sometimes, but rarely, 1¼ inch; and the striking hammers weigh from 8 to 10 pounds. For the new "giant powder" a three-quarter-inch drill is used, and the striking hammers weigh from 3 to 5 pounds. The use of proper copper-tipped tamping bars is rare, but safety-fuse is universally employed, so that the risk in using iron bars is somewhat diminished but is by no means removed.

The following pertinent observations upon blasting and hand-drilling are from notes of a lecture by Mr. Warrington Smyth, of the Royal School of Mines, England:

The introduction of gunpowder has been an immense boon to mining undertakings. It not only enables the miners to work upon rocks of great hardness at an economical rate, but it has led to the enlargement of such excavations as drifts and levels, and so placed the workmen in a better position as to ventilation, comfort, and health. Formerly the miners, when cutting the rock, were compelled, by the narrowness of the levels and smallness of the working places, to inhale the dust made by themselves in piercing the rock, and their lives were shortened in a frightful degree. The mines, since the use of gunpowder, have had to be arranged with greater regard for ventilation, and the cylindrical holes for the gunpowder are now often, while being bored, kept full of water, and the old injury to the breathing faculties are for the most part avoided. There are, of course, occasions and places where gunpowder could not or ought not to be used. Where, for instance, fire-damp is common, and it is necessary to use safety-lamps, the lighting of a fuse with an open match will be most dangerous. In many collieries a certain man is employed to fire the shots, whose duty is to test the places beforehand, and see that no gases are present in quantities sufficient to take fire; but, as we all know, accidents do occur very often, and it is much to be desired that the practice should be greatly restricted, if not done away with altogether. Another case in which gunpowder should not be used is where the seam is much fractured and fissured naturally, so that a shot would result in so large a proportion of small coal as to make the working unremunerative. Again, its use is inadmissible in quarrying marble, or other stone, where it is an object to obtain the rock in large and perfect masses. The methods of employing gunpowder are, to a great extent, the same in principle in all the mining districts of the world. At first in this country, as elsewhere, boring the holes proved a slow and imperfect work, but, nevertheless, it soon came to be observed that by cutting away underneath, and then blowing the rock or seam down by gunpowder, one man could do as much as six with a hammer and gad alone. This, then, at starting renders it possible for a mine to be taken up and worked to profit which could not formerly have been done. The hole is bored, the powder placed in it, either loose or in a cartridge, it is then filled up, or "tamped," to the surface, and a fuse having been arranged, it is fired, and the result is that a portion of the rock is blown down. The hole is bored with what is called in different places a "jumper," a "drill," (Fr. pistolet,) or an "auger"—a piece of iron with a sharp steel ending called "a bit," which may be shaped in various forms, and then struck in the hole with considerable force and dexterity by the workman, until gradually a sufficient depth is pounded out. In most cases it is struck with a hammer wielded by the borer single-handed, but sometimes one man holds the jumper, and turns it after every stroke, while two men strike alternate blows, and thus greatly accelerate the work. The larger augers are usually from one and one-half inch to two and one-half inches in diameter, and in Germany it has been proved by experiment smaller bits are not advisable. The material of which these borers are made has been a question of great importance. About eighteen years ago, the bar of the auger was almost always made of the best fibrous iron, the head being of steel, and the bit or edge of the best shear steel. In Derbyshire, however, they were accustomed to use cast steel, which in the fluor-spars usual there, of very moderate hardness, did very well, and lasted so long that borers bequeathed their augers to their sons; a very different state of things from that of other districts where an auger often would be worn out in a day. Cast steel, however, has been substituted generally for iron; and that because it is not only more economical, but the blow given on the head of an auger of cast steel is transmitted so much quicker to the edge as to give it a decided advantage over iron augers with steel bits. It had long been observed that when the borers had worked for some time with the iron augers some change in the metal was produced, and the blow became more effective than at first. Since 1852 steel augers have, however, become general, in spite of their greater first cost. In a case in North Wales, where very accurate accounts were kept, it was found that the use of steel borers decreased the cost of working nearly ten per cent. The form of the cutting edge varies a good deal. When the ground is moderately soft, the ordinary chisel-shaped edge prevails. In the Hartz it is often curvilinear. In Italy the borers have two edges at right angles, while in Mexico they are swallow-tailed. In all cases, however, the borer must be turned after every blow through a small portion of the circle, so that the edge never falls upon exactly the same place. When the bottom of the hole is clogged with the debris produced by the cutter, the hole is filled with water, which washes out a good deal, and a scraper takes out what is left.

There are many circumstances under which it is necessary to put down holes of a larger character; and then the augers are made larger and longer, and the hammers to strike it heavier. Stages are erected in such instances, so that on each stage several men may be placed to raise the auger, and thus a dozen men may at a word of command all lift and let go together. A jumper of this kind may weigh from two to three hundred-weight. In cases of this kind the spring pole may be used to advantage. This brings us to the question whether or not machinery may be employed for the purpose of boring, and whether it cannot be done at a less expenditure of human labor, and more rapidly.

Among the mining tools that attracted some attention at the Paris Exposition, was an apparatus for enlarging the holes in rock made by an ordinary drill, the object being to secure an enlarged space or chamber at the bottom of the hole for the reception of the powder. The apparatus is described in full detail in the Exposition Reports; but as it does not appear to be of any practical value, it is not repeated here. It is, however, well to mention that, in 1864, a miner from Humboldt County, Nevada, made a drill for the same purpose and in a similar manner. It was known as Linscott's Patent Chamber Drill, and was made, and tested upon granite blocks, at San Francisco. It consisted of a bar of steel or iron, about two and a half feet long, with movable cutters, or steel blades, about two inches long, fitted into recesses, one on each side. These, when passed to the bottom of the hole, would fly out and cut upon the sides of the hole when the drill-bar was struck upon the top with a sledge. In this way, a chamber some three inches in diameter could be made at the bottom of an ordinary one or two inch hole.

The various forms of apparatus for drilling by steam-power or compressed air are described in another chapter.

CHAPTER III.

EXPLOSIVES.

"Nothing is more surprising, considering how early gunpowder was invented and used for the purpose of piercing and shattering the bodies of men, that so great a length of time should have elapsed before its application to the purpose of blasting rocks in mining. The discovery of gunpower for warlike purposes took place in 1354, but it was not introduced into mining until the last century. In a curious old book, published in 1700, entitled 'Familiar Discourse Concerning the Mine

Adventure,' which, among other things, compares the use of gunpowder as a newly introduced system of blasting with the old method of wedging down the material in mines, its use for mining purposes is supposed to have been first proposed at Freiberg, by Martin Weigal, in 1613, but the idea met with little countenance, and it was not till 1631 that it began to be generally employed throughout Saxony, the Hartz, and North Germany. The practice was first adopted in Englend in 1670, at the Ecton Mines, in North Staffordshire, but the blasting at that time was but a clumsy process, and was used to blow in pieces masses of rock which had already been freed from their beds by other agencies. We must not, however, be led astray by statements in books respecting the earlier use of gunpowder in mines, as the older references to 'firing' belong to the still more ancient practice of 'fire-setting,' which dates from a very early period, and was, no doubt, employed by the Romans."*

Even so late as the year 1862, gunpowder had not been introduced in mining in Japan, and it was introduced there for the first time by Mr. Pumpelly and the writer, acting in the capacity of mining engineers to the Japanese government. Up to that time the miners of Nipon and Yesso had cut their way through the rocks by means of the pick and gad, aided sometimes by fire, and they were very greatly astonished when they saw the hard rock at the end of a drift, abandoned by them because it was too hard to cut, thrown down by means of a few ounces of powder.

The consumption of powder for mining purposes upon the Pacific Coast and in our mining Territories has always been large. A part of this is of course used in the construction of roads and grading for railways, but of late the consumption for breaking up the hard cemented conglomerates of the deep placer deposits has greatly increased. For this purpose very heavy charges are employed. Tunnels are driven inwards for 40 to 70 feet from the face of the bank, and cross-tunnels run for 100 feet each way, so that the excavation has the form of the letter T. A charge of from 100 to 500 kegs of powder is placed in the cross-tunnel, and the whole is simultaneously ignited by electricity. The effect is to lift the whole deposit, and to shatter and loosen it to such a degree that the rest of the disintegration is readily effected by water.

Two companies, with adequate capital, are organized for the manufacture of powder in California. The demand for powder for those regions which usually draw their supply from California, is reported to considerably exceed 200,000 kegs annually.

The works of the California Powder Company are the only ones now in operation. At the mills of this company, situated at Santa Cruz, there were manufactured as stated in the following table:

Powder manufactured in California.

Year.	Blasting powder. Kegs.	Sporting, cannon, and musket powder; equivalent to kegs.	Total.
1867	150, 454	7, 269½	157, 723½
1868	63, 033	6, 871½	69, 904½
1869	130, 151	2, 439	132, 590
	343, 638	16, 580	360, 218

* From notes of a lecture by Mr. Warrington Smyth, at the Royal School of Mines, London Mining Journal, January, 1870.

Besides the above there has been some powder made at the Marin Mills, probably not exceeding 30,000 kegs of blasting powder, in the years 1867 and 1868. With the facilities now possessed by the California Company, they can turn out 640 kegs of powder daily. The kegs contain 25 pounds each.

The materials for making powder are abundant and accessible in California, with the exception of niter, which is to a great extent replaced by nitrate of soda from Peru. The peculiar dryness of the air in California for the greater part of the year permits this more deliquescent salt to be successfully used; and, with proper precautions in the manufacture, it makes excellent powder. The capacity of the two mills is over 1,000 kegs of powder daily. A recent modification of the manufacture promises important results. Glycerine is added to the grains in some way not yet made known, and it is said to greatly increase the strength.

Works for the manufacture of safety-fuse have recently been erected in San Francisco, so that the miners can now obtain an article superior to that which is imported.

Notwithstanding the familiarity which all who use powder must gain with the many causes of accident, it is extraordinary that there should continue to be so much carelessness and recklessness in its use. One of the British mining inspectors says that in blasting an iron instead of a wooden or copper rammer is still too often used in getting the wadding and first part of the stemming fairly bedded upon the powder, and shots which have missed fire are still drawn, although experience shows that, even with water in the hole, the drill goes in advance and fires the powder. Accidents are also frequently caused by driving the pricker down into the powder.

The mineral statistics of Victoria, Australia, give exact returns of the quantities of gunpowder issued at each of the mining districts where there are magazines. In the year 1867 the quantity in stock, at the commencement of the year, in all the districts was 71 tons 16 hundred-weight; the quantity issued during the year, 196 tons 13 hundred-weight; the quantity received during the year, 186 tons 12 hundred-weight; and the quantity in stock at the end of the year, 61 tons 15 hundred-weight. In many parts of the colony, however, there are no magazines, and great quantities of blasting powder are used there, of which there is no accurate return.

NEW EXPLOSIVE COMPOUNDS.

In introducing the subject of the new explosive compounds, which are now attracting much attention from engineers and miners, I cannot do better than to cite from the authority mentioned at the commencement of this chapter:

Of all explosives used for blasting powder is the most largely used, and continues to be the most popular. It has been, however, proposed, and that many years ago, to mingle with it various substances, and it has been tolerably well made out on the Continent that the effects of powder have not been deteriorated by a moderate proportion of sawdust being mingled with it. Within comparatively a very few years propositions have been made to completely change our explosive agents—as, for instance, by gun-cotton, which seemed to be peculiarly adapted for blasting purposes. It is difficult to enter upon the comparative merits of different classes of explosives on account of the great jealousies which are indulged in respecting them. This is the case even with powder, every separate manufacture of which has its advocates. Gun-cotton has, however, been most successfully employed in many places, among which may be mentioned the important quarries of the Austrian government up the Danube. In England an improvement in its manufacture was made some time ago, by which it is produced in the form of a rope, and can thus be cut off into convenient lengths. By the newer method, manufactured on a considerable scale by Messrs. Prentice, of Stowmarket, it is made into a pulp, and then compressed so as to take up less space. But even in its rope form gun-cotton has an advantage over gunpowder, as, taking weight for weight, it will do five or six times the work of gunpowder. Besides this, six ounces of powder will occupy eight inches of a bore-hole of given diameter, while one ounce of gun-cotton, which has the same explosive power, will take up only five and a half inches. Then, gun-cotton makes little or no smoke, although the small vapor it leaves is deletorious, if it may be judged by the sensation of headache and dimness of eyes, which it produces. Another important explosive is nitro-glycerine. A year or two ago I might have said a good deal as to its coming into play with advantage, and its general adoption in this country, particularly in North Wales, where it was much used. Indeed, in some mines and quarries, when it was left optional with the men (who for the most part are a careful race, and to be trusted in such matters) to use either gunpowder, nitro-glycerine, or gun-cotton, a considerable proportion preferred nitro-glycerine. They not only found that its explosive force was tremendously greater, but that it was more convenient. Thus, when the bore-hole was completed it had only to be filled full of water, and the nitro-glycerine poured in. By its greater specific gravity the latter sinks to the bottom, and then the introduction of the fuse, in connection with a copper cap at the bottom, was attended with no difficulty or danger, and the results of the explosions were tenfold. Unfortunately, the carelessness of those who had charge of nitro-glycerine gave rise to fearful accidents last summer, and in a sudden panic, as it seems, an act of Parliament was passed, which has practically made its use penal. It is true those who want to use it are allowed to make it on the spot, but every one knows that that permission is of little value, since its manufacture requires a good knowledge of chemistry. Mining agents and managers, therefore, very naturally get rid of the difficulty by giving up its use, and for the present, therefore, in this country it may be said to be tabooed. If, however, the risk attendant upon its conveyance can be got over, it seems a great pity to shut out from mining operations a blasting agent of such enormous power and utility. It has, therefore, been prepared in the form of a powder, called "dynamite," the invention of M. Nobel, of Hamburg.

Before giving a description of this new material, now largely used upon the Pacific coast, the nature and properties of nitro-glycerine will be briefly noticed.

NITRO-GLYCERINE.

Nitro-glycerine was discovered in 1847 by M. Sobrero in the laboratory of Professor Pelouze; but public attention was not directed to it as an explosive until the labors of M. Nobel, a Swedish mining engineer, were made known.

This liquid is obtained by the action of concentrated nitric acid, or of a mixture of nitric acid of 40° strength and sulphuric acid of 66°, upon glycerine. It is formed like pyroxyline, and is, in fact, a trinitrate of glycerine; the reaction being represented by:

$$C^6 H^8 O^6 + 3 NO^5 HO = C^6 H^5 O^3 \; 3 NO^5 + 6 HO.$$

It is a yellow liquid, resembling olive oil, without odor, and possessing a sweet, slightly fragrant taste. Taken into the stomach or absorbed through the skin, as of the hands, it is poisonous, and its vapors give violent headaches. It is soluble in alcohol and ether, but not in water.

It can be heated up to 212° Fahrenheit without decomposition; but at about 360° it detonates with extraordinary violence. It detonates when struck by a hammer on a hard surface or even upon wood, and the mere opening of a wooden box in which tin cans of the oil were packed has been known to explode it.

Pure nitro-glycerine does not appear to be liable to explode spontaneously, but if impure and acid it changes into a mixture of oxalic acid and glycerine, and may explode.

Of gunpowder, according to theory, only 50 per cent. is converted into gas, one volume giving 260 volumes of cold gas, deduction being made for the expansion produced by heat. Practically, however, the combustion is never so complete, and 200 volumes of the cold gas are, therefore, in all probability, above the average result.

In the combustion or explosion of nitro-glycerine seventeen equivalents of oxygen out of the eighteen are absorbed by combining with the carbon and hydrogen, thus leaving one equivalent of oxygen free. Each one hundred parts of the oil when exploded produce by weight:

Water	20.0 parts.
Carbonic acid	58.0 parts.
Oxygen	3.5 parts.
Nitrogen	18.5 parts.
	100.0

And, as the specific weight of the blasting oil is 1.6, one volume produces:

Steam	554 volumes.
Carbonic acid	469 volumes.
Oxygen gas	39 volumes.
Nitrogen gas	236 volumes.
A total of	1,298 volumes

It is assumed that the heat generated by the explosion of nitro-glycerine is at least twice that generated by gunpowder; consequently, if a volume of powder gives 200 volumes of cold gas, expanded by heat four times = 800; a volume of nitro-glycerine gives 1,300 volumes of cold gas, expanded by heat eight times, producing 10,400 volumes; so that nitro-glycerine possesses about *thirteen times* the power of gunpowder when volumes are compared, and eight times its power for equal weights, the specific gravity of powder being taken at 1.0.

It is claimed by the agents for the article in San Francisco that one pound of the blasting-oil will produce effects equal to ten pounds of gunpowder. The first requires but one bore hole, whereas for the powder about ten holes of the same dimensions will be required.

But the sad experience with this dreadful explosive has been such as to prevent its general introduction in mining. Californians will never forget the destruction of life and property which a single box of it wrought in an instant at the office of Wells, Fargo, & Company in San Francisco. This, and the destruction of a vessel at Aspinwall, and several other dreadful accidents in various parts of the world, have been a practical refutation of the theories of the comparative safety and harmlessness of the oil under ordinary circumstances of storage and transportation. These accidents, showing the impossibility of controlling this agent of such wonderful power, led to the introduction of a modification of it in the mixture now known as *dynamite*, or "giant powder."

GIANT POWDER OR DYNAMITE.

The invention of this compound dates from 1867, and it has been in use for nearly two years at some of the mines upon the Pacific coast. It is formed by mingling nitro-glycerine with infusorial earth, and it resembles moist sawdust in appearance. A company has been organized for its manufacture in San Francisco, and the consumption of it is steadily increasing.

The following descriptions of the powder, its properties, and the methods of using it have been supplied to me by the general agents for the Pacific coast, Messrs. Bandmann, Nielsen & Co., of San Francisco:

General properties.—It is an ungrained powder, of a grayish brown color, with a specific gravity of about 1; insoluble in water, and not affected by time or exposure to air or moisture. It congeals at about forty-two degrees Fahrenheit. It sometimes produces a temporary headache when taken into the mouth or stomach. The same effect also follows its continued handling. In the open air, or in ordinary packing, it burns without exploding. Its combustion produces carbonic acid, oxide of carbon, hyponitrous acid, and water.

There are three, and only three, methods of exploding it: 1st. By a violent explosion either in it or into it. 2d. By confining it in a very strong and tight vessel, and setting it on fire, or heating the vessel sufficiently. 3d. By a percussive shock so intense as to produce heat and violence equivalent to an explosion. Unlike gunpowder, its explosion is instantaneous—the entire mass of powder explodes as if it were a single grain. This quality, in connection with its extraordinary evolution of gases, causes its explosive effect to be especially great in solid substances, so much so that the powder cannot be used in ordnance or fire-arms, the gun being blown to pieces instead of being discharged. Its explosion produces carbonic acid, nitrogen, oxygen, and water.

Packing, transportation, and storage.—The powder may be packed, stored, and conveyed in all the ordinary ways. The fact that the powder is explosive, naturally suggests the idea that it is dangerous; but it is in reality no more so than corn meal. Practically, it cannot be exploded by accident. It requires design and careful preparation to explode it. The only practical caution necessary is to keep other explosives away from it. Fire alone will not explode it, nor heat in any form—they will burn it to ashes, like saltpetre paper, without exploding it. Nor will any amount of mere weight upon it, or simple pressure of any kind, explode it. It cannot be exploded by any of the ordinary movements, accidents, or incidents which attend its handling, transportation, or use. The pressing it into cartridges, or ramming it into bore-holes with a wooden rod, however hard, throwing it about, or jostling it in transportation, or even the crushing or violence of overturning wagons, collisions of cars, or explosions of boilers, will never explode it. But heat and pressure combined will explode it, provided they are of the proper kind and degree. It is exploded by any violent explosion either in it or into it, whether of gunpowder, fulminate, nitro-glycerine, giant powder, or other violent explosive. Such an explosion involves the peculiar percussive pressure and heat necessary. The burning or flashing of gunpowder unconfined is not sufficient.

Another method of exploding it is to set it on fire while under confinement in some tight and strong vessel. The burning of the powder produces gases which, finding no escape, at length cause a pressure so great as to produce, with the heat of the burning, an explosion of the unburned powder. By tight and strong vessels is meant iron retorts, quicksilver flasks, gas-pipe, with caps screwed to its ends, and the like. A vessel of the strongest tin has not the requisite strength; this, like cartridges of paper, ordinary packing-boxes, barrels, casks, &c., will be burst asunder by the gases before the pressure is sufficient to cause explosion. These are the only known means of causing an explosion proper, but a partial explosion can be produced by causing a very thin layer of powder to be struck with great force between hard and smooth surfaces, as, for example, striking a minute quantity with a hammer on an anvil, or driving an iron plug upon it in a hole drilled in the iron. In these cases, a slight explosion and detonation follow, but not of sufficient force to explode any part of the powder present, except the few particles in immediate contact with the impinging surfaces.

Utensils for blasting.—Except in special cases, it is better to use the powder in the form of cartridges. It is more economical in both time and powder, and the explosion is more certain. Cartridges of various sizes are prepared and sold by the company. Should others make them, let it be done with strong material, well glued or pasted together, and let the powder be very firmly pressed into them. Cartridges may be cut into such lengths as may be required, care being taken to prevent the loss of powder by rolling the sections in additional paper, or otherwise. Ordinary blasting fuse may be used, but to make sure of a discharge in all cases, and to keep the powder from being burned by fire from a leaky fuse the best gutta percha fuse is recommended, and of a size to fit the caps precisely. Caps manufactured for the special purpose of exploding giant powder are furnished by the company. Common percussion caps cannot be used. As these special caps are more heavily charged with fulminate than ordinary ones, corresponding care should be taken in their handling and use. A pair of cutting nippers, with their edges blunted, used in securing the caps tightly and firmly to the fuse. A tube with a funnel mouth will be useful in charging with loose powder. Tin tubing in sections may be useful in guiding cartridges into submarine bores.

Drill holes, charges, &c.—As to the diameter and depth of holes, and where they should be made, and the direction they should take, and also as to the quantity of powder to be used, and many other matters, no definite or arbitrary rules can be laid down for blasting with any explosive. In these things there must be variation according to the location, character of the material to be blasted, the purpose of the blast, and other circumstances too numerous and complicated to anticipate. Much must, therefore, be left to the good sense and experience of the blaster. The following observations and examples will afford some assistance to a beginner:

As a general rule, the drill holes and charges for giant powder can be, and should be, comparatively small. Experience has proven that ⅞ inch octagon steel with 3½ pound hammers, used by single hand drillers, are best adapted to use the powder to the greatest advantage. Holes one inch in diameter are abundantly large for all ordinary heavy work; for light work, correspondingly smaller ones should be made. A small quantity in a deep hole, whether the hole is large or small; also, a small quantity in a large hole whether the hole be deep or shallow; also a large quantity in a small but deep hole; also, a large quantity in a large but shallow hole, are all examples of misapplications; they are all violations of the general rule applicable to all explosives—that the quantity of powder should not only be proportionate to the resistance, but the hole should be proportionate to the powder.

As by reason of its quickness giant powder in bore holes is nearly as effectual without tamping as with it, it can be exploded with great advantage without any tamping at all in natural fissures and artificial cracks. It is therefore urged that advantage be taken of this extraordinary quality as often as practicable.

Owing to the great difference in the capacity between the old and new powder, the tendency will be to overcharge; it is therefore recommended that each blaster experiment on this point, so far, at least, as to ascertain the minimum quantity of powder which will answer his particular purpose.

Examples.—A solid cast-iron ball, seven inches in diameter, charged with half an ounce of giant powder, in a three-quarter inch hole, three inches deep, without tamping, will be blown into small fragments. The same result will follow the explosion of three-quarters of an ounce at the center of a wrought iron anvil. A six foot cube of solid granite charged with an ounce of giant powder in a three quarter inch hole, nine inches deep, will be cracked into several pieces. Boulders three or four feet in diameter, and particularly flat ones, can be cracked in pieces by exploding an ounce or two of powder on their surfaces. An ordinary rifle will be blown to pieces by a charge of giant powder of one-half of the weight of an ordinary charge of gunpowder. A charge of from one to two pounds of powder in an inch hole from five to ten feet deep, placed ten or fifteen feet back from the face of the wall, in hard rock, will crack off or shatter the whole intervening mass.

Charging.—The charge in the form of cartridges must fit and fill the bottom of the bore, and be packed solid. This is an essential prerequisite to an effective blast. The best way to secure it is this: Take a cartridge, as near as possible, of the same size of the bore, and cut it into sections from one to two inches long. With a hard wood rammer, as long as will run freely in the hole, press these sections into the bore hole one by one with sufficient force until each section is driven to the bottom and expanded laterally, so as to fill the hole solidly in every direction.

Any sized cartridge may be used, provided it is thus put in. Metallic rammers must not be used. In wet holes the sections of cartridge should be rolled in additional paper, and the ends closed to prevent the powder from getting mixed with water. In many mines the giant powder is used *loose* in downward holes. It is poured through the funneled tube into the drill hole. Economy requires that the tube should reach to near the bottom of the hole. The charge should be rammed down in divisions, substantially as directed as to cartridges.

Priming.—After charging the bore, cut off a proper length of fuse and insert its end into one of the special caps up to the fulminate. If the fuse is too large for the cap pare it to a fit; if too small, wrap it with paper. But the difference between the size of the fuse and the caps should be very slight. Then place the edge of the nippers across the cap near its edge, and indent it firmly into the fuse. Never do this with the teeth. Now cut off about one inch of the smallest sized cartridge, and roll it in additional paper, and insert the cap with the fuse attached into the powder about the length of the cap, and press the powder firmly about the cap. Then close the neck of the cartridge about the fuse, and fasten it there by a strong string, or some other means, in such a manner as to prevent the cap from being withdrawn from the powder. To make sure that the cap and cartridge do not get apart, it is better, in all cases, not only to tie the cord about the neck, but also to tie the ends afterwards around the naked fuse close to the mouth of the cartridge. This is called the primer.

Thus prepared, place the primer in the drill hole, and press it with the hand or a wooden rod into contact with the charge.

In using loose powder, if it is within reach of the hand, instead of using a primer a capped fuse can be used to explode it, taking care to press the powder around the cap, and secure the fuse in place by putting a stone upon it, or otherwise.

Tamping.—After priming, fill the bore hole with water whenever it can be done, and when it cannot, blast without tamping.

Considering the slight advantage of any other than water tamping, the time taken to apply it, the danger of disturbing or exploding the cap, and the inconvenience of repriming in case of miss-fire, it is better not to use it.

Explosion of blasts.—The burning of the fuse explodes the cap; the explosion of the cap explodes the primer or charge in which the cap may be. All the other cartridges or charges in the same hole are exploded by the first explosion of powder.

In case the blast misses fire, put in another primer.

A space of several inches, either vacant or filled, between several charges or cartridges in the same hole, will not prevent the simultaneous explosion of all. In case the blast is not effective, it will be because our directions have not been followed, or because the blaster has erred in some matter left to his discretion. The most common causes of failure are deficiency of powder and defective ramming.

It may be stated here that the great advantage claimed for this powder consists not so much in diminishing the cost of powder as an item of expense as in diminishing the cost of using it. The difference in the cost of powder is trifling in comparison with the difference in the cost of drilling, charging, tamping, convenience in wet work, and effectiveness of blasts. Giant powder, as a general rule, throws rock less and breaks it more, and extends its effects much deeper than ordinary blasting powder; and those who use it soon learn not to judge of a blast by first appearances. It frequently happens that a blast which seems to have had no effect proves to have done remarkable execution in cracking and loosening the rock, and preparing the way for subsequent blasts. This is especially the case in tunnels and shafts.

Blasting under water.—Cartridges to be used in water should be made of such paper as will not be destroyed or materially weakened by the water. They should also be weighted with sand in their bottoms, or in some other way, so as to sink. To use such as are not thus weighted, in water, they must be forced to their places, and fastened there by pouring sand upon them or otherwise. In submarine work, where the bore is at a considerable distance below the surface of the water, the tubing, in sections, can be used to guide the weighted cartridge to its place.

If submerged rocks have to be removed, all that is required is to take a large or small box of giant powder, in bulk, as the case may be; bore with a gimlet a hole into the box; fasten, as before mentioned, the cap well to the fuse, and push the cap through the hole its length into the powder, never further; tighten the gimlet hole with some grease or wax; tie additional weight to the box, light the fuse, which only requires sufficient length to allow the box time to reach the rock when sunk, and drop the same on the rock to be blasted. Some use special submarine fuse, which withstands the pressure of the water to any depth. In this way the entrance to the great San Francisco dry dock has been cleared from rocks, under the superintendence of the late efficient engineer, Mr. Pollock. As much as one hundred and twenty pounds of black powder at one blast were lowered, more than once, on a certain rock near or in front of the dry dock and exploded, and nothing was effected but throwing up a beautiful column of water. Mr. Pollock sunk on the same rock a box with ten pounds of giant powder, and the first blast shattered the rock to pieces. Six-pound boxes were then used, Mr. Pollock fearing the enormous effect of larger blasts might injure the dry dock proper; even these blasts proved too powerful, and at last only two-pound boxes were used, which successfully removed all the rocks.

Temperature.—Below 42 degrees Fahrenheit giant powder freezes, and above 212 degrees (the boiling point of water) it throws off noxious fumes, and becomes weakened and finally destroyed. It should, therefore, be kept in some place having a temperature between these extremes. When frozen, it can be thawed by being kept for a time in this proper temperature. When it becomes soft to the touch it is ready for use. As it freezes very slowly, no inconvenient haste is required in its application. If the powder in boxes or cartridges has from accidental causes become wet, if dried again slowly its usefulness is not impaired.

Effect of the giant powder on the health.—Some miners suffered from headache when this powder first came into use; but this was caused by the impossibility of procuring the raw material at the beginning of the business in a pure state. This has long ago been obviated, and since that time we hear of no complaints of headache, except produced by some of the following causes. We have numerous affidavits from miners that it never affected them, and that they never suffered any headache from its use. The causes which can produce a temporary headache are the following: Either from handling the powder too much, tasting it and rubbing it between the fingers, and afterward unconsciously rubbing the face with the hands, when not used to it, or from going immediately after a blast into a badly ventilated tunnel or shaft, which is invariably done by new consumers, to see the effect produced by this new blasting agent. The enormous power of the giant powder in its explosion drives away for a short while the little good air which is at the end of a tunnel; the space is then partially filled with gases. In case the charge is not entirely exploded, but part of it burnt, this burning of the powder creates the noxious fumes which cause headache; or the fumes are caused by improperly securing the cap to the fuse, and the cap and fuse to the primary cartridge. It is of very great importance that this should be done properly. Those who are familiar with its use never experience any inconvenience from its use when the whole charge is properly exploded. A little quicklime placed near the hole to be blasted, or some ammonia placed in a vessel near the blast, will absorb these gases in a few minutes. If men not accustomed to this powder will stay out of the shafts or tunnels which are badly ventilated, after the blast is exploded, only one-half of the time they do after black-powder explosions during the first few days, no complaints of headaches would ever arise. It may not be generally known, but it is nevertheless a fact, that if black powder produced no smoke, (which forces men to stay out a certain time,) and they should go in immediately after a blast, they would experience the same headache. This is sufficiently proved by persons of science. The gases liberated by exploding giant powder are carbonic acid gas, oxygen, nitrogen, and steam, and those from gunpowder are the same; but gunpowder, in addition, has carbonic oxide.

Pipe-clay bank blasting.—It has so far been a very expensive operation for the miners to break up pipe-clay and cement banks to enable them to extract the gold by sluicing. Long tunnels had to be run, with a T at the end, in which were placed from fifty to one thousand kegs of common powder; the tunnel was then filled up again and the blast fired. The bank was always thrown over in large pieces of clay or cement, which were afterwards broken to pieces by picks and gads, and often with small blasts—a very laborious and expensive proceeding. Recently, in this kind of work, giant powder has been introduced, which overcomes all difficulties, and shows itself so far superior to the old process, and saves so enormously in cost, that it cannot fail to be speedily introduced in all bank blasting work. In a bank of pipe-clay about seventy feet high a hole six inches in diameter was bored horizontally, with an auger, twenty-six feet deep and a few feet above the ground. Into this hole one hundred pounds of giant powder, in cartridges six inches in diameter, was introduced and well rammed, and the blast fired. The result was surprisingly successful. The blast did not throw the bank over into enormous pieces to be broken up again, as is always the case where black powder is used; but the blast crushed and crumbled the entire bank, seventy-five feet on each side of the blast, in such a manner that when the water is turned on it can all be washed down without additional work.

Use in vein mining.—The giant powder has been in use for nearly two years at the Oakes and Reese mine, in Hunter's Valley, near the Mariposa Estate. A letter from there, January, 1869, is as follows:

We have used the powder entirely since last April. In its use the steel consumed is of uniform size—three-quarter inch octagon. Hammers (short handles) weighing three and a half pounds. The country rock is hard and tenacious. The veins of quartz are narrow, varying from ten inches to three feet, generally running from one foot to twenty inches in width, with little or no gouge.

The system which Mr. Cassel, superintendent of the mine, has introduced, (and which can only be used to advantage with giant powder,) is to pay the miners by the foot in depth of hole drilled—the miner doing no blasting, nor does he handle any rock, his simple duty being to drill holes where instructed.

The underground superintendent or head blaster—one for each shift—instructs the miner where to drill a hole. When the hole is drilled to the depth required the superintendent measures it and takes a memorandum of the same, and sets the miner at work elsewhere. As soon as the hole is measured the blaster loads it with from two to two and a half ounces of loose powder, fills the hole with water, covers it, and leaves it until the men leave it at time of shift. As soon as the men have left the mine, the blaster with his fuses, with cap or exploder attached, makes his round, and, removing the cover from the hole, drops the fuse into the hole, works the exploder into the powder, which is quite soft, fires the fuse, and in a few minutes will explode all the holes drilled during the working shift. As soon as the explosions are made the rock men and skip men clear away the debris which may be in the way of drilling new holes, and when the men again come into the mine there is work for them ahead in drilling. A blast is only fired when the men are at work on the mine when it becomes necessary to remove material. Thus it will be seen no time is lost in blasting.

My experience since April last leads me to know the following facts in the use of giant powder as against gunpowder:

First. The amount of work which can be performed in a given space in a mine is nearly double.

Second. The consumption of steel is about one-half.

Third. The consumption of hammers is about one-half.

Fourth. The consumption of candles is about one-half.

Fifth. The width of the drifts or stopes is only about one-half, requiring so much less material to be removed or hoisted from the mine.

Sixth. The mining timbers are shorter.

Seventh. The ore raised from the mine is broken by the force of the powder so as to require less spalling for the mill.

Eighth. The progress of the work in the mine is expedited at least forty per cent., and in wet mines the progress is increased fully fifty per cent., if not more.

* * * * * * * * * * *

So far as the miner is concerned, he can earn more money with a three-quarter-inch steel and small hammer, than in any other way. It is true he must earn his money, and is not paid by the day. The price paid in the Oakes & Reese mine is 37½ cents per foot of hole drilled. In October, there was drilled 6,476⅝ feet of hole, costing $2,429 03. The following list will exhibit the amounts earned by miners most expert in the use of single-hammer drills in October, twenty-seven working days.

P. Beicai	$130 20	H. Laity	$97 36
L. Boivin	124 33	F. Gill	94 62
J. A. Wilson	131 77	F. Lastrade	90 70
B. Kendall	103 77	J. Fortuna	94 56
S. Cox	122 25	H. Boyle	91 77
S. Uran	130 74	J. Martin	90 49
B. Picard	104 50	L. Battiola	84 93

and many others ranging below the above amounts, falling short either because not working full time, or from not being expert in use of the single hammer. Still, any system of mining where a miner willing to work can earn as high as $131 77 per month of twenty-seven working days, must inure to the benefit of the miner, and particularly so when the mine owner is willing to pay such wages. One thing is certain, that with giant powder and the use of small steel and hammers, the miner must earn his money, and cannot shirk his work, as is too often the case under the old system of mining.

Mr. L. L. Robinson, the president of the Giant Powder Company, writes under date of January 25, 1869, to the Mining and Scientific Press, as follows:

EDITORS PRESS: Noticing in your paper of the 16th a communication having reference to the use of giant powder in the Oakes & Reese mine, belonging to Mr. McAllister and myself, I beg to state that during the past week our superintendent, Mr. Cassel, has let the following contracts for work on the mine:

1. Sinking the main shaft 50 feet from the 278-foot level, at $60 per foot—contracting parties furnishing everything.
2. Drift west, on Oakes & Reese vein, 50 feet, at $13 per foot—contractors furnishing everything.
3. Drift south, 50 feet, at $10 75 per foot.

The same work has heretofore cost us, with the use of black powder, as follows:

1. Sinking main shaft, $90 per foot.
2. Drift west, Oakes & Reese vein, $30 per foot.
3. Drift south, blue lead, $25 per foot.

Thus it will be seen that in these three contracts the mine owners save as follows:

1. Sinking 50-foot shaft, at $30	$1,500 00
2. West drift, 30 feet, at $17	850 00
3. South drift, 50 feet, at $14 25	712 50
Total saving	3,062 50

In addition to the saving in dollars and cents, is also the important item of saving in time, as the time occupied in finishing contracts with giant powder is only about one-half the time required with use of ordinary powder.

The contractors, even at these low rates, are better satisfied with the prices than under the old prices with the common powder.

Giant powder for railroad work.—The Central Pacific Railroad Company, in running their long "Summit Tunnel," commenced the use of nitro-glycerine, and found it so very effective and advantageous that they were enabled to complete the tunnel in over one year less time than if ordinary powder had been used.

How much this saving of time of over one year has been worth to the Central Pacific railroad can hardly be estimated. It is well known that giant powder possesses about the same strength as nitro-glycerine, without any of its dangerous qualities. At the time the above work was done, giant powder had not been invented, otherwise it would undoubtedly have been preferred to nitro-glycerine. The Western Pacific Railroad Company, the Oregon Railroad Company, and the Virginia and Truckee Railroad Company have used, and are using, the giant powder.

In conclusion, Messrs. Bandmann, Nielsen & Co., give the annexed recapitulation of the chief advantages attending the use of the giant powder:

1. A great economy in labor for boring.
2. The rapidity of blasting operations, which is of vital importance, especially for mines and railway tunnels, can be made with giant powder in one-half the time, or less, than with black powder.

3. Perfect safety in carrying, storing, and handling it.
4. A complete combustion, which leaves no smoke or noxious gases.
5. The quickness of explosion is so great that fissured rocks and clay are easily blasted with it.
6. Great saving in wear and tear of tools, and in consumption of steel and fuse, fewer bore-holes being needed.
7. No tamping but water or loose sand being required, the loading is attended with no risk, but with a saving of time and expense.
8. In boulder blasting in gravel claims it is very superior, as in all ordinary boulders, too large to be easily removed by manual labor, a small charge of giant powder in a hole made with a half-inch drill and three-pound hammer, will shatter the boulders so they can easily be handled.
9. Its use under water or in water-bleeding rock is very simple and the effect very great.
10. It is very useful for blasting heavy blocks of iron, steel, or metal, which cannot be blasted by gunpowder, but easily yield to small charges of giant powder.
11. For military purposes, in springing mines and removing palisades.

A fair trial never fails to prove a complete success. The first blasts are conclusive as to the great superiority of giant powder over gunpowder, but its full economical value can only appear when those who use it use single-handed drills, and at the same time gain experience enough not to waste its power by overcharging or requiring impossibilities of it.

The consumption of giant powder in California is reported (1869) to vary from 12,000 to 15,000 pounds per month, and to be increasing.

EXPERIMENTS WITH GIANT POWDER.—In offering the giant powder to the several steamship, steamboat, railroad, and express companies to be transported, some doubts were expressed as to its safety; invitations were therefore given to several officers of these companies to witness a few experiments with the powder, designed to test its qualities in this respect and satisfy such doubts.

Accordingly, on the 27th day of March, 1868, near the company's works in San Francisco, the powder was subjected to the following tests, in the presence of Charles E. McLane, of Wells, Fargo & Co.; C. J. Brenham, of the California, Oregon and Mexico Steamship Company; B. M. Hartshorne, of the California Steam Navigation Company; W. M. Hughes, of Hughes & Keys, of Stockton, and several other gentlemen. The following is the record of results:

First Experiment.—A box strongly made of ½-inch pine boards, and filled with about 3 lbs. of giant powder, firmly packed, was thrown from a perpendicular height of 30 fee- upon a rock. The end upon which the box struck was broken in and the powder cont siderably displaced and compressed, but not exploded.

Second Experiment.—At the suggestion of Mr. McLane, 8 cartridges, each containing 4 ounces of powder, were firmly bound together with a strong cord and thrown repeatedly from the same height upon the rocks below. Several of the cartridges were indented, bent and bruised, but not broken. Finally the cord was cut by the rocks and the cartridges separated. No explosion.

Third Experiment.—A similar bundle of cartridges was placed upon a large rock, with a rough surface, and heavy stones, weighing from 10 to 30 lbs. each, thrown from the same height upon it. The cartridges were flattened and broken open, and some of the powder spilled and ground into the rock. No explosion.

Fourth Experiment.—A box of the same size as in the first experiment was filled partly with cartridges and partly with loose powder. A common fuse, without any ca p, was inserted in the loose powder, and the cover of the box screwed on and the fuse lighted. The loose powder was set on fire, causing a formation of gases, which forced the boards apart, and escaped with a hissing noise like steam. There was no explosion. The loose powder was burned while the cartridges were unaffected except by being scorched. In this state one of the cartridges was taken from the box and exploded in the ordinary manner, with terrific effect.

Fifth Experiment.—A similar box was now filled with cartridges, from which Captain Brenham selected one at random, for the purpose of testing it. The box was then closed tightly, and placed upon an open fire and consumed, powder and all, without exploding. During the burning, slight noises were heard from time to time, indicating the bursting of the cartridges. The cartridge selected by Captain Brenham was now exploded in the usual manner, with the usual effect.

Sixth Experiment.—A heavy tin cylinder, 1 inch in diameter and 8 inches long, was packed full of loose powder, a fuse without a cap inserted, and the end of the cylinder then tightly plugged. A small portion of the powder about the fuse was burned, the plug forced out with a noise like the drawing of a cork, and the fire extinguished. The cartridge was then thrown into a fire and consumed without exploding.

Seventh Experiment.—Six cartridges, each containing 4 ounces of powder with a capped fuse in one of them, were placed 2 or 3 inches apart in a horizontal crevice in a cliff of hard rock, without tamping or other means of confinement. The cartridges were all exploded together; there was but a single report. The bluff above the crevice, to the extent of many tons, was completely shattered.

Eighth Experiment.—The box of powder used in the first experiment was now placed on a flat, hard stone, about 9 square feet surface, and fifteen inches thick, and exploded in the proper manner. The rock was broken into fragments, none of which was larger than a man's fist, and the ground was torn up and blown out to a considerable depth.

Ninth Experiment.—Two handfuls of loose powder were exploded upon a rock similar to that in the eighth experiment, but imbedded in the earth. The portion of the rock above ground was crumbled into small pieces, while that below was cracked and shivered in every direction.

Tenth Experiment.—A section of 2-inch common gas pipe, about 4 feet long, was placed upon the ground, a 2-ounce cartridge inserted loosely in each end, leaving the tube between the cartridges—a space of about 3½ feet—entirely empty. In one of the cartridges was placed the usual fuse and cap and nothing in the other. No tamping was used, or other filling or fastening. The ends of the tube were not more than half filled by the cartridges. Both cartridges exploded at once. Each end of the pipe for about a foot was blown off, and into small fragments, leaving half of the remainder split open and flattened out as by a hammer, and the other end flaring and jagged.

DUALIN.

Another powerful explosive compound has recently been brought before the public and patented in the United States. It is known as *dualin*, and appears to be a mixture of nitro-glycerine and nitrogenized cellulose, made from sawdust. It was first introduced into Germany in April, 1869. In many mining districts, especially in mines belonging to the Prussian government, it is now used in the place of common powder, and has taken the place of nitro-glycerine and dynamite, (giant powder.)

Lieutenant Dittmar, the inventor, and the manufacturer of the article at Boston, describes dualin as a powder:

It is fabricated in six different degrees of strength, the use of which will depend on the degree of hardness and toughness of the material intended to be subjected to the action of the powder. Dualin will, if lighted in the open air, burn without exploding; but, if confined, may be made to explode in the same way as common powder. It is not sensitive to concussion; will not decompose by itself, nor cake or pack together, and may be readily filled into cartridges or blast-holes, requiring no other than water-tamping. It matters not whether the place where it is stored be warm or cold, dry or damp. Dualin has from four to fifteen times the strength of common powder, and is, therefore, stronger than nitro-glycerine or dynamite. The advantages claimed for dualin over other explosive agents are—

First. It may be stored, transported, manipulated, and applied with less risk than common powder.

Second. It may be used in cold weather without first requiring the warming process, which nitro-glycerine and dynamite require, as they frequently become inexplosive at a low temperature.

Third. Its explosion does not develop any noxious gases.

Fourth. Absolutely cheaper than either nitro-glycerine or dynamite, dualin is also relatively cheaper than common powder, for, possessing four to fifteen times the strength of the latter, its use will proportionably reduce the labor and cost of mining and blasting operations.

Fifth. The effect of a dualin explosion is to tear and rend the material exposed to its action, less than to pulverize it, as is the case with nitro-glycerine when applied to mining and blasting operations in coal and rock.

Sixth. Dualin, when confined, does not necessitate the application of an exploder, but may be exploded by a blasting fuse, like common powder.

Seventh. Its great want of sensitiveness to concussion, renders dualin a suitable material for the bursting charge of shells.

Eighth. Dualin may be stored for long periods without losing any of its strength.

Ninth. Dualin may for days be subjected to the action of water without losing any of its strength. Tin cartridges are, therefore, never required, not even for submarine blasting or blasts where water-tamping is used; and in shipping dualin packed in paper or thin wooden cartridges, ready for use, the only object is to save the consumer time in charging his blast.

Directions for use.—Dualin is shipped in boxes containing the cartridges, all ready for use; the degree of the powder, the number of cartridges contained in each box, the weight, diameter and length of each cartridge being plainly marked on the box.

1. The common blasting fuse may be used whenever rock, sand, brick or clay is used for tamping. In this case the treatment of dualin is entirely analogous to that of common blasting powder.

2. Exploders are required for firing charges.

A. When no blast-hole having been drilled, the powder is simply placed on the surface of a boulder, &c., which it is intended to break.

B. When submarine blasts are to be made, or water is used for tamping, or the blast-holes contain water.

C. When electricity is employed as a means of igniting the charge.

For heavy charges it will be well to use more than one exploder. The effect of the explosion depends greatly on the cartridge exactly fitting the blast-hole. Whenever ordinary tamping is used it should be packed as compactly as common powder requires. Blast-holes that will hold water require no other but water-tamping.

Mr. F. Shanly, the contractor upon the Hoosac Tunnel, has had some experiments tried with dualin at the tunnel, and certifies that he has used about 20 pounds, manufactured by Lieutenant Dittmar, and, so far as an opinion could be formed upon so limited a quantity, he considered it fully equal to nitro-glycerine in its results, while for safety in handling, it was proved by the most severe tests to be vastly superior.

In several of the blasts water-tamping was used. The charges were fired by means of electricity, using Mr. H. Julian Smith's battery. The same battery has been in service for some time past, in the operations of the Hoosac Tunnel, and it is but just to state that in regard to the density of the spark developed, as well as to simplicity of construction and compactness, a more serviceable battery could hardly be recommended to the attention of all engaged in mining or blasting operations. This battery will be described in a future chapter. Another compound called xyloïdine is manufactured at the same establishment.

The Journal of Applied Chemistry observes as follows in respect to the qualities and strength of dualin:

This compound, which, according to its inventor, Mr. Dittmar, possesses the explosive power of nitro-glycerine, together with the slow combustibility of ordinary gunpowder, consists principally of nitrate of ammonia and fine sawdust, that has been acted upon by nitro-sulphuric acid. This material, according to Fuchs, is undoubtedly endowed with a greater explosive force than ordinary powder; it is also considered as being less dangerous in regard to spontaneous explosion. In its composition it is similar to that of gun-cotton, being also subject to gradual decomposition in moist air. In regard to the efficacy of the dualin, as compared with dynamite, (which is a mixture of nitro-glycerine and infusorial sand,) the inventor states that they are both equal in this respect. However, it is extremely difficult to get at comparable results in blasting experiments; in most instances, the experimenter must be satisfied with the average results of a great number of trials undertaken under various conditions. But it is nevertheless easy, in one respect, to fix a difference between the two materials, which leaves no doubt as to the superiority of the dynamite. If equal quantities of dynamite and dualin, provided with primers, are allowed to explode upon air plates of equal strength, the effect indicates such an evident difference that one must adjudge to the former a much more rapid and violent action. This will certainly be recognized in blasting rocks. In price dualin is cheaper than dynamite. When coming in contact with fire, it will certainly cause explosion, as it burns quite as rapidly as ordinary powder. Of the dynamite, however, it is sufficiently established that it will never explode on holding a flame near it, but simply burn quietly, even if inclosed in strong wooden boxes. Against pressure and concussions, both blasting materials are equally inert, and, finally, dualin possesses the advantage over dynamite that it does not freeze, while the latter, when in a frozen state, cannot be directly exploded. But as blasting is mostly suspended during frost, this circumstance is not of very great importance; moreover, the use of dynamite is not excluded at all, if frozen, as it will readily yield by the explosion of a small cartridge containing non-solidified dynamite. The great superiority of dynamite, above all, consists in its non-liability to become moist; this property allows its direct application under water and in bore-holes, while dualin, like gunpowder, does not bear contact with water.

The objection thus urged against dualin is contradicted by the inventor, who declares it to be insensitive to moisture.

PYROXYLINE, XYLOÏDINE, GUN COTTON.

The name pyroxyline is given to the very inflammable and detonating compound produced by the action of concentrated nitric acid upon cellulose, or substances such as cotton, linen, hemp, paper, and sawdust. The name xyloïdine was given by Braconnet, in 1833, to the white, pulverulent, and very explosive substance he had obtained by treating starch with many times its weight of concentrated nitric acid.

The preparation of gun cotton for mining purposes has been greatly improved. It is now made into pulp, and then compressed into solid cylinders, which burn harmlessly when ignited in the open air, but explode with intense violence when confined and ignited by a detonating compound.

In its old form, it was experimented with at the Gould & Curry mine, in Nevada, with apparently good results. A report of these experiments states that a 1¼-inch hole, twenty-eight inches deep, in hard and tightly-bound rock, charged with six inches of cotton and exploded, threw down as much rock as an ordinary charge of gunpowder, without producing any smoke.

OLIVER'S POWDER.

A new powder, under the above name, has been manufactured near Wilkesbarre, Pennsylvania, for some months past, by the Luzerne Powder Company, a corporation organized by some of the principal coal operators of that region. It is believed that the invention is calculated to be of great public benefit, by reducing the risk and danger in the manufacture of powder, and by producing, at the same time, a safe and powerful explosive. General Oliver's patents refer to both the ingredients used and to the machinery employed in the manufacture of the powder. In composition, the principal difference between this and other powders is the substitution of peat for charcoal; and this, together with the method of manufacture, produces an article which, it is claimed, has invariably shown, in the "powder prover," a strength from twenty to thirty per cent. greater than that of Dupont's, Hazard's, Smith & Rand's, or any other powder now in use in the coal region. The sporting powder of the Luzerne Powder Company, as compared with the finest brands of rifle powder, is stated to give a much higher velocity, and consequently a greater penetration to the ball; to foul the gun less; and, like the blasting powder, to produce less smoke than do the powders now in use. The machinery used in the manufacture is very simple and inexpensive, and only a very small quantity of powder is at any one time in the mill, and that, while unconfined, is inexplosive. The success attending the manufacture by the Luzerne Powder Company has been sufficient to induce the company to determine on building a second mill near Hazleton, Pennsylvania.

Another substitute for charcoal, which has been tried with favorable results in the manufacture of gunpowder, is the mineral known as Grahamite, and occurring in West Virginia. Its application for this purpose has been patented by Dr. Van der Weyde, of New York.

CHLORATE OF POTASH POWDER.

A so-called "safety explosive compound" has been patented in England, by Mr. Percy A. Blake, of Aberdeen Park. The constituents of this compound are sulphur and chlorate of potash, in the ratio of one of the former to two of the latter. These substances are kept separately and dry, and are mixed when required. The powder burns slowly when ignited, but explodes under percussion. This explosion is effected by means of a detonating tube of metal, about an inch long and $\frac{7}{32}$ of an inch in diameter, partly filled with the compound and with fulminating mercury, and lastly with powder. This powder may be ignited by any ordinary ignition apparatus.

The first attempts to make powder with chlorate of potash, sulphur, and carbon, were those of Berthollet, in 1788. In 1792, experiments in its manufacture were made at the works of Essonne under his direction; but they were stopped by a terrible explosion which destroyed the lives of the director of the works, his daughter, and four workmen. Berthollet, who was with the director, had a wonderful escape. The explosion was caused by the end of the director's cane striking some of the powder upon the floor.

It has also been attempted to use various mixtures of the chlorate with white sugar and prussiate of potash and with charcoal and sulphuret of antimony and starch; but all these compounds are exceedingly dangerous to manufacture or transport, and it does not appear probable that they can ever come into general use.

For mining purposes a mixture of tan-bark, chlorate of potash and sulphur has been made at Plymouth, England. The tan is soaked in a warm solution of the chlorate, and afterward covered with a film or layer of powdered sulphur. This preparation is said to burn but slowly in the open air, but when confined, as in the hole of a boring, it explodes with great energy.

Picrate of potash has also been experimented with, and used for torpedoes, but its preparation has led to some frightful accidents; that at the Sorbonne, in 1869, killing five persons and wounding many more.

EXPLODING CHARGES BY ELECTRICITY.

Franklin, in 1751, and Priestley, in 1761, suggested the possibility of applying the electric spark for the ignition of gunpowder charges; but electricity was not practically applied until about thirty years ago, by the French military engineers, since which its use has become general. It was employed to ignite the great blasts that destroyed the Round Cliff at Dover, and to remove the wreck of the Royal George; and has been largely used in heavy blasting with powder and nitro-glycerine in California and for exploding torpedoes under water.

The variety of contrivances is very great. Many exploders have been devised to act either by heating a piece of thin wire, introduced in the circuit of a battery and placed in the charge, or by the passage of a spark produced by an electro-magnetic machine or Ritchie coil through a sensitive explosive compound, thus causing a local explosion sufficient to ignite the whole charge.

Among those who have given great attention to this subject, Baron Von Ebner, of the Austrian military engineers, may be specially mentioned, and Mr. Abel, of the British war department, who has devised one of the best exploders known. A spark generated by revolving magnets is made to pass through a mixture of subphosphide and subsulphide of copper and chlorate of potash—materials of high conducting power and extremely sensitive to the spark. One of the great difficulties in the way of making such exploders is the liability of the materials to be merely thrown aside and not exploded by the passage of the spark.

In the United States inventors have been active in devising different forms of apparatus for igniting explosives. They all depend upon either the direct passage of a spark or the heating up of an imperfect conductor, immersed in an explosive mixture. This mixture and the arrangement of wires are inclosed in a small cartridge of paper or wood, which can be readily placed in the midst of the powder in the hole to be exploded. Mr. Stowell patented, in 1862, a peculiar form of cartridge containing the ends of the conducting wires and a strip of platina. Beardslee, in 1863, patented a very simple mode of making an imperfect conductor between the ends of two wires, by drawing a pencil mark, of graphite, upon the surface of a piece of dry wood. Mowbray, in July, 1869, patented an improved electrical fuse for exploding charges of nitro-glycerine. It consists of a small cartridge of powder, in the top of which is placed a small quantity of a composition, like that used by Mr. Abel, made of sulphide of copper, 9 parts; subphosphide of copper, 2 parts; chlorate of potash, 3 parts, the whole intimately mixed. The ends of the wires are immersed in this mixture. It is designed especially to be inserted in cans of nitro-glycerine, to be exploded in oil wells.

The dealers in the new explosive compounds, such as nitro-glycerine, dynamite, and dualin, furnish exploders especially designed for the several preparations. These various exploders may be fired either by the voltaic current or by a spark from a suitable electrical machine, or the Page coil. An electrical machine has recently been invented and patented by Mr. H. J. Smith. The following is a description and the claim: *

The object of this invention is the production of an electrical machine constructed with especial reference to portability, and to working in all conditions of the atmosphere. It is designed more especially for igniting charges of powder by means of the electric spark which it evolves.

It is well known that the electrical machine, as commonly constructed of glass, becomes wholly inefficient in a damp atmosphere, such as prevails in tunnels and mines. This is due to the fact that glass so very readily condenses moisture upon its surface, in the form of a continuous film. Vulcanite, on the contrary, does not so readily condense moisture. Nor does it condense moisture in the form of a film, but rather in the form of detached drops.

The machine consists of an outer covering or shallow box, containing a frame plate, a Leyden jar or condenser, a generating plate of vulcanite, and devices for operating the generating plate and condenser in connection.

The frame plate, the condenser, and the generating plate are placed parallel to each other, and parallel to the sides of a box about a foot in diameter.

The condenser is connected to the frame plate by four posts, 1, 2, 3, and 4.

The generating plate of vulcanite lies between the condenser and frame plate, and is revolved on its axis by means of a handle or crank.

The axis of the generating plate passes tightly through a stuffing box, which may be made to grasp the axis more or less tightly, by means of a packing screw.

The outer end of the axis has its bearing in a small hole sunk in the outer vulcanized plate of the condenser.

The generating plate of vulcanite revolves between two cushions, the surfaces of which are coated with an amalgam, as is usual with electrical machines.

The cushions are provided with flaps, which flaps serve to prevent the electricity from escaping from the generating plate until the excited portion of its surface arrives in the neighborhood of the collectors, which are serrated strips of metal, placed one on each side of the generating plate, and both collectors are attached to and in metallic

* Vide letters patent, No. 93,563, August, 1869.

connection with the frame post 4, and by it are brought into connection with the inner plate or surface of the Leyden jar or condenser.

The two outer plates or surfaces of the condenser are in metallic connection with the post 2, and also with the cushions by means of post 3.

The inner plate connects with post 1, as well as with post 4.

The condenser is constructed in the following manner:

When the vulcanite is in a plastic state, upon a layer of vulcanite is placed a layer of tin-foil. Over the layer of tin-foil there is placed a second layer of plastic vulcanite, and then a second layer of tin-foil. A third layer of plastic vulcanite, a third of tin-foil, and a fourth of vulcanite, complete the jar or condenser.

The first and third layers of tin-foil form the outer surfaces of the condenser, the middle layer forming the inner surface.

Care must be taken that the diameter of the tin-foil plates be less than that of the layers of plastic rubber, excepting a small projection from each tin-foil plate, intended to connect with the posts of the frame. The condenser, thus made up, is then submitted to the baking or vulcanizing process, at the end of which it becomes hard and rigid. Its surfaces will forever remain in a perfectly dry condition.

The posts 1, 2, 3, and 4, are now screwed into the condenser, posts 1 and 4, as before stated, connecting with the inner surface, while posts 2 and 3 connect with the outer surfaces.

To the outer casing are attached two knobs. These knobs are electrodes, or paths for the discharge of the electricity when they are brought into contact with the inner and outer surfaces of the condenser, which is done by turning the handle of the machine backward a little, until the post 1 comes into contact with a projection from one knob, and the post 2 comes into contact with the projection from another knob.

There is a stop, which serves to prevent the framework of the machine from revolving by the action of the crank, except through a small arc. The post 1 is limited in its forward motion by the stop, and in its backward motion by the projection from the knob.

The casing is made of vulcanite. Two forms of casing are made: one, a box in halves, which are screwed together, with a packing of soft rubber or other air-tight material between them; the other, a box with a cover, having a rubber band placed over and around the outer edge.

The operation of the machine is as follows:

By turning the crank the generating plate is revolved between the cushions. The electricity generated is collected by the collectors, and from them carried by post 4 to the inner surface of the condenser. The opposite electricity appearing at the rubbers, is conducted from them by post 3 to the outer surface of the condenser.

By continued turning of the crank, the condenser may be charged sufficiently to give a spark of three-eighths or one-half an inch in small machines of five or six inches in diameter.

The first motion of the crank turns the frame, as well as the generating plate, until post 1 strikes the stop. Turning the crank backward brings posts 1 and 2 in contact with the knobs, when the condenser may be discharged. It is desirable that the condenser be discharged by the posts 1 and 2, rather than by posts 3 and 4, which are used for charging, as the tendency to escape during accumulation is thereby avoided.

The frame plate and the generating plate are both made of plastic rubber, and vulcanized.

The capacity of a Leyden jar or condenser constructed of plastic rubber and metallic plates, as above directed, may be increased by adding successive layers of metal and vulcanite. Such a condenser will be of use for electrical purposes independently of the generating apparatus herein described.

The inventor claims:

1. A generating plate and a flat condenser, placed parallel to each other within the same casing, substantially as described.

2. A Leyden jar or condenser constructed of vulcanized rubber and metallic plates, substantially as described.

3. So arranging the jar or condenser that the forward motion of the crank, to generate electricity and charge the jar, moves the jar forward through a small arc, whereby its terminals are moved away from the discharging knobs.

4. The device for discharging the jar by the retrograde motion of the crank bringing the posts 1 and 2 into contact with the projections from knobs V and W.

5. Placing the firing points of the condenser at a distance from the collecting points, substantially as described.

6. The stop X, limiting the forward movement of the jar, substantially as described.

7. The combination of a generating plate, a condenser, and a casing, made air-tight, as described, by packing or a rubber band, together with knobs in the casing, and their projections, by which the condenser is discharged, substantially as described.

SECTION II.—BORING AND EXCAVATING BY MACHINERY.

CHAPTER IV.

MACHINES FOR DRILLING ROCKS.

Machines for rock-drilling originated in the United States, where one was put into practical operation as early as 1838. The attention of mechanicians and inventors being thus early directed to this great desideratum, a machine that could be economically and easily substituted for hand labor, so great a variety of contrivances and forms have been proposed and experimented with, that their number renders it difficult even to enumerate them. Our Patent Office and the patent offices of Europe contain many models of machines; but most of them are of the class known as "drop drills," where the tool cuts by percussion. There are other forms of machines, fitted with revolving disks or cutters, and designed to bore out the drift or tunnel to its full size at one operation; and others, again, in which a number of drills are mounted in a frame, so as to cut an annular space around a central core of rock, which can afterward be broken out with powder or otherwise. There is still another type, in which diamonds are made to do the cutting by pressure and rotation, without percussion. Rock-drilling machines may therefore be grouped in two great classes: 1. Those that bore by percussion; 2. Those that bore by constant pressure and rotation.

The drop drills belong to the first class, and will be first considered. In these machines the drill or bar of iron or steel—either a single rod or provided with a steel bit or point at the lower end—is raised by means of a crank, cam, or other mechanism, and then allowed to fall by its own weight upon the rock to be bored. There are also numerous contrivances to accelerate the speed of the fall and increase the force of the blow. Metallic and rubber springs have been used, and, in some cases, the elasticity of air; but in all these modifications but little has been gained over the form in which gravity acts unaided. With springs, the greatest compression and force is exerted when the drill is at its highest or furthest from its striking point, and as the drill descends this force becomes less and less—the reverse of the most desirable condition given by gravity.

It is desirable to note a few of the more important of these inventions which have been in use practically during the past thirty years, and which, by successive modifications and improvements, have led to the present very considerable degree of perfection of rock-drilling machines.

As early as 1838, Messrs. J. M. and John N. Singer experimented with a large drop drill on section 64 of the Illinois and Michigan Canal, about thirty miles below Chicago. This machine was patented in May, 1839, and some ten or twelve machines were built for, and used upon, the canal until the suspension of that work in 1841–'42. They were also used in the Mount Washington cut, near Hinsdale, for the Western railroad of Massachusetts. Two machines were built at Lockport, in 1840, and used upon the enlargement of the Erie Canal. Modifica-

3 M

tions of these machines are even now in use in various parts of the country. They are all drop drills, and their operation is restricted to vertical holes.

The original Singer drill, as applied in Illinois, is considered to have been the first successful machine for its purpose. It was extensively copied, and many improvements upon it were claimed from time to time. The first substantial departure from it was made by J. J. Couch, aided by Joseph W. Fowle, of Boston, in the year 1848. They constructed a steam drilling machine, in which the drill-bar passed directly through the piston of the engine and was alternately caught, drawn back, and thrown against the rock. It was only used a short time in experimenting, and was finally taken apart and sold at auction. Although not a success, this machine marks the second phase of the rock-drilling machines, and was the first attempt that approached success in the direct application of steam-power to rock-drilling.

From the time of this experience the two inventors separated, Mr. Couch following up the general idea of a hollow-piston drill, while Mr. Fowle, discarding the idea of the hollow piston, conceived that success would be gained by placing the drill directly upon the end of a solid piston-rod. During a period of five years Mr. Couch produced a number of drilling engines, variously constructed, but all upon the hollow-piston plan. Some of these were in a measure successful, but not sufficiently so to insure their general adoption. They required very nice adjustment and presented practical difficulties; and finally this style of machines was abandoned.

Mr. Fowle, adhering to his plan of attaching the drill directly to the piston-rod or cross-head of an engine, experimented and struggled against many obstacles for several years. He built, in all, some five machines, but did not succeed in carrying his plan to perfection, until, discouraged and disabled by sickness, he suspended his efforts.

In the year 1861 machine drilling was experimentally begun by Sommeiller, at Mont Cenis, with machines virtually upon the principle of Fowle's, though different in construction. To M. Sommeiller belongs the credit of driving such machines with compressed air, a very important application of this power for all tunnel or mining work, especially where artificial ventilation is required.

The magnitude of the undertaking to tunnel the Hoosac Mountain, in Massachusetts, upon the line of the Troy and Greenfield railroad, prompted the commissioners having it in charge to seek all means of accelerating the work, and their attention was naturally directed to the reports of rapid progress by machine drills at Mont Cenis. The report being favorable as to the results, while the machine of Sommeiller was not regarded as specially adapted to the work on the Hoosac Tunnel, it was decided to devise and perfect a drill for the purpose. As a first step, Couch's patent of the hollow piston-rod was purchased for New England, and scientific mechanics were employed to work upon it. One of these machines, constructed by Mr. Hanson, is known as the

HANSON MACHINE DRILL,

which promised some success, but on trial proved a failure. It had a cylinder and valve-motion, similar to those of a steam-engine. The piston was hollow, with the drill-bar, of any required length, passing through it and moved by the piston, by means of four wedges or cams at each end. These cams were pressed upon the drill-bar by means of sliding collars, forced upon them by a complex arrangement of mechanism, acting alternately upon one and the other, for the purpose of catching and throwing the drill-bar. The rotation of the bar was effected by means of a ratchet, worked by a spiral groove in the shield of the machine. There were 120 pieces in this machine, and it weighed 590 pounds. It did not work well horizontally. The main difficulty was with the cams and collars for seizing the drill-bar.

A second machine, called the

BROOKS, BURLEIGH, AND GATES MACHINE,

made under the direction of the commissioners at Fitchburg, was put upon the works and used for several months. This machine also had a hollow piston, the drill-bar or holder being a screw, passing through the piston and moving with it. The feed was given by means of a nut on the end of the piston-rod, held by means of a cap or union nut, the latter being screwed on to the coupling, and the coupling-nut screwed to the piston-rod. The feed nut turns in the union nut, and protrudes from it. A ratchet, moving with the piston, works upon this feed nut, and is governed in its action upon the nut by a spiral groove in a shield attached by screws to the cylinder. On the ratchet band there is a pawl, with two springs, one under the other; one serves to hold the pawl in gear, the other to hold it out of gear. As the piston descends, the outer spring comes in contact with a trip on the shield, and is lifted up, allowing the under spring to throw the pawl into the ratchet; and as the piston returns, the outer spring turns the nut round, and thus feeds the screw, or the drill-bar, forward. At the end of the back stroke, the pawl strikes another trip on the shield and is thrown out of gear, and is held so by the outer spring, made with a catch. The rotary motion of the drill-bar is given by a ratchet on the coupling-nut, covered by a ratchet band, the arm of which moves in a spiral groove in the shield, similar to the other. The crosshead is held between two check-nuts, on the coupling-nut. It carries a bar, governing a valve which opens the port when the piston and drill-bar move back, and shuts it when they move forward; the air is always pressing during the backward stroke. The area of the back of the piston being greater than the front, the forward pressure preponderates and carries the piston forward, and when cut off the backward pressure returns the piston.

The piston-head of this machine has a diameter of $4\frac{5}{8}$ inches and the diameter of the piston-rod is 4 inches at the large end and $2\frac{1}{4}$ at the small end. There are, therefore, 12.87 square inches of area on the back, upon which the compressed air acts to drive the drill forward against the rock, and 4.23 inches area on the forward end upon which the air acts to throw the drill back out of the hole. As the pressure was not removed from the front of the piston the motion forward was due to the difference of area between the back and front of the piston, viz: $12.87 - 4.23 = 8.64$ square inches.

This machine was automatic, and it generally continued to work until some part gave way. No part of it was found to be strong enough to withstand the shocks for any considerable portion of time. The union nut was its weakest point; and the breaking of this nut generally destroyed the part of the piston to which it was attached. The springs of the feed ratchet-band were also almost continually breaking.

This machine had 80 pieces; of these 23 were screws, 15 pins, and 7 pieces of cast iron. It weighed 240 pounds, made about 200 strokes per minute, and cost about $400. Its longest run, without breaking, was five days. To run for two days without breaking some part of the machine was considered fortunate. More than one breakage a day was the average.

The experience with these machines at the Hoosac tunnel was discouraging. About forty machines were used there, and of these eight or ten were originally vertical, and intended for use in sinking the central shaft. Owing to the many breakages it was difficult to keep up a supply, and the progress of the work diminished in proportion to the giving out machines. It was the opinion of the engineer that if a constant supply of machines could have been furnished the progress would have been much greater than that attainable by hand labor. The average "life" of one of these machines was about eighty hours, and it is said by those familiar with the operations at the tunnel at that time, that soon after starting them at work the tunnel seemed to be a highway, along which a crowd of people was continually passing, each person carrying a portion of a drilling machine, or tools and materials for repairs.

This unsatisfactory experience led to the gradual abandonment of the Brooks, Burleigh, and Gates machine, and the substitution for it of a new and simpler machine, made by Mr. Charles Burleigh.

THE BURLEIGH ROCK DRILL.

Abandoning the idea of constructing a machine upon the Couch or hollow piston principle, Mr. Burleigh purchased the Fowle patent, and commenced the construction of machines with solid pistons, arranging the details of construction so that the parts should be few in number, and strong enough to bear the great shocks of working. In this he claims to have been successful; and it is stated that sixteen out of the twenty machines furnished for use at the east end of the tunnel were still in operation at the close of the summer of 1869, some of them having been in use since November, 1866.

According to a report made by a joint committee of the Massachusetts legislature, the construction of this drilling machine, in 1867, was substantially as follows: It has a solid (so-called) cast-steel piston, to one end of which the drill or bit is attached, while the other end within the cylinder, by means of suitable mechanism, operates the valves. The piston-head has a diameter of 4.25 inches; the piston at the large end 3 inches, and at the small end, 2.75 inches. The number of inches of air area is thus 8.20 when the drill is thrown out upon the rock, and 7.07 when returning. On the back end of the piston is a section of a ball used as a cam, which works the valve and the feed motion. The movement of the piston brings the ball into contact with these cams, and, by rocking them back and forth, opens and closes the valve. The cylinder is supported upon parallel ways or a bed-plate, upon which it slides up and down as moved by the feed-screw. This feed-screw passes through a gallows frame, attached to the upper end of the ways, and the lower end of the screw, passing through a feed-nut, enters the cylinder. The end of the piston is drilled out, so that the feed-screw is not struck during the oscillations. The feed-nut is secured between two collars, so that it turns easily, and its outer edge is cut into a ratchet, into which works a pawl, operated by the piston, turning the nut upon the fixed feed-screw, and moving the cylinder, drill, &c., forward. This machine weighed 372 pounds, including the ways or bed-piece; without the ways the weight was 212 pounds. It comprised eighty pieces, and had the same number of screws and pins as the Gates, Brooks, and Burleigh machine. Its number of strokes was 300 a minute. They stood the work much better than the former machines, and their average "life" in the tunnel without repairs was about five days. One worked for fourteen days without repairs.

The external appearance of the Burleigh drilling-machine as now made is shown by the figure. It is simpler and stronger than the machine of 1866. It has 27 pieces less than that machine. Five sizes are made, drilling from $\frac{3}{4}$-inch to $5\frac{1}{2}$-inch holes, and feeding from thirty inches to eighty-four inches without change of drill-points. The piston-bar, to which the drill-point is directly attached, is made of solid cast-steel. The machine is so constructed that the piston-bar is the only part of the machine which receives the shock resulting from the blow upon the rock. With a pressure of 50 pounds to the square inch, the drill strikes from 250 to 300 blows per minute. It weighs from 150 to 1,000 pounds, according to size, and can be operated either by steam or by compressed air. The size recommended for general mining is the tunnel-size, weighing about 400 pounds, drilling $1\frac{1}{4}$ to $2\frac{1}{4}$-inch holes, and feeding 36 inches without change of drill-points. It will drill from 2 to 6 inches a minute, according to the hardness of the rock.

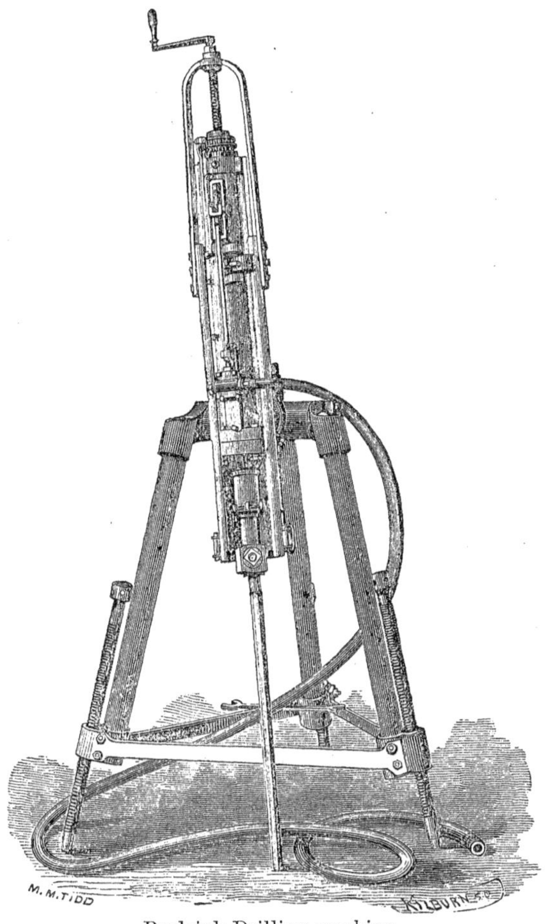

Burleigh Drilling-machine.

Besides being in operation at the Hoosac Tunnel, these machines are or have been in successful working operation in New York, Chicago, Jersey City, Hell Gate, Scranton, Lake Superior, Colorado, Nova Scotia, Union Pacific railroad, Boston and Hartford railroad, &c., and in deepening the beds of the Illinois and Michigan Canals at the Des Moines Rapids.

In Colorado, Mr. Burleigh is running a tunnel to intersect several lodes at a considerable depth. It is found advantageous to make this tunnel larger than is usual, in order to have room for the machines and two tracks. It is, therefore, cut eight feet high and nine feet wide. A double track is laid with iron rails as the work advances. Two inside shifts of men, four in each, are worked regularly; and with the drilling machines the progress in a hard crystalline rock has been, of late, as great as 60 feet per month. In one week, 15 feet of advance was made, and at a cost per foot of $37 50, including all expenses. The tunnel has now penetrated 415 feet in the solid rock, and the average rate of progress for some months before the machines were carried to their present degree of perfection was 40 feet per month, which was at least four times as great as could be accomplished by hand labor. The expenses of running a tunnel in Colorado, near Georgetown, are much greater than at the East. Miners' wages are $4 per day; blacksmiths', $6; powder, $8 per keg; wood from $5 to $6 per cord, and all supplies are costly. The cost of driving the tunnel up to March, 1870, had been $62 per running foot; which is much less than it would have cost by hand labor alone.

The Baltimore Tunnel, in the vicinity, is being driven with three shifts, of three men in each, at a rate of 50 feet per month. Another tunnel, worked by hand labor alone, is advancing only 8 feet per month. Mr. Burleigh thinks that he can drive the large sized tunnel more rapidly and cheaply than one of the ordinary dimensions.

At Hallett's Point, near New York, these drills have been advantageously used; and it is believed that they accomplish from three to four times as much as can be done by hand for the same cost, and in much less time.

At the Hoosac Tunnel, (January, 1870,) the Burleigh drills are used in driving the "headings" only at both ends of the tunnel—nine machines at the eastern end and eight at the western end. The heading or advanced opening is 8 feet high and 24 feet in width; and in the eastern end is made on the floor, and in the western end, next the roof. The enlargement is at present carried forward entirely by manual labor; but arrangements are making for the use of the machine drills for the enlargement of the eastern end. The rock is a compact mica slate, in which, at the western end, veins of quartz, sometimes many feet in thickness, are of frequent occurrence. In the eastern end, however, the mica slate is comparatively free from these veins or bands, and the rate of progress there is much greater.

In the western end eight drills are kept constantly at work. Four drills are mounted upon a carriage, which, with its load of drills, tools, &c., weighs, by estimate, about five tons. There are two carriages, which are brought into position upon parallel railways, laid as the work progresses. The holes are commenced with 2-inch drills, and finished with 1¼-inch drills, or drills which cut holes of those diameters. The average depth of the holes is about 50 inches. At the western end, where the quartz veins are so frequent and hard, the working of the drills is so constantly interrupted by stoppages that it would require very extended observation of one machine to determine the work it is capable of performing. One of the machines, in the presence of my brother, drilled about twelve inches in ten minutes, making, as nearly as he could estimate, something over 200 strokes per minute. The rock consisted largely of quartz. In boring a hole 5 feet in depth in such rock, the drills are often changed as many as ten times. According to Mr. Roscoe, manager of the western end of the tunnel, one of the new drills had drilled a hole 5 feet in depth in quartz rock, such as frequently occurs there, in 25 minutes. At the eastern end, where the rock is mica slate without the heavy quartz veins, a hole of equal depth is often drilled in from 10 to 12 minutes. According to Mr. Shanley, from 800 to 900 inches are drilled in the western heading during every shift of eight hours; and the daily progress of the tunnel is about 4 feet. In the eastern end, however, with nine drills, from 1,600 to 1,800 inches are drilled every shift, and the daily rate of progress is about 6 feet. Blasting is done twice in every shift.

It is the opinion of the superintendent that in the eastern end the cost of drilling by the Burleigh drill is to the cost of drilling by hand, as 4½ to 7. In the western end, however, it is believed that the machine drilling, owing to the numerous stoppages, is as expensive as it would be by hand.

Each drill requires the constant attendance of two men. In hard rock it is found necessary to feed the drill by hand instead of employing the automatic arrangement provided for that purpose. Hence, at the western end, where the rock is so highly quartzose, the feeding is done entirely by hand; but in the eastern end, where the rock is less hard and of more uniform character, the feed is automatic.

At both ends the wear and tear on the machine drills is necessarily great; but in the western end particularly so—so great, in fact, that on an average two drills are in the shop for repairs to one at work in the "heading." But this end had not been fully supplied with the *new* Burleigh drills.

As before stated, these drills may be operated by either compressed air or by steam. For all underground operations the former is used. At the western end of the Hoosac Tunnel four of Burleigh's air-compressers are used for the compression of air to work the drills. The compression is rapidly effected by pumps, worked by a steam engine.

The reservoir at that place consists of two cylindrical vessels of boiler iron, 25 feet long and 5 feet in diameter, in which the compression is carried to from 50 to 60 pounds to the inch, or three and one-third to four atmospheres. The air is conveyed in iron pipes 8 inches in interior diameter.

COMPRESSED AIR AS A MOTOR IN MINING.

The annexed figure shows the form of the new machines used by the Burleigh Drill Company for compressing the air by which the drills are worked in the end of a tunnel, or for other purposes where compressed air can be used to advantage.

It is obvious that for underground operations, in deep shafts, and in tunnels, steam cannot be used as a motor. Aside from the difficulty of conveying it great distances in pipes without great loss by con-

Burleigh Air-compressor.

densation, its discharge in the confined galleries of a mine would render working impossible. Compressed air, on the other hand, when conveyed from the exterior to the interior of a mine, and discharged there, gives a constant supply of fresh, pure air, promoting the health and comfort of the miners.

The compressors now used with great success, consist of a steam-engine connecting by means of a crank shaft with two single air pumps, arranged as seen in the figure. It is very compactly and strongly built, and, by a nice adjustment of the cranks, the greatest power of the engine is applied at the point of greatest resistance. These compressors are made of three sizes, rated as Nos. 1, 2, and 3, and with the following dimensions:

Dimensions of air compressors.

	Number One.	Number Two.	Number Three.
Steam cylinder	6¼-inch diameter ... 15-inch stroke......	9-inch diameter .... 18-inch stroke	10¼-inch diameter. 18-inch stroke.
Air cylinders, each	10½-inch diameter ... 10-inch stroke......	12-inch diameter .... 15-inch stroke.......	14¾-inch diameter. 15-inch stroke.
Size of base	45 × 35 inches	45 × 56¼ inches	48 × 64¼ inches.
Extreme height	7 feet 5½ inches	9 feet 3½ inches......	9 feet 3½ inches.
Weight	3,800 pounds	7,600 pounds	11,000 pounds.
Cubic feet of free air compressed per minute at 90 revolutions	90.19 cubic feet......	176.70 cubic feet.....	266.97 cubic feet.
Size of discharge pipe	2 inches.............	2½ inches............	3 inches.

The air, when compressed, is taken into a tank, or air-chamber, and thence carried to any desired point in pipes, in the same manner that steam is carried. Connection between the permanent pipes and the rock drills upon the carriages is made by flexible rubber pipe, which is uncoupled when the carriage is run back for a blast.

The constructors of these compressors claim that, with eighty pounds of steam, they have compressed air to an equal degree, so as to produce an equilibrium between the condensed air in the receiver and the steam in the boiler.

In regard to the economy of transmission of power to a distance by means of compressed air, the practical results at the Hoosac Tunnel are extremely favorable, and show, as already mentioned, but a slight difference of pressure—about two pounds—between the two extremes of a pipe 7,150 feet long and eight inches in diameter. The following table shows the result of some experiments made while from five to nine drills were in operation:

Results of experiments upon the loss of pressure by the flow of air in an 8-inch pipe.

Time.	No. of compressors running.	Revolutions per minute, No. 1.	Revolutions per minute, No. 2.	No. of drills running.	Pressure per inch at compressors.	Pressure per inch at heading.	Difference in pressure.
					Pounds.	*Pounds.*	*Pounds.*
1 p. m.	2	76	80	6	67	65	2
1.10 p. m.	2	90	92	9	63	62	1
1.20 p. m.	2	104	96	7	64	62	2
1.30 p. m.	2	112	104	6	65	62	3
1.40 p. m.	2	90	96	7	67	64½	2½
1.50 p. m.	2	96	96	5	66	63½	2½
2 p. m.	1	....	94	4	67	64	3
2.10 p. m.	2	88	92	6	66	64	2
2.20 p. m.	2	86	92	6	67	66	1
2.30 p. m.	2	90	90	8	66	65	1
2.40 p. m.	2	88	88	5	67	65	2
2.50 p. m.	2	92	90	6	65	64	1
3 p. m.	2	92	90	6	65	63	2

Average loss of pressure, 2 pounds. Average number of drills running, 6. Length of 8-inch air-pipe from compressors to heading, 7,150 feet.

These results are in accord with those obtained by the engineers at Mt. Cenis, where, at the date of the report of progress of the work in the year 1863, the air was conveyed a distance of nearly 2,000 metres, and worked nine drilling machines with a force of two and a half horse-power each. The tube, like that at the Hoosac, was nearly eight inches in diameter. The air was compressed to six atmospheres, and its velocity in the tube was about three feet per second. The transmission under these conditions was not attended by any sensible loss, and the pressure was the same when the drills were all in operation as when they were at rest.

A series of experiments were made at Coscia by order of the Italian government in 1857, upon the resistance of tubes to the flow of air through them, and the following conclusions were deduced:

1. The resistance is directly as the length of the tube.
2. It is directly as the square of the velocity of the flow.
3. It is inversely as the diameter of the tube.

The whole subject of the transmission of power by compressed air is most thoroughly and ably discussed by Professor F. A. P. Barnard, in his report upon the Paris Exposition* of 1867, to which reference is made for further details upon this most important subject.

The compression of the air at the eastern end of the Hoosac Tunnel is effected by water-power. Four 24-horse turbines operate 16 air-pumps, each of 13½-inch bore and 20-inch stroke; but these are not all used to-together.

The use of the machine drill in sinking the central shaft, now down over 800 feet, has been discontinued.

Directions for running the Burleigh drills.—Before attempting to start a drill the parts should be thoroughly oiled by introducing oil through the plug marked "oil," and also behind the "feed lever," beneath the "momentum piece," between rotating ratchet and friction ring, and between rotating ratchet and inside sleeve.

In setting the drill carriage preparatory to drilling, the rear part of the same should be raised three to four inches above a level by turning down the back jack-screws. The machine is now ready to receive the drill point. This is done as follows: Raise the piston sufficiently to admit of the drill point entering the chuck. In doing this be careful to observe that the "momentum piece" is knocked back so as to clear the ball on the end of piston which moves the "momentum piece" and valve. Now let the piston drop down on the drill point and firmly secure the same by tightening the bolts in the chuck. Now feed down the cylinder by the crank on feed-screw, until the drill point touches the rock, and then feed it down three-quarters of an inch more if a "Tunnel pattern," or one inch if a "New York pattern," so that the piston will not strike the lower cylinder head when the drill is at work.

The drill is now ready for work. Let on steam, and if it does not at once start, knock the "momentum piece" (with a mallet or stick of wood at the knob upon the same) forward and back. If the piston raises and strikes one blow and stops, the valve gland must be tightened a little to prevent the valve from falling back over the port and cutting off the steam. Now strike the "momentum piece" as before, and the drill will start, unless the valve gland has been tightened so much as to prevent the full throw of the valve. (Experience will guide in this matter.) Again, if the cylinder is fed down *more* than three-quarters of an inch, as above described, it will not start, in which case turn back the feed-screw a little.

Having once started, if the drill rotates more than one tooth at a time, the lower "stuffer" should be screwed up sufficiently to increase the friction on the piston rod to reduce the rotation. In case the drill will not rotate, screw up the set-screw in the friction pad, which will cause rotation. Observe that the spring over the rotating pawl is of sufficient strength to cause the pawl to throw into the notch, as the drill rotates. The same care should be used with the spring over "qualifier," for if too weak, or from any cause broken, the drill will feed itself down, cutting off the stroke, and in consequence stop.

By carefully following the above directions, the successful working of the drill is secured. Great care should be taken to prevent the piston from striking the lower cylinder head. This occurs if for any cause it does not feed fast enough, which will be

* Machinery and Processes of the Industrial Arts, &c., pp. 137–150.

the case if the spring over feed lever is not of sufficient strength, or a soft place in the rock is reached, or if the drill strikes through into a seam or cavity. This will be immediately detected by the difference in sound of the blows, and when it occurs the steam should be at once shut off, or the drill rapidly fed down by the crank on end of feed-screw.

To change drill points.—Having drilled the length of the first drill point, if a greater depth is desired, the drill points will be changed by following these directions: Loosen the bolts in the chuck, allowing the drill point to drop out. Bring the frame or carriage to a level by turning the back jack-screws, which will allow the passage of the longer drill down past the cylinder; raise the piston as before described, until the drill enters the chuck—then raise the rear of carriage to its former position—secure the drill and proceed as before.

Sharpening the drill points.—In sharpening the drills, care should be taken to form the points in the shape of a letter X, and not square like a +. On the two-inch (tunnel or mining bit) there should be a difference of at least ⅛ inch between the lips of same. On the three-inch or New York pattern there should be ¼ inch.

If these directions are not followed the hole will be five-sided and cause the drill to bind.

In drilling, water should be occasionally fed into the hole to keep the point cool and wash out the debris. In case the drill binds from running off or any cause, the bolts in the clamp which holds the drill should be loosened to relieve the same.

The above directions for running a drill apply more particularly to vertical drilling, but are generally applicable to various kinds of drilling.

To take the machine apart.—Take out the bolts in the lower cylinder head; all the set-screws on the side of cylinder, feed-lever, momentum piece, rotating pawl, and friction pad; then pull the piston down with a jerk and it will start the inside sleeve. By continuing this operation the inside works can be removed. In putting the drill together, when the inside works are put in observe that the upper end of inside sleeve is flush with the lower end of rotating pawl, and that the back ring is opposite to the back set-screw. Turn the set-screws down firmly and replace the other parts as before.

SOMMEILLER'S ROCK-DRILLING MACHINES.

The following notice of rock-drilling by machinery at Mont Cenis is compiled from the report by Messrs. Geyler and d'Aligny. It is generally known that these machines are worked by compressed air:

On the Italian side of the Alps, at Bardonnèche, (the Piedmont entrance,) the air compressors are a kind of hydraulic ram, the valves of which are arranged in such a way that, at each lift of the valve admitting water, a certain quantity of air, at a pressure of five atmospheres, is forced into a reservoir 10 metres long and 17 cubic metres capacity.

The air compressors at Modane (north side) are composed of a horizontal cylinder full of water, in which a piston works, and of two vertical cylinders receiving the air, and provided with valves in their upper part. By the motion of the piston a quantity of air, equal to that of water displaced by the movement, is introduced and expelled at each stroke. The air is conducted to the boring machine by cast-iron pipes of $0^{m}.20$. It has been ascertained that the loss due to friction is about one-tenth of an atmosphere.

The boring machines of Mr. Sommeiller are essentially composed of a cylinder in which the compressed air works. The piston rod traverses the heads of this cylinder, and carries on one side a screw which commands the distributer. A machine similar to a steam-engine commands the slide valve of this distributer. This arrangement was adopted inasmuch as the stroké of the piston woich carries the drill varies with the hardness of the rock and the position of the drill in the hole, and no reliance could be placed upon the introduction of the compressed air by means of the percussion alone.

The whole apparatus weighs 200 kilogrammes. It rests upon a frame open in the center; the sides are $0^{m}.03$ wide by $0^{m}.05$ high, and $0^{m}.09$ apart; their length is $2^{m}.70$. They are cut upon their inside faces with a screw thread, in which a screw moves, and the edge of their lower faces is cut with rack teeth, in which a pawl works.

The cylinder of the distributing machine is $0^{m}.06$ in diameter. The stroke of the piston is $0^{m}.10$. It is furnished with a connecting rod and a crank, and by means of gearing gives a rotary movement to a square stem, upon which is fixed, first, a pawl, which advances tooth by tooth a ratchet wheel provided with sixteen teeth, and fixed invariably on the prolongation of the piston rod in such manner that, after sixteen blows of the drill, the ratchet, the piston, and the drill have made a complete revolution; second, a plate furnished with a cam which moves the slide rod, and if we suppose that the slide valve, pushed by this cam, advances and stops the aperture for admission, the air which acts escapes through the opening which communicates with the atmosphere by the hollow passage in the slide valve, and the piston is carried to its original position by the constant pressure which is exerted on its front face. At this instance the valve, abandoned by the cam, is pushed back suddenly to its initial position, by the difference of pressure which is exerted upon the two faces, and thus opens the inlet port.

The diameter of the piston of the boring machine is $0^{m}.06$; its stroke, $0^{m}.20$; and it gives 200 blows per minute. This machine is single-acting. The compressed air enters by the opening in constant communication by the conduit with the front part of the cylinder; when the piston is at the end of the stroke, the slide opens the inlet port, and the piston only advances in consequence of the difference of the pressure of air on its back face fitted with a slender rod, and on its internal face, of which the area is reduced by the large shaft of the tool-carrier. The impulsive force upon the piston is, for some of these machines, 95 kilogrammes, and for others, 150 kilogrammes.

We have before explained how the drill is made to rotate. It remains to show how it is made to advance, and how it can be rapidly taken out in case of need. If the screw, constantly geared into its nut formed by the internal filleted faces of the beds, were fixed permanently upon the shaft, it would follow that in each rotation of the drill it would advance the cylinder by a length equal to the pitch of the thread; but it should, on the contrary, only advance at the same speed that the drill enters the rock; therefore the screw works loosely upon the shaft, and only turns when a clutch box catches it, this clutch being continually pushed by the action of a spiral spring, which is retained by a rod connected with the clutch, and carrying at its front extremity—

1. A fork, the teeth of which rest against those of the rack on the lower part of the bed plate.
2. A prolongation terminated by a semicircular appendage.

If we now suppose that the piston is reaching the end of its stroke, with the drill scarcely touching the bottom of the hole, a tappet fixed upon the shaft of the tool-carrier strikes the above-mentioned appendage, forces it to drop, and detaches the tooth from the rack. Then the clutch box, impelled by the spring, catches and turns the screw, and the striking cylinder advances till the fork is caught by the following tooth of the rack, and thus disengages the clutch.

It may be conceded that Mr. Sommeiller has constructed an ingenious machine which fulfills the following conditions:

1. It strikes hard and rapid blows upon the rock.
2. It transmits a self-acting rotary motion to the drill, required to prevent it from becoming fixed in the hole.
3. It imparts also a progressive, self-acting, and regular advance to the drill as the hole deepens in working.

4. And lastly, it can be rapidly drawn back to change the tools.

The tool is a drill, with the cutting-edge in the form of a Z. It makes a hole of 0 .09 and $0^{m}.04$ in diameter; but in the first case it is furnished for $0^{m}.20$ behind its head, with a bulge which trims or reams the holes to full size. The stroke of the machine is but $0^{m}.80$, but it can make a hole to a depth of $0^{m}.90$, by reason of the length of the drills, which vary from $0^{m}.50$ to 2^{m}.

The apparatus placed before the breast of the gallery to be attacked carries 8 drills, which cover a section 4 metres wide by 3 metres high, equal to an area of 12 square metres. Eighty holes are bored, 6 of $0^{m}.09$ and 74 of $0^{m}.04$ diameter, and $0^{m}.90$ deep. The daily work has varied evidently according to the hardness of the rock. In March, 1863, it was $1^{m}.10$ in twenty-four hours; in April, $1^{m}.40$, and in some parts of the strata even $2^{m}.50$; but when the bank of quartz was met, which was 308 metres thick, the advance was hardly $0^{m}.50$ per day.

During the month of March, 1863, it was shown that each explosion of $0^{m}.70$ to $0^{m}.80$ required six hours for boring the holes, and four hours for the miners carrying away the rubbish.

The staff employed for the boring of the holes during twenty-four hours was as follows:

	Men.
Two shifts	16
Miners	2
Laborers for taking away the débris	8
Superintendents	2
Total	28
The compressors required	9
Total	37

In 1863 for 8 machines working there were 60 in the shop. In 1867 when the work was carried on both from the French and Italian sides the number of machines working was 16, and of those in the shop for repairs 200.

In 1863, for repairing 8 perforators working in a coarse sandstone, (*grès à gros grains*,) the staff attached to the workshops consisted of 24 men.

In 1867 the number was much greater, but exact information could not be obtained. The work had, however, been offered to a company at 6,000 francs per running metre, the company taking all the apparatus and agreeing to repair the tools and clear away the débris. This was refused, although the price was equal to 500 francs per cubic metre. The enormous shocks which the machine was subjected to obliged them to change the iron beds for Krupp steel ones; the springs often broke, and the drills did not advance $0^{m}.20$ or $0^{m}.30$ without requiring repairs.

DÖRING'S DRILLING MACHINE.

Mr. Döring, of Ruhrort, in Westphalia, has constructed a drilling machine that has been used to great advantage in the zinc mines of the Vieille Montagne Company at Moresnet, near Aix-la-Chapelle. The director of these mines stated in 1867 that 11 of these machines, two of them of a recent construction, had been in actual use there, and that in one of the levels, where the rock was a very hard quartzose dolomite, they had made an advance of 3 metres in 14 days, where by hand driving 1½ metres only could be achieved. Sometimes the machine could advance

4 metres in that time, and with only 2 men instead of 6. A six horse-power engine is required to work 2 machines; the air is compressed to $1\frac{1}{2}$ atmospheres. For one working machine it requires 2 in reserve. The speed per minute is $0^{m}.03$, including replacing the drills. Each drill will not bore more than $0^{m}.20$ to $0^{m}.30$ without being replaced. Its speed of advance at Vieille Montagne over ordinary borers may be considered to have been treble in hard rock, but only double in soft rock.

This apparatus of Döring weighs 45 kilogrammes, and constitutes the borer, properly so called. It is erected upon a special carriage, which allows any direction to be given to the drill that is desired. The pressure of the air varies from $\frac{3}{4}$ of an atmosphere to $1\frac{1}{2}$. This machine is composed of a cylinder $0^{m}.400$ in diameter, and $0^{m}.300$ long. In this cylinder a piston moves, to which is fixed the stem of the drill. The compressed air is distributed by means of a slide valve, and, after acting freely, escapes into the air. Two ratchet wheels, furnished with dogs, are placed at the back of the cylinder, and are put in action by the prolonged rod of the piston by means of a fork which commands the dogs. One of the ratchet wheels serves to give to the drill a rotary movement on its axis; the other ratchet, which is nearest to the cylinder, by means of a toothed wheel advances the tool upon the support. The arrangement is such that the drill advances only when the piston has run its stroke. A jet of water is constantly thrown into the hole for the removal of the débris. The drill most used is pointed in the form of the letter Z; and it is found that when worked in the machine it does not blunt as rapidly as when worked by hand.

Mr. Döring has put his machines into operation in a very deep mine—the Tincroft, in Cornwall—where the rock is the hardest in that country, and one is to be introduced at the Dolcoath mine. It is represented as making good headway in the hard rock of the Tincroft.

BERGSTRÖM'S DRILLING MACHINE.

Bergström's drilling machine originated in Sweden, and has been in use there at the Persberg mine. A machine exhibited at Paris in 1867 was said to have worked for 700 days under ground, and to have bored in the aggregate 1,000 metres. Upon hard granite, in trials with the drill, it bored 2 metres in 1 hour. The drill is impelled by compressed air, in a cylinder similar to that of Döring's machine, but without an automatic advance movement. It gives from 300 to 400 blows per minute, and the diameter of the drills varies from $0^{m}.018$ to $0^{m}.025$. The weight of the whole apparatus is only 120 pounds, and it is supported upon a steel bar, which must be fixed in a direction parallel to that of the intended bore-hole. The cylinder is made to travel along this bar.

It may here be mentioned that in 1856 Karl Schumann, of Freiberg, Saxony, constructed a boring machine, to which those above described and the drill of General Haupt are similar in some respects.

HAUPT'S DRILL.

This percussion borer differs essentially in its construction from those described. It works by means of steam. The drill passes down a hollow piston rod, to which it is fixed by the extremity which is before the workman. The reciprocating movement is communicated directly to the drill, and by a special arrangement of the slide valve the introduction of the steam into the cylinder is avoided until the piston has arrived at the end of its forward stroke.

The force of the blow of the drill upon the rock depends on the pressure of the steam upon the piston. It will be observed, besides, that the useful effect of the drill depends much more upon the section of the piston and the pressure of the steam, than on the length of the stroke of the piston, and that the consumption is proportioned to this last dimension. The length of the stroke of the piston is $0^{m}.102$, and the number of blows per minute is 375.

The movement of rotation is given to the drill in the following way: The box in which the shaft of the drill is held, and which turns with it, carries a ratchet wheel on one part of its circumference, and around this wheel is a ring furnished with a pawl, which catches in the teeth of the ratchet wheel. This ring also carries a projecting tappet, which passes in an inclined groove left in the outer envelope of sheet iron which surrounds the steam cylinder. The tappet participates in the movement of the piston and drill, and by sliding in the inclined groove turns a screw with which it is combined, and by means of the pawl gives the ratchet wheel and the drill a rotary motion.

This arrangement would be insufficient alone, since the tappet moving in both directions in the groove destroys, to a certain extent, during the forward stroke, the useful effect produced during the back stroke. To obviate this imperfection, and to maintain the rotation transmitted to the drill, there is a second ratchet wheel placed at the front end of the box that carries the drill. A steel spindle placed in a recess formed by the cylinder jacket locks into the teeth of this second ratchet wheel, so that the movement of rotation only takes place one way. The first ratchet wheel allows the transmission of the rotating movement to the tool; the second forces this movement to be always effected one way.

Mr. Haupt has contrived a special arrangement which causes the drill to always strike upon the rock with the same force, and to vary its advance according to the hardness of the rock. If the drill is put into the drill-carrier in such manner that at any given time the motion of this latter can be suddenly arrested while the tool itself continues to move, it is clear that each stoppage of the tool-carrier will be followed by an advance of the tool; but as this stoppage would diminish the force of the blow upon the bottom of the hole, it is only allowed to take place at intervals.

Mr. Haupt estimates that three horse-power is required for each borer, and that the rate of progress in rocks of ordinary hardness is $0^{m}.05$ per minute.

BEAUMONT AND LOCOCK'S DRILLING ENGINE.

This machine is worked by compressed air; its object is to pierce a gallery of two metres diameter entirely by the machine, aided by powder for disengaging the core of rock which is left in the middle of the annular trench cut by the drills.

This machine is composed of a cast-iron plate which carries on its circumference thirty-six drills made of cast steel, and in its center a similar drill. The diameter of the plate is about two metres, and is the same as that of the gallery to be driven. It is fixed on a hollow iron shaft, about two-thirds of its length being a piston, which moves in a cylinder.

The stroke of the piston is about $0^{m}.30$. A slide valve introduces the air (compressed to two atmospheres) to each face of the piston, and gives it an alternate movement of 250 blows per minute. A worm, worked by a special mechanism, turns the axle with the drills by means of a screw wheel combined with the axle. The carriage on which the piston shaft is mounted receives a forward motion by a special arrangement. The water which is thrown into the groove formed by the drills enters the interior of the shaft, and by pipes branched upon this axle is conducted to the circumference of the plate.

This is evidently one of those machines that cannot long withstand the extreme violence of the impact essential to rapid drilling. If it is almost impossible to construct a machine with one drill that will work long enough without repairs to make it an economical success compared with hand labor, how much can we expect from an engine armed with thirty-seven drills, all rigidly attached to one piston?

FORD'S DRILLING MACHINE.

A power-drilling machine has been constructed and put into operation in one of the mines at Sandhurst, Australia, and is said to effect a very considerable saving over the ordinary process of drilling by hand. Mr. Joseph Millin, the manager of the Hustler's Reef Company, states that drilling in ground that would cost forty shillings per foot with hand labor can be wrought with the machine for thirty shillings; or, if with hand labor at sixty or eighty shillings, with the machine for forty shillings. The harder the ground the greater the saving. The machine appears, from the description given, to be similar in construction to the Burleigh drill. The constructor, Mr. R. G. Ford, of Sandhurst, describes the drill as follows:

In Ford's rock-boring machine the motion of the rock-boring tool is reciprocating, and the motive power is compressed air or steam, at a pressure of sixty pounds per square inch, acting on a piston in a cylinder. It presses constantly on a small annular space in front of the piston, and intermittingly on the whole area of the back of the piston; a percussive action is thus given by the borer carried by the piston rod. The ports for the alternate admission of the compressed air behind the piston, and for the exhaust, are opened and closed by a valve worked by a small piston, thus securing the full pressure on the back of the piston, and giving a free blow and a clear exhaust for the return stroke.

The air-ports and the movement of the valve are so arranged that the piston cannot strike the front and back of the cylinder. The rotation of the boring tool is self-acting, and is caused by the piston rod working a ratchet and click round a cylinder attached to the front of the working cylinder, and as the piston reciprocates it carries itself round the cylinder and makes a complete revolution every twenty-one blows, by which means the machine bores a perfectly round hole, and the drill cannot move more or less than a twenty-first part of a revolution at each stroke. The feed is self-advancing and self-adjustable and variable, feeding with precision as fast as the tool has power to penetrate the rock, but no faster, varying its feed in the same hole with the varying hardness of the rock or sharpness of the tool. This is effected by the working cylinder being provided with an exterior cylinder in which it can slide, and the compressed air is constantly tending to propel the working cylinder forward, but is retained by a screw, which is prevented from turning by a pawl, which the piston strikes when it makes a full stroke, thus releasing the screw and permitting the working cylinder to advance forward as the hole increases in depth.

An ordinary drill is used; the only alteration required is the head, which is made to fit the machine. The drills can be made to bore holes from three-quarters of an inch to two inches in diameter. The weight of the blow struck by the machine can be varied from 1 pound to 510 pounds, and the number of blows from 20 to 600 per minute, by the attendant simply moving the handle of a small air-cock.

The air-compressor used at this mine with Ford's machine is very simple, consisting of a cylinder nine inches in diameter, bent like the letter U, with a piston working in one leg only, the other being filled with water. The piston has a stroke of two feet, and as it moves up and down in one leg the water rises and falls in the other, thus making it double-acting. The piston works through a stuffing-box at the bottom, and the inlet and outlet valves are placed at the top. A small supply of water is admitted at the inlet valve with each stroke, and is thrown into the receiver at each return stroke, thus circulating through the apparatus, and carrying off the heat given out by the air when compressed. An old boiler is used as the receiver, and the compressed air is conveyed to the drilling machine in iron gas-piping.

LESCHOT'S ANNULAR DIAMOND DRILL.

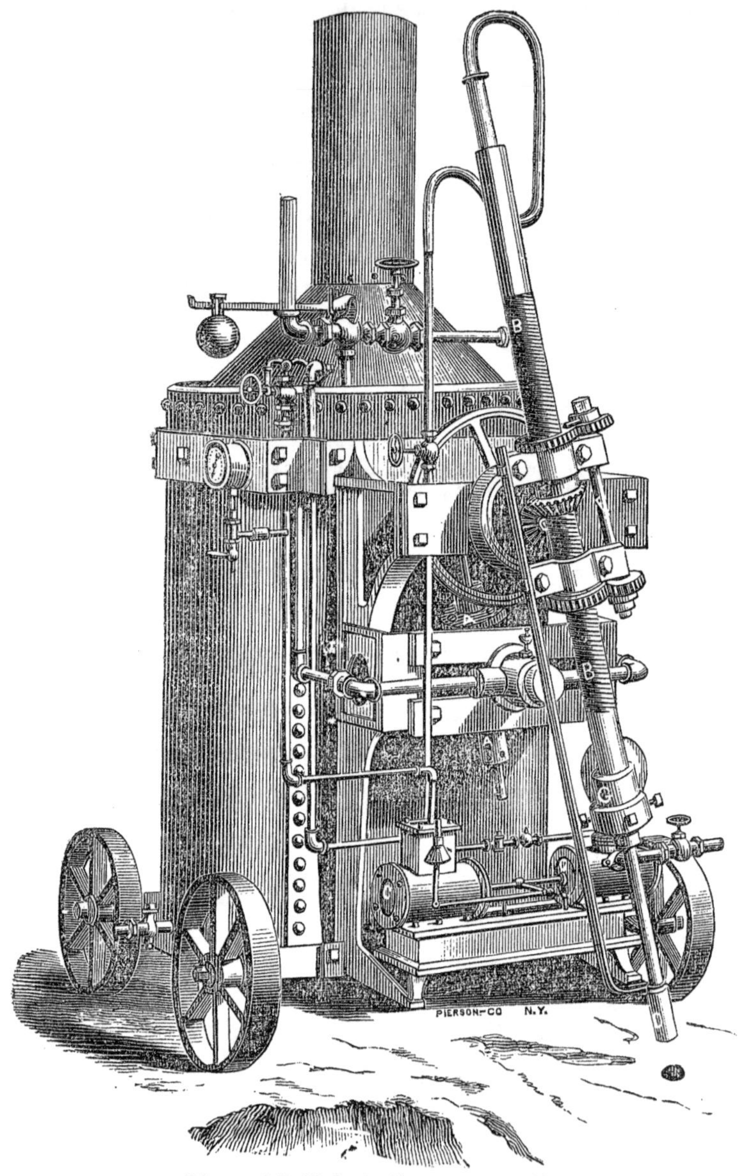

Diamond Drill for testing or prospecting.

The drills about to be described work upon an entirely different principle from those noticed in the preceding pages. The latter are all of the class of percussion drills, and cut by the force of the blow concentrated at the point of the drill. The diamond drill, on the contrary, is not used percussively, but by virtue of its extreme hardness it is made to cut away the rock by contact and pressure. The drill is pressed firmly, and is rapidly rotated against the rock to be bored.

The application of rough black diamonds to boring and cutting into rocks was made in 1860, by Mr. Rodolphe Leschot, a civil engineer residing in Paris, and formerly a student in the École Centrale. He found by experimenting that such diamonds, firmly set in the end of an iron or steel tube or cylinder, could be made to bore holes in rock to great depths and with a rapidity before unknown.

A short section of a cylinder of soft steel is used for the purpose. It varies from one to three or more inches in diameter, according to the size of the hole to be drilled, and is only about one-quarter of an inch thick. Cavities are drilled in the end of the cylinder, and into these cavities black diamonds of the common or bort variety are firmly set, by hammering up the soft metal around them. They are allowed to project about half a millimetre in front and slightly beyond the outer and inner surface of the cylinder or ring. This ring is secured by means of a bayonet joint or screw thread upon the end of a long hollow rod or drill bar, to which a rapid rotation is given. By pressing or feeding this revolving diamond-mounted ring against the rock to be cut, and at the same time supplying it freely with cold water, the rock, whether of soft or hard materials, of clay, slate, or of flint, is rapidly worn away, and an annular cutting results, leaving a central core of rock, which passes into the center of the drill and drill holder, and may be broken out when the drill is withdrawn, thus leaving a truly cylindrical hole with smooth sides.

The rapidity with which this apparently delicate ring cuts its way into the hardest syenite, quartz, or granite is surprising. The first experiments showed that two men with a machine like an ordinary feed drill could bore $0^{m}.025$ in depth per hour. The cylindrical core left in the center was $0^{m}.031$ in diameter and the annular groove $0^{m}.043$ in diameter; consequently the part cut out was equal to a cylinder $0^{m}.012$ thick. But this method of feeding or advancing the drill was clearly very defective, no allowance being made for the varying hardness of the rock. Since that time very great improvements in the way of mounting, operating, and feeding the drills have been made.

The wood-cut represents the drill and its mounting, as manufactured by Messrs. Severance & Holt, the assignees of the patent for the United States. This form is known as the "testing or prospecting drill," and it is designed chiefly for testing the character and value of mineral deposits, although it is adapted to a variety of other work, such as drilling holes in quarries for blasting, and for well-boring.

It consists of a small, upright boiler, to one side of which is firmly bolted the cast-iron frame which supports the engine and swivel, drill-head, gears, and screw shaft, as shown in the engraving. The engine—an oscillator of from five to seven horse power—is shown at A. B is the screw shaft with drill passing through it. This shaft is made of hydraulic pipe from five to seven feet in length, with a coarse thread cut on the outside. This thread, a portion of which is shown in the cut, runs the entire length of the shaft, which also carries a spline by which it is feathered to its upper sleeve-gear. This gear is double, and connects by its lower teeth with the beveled driving-gear, and by its upper teeth with the release-gear (E.) This release-gear is feathered to the feed shaft, (F,)at the bottom of which is a frictional gear fitting the lower gear on the screw shaft, which has one or more teeth less than the frictional gear, whereby a differential feed is produced. This frictional gear is attached to bottom of feed shaft (F) by a friction nut, thus producing a combined differential and frictional feed which renders the drill perfectly sensitive to the character of the rock through which it is passing, and maintains a uniform pressure upon the same. The severe and sudden strain upon the cutting points incidental to drilling through soft into hard rock with a positive feed is thus avoided. The drill proper (passing through the screw shaft B) consists of a tubular bar, made of lap-weld pipe, with a steel bit or boring-head (D) screwed on to one end. This bit is a steel thimble about four inches in length, having three rows of black diamonds in their natural rough state firmly imbedded therein, so that the edges of those in one row project forward from its face, while the edges of those in the other two rows project from the outer and inner peripheries respectively. The diamonds of the first-mentioned row cut the path of the drill in its forward progress, while those upon the outer and inner periphery of the tool enlarge the cavity around the same, and admit the free ingress and egress of the water as hereafter described. As the drill passes into the rock, cutting an annular channel, that portion of stone encircled by this channel is of course undisturbed, and passes up into the drill in the form of a solid cylinder. This core is drawn out with the drill in sections sometimes of from 8 to 10 feet in length.

The sides of the hollow bit are one-fourth of an inch thick, and the diamonds of the inner row project about one-eighth of an inch, so that the core or cylinder produced by a two-inch drill (the ordinary size for testing) is one and a quarter inches in diameter.

Inside the bit (D) is placed a self-adjusting wedge which allows the core to pass up into the drill without hinderance, but which impinges upon and holds it fast when the action of the drill is reversed—thus breaking it off at the bottom and bringing it to the surface when the drill is withdrawn.

In order to withdraw the drill it is only necessary to throw out the release-gear (E) by sliding it up to the feed shaft, (F,) to which it is feathered, when the drill runs up with the same motion of the engine which carried it down, but with a velocity sixty times greater; that is, the speed with which the drill leaves the rock, bringing the core with it, is to the speed with which it penetrates it as sixty to one—the revolving velocity in both cases being the same.

The drill rod may be extended to any desirable length by simply adding fresh pieces of pipe. Common gas-pipe, or, better, lap-welded iron tube, is found to serve admirably for this purpose, the successive lengths being quickly coupled together by an inside coupling four inches long, with a hole through the center of each to admit the water. The drill is held firmly in its place by the chuck (G) at the bottom of the screw shaft.

The small steam pump (C C) is connected by rubber hose with any convenient stream or reservoir of water, and also with the outer end of the drill pipe by a similar hose having a swivel-joint, as shown in the picture. Through this hose a steady stream of water is forced by the pump into the drill from which it escapes between the diamond teeth at the bottom of the bit, (D,) and passes rapidly out of the hole at the surface of the rock, carrying away all the grit and borings produced by the drill. Where water is scarce or difficult of access, a spout is laid from the mouth of the hole to the tank or reservoir and a strainer attached to the connecting hose, so that the same water may be used over and over again with but little loss. This pump also supplies the boiler.

The same parties manufacture another style of prospecting drill, similar in its construction to that just described, but larger and more powerful. It has a horizontal tubular boiler 3½ by 7 feet, with flues three inches in diameter, and steam capacity equal to twelve horse-power. The engines are two oscillators of 4¾-inch cylinder, five-inch stroke, and both attached to the same crank shaft. The whole is mounted upon wheels so as to be portable. It is geared to run with twice the speed of the first-described machine. Its construction and general appearance is shown by the cut. The pump P and water hose H fill the same offices as those in the upright machine. This pattern is mounted on large wheels with broad felloes for easy transportation in rough mining districts, and, like No. 1, is all complete in itself.

It is especially adapted to well boring, draining, and prospecting, and will bore holes from two (2) to five (5) inches in diameter, as desired, and to any required depth. The total weight is about 3,800 pounds.

An open cut or quarry drill is also made. It is similar in its construction to the last-described machine without the boiler, and has two oscillating engines, B B, of five horse-power each, and is geared three to one. This machine gives to its drill rod 900 to 1,000 revolutions per minute, and drills in ordinary rock at the rate of fifteen to twenty feet per hour. It is adapted to either compressed air or steam. A powerful plunger pump is represented at A.

Severance & Holt's Portable Prospecting Drill.

The speed of boring of course depends upon the character of the rock, ranging from five feet per hour in very hard rock to fifteen feet per hour in limestone, sand rock, and shale. The rate of speed in drilling appears to be limited only by the velocity with which it is possible to rotate the drill. It is claimed that with one thousand revolutions per minute the hardest rock may be drilled from eight to ten feet per hour, the diamonds cutting only the one-four-hundredth part of an inch at each revolution, and the drill thus advancing one inch for every four hundred revolutions. This is the finest or slowest "feed," and is used only in flint or rocks of greatest hardness; while in ordinary rock the drill is fed at the rate of three hundred revolutions to the inch—the diamonds, of course, cutting the one-three-hundredth part of an inch at each revolution; and in marble, sandstone, &c., at the rate of an inch for every two hundred revolutions. The pressure of the bit or drill head against the rock does not depend upon the length and weight of the drill rod, and is no greater at the depth of a hundred feet than when entering the rock at the surface. The variations in the feed are effected by simply changing one gear-wheel, requiring less than five minutes' time. The same machine will bore holes from one to four inches in diameter, as desired.

The diamond teeth are the only parts of the tool which come in contact with the rock, and their hardness is such that more than two thousand feet have been drilled by the same points with but little appreciable wear. The cost of resetting the diamonds so as to present new points is very slight, and no special skill is required for the operation.

Other repairs are seldom needed. The diamonds vary in price from six to seven dollars per carat, gold. Some of them are light-colored, translucent stones, nearly one-quarter of an inch in diameter. The usual diameter of bits for drilling blast holes in mines is one and a half inch, carrying six diamonds.

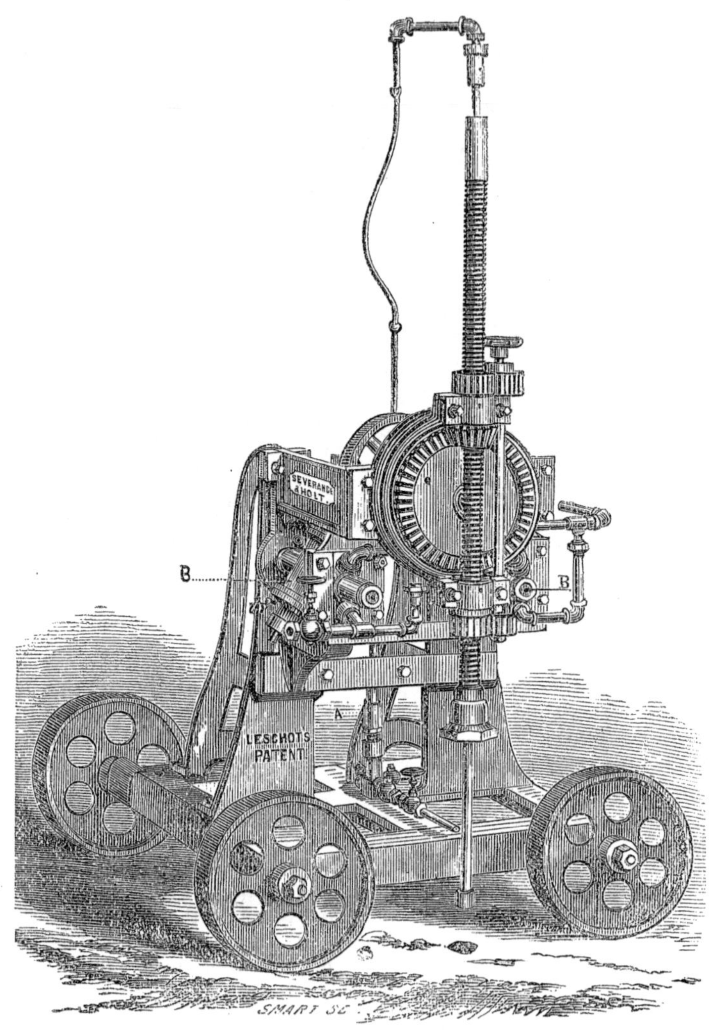

Open Cut or Quarry Drill.

The peculiar shape of the boring bit prevents the drill from running out of line; hence the hole bored, however deep it may be, is perfectly straight and there is no friction of the drill against the rock.

The manufacturers have made another boring head of similar construction, but having the annular opening partially closed and the diamonds so arranged as to bore out the entire hole instead of producing the core. This form of bit, however, is not desirable, as it requires far more power to drive it, consumes more diamonds, and is not available for boring deep holes on account of its tendency to deviate from a true line.

The annular diamond drill has been used for testing the nature of the rocks at considerable depths in many places, and it is evidently destined to be of very great service to mining industry. Rock-cylinders or cores have been repeatedly taken out from a depth of 300 to 400 feet, and they give a perfect record of the succession of the rock deposits, or veins passed through. At the lead mines in St. Francis County, Missouri, test holes have been bored at several points from sixty-five to one hundred and fifty feet in depth, and have proved the existence of deposits of ore not before known. At the Portland, Connecticut, sandstone quarries, a test hole has been bored and cores obtained to a depth of 312 feet. In Essex County, New York, the drill has been used upon the ore-bed of Witherbees, Sherman & Co., and gave a continuous core to a depth of 340 feet in very hard rock, and in the compact iron ore, thus showing the nature of the formation to that depth. In Pennsylvania, at the William Penn Colliery, the drill has been used to prospect for the "Mammoth Vein." The drills were put into operation at the bottom of a shaft already sunk 170 feet. In six hours and forty-seven minutes, actual running time, the drill penetrated to an additional depth of 104 feet 11 inches. Of this, 46 feet and 1 inch was through slate and coal alternating and mixed, and 58 feet 10 inches through anthracite coal, the bed dipping at about 45 degrees. The average rate of boring was 3.06 inches per minute for the whole depth, or about 15½ feet an hour. The proprietors write:

We are satisfied that we could have bored through hard rock at the same uniform rate, for the slate bored through contains "sulphur balls" of the size of a goose egg, and upward, of sulphuret of iron, of intense hardness, but which formed no more serious obstructions to the drill than the conglomerate rock. With the exception of one imperfect diamond, we could not perceive the least effect or abrasion on the surface of the diamonds, even with a magnifying glass. We afterward tried the same machine for boring blast holes in the coal at bottom of shaft with equally satisfactory results. The coal was such as experienced miners could drill five feet per hour in by hand; the machine bored it at the rate of twenty-two inches per minute, to the no small surprise of our veteran miners.

It is found to work well upon hard trap rock, in which it is almost impossible to drill a hole of uniform size with hand drills, or to drill more than about ten feet in depth. In this rock, upon the New Haven and Willimantic railroad, it is found by experience that where only from 8 to 12 feet of drilling could be made by hand in one day by three men, working by the foot, a machine will drill from 30 to 36 feet. Two machines are used and they give holes two inches in diameter and uniform throughout their depth—from 18 to 30 feet. It is found very advantageous to drill from two to four holes and to explode the charges in them simultaneously. By boring five holes to the depth of the grade, and exploding the charges all at once by the battery, it is possible to remove twenty-four feet in length of the rock in the cut at one blast.

Some interesting results have been obtained with the drill in submarine boring at Hell Gate. The reef of rock to be removed lies from twelve to twenty feet below the surface of the water at high tide. The machine was so placed, just above the water, upon a trestle-work or staging, that the drill could be placed in contact with the rock twelve feet below. The drill penetrated at the rate of 6½ feet per hour, and two holes 32 feet deep and 2½ inches in diameter were drilled in a short time. Its performance at that place has given great satisfaction.

The annexed figure shows the construction of a machine for drilling in mines or tunnels varying from four to sixteen feet high. It is operated by steam and is portable, being nearly balanced upon the two wheels. By depressing the handle H it can be trundled about.

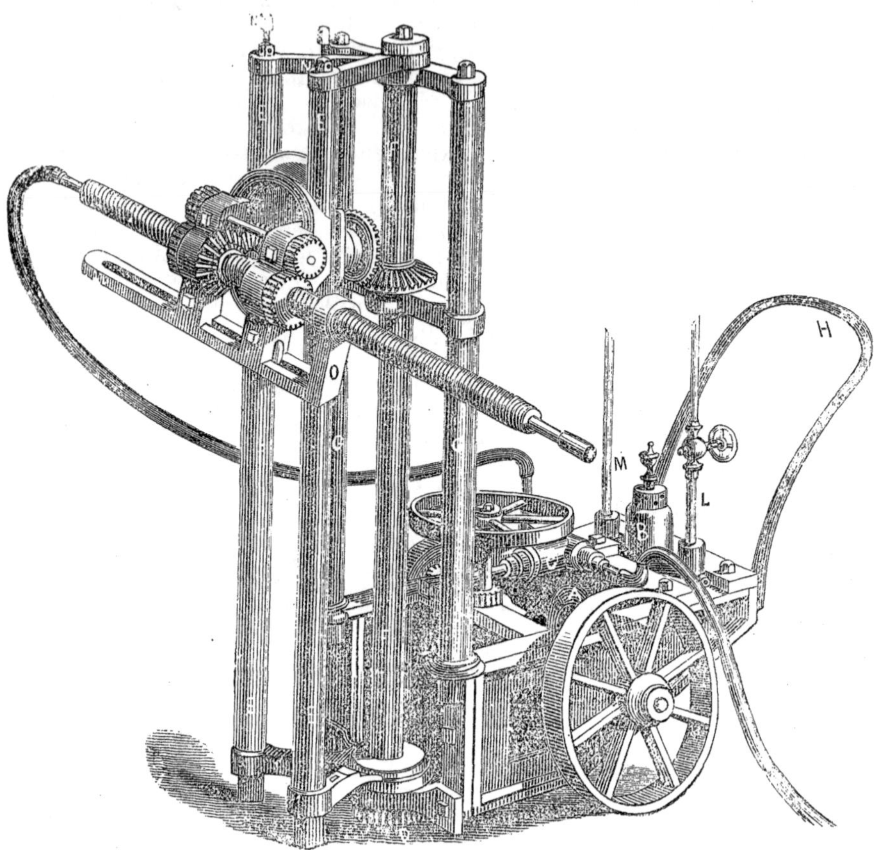

Diamond Drill for mines.

The upright frame (E E) which supports the swivel drill-head with its gears and drill, is attached by hinge-plates to the top and bottom of the driving shaft (F) and may be swung to the right or left, describing a semi-circle. This permits drilling at any angle of the horizontal arc thus described without moving the machine, and also placing the drill-rod close up to the side wall of the tunnel. The drill-head also slides up and down this adjustable frame (E E) and can be secured at any point so as to bore a perpendicular row of horizontal holes, without incurring more than three or four minutes' delay in adjusting the drill to each successive hole.

The drill itself with its feed-gears and sliding guide (O) may be turned completely round by simply loosening a nut on the back of the swivel head so that the point of the drill shall describe a vertical circle, at any angle of which it will bore equally well.

The two uprights (G G) are used to support the driving shaft, (F.) They are made of common hydraulic pipe, and may be lengthened or shortened at pleasure, according to the height of the tunnel. The driving shaft (F) has a sliding gear attached by feather and spline adjustable at any position as shown in the cut. The sliding brace just beneath this gear is used to steady the driving shaft. Motion is communicated to this shaft by means of the gear at the bottom, (D.) The hollow frame posts (E E) are set firmly against the upper wall by means of extension screws (N N) which may be run up two or three feet if desired. The engine, water apparatus, feed-gears and bit, are the same as in the prospecting drill, and the mode of operation is essentially the same. When it is desired to produce holes less than one or one and a quarter inches diameter, it is usual to set the diamonds so as to cut out all the rock, but otherwise the annular bit is preferable. The steam or compressed air is brought through rubber hose from any convenient distance and introduced into the engine by pipe, (L.) (M) is the exhaust pipe. This drill being used to bore short holes, may be run much faster than the other, 900 revolutions per minute being a fair rate of speed. The feed may be varied at pleasure, and according to the hardness of the rock from 90 to 340 revolutions per inch, which gives from two to ten inches per minute. The same advantages are secured by friction feed in this drill as in the larger one.

The Leschot drill has recently been introduced in California and is in practical operation in Colorado Territory, at Clinton Gulch, in a tunnel belonging to the Consolidated Bullion and Incas Mining Company. It was desired to prove the ground in advance of the end of the prospecting tunnel, 600 feet long, and by means of the drill a hole was made 417½ feet, horizontally, in advance, and a core brought out so as to show the nature of the rock for the whole distance. The machine was placed in the tunnel 600 feet from the outer air and was moved by compressed air, supplied from a compresser outside.

At Shenandoah, Schuylkill County, Pennsylvania, the drill has bored a hole 274 feet deep, through shale, sandstone, and coal, at the rate of from 20 to 25 feet a day, including the time occupied in taking out the core. Where it is not essential to obtain a test core, a much more rapid rate of progress may be attained.

DE LA ROCHE-TOLLAY AND PERRET'S BORING APPARATUS.

In France considerable attention has been given to perfecting machinery for supporting in the proper positions and giving motion to the diamond drill, and at the Paris Universal Exposition of 1867 the drill could be seen daily in operation, driven by water power and boring holes into the hardest granite. The motor was a small water-pressure engine, contrived by Mr. Perret, of Bordeaux. This consists of a brass cylinder, $0^{m}.055$ inside diameter, in which a piston works back and forth by the alternate pressure of the water on the faces. The length of stroke was $0^{m}.120$, and the motion was changed from reciprocating to rotary by a connecting rod and crank. It was run with water, the pressure of which varied from 3 to 9½ atmospheres; and it is claimed that under the maximum pressure from 47 to 57 per cent. of the theoretical effect was realized.

The drill-bar consists of a six-sided cast-steel shaft, $1^{m}.45$ long, bored throughout its entire length with a hole $0^{m}.016$ in diameter. The diamond-armed ring is mounted upon one end of this hollow hexagonal drill-bar, and at the other end is a brass piston, $0^{m}.11$ in diameter, upon which the water is allowed to press, so as to keep the ring firmly against the face of the rock to be bored. This pressure is varied with the hardness of the rock. A pressure of eight atmospheres is sufficient for hard rocks, such as quartz and granite. For calcareous rocks, such as limestones and marbles, five or six atmospheres is sufficient. The tool makes about 200 revolutions a minute. By the injection of water through the hollow drill-bar the powder of the rock is washed out as fast as formed and the drill is kept cool. The drill-bar receives its motion by means of bevel gearing.

The following are some of the results of the experiments made during the progress of the Exposition. The pressure upon the feeding or advancing piston, forcing the drill forward, was equal to eight atmospheres, and the speed of rotation varied from 200 to 280 revolutions per minute. The rate of advance was as follows:

In solid Mont Cenis quartz .... $0^{m}.054$ per minute.
In Morvan porphyries .... $0^{m}.042$ per minute.

In granite.................................... $0^m.050$ per minute.
In hard calcareous dolomite...................... $0^m.080$ per minute.

The holes were cylindrical, and the sides were left quite smooth, and were thus very well adapted to the use of cartridges.

The weight of the apparatus is equal to that of the percussive drilling machines used at Mont Cenis—about 200 kilograms—and its price, including the engine but not the support, is 2,500 francs. It bores holes $0^m.035$ to $0^m.06$ in diameter and from $0^m.90$ to $1^m.00$ deep. The ring used was $0^m.035$ outside diameter and the core left was $0^m.014$ in diameter. In regard to the cost of the diamond drill or the cost and wear of the diamond, it is stated in the reports upon the Exposition:

It is true that when the ring was first used a difficulty existed in the selection of the diamonds, as to which, from the nature of their cleavage, would be the most serviceable. The setting was not always performed as solidly as could be desired; but these difficulties have disappeared. We have examined two rings which were worked for seven months at the Exposition, and which have perfectly resisted. We believe that we can affirm that in a hard stone like granite, a ring properly worked will cut holes to an aggregate depth of 150 metres. A ring for boring holes $0^m.036$ diameter costs about 150 francs, but as the black and opaque diamonds used in its construction are ordinarily employed in the shape of dust for polishing transparent diamonds, and as their wear during the act of perforation is very slight, they can be extracted from the socket in which they are set, and be returned to the trade with a depreciation proportionate only to the diminution of weight. The diamonds extracted from a worn-out ring generally fetch from seventy to eighty francs—that is to say, about one-half of their first cost.

It is the opinion of Messrs. Huet and Geyler, who, with Mr. D'Aligny, reported upon this drilling machine, that it must, in time, supersede the percussion drills; and they are confident that it could be used most advantageously to replace the percussion drills at Mont Cenis. They remark:

We cannot refrain from making a comparison between this perforator and the one employed at Mont Cenis. Its solidity, proved by seven months' work, gives the assurance that twenty to twenty-two of these perforators would be sufficient for the heads of both galleries, including duplicates, instead of at least two hundred and twenty actually existing. Mr. Sommeiller's perforators cost the same as those of Messrs. De La Roche-Tollay and Perret. The staff would be four times less, for one man can easily attend four perforators; thus four men instead of sixteen would suffice for twenty-four hours at the two galleries.

The repairs to the rings require neither forges, lathes, nor workshops; and we are convinced that a workman to each gallery would be sufficient for the repairs of all the perforators. We have stated that the rate of advance in the Mont Cenis quartz was $0^m.054$ per minute, under a pressure of 874 kilogrammes on the propelling piston; therefore a hole $0^m.90$ could have been driven in 16 minutes, say 20, and as each perforator should make 10 holes, say 3½ hours, even doubling this time for preparing the work, it will be seen that five stopes can be done in two days, including the time for blasting and clearing away the debris, which is equivalent to an advance of $2^m.25$ per diem, instead of barely $0^m.50$, the actual rate of advance.

The apparatus of Messrs. De La Roche-Tollay and Perret is not subjected to any shock; the pressure is exerted on the rock irrespective of the speed of the tool, and such pressure can be regulated as may be desired; and when water power is obtainable, which is generally the case in mines and tunnels, the motive power actually costs nothing.

Mr. Perret's machine can also be worked by compressed air, and for this it would be sufficient to add a hydraulic accumulator to the perforator carriage. Such an accumulator would be but small, since the volume of water required for advancing the piston one meter is 9½ litres, it would be sufficient to add two or three litres per hole one, meter deep for washing out the holes.

VALUE OF THE ANNULAR DRILL.

A conviction of the very great value of the diamond drills, especially as now made and worked by Messrs. Severance & Holt, must be the excuse, if any is necessary, for giving so much space to the description of them. After having seen the operation of the drills, and the great variety of samples of cores of the hard rocks, such as syenite, granite, trap, compact quartz, magnetic iron ore, marble, &c., which have been taken out by their use, and after reading many of the letters from various parts of the country, giving the most satisfactory reports of the operation of the drill in prospecting and in quarrying, I am satisfied that it should be commended to the attention of miners and prospectors everywhere, as one of the greatest aids they can have in ascertaining the nature of veins and beds at considerable distances, either from the surface or from the deepest or remotest points reached in their mines. The prospective value of many mines may, by means of this drill, be very closely and economically ascertained. It may be made of immense service not only in mines where the veins are pinched and of doubtful value, but in those veins that have always been of good size and value. It would, for example, be important and highly satisfactory to ascertain whether the rich vein of the Eureka Mine, at Grass Valley, California, continues to have nearly the same character and gold-bearing value for 400 or 500 feet below the present workings. The shafts and preparations for working could then with great propriety be projected upon a scale commensurate with the work evidently to be done. So, also, in respect to the Amador Mine, Sutter Creek, the Sierra Buttes, and other noted mines of California, and the Comstock lode in Nevada. There is at least one prominent case where this testing drill could be made of great service—at the Princeton vein, on the Mariposa Estate. The shoot of ore in this vein plunges at an angle of about 17° to the southeast, and has been worked about as far as it can be economically in that direction; and it is very desirable to know whether the shoot continues with the same inclination and richness far beyond the present excavations. If it does, it will be advisable to sink another shaft to intersect that part of the lode. A test hole could be sunk in a few weeks by means of this drill, and a core, showing the thickness and nature of the vein at that point obtained at trifling expense, compared with the cost of sinking a shaft or running a tunnel.

It is probable that the annular diamond drill may be advantageously used for cutting shafts of large diameter, inasmuch as the ratio of the quantity of material cut away to the size of the hole bored becomes less and less as the diameter of the bore increases. A large core would be left, but this could be readily broken out by blasting in a central hole. Among the great advantages of such shafts would be their truly cylindrical form and smooth sides.

CHAPTER V.

BORING DEEP WELLS FOR WATER OR OIL.

Within ten years seventy-five artesian wells have been bored in the desert of Sahara, yielding in the aggregate 45,000 litres of water per minute, or 64,800 cubic metres in twenty-four hours. A part of this desert has been made fertile; two villages have been created in the midst of the former solitudes, and 150,000 palm trees have been planted in more than a thousand new gardens. This is an indication of the great results in store for those who may undertake the work of supplying water to the marvelously rich soil of the Colorado desert in California. The strong arm of the government should be reached out in the initiative to restore fertility to such a broad area of the public lands, now not only worthless but a positive barrier to the settlement of that part of the country, and to transportation between the coast region and the interior.

Artesian well-boring has been practiced in California since about 1852, when several wells were pierced in the recent strata overlying the rock formations of San Francisco. Since then a great number of borings in the Santa Clara and San José valleys, and in other portions of the State, have been very successful. At Stockton a well has been pierced to a great depth, and an abundant supply of potable water obtained, which rises above the surface and supplies the city. The great trough-like valleys and basin-shaped depressions throughout California, Nevada, and adjoining regions present conditions favorable to the success of artesian borings; and although an overflowing fountain cannot in all cases be expected, yet there is little reason to doubt that an abundant supply may be obtained from the borings by pumping. The Sacramento, San Joaquin, and Tulare valleys, all invite a resort to artesian borings for water to irrigate their lower and more arid portions, where in mid-summer the drought is excessive. The Colorado desert, already mentioned, is another region where artesian borings may supply the only requisite for extreme fertility.

The most simple and the most ancient form of apparatus for piercing the earth to great depths is that adopted by the Chinese. It consists of a rope armed at the lower end with a tool of iron or steel. We are indebted for some of the earliest information in detail upon this subject to the missionary, Imbert, in 1827, who reported that in the Province of Ou-Tong-Kiao there were many thousand borings within an area of four leagues by ten, carried to a depth of nearly 1,800 feet in search of saline water and petroleum. Some of these borings, after the exhaustion of their brine, had been pierced to the depth of 3,000 feet, and had reached sources of carbureted hydrogen gas, which was used to produce the heat necessary for the concentration of the saline water.

A simple derrick, with a pulley above, and reel below from which the rope is unwound as the hole deepens, is nearly all that is required besides the perforating tools. Cords are attached by means of clamps to the rope between the pulley and the reel, and by pulling upon these cords the drill is alternately raised and dropped. The vertical movement of the drill ranges from one to two feet or more. The drills are made in various forms according to the nature of the rock to be penetrated. A French engineer, M. Jobard, uses a heavy cylindrical head of chilled cast iron attached to a long iron rod, as shown in section by the figure. The extremity of this rod is armed with a steel point, which projects below the cutting face of the cylinder, and serves to center the hole like the point of a carpenter's center-bit.

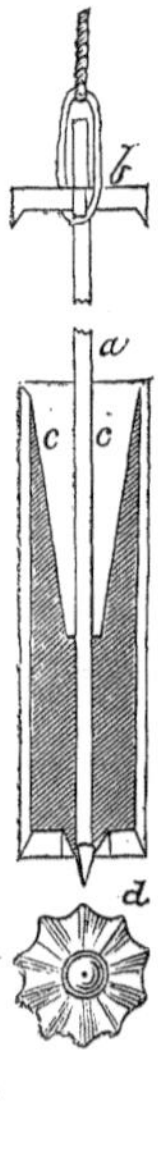

The surface of this cylindrical drill-head is channeled, so as to give room for the powder formed by the cutting to rise around it, and the upper part is provided with a conical cavity, *c c*, into which the loosened materials fall, and are removed from the hole when the drill is drawn out. The small figure, *d*, below the section, is a view of the end of the drill, and shows the arrangement of the cutting edges and grooves. The rod *a* may be several yards long, and is provided at the top with cross-bars of steel, *b*, intended to act as guides to keep the tool vertical. If it is desired to make the hole larger, in order to introduce tubing, it is only necessary to suspend the tool a little to one side of the axis, it will then hang with more less inclination in the hole, and cut out the sides in its descent. This would not be safe in loose rock.

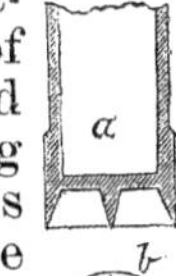

Another form of drill was designed and has been most successfully used by M. Goulet-Collet, of Rheims. It consists of a cylinder of heavy sheet-iron, two metres in length, suspended by a chain, and armed at its lower end with an annular cutting head of steel, *a*, in which two knives or chisels are placed across the opening, as shown in the end view at *b*. These chisels serve to cut the rock, while the water and sand are free to rise through the cylinder. The removal of the debris is effected by another tool, although this cylinder may be provided with valves like a sand-pump, and thus serve the double purpose of drill and pump.

When the rocks are not too hard for this form of tool they may be pierced with great rapidity. According to M. Debette, from whose description the foregoing is compiled, M. Goulet-Collet, with two workmen, could bore from eight to eleven metres a day in the chalk of the cretaceous formations of Champagne. He would also contract to bore wells to any required depth for nine francs per metre. He had made in the course of several years nearly one hundred borings, and each had given good water, for a total cost ranging from 150 to 300 francs. The apparatus did not cost over 500 francs.

The methods of boring employed in California are substantially the same as those for oil wells, to be hereafter described. The rope is used in preference to rods, and there is no peculiarity in the method worthy of special notice.

In Europe boring with rods rather than rope is preferred. These rods are made of elastic wood, or of the best quality of iron. In the latter case the sectional area depends upon the depth to which the hole is to be bored, varying as shown by the annexed table:

Depth of hole.	Diameter of hole.	Sectional area of rods.
Metres.	*Metres.*	*Metres.*
0 to 50	0.05 to 0. 6	0.025
50 to 100	0.06 to 0.10	0.030
100 to 200	0.10 to 0.15	0.032
200 and beyond.	0.15 to 0.25	0.045

At Cessingen a well has been bored to a depth of 535 metres, with rods of $0^{m}.025$ section. The length of rods is limited only by the height of the derricks. It is usually between four and eight metres.

As already remarked, great improvements have of late been made in the apparatus for boring to great depths, and especially for sinking wells several feet in diameter. The success attending the boring of the celebrated well at Grenelle, Paris, has led to the sinking of still larger ones, in order to give a more abundant supply of water and meet the necessities of a rapidly increasing population. In 1867 two wells were in progress—one in the suburb of La Chapelle, in the northern portion of the city of Paris, by MM. Degousée and Laurent, and the other at Butte-aux-Cailles, in the extreme south of the city, by M. Dru, formerly Mulot & Dru. These new wells were to be, the one five feet in diameter, and the other about four feet. The following are the depths and dimensions of the older wells: Height above the sea, at Grenelle,

121.3 feet; at Passy, 305.2 feet; depth of bore-hole, at Grenelle, 1800.7 feet; at Passy, 1923.7 feet: internal diameter of tube, or lining of hole, at Grenelle, approximately, 9 inches to 6 inches at bottom; at Passy, 2.4 feet. The full diameter of the Passy bore-hole was one metre, or 3.28 English feet.

The Universal Exposition of 1867, at Paris, contained fine illustrative specimens of the tools and apparatus now used by Messrs. Degousée and Ch. Laurent. In the notice of them, and of the operations of boring which follows, I have used not only my own notes, made upon the spot, but portions of the report of the United States commissioner to the Exposition.

The apparatus, doubtless, does not present, for the most part, the interest of a new invention; but in examining the details of its construction, it is easy to see that the novel and diversified condition in which the sinkings have been executed, and the unforeseen accidents which these have produced, have been studied with great care and intelligence by these able engineers, and that all the teachings of practice have been profited by and have led to many important modifications and simplifications of the forms of the tools.

The boring rods applicable to artesian wells, before the wells of Passy were sunk, did not exceed $0^{m}.30$ in diameter. The two wells undertaken by the city of Paris—one at La Chapelle, by Messrs. Degousée and Ch. Laurent, the other at La Butte-aux-Cailles, near the Ivry station, by Messrs. Dru Brothers—have been commenced at a diameter of $1^{m}.80$.

The boring apparatus comprises two essential parts—the tools which serve to excavate the earth, and the appliances at the surface for working or handling the tools, which become much more important as the diameter of the wells or shafts is increased.

The following are some of the details of the construction and dimensions of the tools used by Messrs. Degousée and Ch. Laurent at the artesian wells of La Chapelle:

The machine is worked by a horizontal steam-engine of 15 horse-power. The fly-wheel shaft makes 50 revolutions per minute. It carries, first, a pinion of $0^{m}.30$ diameter; secondly, two brakes; thirdly, two clutches; fourthly and lastly, a pulley of $1^{m}.50$ diameter.

The pinion of $0^{m}.30$ diameter drives a toothed wheel fixed on the axle of the drum of the capstan, upon which the chains for lifting the shafts of the borers are wound, and also the percussion and cleansing apparatus. The diameter of the drum of the capstan is $0^{m}.55$; its length is $1^{m}.60$. It has a spiral groove which guides the chains and causes them to wind regularly upon it. The pulley of $1^{m}.50$ diameter is belted to another pulley of $1^{m}.00$ diameter, fixed at the extremity of an axle which carries at the other end a pinion $0^{m}.40$ diameter. This pinion is geared with a wheel of $2^{m}.00$ diameter, fixed on a second axle, where is also fixed the crank-plate which, by means of a connecting rod, gives a reciprocating motion to the striking beam. This beam is supported at a point about two-thirds of its whole length distant from the connecting-rod end.

The two clutches mentioned serve, on one part, to throw into gear the pinion of $0^{m}.30$ with the driving wheel of the drum of the capstan, and, on the other part, to drive the pulley of $1^{m}.50$ diameter, keyed on the fly-wheel shaft, by which motion is given to the striking beam, at the end of which the boring tools are attached.

The two brakes placed upon the fly-wheel shaft are for the purpose of regulating the speed of the descent of the tools, the weight of which might cause a great acceleration of speed, and, consequently a fracture, which is always to be dreaded.

The timber framing which forms the derrick or tower for the sinking of the wells is more simply arranged than that adopted by Mr. Kind in his construction for sinking large shafts. The tools, in place of being received upon a platform about ten metres above the surface, are upon the surface itself, and it is, consequently, much more easy to work them. The linked chain for lifting the tools has stood the wear of ten years without any accident; while the breaking of the cables employed in the system of Messrs. Kind and Chaudron have occasioned serious accidents and delays.

At the boring of the wells of Passy, undertaken by Mr. Kind, there were two machines of 25 horse-power, one of 10 horse-power working the striking beam, and one of 15 horse-power working the capstan drum. The trepan, at the shank, did not weigh more than about two tons. Messrs. Degousée and Ch. Laurent used an engine of only 15 horse-power to work their trepan, which weighed about four tons, and to bring the broken or bored earth to the surface. This engine did not require any repairs, except such as are ordinarily necessary during a service of two years.

BORING TOOLS OF DEGOUSÉE AND LAURENT.

The construction of the trepan employed at the artesian well of La Chapelle differs completely from that of Mr. Kind. It is composed of six branches, so arranged as to break up the earth in an annular belt or zone, leaving a central core. The six teeth, which are keyed into the blade-holder, are $0^{m}.35$ wide, and the mode of fixing them into the six branches is so secure and solid that, up to this date, no accident has happened. Even when a tooth becomes unkeyed it cannot get out of the blade-holder, while at the shaft of the Hôpital there have been twenty-three teeth out of their sockets, all of which fell into the shaft. One of these accidents caused a stoppage of a month.

The percussion of the trepan with the regular rotating movement cuts out an annular channel of $0^{m}.45$ to $0^{m}.50$ large, leaving in the center of the shaft an unworked piece of earth, or core, of $0^{m}.80$ or $0^{m}.90$ diameter. This mass, when in slightly coherent earth, crumbles down and forms an irregular cone. In this case they bolt on one side of the center of the tool a radial or a transverse blade, which triturates the core.

This trepan weighs about four tons. Its first cost is greater than that of Mr. Kind's, but it proves in practice to be much more solid and durable, and it works better.

Messrs. Degousée and Ch. Laurent have been very successful in giving a free fall or drop to their trepan. With more than ten thousand blows, the trepan has not once failed to be caught again upon the descent of the rods, and its fall has always worked with the greatest regularity, while at the shaft of the Hôpital eighteen fractures of pieces of the slide have occasioned a stoppage of more than a month. The contrivance for the free fall of the trepan is constructed as follows: A movable piece surrounds the shaft above the hooks and terminates in a fork, of which the two branches extend below the cutters and touch the bottom of the bore. This piece is not lifted, unless the borer is raised more than the stroke allowed by the collar which attaches around the hooks. The upper part of the hooks lifted by the boring rod slides, therefore, in the collar, and, meeting a striker which makes them open, the tool immediately falls with all its weight on the bottom of the bore.

The boring rod, being lowered, catches the tool again by the hooks, and this action is repeated so as to obtain a succession of blows.

The suspension rods employed by Messrs. Degousée and Ch. Laurent are of iron. They have a section of $0^m.045$ square, and are $12^m.00$ long. These rods have worked for two years without accident, and they are better than those made of wood, for the following reasons: It is evident that wood at a great depth will acquire from the pressure of the water a density at least equal to that of the water; and, moreover, the iron fittings add to the weight in a certain proportion; and if we compare the sections of the shafts or wooden rods of the wells at the Hôpital with those of iron at the wells of La Chapelle, it is seen that the metre in length of the first weighs at least 35 kilograms, (70 pounds,) while that of the second does not exceed 16 kilograms, (32 pounds.) It is true that, as the wooden rods displace a greater quantity of water, their weight is diminished; but this small advantage is largely overbalanced by their rapid deterioration, whether in store or at work. The wood in drying heats and loses its qualities. Well made, their construction appears sufficiently costly to make the matter of renewing them at each sinking rather an important item; they augment sensibly the cost of work to be done. On the other hand, the iron shafts that can be balanced, as practiced by Messrs. Degousée and Laurent, require for their descent and elevation but a little more force, and with steam-engines this increase of expense is so little that it may be disregarded.

The draining and cleaning tools of the wells at La Chapelle differ equally from those of Mr. Kind, and they are, perhaps, superior. The modification of the trepan intended to work out the annular groove or zone led to a modification of the auger, which is annular and composed of nine augers joined together, of $0^m.35$ diameter.

The spoon or bucket which lifts the detritus in the middle of the wells is a cylinder $1^m.00$ in diameter, and $2^m.50$ in height. The bottom, in place of carrying two valves, is pierced with seven round holes, which are closed by hemispherical hollow valves, carrying in their axis a shaft which traverses the whole length of the spoon. This shaft is terminated by a handle which permits the workmen to lift up the valve in order to empty out the mud when the bucket is withdrawn from the well. This arrangement is intended to obviate the inconvenience of the hinged valves, which often, by not completely closing, let the matter in the bucket escape during the ascent of the dredge.

The bucket at La Chapelle is emptied with great ease, it being lifted one metre above the surface and placed on a little truck, which carries it immediately under a crane placed at the side where the contents are to be emptied.

The recovering tools are composed simply of the ordinary screw bell, (*cloche à vis*,) a grapnel, and a new form of pincers, with four branches. These four branches are arranged in a parallelogram, and one of their ends is fixed to a single piece bored and tapped in its center. It is easy to understand the part this plays: in raising or lowering the nut in the screw, which is attached to the boring rods, the four branches expand or contract at will, and, resting on the bottom of the well, they seize the objects which may be there.

TUBBING.

The artesian well of La Chapelle traverses the Tertiary strata of the Paris basin, and penetrates the chalks and marls of the Secondary.

According to the agreement between the contractors and the city, the boring is expected to be 600 metres deep before it reaches the water-bearing bed of the green sand formation. After working two years, the well has already (1867) reached a depth of 337 metres, but it has been found necessary to tub or line the shaft to avoid the caving which would inevitably happen without it.

A first column of sheet-iron lining, $1^m.80$ diameter, $34^m.50$ high, and weighing about thirty-six tons, was put in immediately below the preparatory pit, which last was lined with masonry to a distance of about six metres below the surface, where the working platform was placed.

A second column, $1^m.70$ diameter, 135 metres high, and weighing 11 tons, was next put in; and lastly, a third column was put down just to the chalk. This column has a height of 139 metres, its diameter $1^m.37$, and its weight about 110 tons.

The columns are made of sheet iron of a mean thickness of $0^m.02$; the height of each section being determined by the breadth of the iron plates. These plates were fastened together by rivets with countersunk heads, so that the interior and exterior surface of the lining were quite smooth.

To form one of these cylinders, *two* sheets of iron of the thickness of $0^m.01$ are taken and riveted together in such a manner that one of them, the inner one for example, projects slightly beyond the other, and thus forms a shoulder to which the next section above can be riveted. By this arrangement it will be seen that each column of tubbing presented the same diameter throughout its length. When the sections of the column are thus prepared, they are lowered and put together as they descend into the well.

This operation is performed in the following manner:

A wooden frame is made and supported upon a wheeled truck. This frame is composed of two strong vertical walls of a height of four or five metres, connected at their upper part by a cap or top, to which four nuts are fixed to receive four screws intended to sustain the pipe in its descent. Each of these screws is worked by two men by means of a crank and bevel gearing conveniently arranged.

The lower part of these four screws is fixed to a strong circular wooden plate, about $0^m.50$ thick, and equal in diameter to the inner diameter of the column that is to be lowered.

Upon the working platform a species of tubbing in wood is placed, the interior diameter of which is equal to the exterior of the iron tubbing or cylinder. The height of this tubbing is two metres; the segments of which it is composed are united together, and can be drawn together or expanded by means of screws, so as to squeeze the column and act as a clamp or support during its descent. When this kind of tubbing is put in place, and the frame which carries the screws is put in the axis of the well, the first section of pipe is brought forward and placed over the well. Previously several iron ears are bolted upon the interior face of the tub, and about a metre below its upper edge, the use of which will be presently explained. Other projecting ears are fixed in the inside of the tub, and on these ears the lower part of the wooden plate is allowed to rest, and is then bolted to them. When the work is thus prepared, this first tub is lowered until the outer ears rest upon the upper edge of the wooden tubbing which surrounds the column on the outside. The inside ears are then removed and the pipe is supported upon the outer tub. The inner plate of wood is then lifted up by the aid of the screws, and the rivet holes of the ears are closed up by hot rivets with countersunk heads. The second cylinder is then placed in the axis of the well. This second cylinder has inside and outside ears like the first, and the circular plate is introduced and bolted to the ears. These hold it at its upper part, and it is then lowered regularly, with the aid of the screws, until the lower part fits into the first cylinder. The two sections are then riveted together by hot rivets. The tub is then lifted a little in order to remove the outside ears of the first section of the cylinder, and the whole is allowed to descend by its own weight till the outer ears of the top cylinder rest in their turn upon the upper part of the wooden tubbing. They proceed in the same way for all the other sections of the column or tubbing of the well until it is finished.

The lowering screws are each calculated to withstand a strain of fifty tons; but to prevent a too rapid descent of the lining when it has attained a considerable weight, Messrs. Degousée and Ch. Laurent make use of the species of tubbing upon the surface of the working pits already noticed. This tubbing not only serves to guide the column and to make it descend vertically, but also, and above all, to act as a powerful brake, and thus enable the workmen to control the velocity of the descent at will.

Tightening the segment screws gives a strong compression and friction over a height of two metres, sufficient to control the descent of the tubbing.

The three columns of sheet-iron lining, which have been mentioned, were put in place by this system of operating with the greatest ease, at the rate of four metres a day, including the time spent in riveting the sections of the tubbing.

When the artesian well of La Chapelle is sunk to the depth of 600 metres, a tub in one column will be lowered to the same depth. Messrs. Degousée and Ch. Laurent propose to employ the same method of lowering, and there is no doubt that these able engineers will succeed completely in this magnificent work.

The false bottom for the tubbing, which is used by Messrs. Kind and Chaudron, would not answer in this case, because it would prevent the water from rising in the well. The work carried forward at La Chapelle proves that by the system *à niveau plein*, of sinking from the surface, large shafts for mines can be executed by the tools and method of Messrs. Degousée and Ch. Laurent with great success in similar formations.

At the well bored by the Messrs. Dru, the depth at the end of April, 1867, was nearly 500 feet. The weight of the boring tool was over 2 tons 18 cwt. The rods were, for the most part, of wood, with iron connections, and 10 metres long; two rods, or a length of 20^{m}, were raised and lowered together.

BORING FOR COAL.

One great use of boring apparatus abroad is, to ascertain the thickness and nature of the strata that over-lie coal beds, and thus to know the position of the coal and the probable difficulties and expense of sinking shafts to reach the beds. It is also employed to ascertain the nature of the faults and dislocations of the beds; the extent of ancient pits and workings, and to drain such places by piercing to them in advance of the new galleries. In the coal district at Zwickau, Saxony, mining concessions are not granted until coal has been discovered by a bore hole or other means. The Brückenberg company prospected their ground by boring to a depth of 363 fms. before they found coal. The following are the dimensions of the hole in Saxon measure:

	Diameter.
1st 24 feet	6 feet.
265 feet	20 inches.
180 feet	18½ inches.

	Diameter.
315 feet	$17\frac{1}{8}$ inches.
440 feet	$15\frac{3}{4}$ inches.
360 feet	$14\frac{1}{4}$ inches.
250 feet	$12\frac{4}{5}$ inches.
122 feet	$11\frac{1}{3}$ inches.
198 feet	10 inches.
73 feet	$8\frac{1}{2}$ inches.
47 feet	7 inches.
50 feet	6 inches.

For many such operations, the diamond drill, already fully discussed, may be found superior to the apparatus ordinarily employed.

BORING FOR OIL.

The discovery of petroleum in quantities in Western Pennsylvania, West Virginia, Ohio, Canada, and other localities, has given a great development to the art of well-boring in the United States. The cumbrous pole-tools have been rejected, and the cable, upon the ancient Chinese system, substituted.

The great advance has been in the construction of the tools, and in the adoption of simple apparatus for giving motion to the drill by means of steam-power. For prospecting and for sinking to moderate depths of 50 to 150 feet, the spring-pole, worked by hand, is frequently employed. This was the apparatus chiefly used in California a few years since, when the oil regions were prospected.

The constructions in common use in Pennsylvania at the oil-wells, and used for a time during the oil excitement in California, consists of a derrick, bull-wheel, band-wheel, sansom-post, and walking-beam, and a portable steam-engine. The descriptions and dimensions given below represent the average as determined by experience.

The derricks are usually constructed of plank and boards, when they can be obtained, or of unhewed poles. They rise to a height of 50 to 60 feet, and taper upward from a base about 15 feet square. The standards are of two-inch plank, 8 inches wide, and the cross-braces 8 inches wide and 1 inch thick. The tools are suspended by the cable, which, passing over the pully at the top, descends at the side, and is wound upon the drum of the bull-wheel, the shaft of which rest on bearings in the standards. The drum of the bull-wheel is about 10 inches in diameter.

The walking-beam, of wood, 26 feet long, is supported at the center upon the top of the sansom-post. One end is connected by a pitman, with a crank of 22 inches radius, upon the end of a shaft receiving motion by a belt from the engine; the other end, projecting within the derrick and directly over the well, carries, suspended, the tem-

Rope Socket.

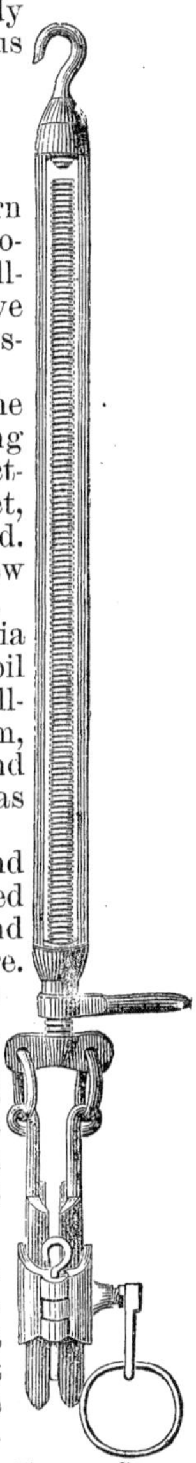

Temper Screw.

per-screw, to which is attached a clamp for seizing upon the rope. The rotation of the crank-shaft gives a reciprocating motion to the end of the beam, and this is imparted to the rope, carrying the tools at its lower end.

The form of the temper-screw is shown by the figure. By this the drill may be lowered or "fed out" to a certain extent during the progress of boring. The rope is seized and held fast by the clamp; and when the whole length of the screw is fed out the position of the clamp is changed.

The drilling tools consist of center-bits, reamers, an auger-stem, sinker-bar, and the "jar," besides a socket for attaching them to the lower end of the rope, and wrenches, and other accessories to aid in attaching and unscrewing the bits. There are, besides, a variety of tools for recovering broken bits or other parts of the apparatus lost in the well, and sand pumps for removing the débris.

The bits are represented by the annexed cuts. They are $3\frac{1}{2}$ inches broad on the face, and the reamers are $4\frac{1}{2}$ inches. They are made, however, of various sizes, and all have strong square shanks, so that they may be firmly screwed into the auger-stem, made of $2\frac{1}{4}$ inch iron and 20 feet long.

The Wrenches.

The "jar" is a contrivance by which the auger-stem and bit is, in a measure, detached from the rope. By it a blow or sudden jerk may be given upwards so as to loosen the bit in case it becomes wedged in the hole, while the same device serves to give a blow downward upon the auger, after the bit strikes the bottom, thus doubling the efficiency of

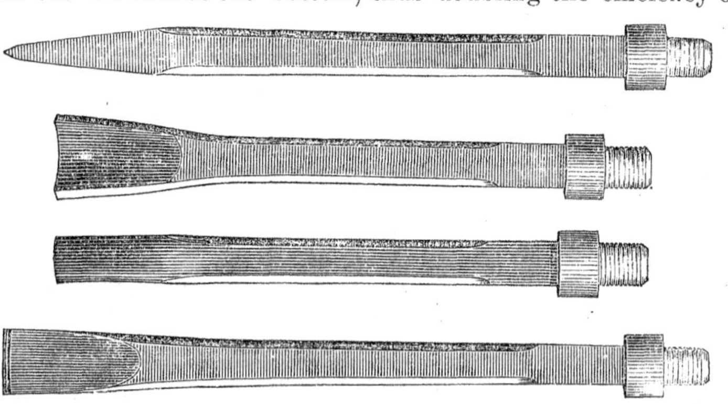

Bits and Reamer for drilling.

The Jar.

each stroke. It serves also to maintain the tension of the rope during the stroke. These jars are made of $1\frac{1}{4}$-inch iron on the sides, with 12-inch heads, and 18-inch stroke.

The sinker-bar, 10 feet long, is attached by a screw to the upper end of the jar, and above this is the rope-socket, securely united by means of rivets to the end of the rope.

The bits and other parts of the drilling tools are connected and disconnected by means of two large wrenches, 3 feet 9 inches long, with broad flat heads, shaped as shown in the figures.

The drilling ropes or cables vary from $1\frac{1}{4}$ inch to $1\frac{3}{4}$ inch diameter, and weigh from 48 pounds to 86 pounds per 100 feet.

The sand pumps made of heavy sheet-iron, or of galvanized iron, sometimes of copper; are about 5 feet long, and from 3 inches to 4 inches in diameter, and are fitted with leather valves resting upon iron seats, as indicated at the lower end of the figure.

These tools, and the iron fittings for the walking-beam, wheels, and other parts of the apparatus for well-boring, are manufactured by Messrs. Hart, Ball & Hart, of Buffalo, New York, to whom I am indebted for the illustrations. The steam-engines in use are portable, and generally from 8 to 10 horse-power. A 900-foot well can be drilled with an 8 horse-power engine. Rope for a well 900 feet deep, with the tools, will weigh about 800 pounds.

Before commencing to drill it is usual to drive down a cast-iron pipe through the loose soil and alluvial deposits until the firm bed-rock is reached. These pipes are made in lengths of eight feet, and are from five to six inches in diameter. They are joined together, end to end, by means of wrought-iron bands carefully welded and sized to shrink on to a shoulder turned upon each end of the pipe in a lathe, so that a flush joint is formed by the band. The lower end is made sharp, and the band is edged with steel. This form of joint has been patented by Mr. Bolles, whose name it bears, and it gives great satisfaction. The five-inch lengths weigh 55 pounds per foot, or 440 pounds in all; and the six-inch 69 pounds per foot, or 552 pounds per length.

For lining the wells wrought-iron tubing is used, made with screws and sockets or with flush joints, but always smooth-finished inside. The sizes vary. For the light kinds, from one and a half to four inches for the inside diameter, and from 1.66 pound to 6 pounds per foot. The heavier tubing ranges from one and a half inches in diameter, and 2.70 pounds per foot, to 6 inches, weighing 18.7 pounds per foot. These large sizes are seldom used for oil wells.

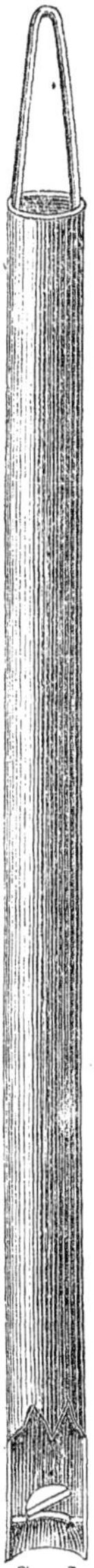

Sand Pump.

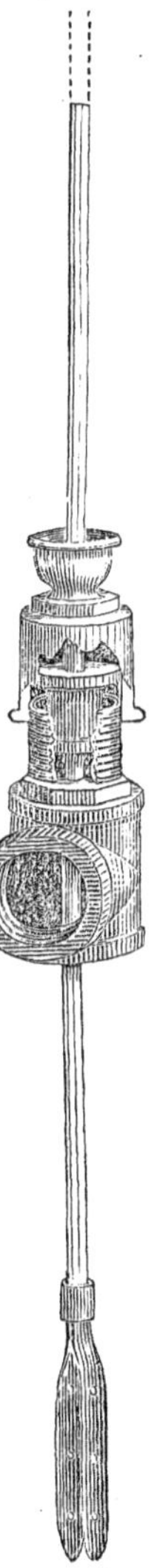

Stuffing Box.

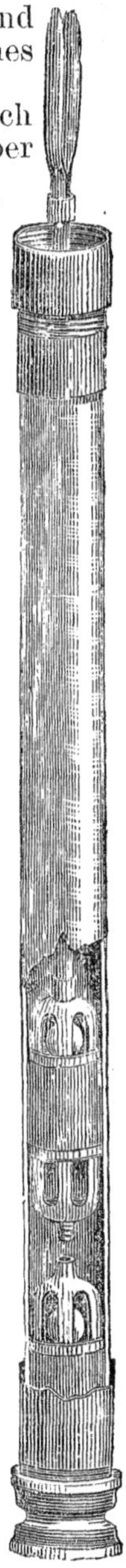

Oil Pump.

Pumps are made of wrought-iron pipe lined with heavy seamless brass tubes bored perfectly true, or of heavy brass tube alone. One of the last-mentioned construction, five feet long, is shown by the annexed figure, in which a portion of the interior is seen with the two valves and boxes. These valves are made of gun-metal, and are fitted with great care. The packing is made of the best oak-tanned leather. Ball valves are generally used. The pump here represented is manufactured by the Messrs. Hart, and they have made an improvement upon the ordinary construction, by which the lower ball valve may be loosened from the top of the guard over the valve seat, to which it sometimes becomes attached by the accumulation of a deposit. A projecting point at the bottom of the upper box enters the hole in the top of the lower box, and thus forces down the ball. The portion of this projection nearest to the box has a screw thread cut upon it, and may be screwed into the box below, so that they may both be drawn out together. The pump barrels are usually five feet in length.

At the top of the well a stuffing box and elbow pipe is fitted. The construction of this box and the form of the joint for attaching to the sucker rods is shown in the figure. The stuffing is kept in place and is pressed firmly upon the plunger-rod or piston by means of the follower, made of brass. The plunger-rods are five feet long, are made of one-inch diameter cold-rolled iron, and are perfectly polished.

One other important adjunct of a complete oil well is the seed-bag, the use of which is to form a water-tight joint or packing around the tube or lining of the well, and thus shut off all communication between the water of the upper strata and the oil-bearing crevices or chambers below.

This bag is made of leather, and is filled with flax-seed. It is put around the tube and is pushed down to the proper place, and soon becomes so much swollen by the absorption of water, that it fills the space between the tube and the walls perfectly, and shuts off all communication around the tubing for either water or oil from above or below.

THE AMERICAN TUBULAR WELL.

A very expeditious and simple apparatus for obtaining water, where it is not at very great depths below the surface, and in alluvial soil, is here worthy of mention. It is known as the tubular pump, or tubular well, and consists merely of a wrought-iron tube an inch or two in diameter, which forms the pump barrel. This is fitted with a valve near the bottom, and tipped at the end by a sharp-pointed steel plug. This sharp point permits the whole tube to be driven down into the soil until the watery ground is reached, when, by raising the pipe a few inches, the plug is detached, and the lower end of the pipe is left open, while, at the same time, a small water chamber is formed. By inserting a pump-rod, with a lift-box, water may be pumped to the surface in a continuous stream.

This simple pump has worked well in sandy and gravelly soils, and is said to have been of great service to the British forces in Abyssinia. It could doubtless be used to great advantage in many places throughout the Great Basin and in California.

CHAPTER VI.

BORING LARGE MINING SHAFTS.

The methods of boring shafts of large diameter have of late years been carried to great perfection abroad, especially in France and Belgium, and there is little doubt that they might be introduced with advantage in some sections of the western coal-fields; and perhaps, also, in the metalliferous regions among the harder metamorphic rocks. It is therefore deemed appropriate to give a short description of these methods and of some of the great results which have been achieved.

Probably the most important advance in the art of mining, of late years, is in the sinking of large shafts by boring. Boring into the earth to great depths is no longer confined to explorations in search of water or oil, liquids which will freely flow out in quantity through small openings, but it is now resorted to for the construction of deep shafts through which solids, such as coal and metallic ores, are to be hoisted.

Even artesian borings have been increased in size until they resemble rather mining shafts than the former borings, only a few inches in diameter. The art of boring has received a great impetus from the necessity of boring larger and deeper wells for the supply of the city of Paris with water. Several wells have been commenced with a diameter of more than three feet, accounts of which were given in a former chapter.

In order to bore shafts and wells of such great diameter it is necessary to use tools of immense size, weight, and strength, and steam-power to move and work them. The great improvements are due chiefly to Messrs. Fantet, Dru, Degousée and Mulot, in France; Sello, Kind, and Oeynhausen, in Germany; Jobard, Guibal, and Chaudron, in Belgium.

The most striking feature, next to boring, of this system of shaft-sinking, is that the work is executed and the shaft is lined without pumping the water out of the excavation. The sinking proceeds under water, and the shaft is not drained or entered by miners until it is completed and lined from top to bottom.

The method thus finds the most useful application in regions where the strata to be passed through are highly charged with water, and, in fact, it owes its perfection to the necessity of penetrating through watery and difficult ground in the northern French coal-fields. The expense and extreme difficulty attending such operations in the ordinary way is well known. Burat estimates that a capital of upwards of $600,000 is expended in opening a coal mine with a productive capacity of 100,000 tons annually. Examples of a still greater outlay are not wanting. Warrington Smyth, the great British professional authority upon mining, states that, in consequence of the difficulty of piercing through the strata overlying the coal in Durham, England, sums of £40,000, £60,000, and, it is even said, £100,000, have been expended on a single shaft.

As early as 1860 M. Chaudron succeeded in sinking an air-shaft at Péronnes, where the watery beds extended from the 43d metre to 105 metres in depth; and M. de Vaux, inspector general of mines, Belgium, reported in 1861 that the work had been executed for less than one-quarter of what it would have cost if sunk in the ordinary way.

In the coal basin of Saarbruck, in the north of France, at L'Hôpital, the Saint Avold Company desired to sink two shafts, one for ventilation, and the other for extraction. There were 150 metres in thickness of water-bearing strata to be passed through. After numerous unsuccessful efforts before the year 1858, and an expenditure of more than 21,000,000 francs, about $4,200,000, the attempt to execute the work in the ordinary manner was abandoned, and recourse was had to the engineers Messrs. Kind and Chaudron, who, by the boring process *à niveau plein*, succeeded in sinking and lining the two shafts in the most satisfactory manner in less than thirty months, and at a cost of less than 700,000 francs, which includes the cost of installation and the tools—nearly one-seventh of the whole sum. The tools used in this work, and sections of the cast-iron lining or tubing, were exhibited at the Exposition of 1867, and have been reported upon in the series of reports by the United States commissioners. They are also described in the reports of the international jury, and I am indebted for many of the figures here given, supplementary to my own notes at the Exposition, to the report of M. Gernaert.*

The tools consist of enormous trepans, one of which weighed no less than 14,000 kilogrammes, about 15 tons, so large and ponderous that it was hardly possible to conceive of its being suspended in a shaft, and made to rise and fall upon the rocks at the bottom. The general construction of the trepans will be understood from the annexed figures. The massive framework is armed at the bottom with stout chisel-like teeth of steel, securely attached in conical sockets, and, in the most approved forms of the apparatus, bolted in, or so strongly keyed that they cannot be loosened and lost out in the pit during the violent shocks of working. The annexed figure shows the form of a full-blade trepan, (*à lame pleine*,) as used by Messrs. Dru Brothers, successors to Messrs. Mulot, in boring at the *Butte-aux-Cailles*. One of the preceding figures shows the construction of a trepan with a guide rod at the bottom, as used by M. Kind, for enlarging holes already bored by a smaller tool. This form is made with a detaching apparatus at the top, (not shown in the figure,) so that it can be raised and dropped in the hole. It cuts by the percussive force of the blow.

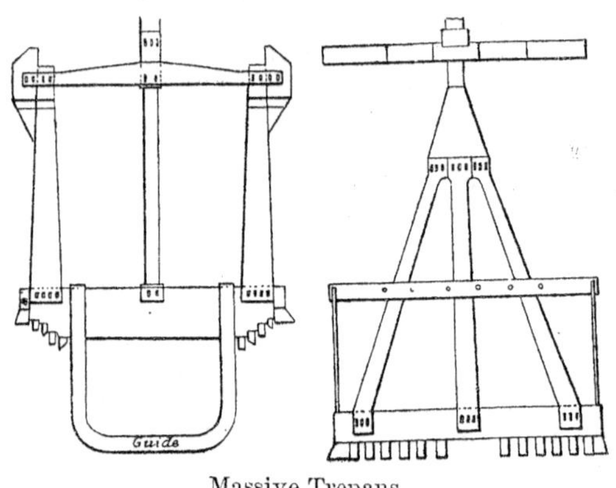

Massive Trepans.

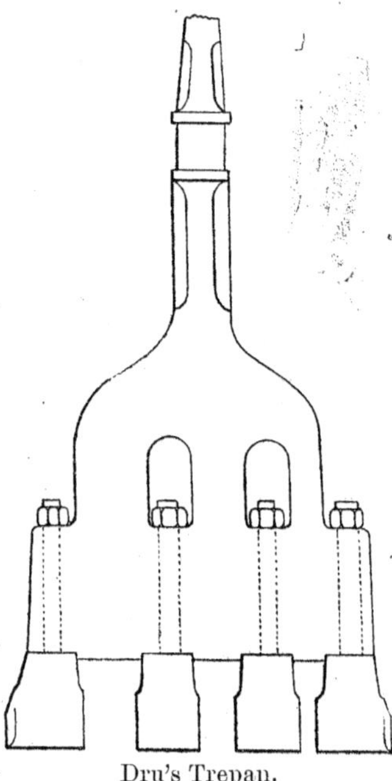
Dru's Trepan.

The notable example of boring large shafts by the method indicated, was, as already mentioned, the construction of two shafts in the department of the Moselle, France, at L'Hôpital, for the St. Avold Company. Two borings were made; one for an air-shaft (No. 1) with a diameter of $1^{m}.80$ within the tubbing, and $2^{m}.56$ in its greatest diameter; the other (or No. 2) for a winding or hoisting shaft was bored with a diameter of $4^{m}.10$, and was $3^{m}.40$ when finished. The operations, according to this method, succeed in the following order:

* Report of M. Gernaert in the jury reports.

1. Construction upon the surface—buildings and derricks.
2. Boring the pits.
3. Lowering the tubbing.
4. Puddling or packing.
5. Packing at the base of the tubbing.

1. *Surface preparations.*—The preliminary operations consisted in the construction of the necessary buildings for the engines and tools, and the erection of a derrick over the site of the pit. All these were of temporary construction, intended to be used merely during the progress of the work.

The derrick was made of four supports strongly framed together, and sustaining a platform about thirty feet above the surface of the ground. Upon this a railway or tram-road was laid for the trucks, which carried the boring tools and rods.

The engines for sinking comprised the *capstan*, the *jumper*, and the *donkey-engine.* The capstan was used for lowering and hoisting the boring tools in the pits, and for lowering the tubbing or lining of the shaft. The engines had a nominal force of 25 horse-power. The diameter of the cylinder was $0^{m}.56$, and the length of the stroke $0^{m}.70$. The respective diameters of the gearing were $1^{m}.70$ and $0^{m}.35$. Admitting an effective pressure of three atmospheres, the initial force upon the driving shaft was 48,513 kilogrammes.

The first rope used at the air-shaft had a section of 54 square centimetres, capable of sustaining a strain of 5,400 kilogrammes. It was made of good hemp; but after working for one year, it broke in lifting a trepan weighing 3,858 kilogrammes. The tool fell from a height of 86 metres, taking with it 17 metres of the rope. This accident occasioned a stoppage of nine days. The cable was replaced by another having a section of 85 square centimetres, and after using it for fourteen months the work was suspended for three days in order to make a new splice.

The second machine—the jumper—was made of an engine cylinder, open at the bottom and closed at the top. The piston-rod was connected directly with the wooden beam, carrying the tool for cutting and boring at its other end. By the alternate lifting and falling of this tool with the attached beam, the rock was cut away. The diameter of the piston of the jumper was $0^{m}.60$, and the greatest length of stroke was one metre. The jumper did not require any repairs during the whole operation of sinking the shaft.

The third machine—the donkey-engine—was used to work a pump for hot and for cold water. It is indispensable for the supply of the boiler, as the capstan and the jumper work irregularly. Experience has shown that the feed-pumps should be in duplicate, so as to avoid the necessity of stopping for repairs.

The preparations for sinking the air-shaft were commenced in October, 1862, and were finished in the following month of April. The expense was as follows:

	Francs.
Buildings	28,302.65
Machines and tools	37,326.91
Total	65,629.56

Boring the pits.—Before commencing the sinking with the special tools, a preparatory pit was sunk to a depth of $21^{m}.40$, and was lined with masonry to a diameter of $2^{m}.80$ up to within 5 metres of the surface, where the diameter was increased to 4 metres. This shoulder in the stone lining afforded a foundation for a platform.

The sinking was accomplished by two different operations. First, a central pit of $1^m.37$ was sunk and then enlarged to $2^m.26$. The débris of this enlargement fell into the first pit. The tubbing was inserted in the enlarged pit.

The boring tools employed in these operations will now be described; the scraper, the scrape-hook, and other apparatus was used indiscriminately in the two pits.

The little trepan first employed weighed 2,085 kilogrammes, and was formed of two principal parts—the fork and the blade. The blade was $1^m.26$ long, and had teeth of cast-steel, or of iron faced with steel. These teeth increased the diameter of the trepan to $1^m.37$. The blade was joined by means of keys to two strong iron arms, which were united above with a central shaft, which was connected by a slide with the suspension apparatus.

This trepan worked easily through the sandstone of the Vosges—*grès des Vosges.* The fall given was $0^m.30$. The progress per day was at first $0^m.79$, and it diminished to $0^m.52$, and then to $0^m.28$ at a depth of 121 metres; but at 135 metres in depth, in a stratum of strongly aggregated silicious red sandstone, the progress was only $0^m.15$ and $0^m.11$. It was soon found that this trepan was too light to stand the shocks of the blows, and three successive ruptures of the stem made it necessary to procure a stronger trepan, weighing 3,858 kilogrammes, divided among the various parts, as follows:

	Kilos.
Body of trepan	2,700
Guide	340
Blade	230
Four teeth of the head	148
Four intermediate teeth	88
Plates and keys	352
Total weight	3,858

The teeth are fixed upon this mass of iron by means of keys. The sockets for the reception of the tenons are conical, and are $0^m.10$ in diameter at the base and $0^m.09$ at the top. The progress in the work made by this trepan, from the commencement, was from $0^m.28$ to $0^m.32$, and even as high as $0^m.83$, giving a mean of $0^m.39$, being three times as much as made by the first trepan. This shows clearly that the heavy trepans are best for the hard strata.

The trepan which was first used for the enlargement of the pit to the diameter of $2^m.56$ had a blade $2^m.46$ in length; it was formed like the little trepan first used, and had a blade fixed upon a fork, and weighed in all 3,980 kilogrammes, divided as follows:

	Kilos.
Fork	2,500
Blade	906
Six teeth of the head	102
Three intermediate teeth	48
Two plates	430
Total weight	3,980

In order to avoid the frequent breaking out of the teeth, this trepan was lifted only $0^m.20$. The progress made with it daily was from $1^m.10$ to $0^m.18$ at the last, when a stratum of hard sandstone was encountered and the weight of the trepan was found to be insufficient. Two blades, one above the other, were then united to the fork by rings and bolts. Each of these blades carried the teeth so as to cut the strata in two steps. This new tool weighed about 5,000 kilogrammes. It worked four months, and required frequent repairs. The rate of progress per day was only $0^m.11$. It was then decided to replace this trepan by a more massive one, weighing 8,000 kilogrammes, and $2^m.50$ in diameter. With this the progress was increased to $0^m.34$ a day, thus showing a second time that in hard rock heavy trepans are required.

The diameter of the pit at the beginning was $2^m.56$; at 134^m depth it was reduced to $2^m.45$; at 155^m depth it was reduced to $2^m.40$; from $155^m.00$ to $155^m.50$ depth it was reduced to $2^m.33$; from $155^m.50$ to $158^m.00$ depth it was reduced to $2^m.25$. At this depth the little pit was continued for a depth of seven metres, and a circular curb of $0^m.40$ was fixed to receive the base of the tubbing.

The work of sinking this air-shaft lasted about twenty-eight months and a half. The central pit required 392 days, including 46 days during which work was stopped, so that only 346 of actual work were necessary. The enlarging operations to a diameter of $2^m.56$ occupied 469 days, including 148½ days of no work. The depth of the central pit being $143^m.70$, (equal to 471.46 feet,) the mean progress for each working day was $4^m.15$, (13 feet,) and the enlarging to $2^m.40$ gave a daily mean of $4^m.25$ for a depth of $136^m.60$.

The expenses of boring were as follows:

	Francs.
Salaries and wages	55, 039. 81
Fuel	12, 513. 11
Oil and grease	2, 381. 71
Ropes	2, 987. 20
Iron, steel, and repairs to tools	12, 530. 90
Cartage and sundries	7, 560. 66
Total	93, 013. 39

TUBBING.—Before entering upon a description of the operation of tubbing the air-shaft, it will be best to explain the system adopted by Messrs. Kind and Chaudron.

The tubbing of the pits is accomplished by lowering into them a metallic cylinder, which finally rests upon a proper seat or foundation, carefully cut for it at the bottom. This cylinder is made smaller than the bore of the pits, and the space between the cylinder and the walls is afterward puddled or filled in with concrete, so as to make a solid continuous lining. The metallic cylinder or tubbing is formed in sections of a cylinder, made of cast iron, and provided with flanges projecting inward, by which they are securely bolted together. One section or length is added after another to the top as the whole descends in the pit, so that at the completion of the work the whole pit is lined with iron from the top to the bottom. The outer surface of all these sections of the cylinder is quite smooth; but in the inside, besides the flanges for the bolts, there are horizontal ribs or webs cast with each segment, and intended to strengthen them.

The thickness of the tubbing will evidently vary with the diameter of the pits and that of the different segments, according to their position in the pit. Messrs. Kind and Chaudron determine the thickness by the following formula:

$$E = 0^{m}.02 \times \frac{R \times P}{500}.$$

E represents the thickness of the tub, R the radius, and P the pressure expressed in kilogrammes upon the square.

M. Gernaert, of the International Jury of the Paris Exposition, says that the principal merit of the success at L'Hôpital should be given to the inventors of the method of lining the shafts while full of water. The jury awarded the highest order of prizes under the title of co-operators to the engineer, M. Kind, of the kingdom of Saxony, and to M. Chaudron, of the mining corps of Belgium, particularly for the improvements in lining or tubbing, which form an indispensable complement to the process of boring shafts in watery strata, and without which the perforations, however large, would not have any great practical value.

The operation of boring was not new. Many engineers had succeeded in excavating shafts of large diameter in this manner, but the great difficulty was to secure a firm and water-tight lining for them. M. Kind had proposed to lower tubbings made of wooden staves held by metal hoops. Many shafts were lined in this way, but all or nearly all were failures. A shaft was finished in this manner at Dalbuch, in Westphalia; but when the water was pumped out, down to a certain level the pressure displaced the staves and it became necessary to insert very heavy iron rings throughout the whole extent of the tubbing. But notwithstanding these expensive efforts the quantity of water which forced its way through the vertical joints was sufficient to supply a powerful pump.

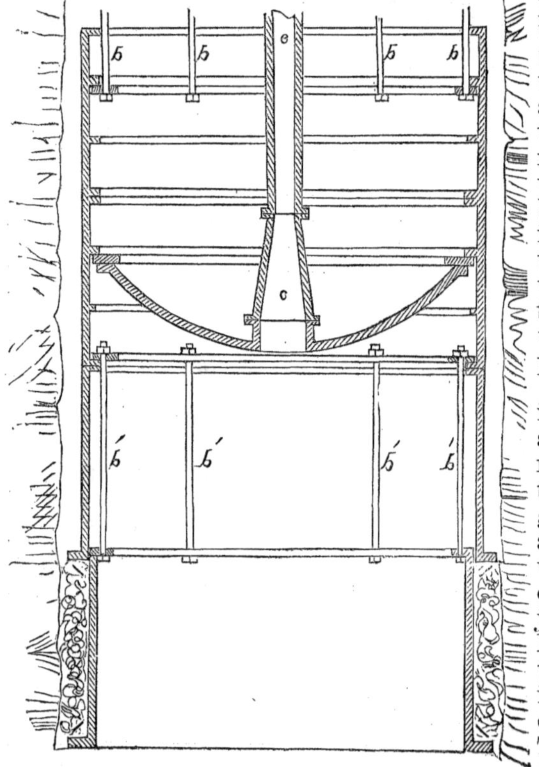

Cylinder and Moss Box.

Cast-iron tubbing made in segments of a cylinder and bolted together was next employed; but even these, notwithstanding the great care used in fitting and placing them, allowed water to penetrate, especially along the vertical joints. But at L'Hôpital, M. Chaudron avoided these difficulties by casting sections of the cylindrical tubbing in one piece. These sections were made about $1^{m}.50$ high and $3^{m}.40$ in diameter and varied in thickness from $0^{m}.060$ to $0^{m}.028$, but were strengthened by ribs and flanges on the inside, which served also for bolting one section to another.

The opposing faces of these cylindrical sections were truly turned or planed down at right angles with the axis, so that they fitted accurately one upon another. The joint was made more perfect and tight by a packing of heavy sheet lead.

The shaft having been bored to the proper depth through the watery ground, and a firm seat or socket secured at the bottom in solid and comparatively impermeable rock, the next operation was to lower the cast-iron tubbing to its place. This was accomplished in the most ingenious manner by M. Chaudron, by tightly closing the bottom segment of the cylinder with a hemispherical cap, so secured that it could be afterward removed, and then floating the cylinder in the water of the pit. But in order to secure the descent as section after section was added at the top a central open column or tube *e e* was bolted to the bottom, and through this, by means of holes drilled at proper distances, water was allowed to enter the inside of the cylinder for the purpose of sinking it, and to aid in keeping it in a vertical position. The annexed woodcut shows, in section, the cylinder, the convex bottom, the central or equilibrium column, the moss-box, and the suspending rods *b b* and *b′ b′*. The moss-box is a contrivance similar in its objects and application to the seed-bag used by the borers of petroleum wells to cut off the ingress of water from strata around the pipe. By means of the moss, expanded laterally when the cylindrical column of cast-iron tubbing is allowed to rest upon it, a tight joint is formed between the firm rock at the bottom and the cast-iron tubbing, thus effectually shutting out the water.

The entire cost of sinking the first shaft (or shaft No. 1) at L'Hôpital through the watery strata to a depth of 140 metres, the internal diamter being $1^{m}.80$, amounted to 255,041.27 francs, divided thus:

	Francs.
Preliminary works	65,629.56
Sinking the pit	93,013.39
Tubbing	78,577.53
Concreting	11,811.20
Packing	6,009.59
Total	255,041.27

Which gives an expense of 1,600 francs per running metre.

The cost of shaft No. 2 is estimated as follows:

	Francs.
Preliminary works	104,571.77
Boring the shaft	141,659.31
Piping	169,220.07
Concreting	15,000,00
Packing	10,000.00
Total	440,451.15

or at the rate of 3,100 francs per running metre.

The preliminary work commenced in September, 1863, and on the 6th of April the concreting was finished; the work lasted three years and a half.

CHAPTER VII.

MACHINES FOR CUTTING OUT COAL.

Before proceeding to throw down coal from its place in the bed it is necessary to undercut it, that is, to excavate a space at the floor of the seam, partly in the floor and partly in the coal, thus undermining the coal so that its gravity assists in bringing it down. This undercutting operation is known as holing, baring, kirving or undercutting, and is one of the most laborious and difficult duties which the miner is called upon to perform. It is often effected under the greatest disadvantages, especially when the seam of coal is very thin, and is cut on the end, to improve its salable qualities. The work is usually accomplished by means of a pick in the hands of a miner, while he rests extended upon his side. An experienced miner makes about forty blows a minute with a pick and cuts from three to four feet under the coal, at the rate of one to one and a half linear yards per hour. In order that the miner may have the necessary space for his body in working so far under the coal, much of the coal has to be cut away and destroyed. It is estimated that the miner under such circumstances exerts about one-sixth of a horse-power, which is applied percussively. He works into the coal as a mechanic with a hammer and cold-chisel used to cut away iron before planing and slotting machines were invented. The proposition to substitute machines for manual labor in cutting out coal was made some twenty years ago, by Mr. Peace, of Wigan. He invented a machine called the iron-man, but it met with ridicule and contempt. Much attention has of late been given to the construction of machines for the purpose, and a very considerable degree of success has been attained; but it cannot be said that any of the machines yet put into operation give entire satisfaction under all conditions. Most of the efforts in this direction have been made in England, where several machines have been brought prominently before the public by means of descriptions and advertising, and by the exhibition of the machines or models at the Paris Exposition of 1867.

The following observations upon the value and importance of machines for excavating coal are taken from the Colliery Guardian, November, 1869:

How to win and work coal most economically, is a problem the satisfactory solution of which is of the highest moment to the colliery owner, the mining engineer, and the public at large. In this matter producers and consumers are alike interested, and the question is one the growing importance of which is becoming daily more evident. In these times of keen competition, the most successful man in any branch of industry will generally be the one who has at his command the most efficient appliances in the way of improved machinery and skillful modes of operation. To this rule—applicable to trade and manufacture generally—coal-mining is no exception. A saving of a very insignificant amount—say but a few farthings—per ton, upon the whole of the out-put of a large colliery, will make a marvelous difference in the financial prosperity of the concern, and will present a very satisfactory result in the profit and loss account. To this fact colliery owners and managers are fully alive. Hence, in the meetings of the North of England Institute of Mining Engineers, and other kindred associations established in the several mining districts of Great Britain, attention is perpetually directed to this one point, and a patient and painstaking examination is given to every proposal, the professed object of which is to facilitate any of the numerous operations connected with mining industry. Any improvement in boring or sinking—in coal-getting or underground conveyance—in winding or shipping the produce of the mine, need only be fairly brought under the notice of the mining community to insure for it careful consideration and impartial judgment. Special attention has of late years been directed to the subject of coal-getting by machinery. More than a century has elapsed since the first apparatus designed for the effecting this object was patented, and since that time "iron men" and coal-getters in great numbers, and almost equally great variety, have been presented to the mining public. Additional impetus was given to inventive genius by the appointment of a committee of the North of England Institute, commissioned to investigate the subject, and to report upon the value of existing patents; by the prizes offered by the South Lancashire and Cheshire Coal Association for the best coal-cutting machine; and by the encouragement afforded by mining engineers, both in their individual capacity and when incorporated into associations. It was felt that, looking at the success which in other departments of industry has attended the substitution of machinery for hand labor, there was good ground for the belief that machinery might also be advantageously applied to the cutting of so uniform a substance as coal, and the driving of airways through it. The purely mechanical operation of cutting, by means of a light pick, a groove of from 2½ feet to 4 feet deep along the face of coal which is to be removed, is not only slow and laborious, but also wasteful, inasmuch as a considerable amount of the seam is necessarily cut into slack; and forming, as this process does, the chief item of expense in the excavation of coal, it has of late been more seriously forced upon the attention of coal owners by the irregularities and strikes of the workmen, which have so often brought the operations of coal mines to a ruinous stand-still. The introduction of efficient machinery is also calculated to have an important bearing on the safety of mines, enabling them to be more rapidly opened out, and the seam to be intersected or the winning to be surrounded by air-ways so as to drain off the dangerous gases. It is not to be wondered at, therefore, either that an efficient machine for getting coal should have become an acknowledged want, or that so many ingenious inventors should have applied themselves to the production of apparatus to meet that want. It is true that many of the inventions have been crude, and some of them designed without much regard to some of the first requisites to extended application, but others have been tested in actual working, and found to give satisfactory results.

Machines for coal-cutting may be classed under two distinct types, being, like the machines for rock-drilling, made upon two very different principles. One type is percussive, and imitates the cutting operation of the pick as swung by the miner; the other concentrates and applies the power continuously through cutters which are pressed against the coal and shave it off little by little. Prominent among the machines of the second type is that of Carret, Marshall & Co., of Leeds, England.

CARRET, MARSHALL & COMPANY'S COAL-CUTTING MACHINE.

This machine works like a hand-plane; and it is claimed that it has the power of eighteen men, that it can work effectively in a space only two feet high, and cut into coal as a scoop cuts into cheese, accomplishing more in one minute than 700 blows from a pick can in the same time. It is about two feet high, weighs one ton, has four legs of adjustable length, and is provided with a holding piece adjusted so as to touch the roof of the drift and hold the machine firmly to its work. The motor is water, under a pressure of about 20 atmospheres or 300 pounds, and supplied through a 2-inch pipe at the rate of 30 gallons per minute. This water pressure acts vertically on a 5-inch piston pressing against the roof, and horizontally on one about the same size, reciprocating 18 inches and 15 to 20 times in a minute. There is a pressure of 5,000 pounds against roof, and the same pressure acting horizontally, forcing three steel cutters shaped like cheese scoops into the coal. These cutting tools are 3 inches wide, and penetrate 4 feet, with a power equal to 3 horses or 18 men; and this is effected by a consumption of 50 pounds of coal per hour to feed the boiler of the engine, which makes the water pressure, and pumps the same over and over again.

The construction in detail is shown by the figures,* which embrace a front elevation, a ground plan, and an end view, all drawn to a scale of three quarters of one inch to one foot, or one-sixteenth the real size.

The machine in operation fixes itself dead fast upon the rails during the cutting stroke, and releases itself at the back or return stroke, and traverses forward the requisite amount for the next cut without any

* Supplied for this report by Messrs. Carrett, Marshall & Co., the manufacturers.

manual labor. Should the tools be prevented making the full stroke at one cut, they will continue to make more strokes at the same place, until the maximum depth is attained, when, the machine will move itself forward the required amount for the next cut. Thus, at *one operation*, a uniform straight depth is attained, parallel with the rails, inducing an even fracture when the coals are brought down, and thereby a straight line for the new coal face. There is no percussive action, either against the roof or into the coal, but simply a concentrated pressure, producing a steady reciprocating motion at fifteen strokes per minute. There is, consequently, no dust or noise, and little wear and tear.

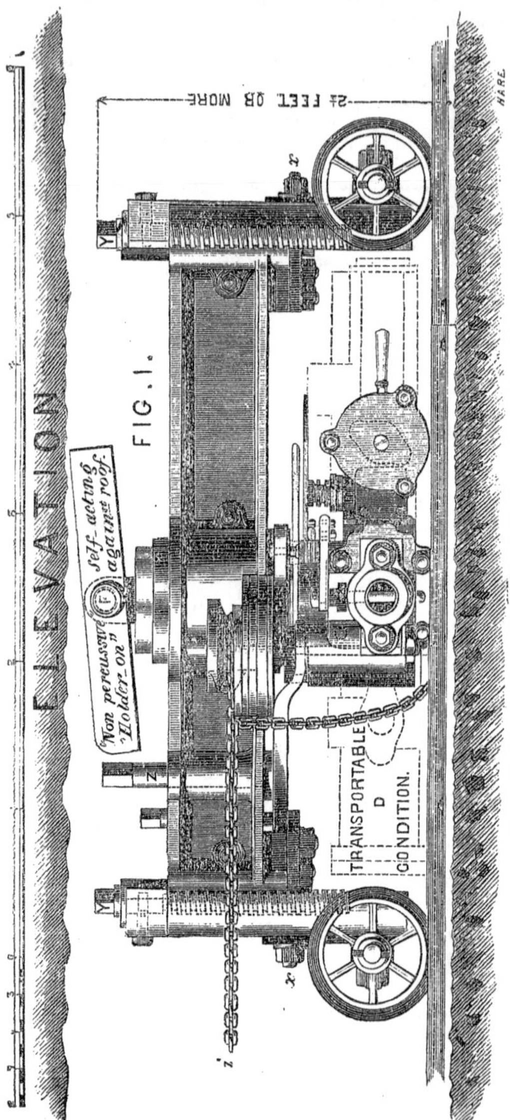

Carrett, Marshall & Co.'s Coal Cutter, front elevation.

For the same reason, when cutting pyrites, the tools throw out no sparks, and the workman can hear any movement in the coal or roof.

The required height from the line of rails in the "holing," "kirving," or "baring," varies in different mines, it follows that the hydraulic cutting cylinder, and its direct action cutting tools, have sometimes to be arranged *above* the carriage, and sometimes *beneath* the main carriage, or close down upon the rails, as is illustrated in the elevations. The first figure is the main carriage, with four wheels far enough apart to allow the machine to be placed longitudinally when being transported from place to place. The screws YY are for raising and lowering the carriage and its cylinder and cutting tools. The pinion Z and the segmental rack H regulate the desired angle of the tools cutting into the coal face, and the two nuts *xx* at each end of carriage regulate the angle required, when necessary that it shall not be in the same plane as the rails.

AAA are the cutting tools, B the cutter bar, N a guide roller for the same; D is the main cylinder, with its self-acting hydraulic valve mo-

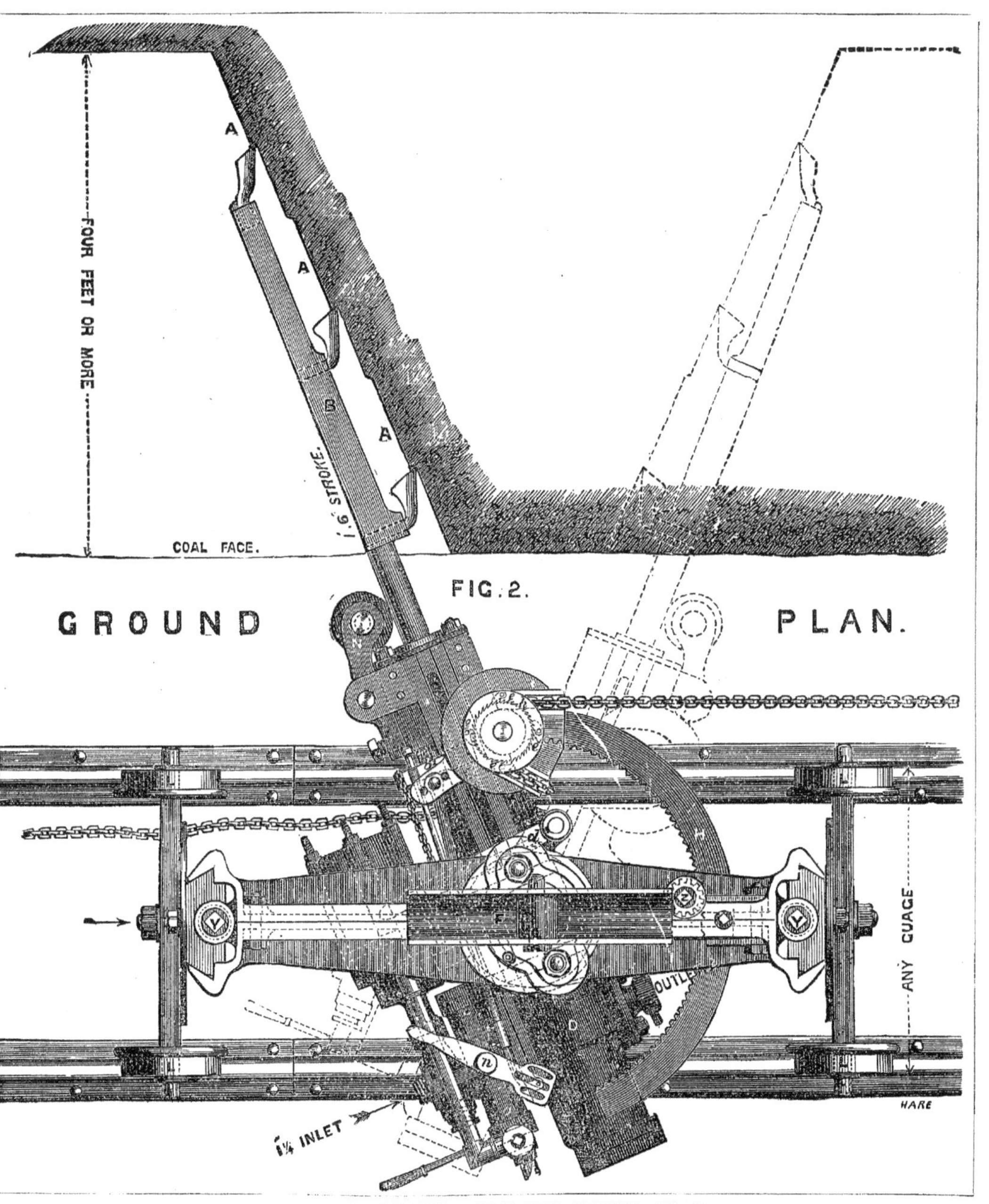

CARRETT, MARSHALL & CO.'S COAL CUTTER—PLAN.

tion, which passes a portion of its water alternately above and below the piston of the holder-on, which thus rises and falls without percussion, and follows the uneven line of the roof of the mine, so that the re-required stability is given to the machine for the time being, an instant before the cutters enter the coal.

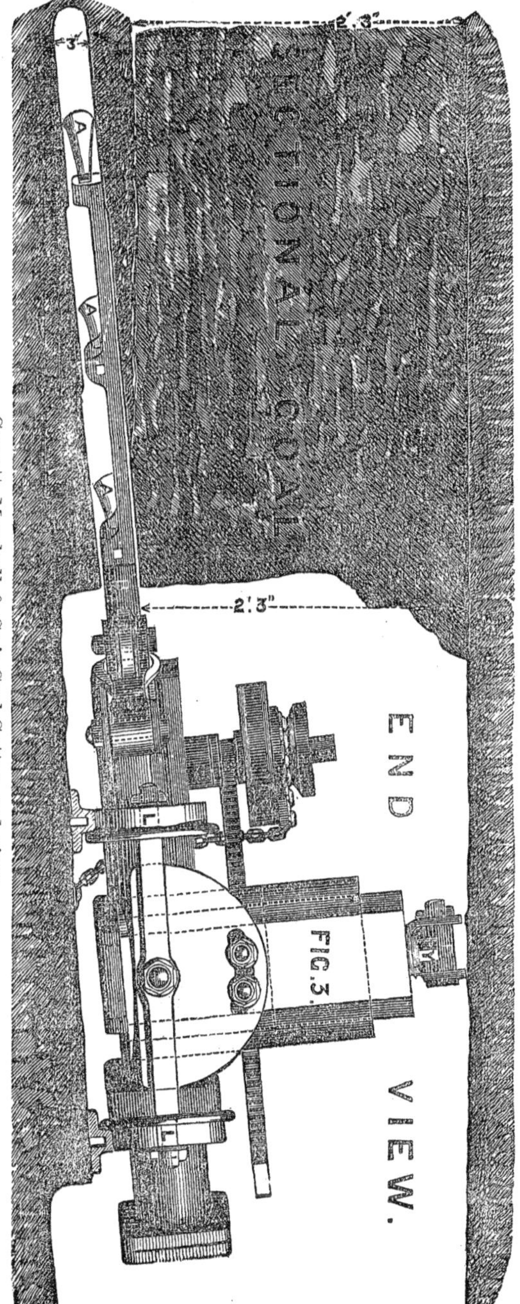

Carrett, Marshall & Co.'s Coal Cutter, end view.

The "holder-on piece" can be any length necessary to bridge over gaps in the roof; it is loose on the pin F and droops at its leading end to enable it to ride over the varying projections in roof.

The traverse motion is actuated by the pin *b*, which connects the cutter bar with piston rod, and at the termination of each end of its stroke actuates the lever *d* in both directions, which operates on the pawl *e*, which causes the chain pully to revolve on the chain *i*, made fast ahead by an anchor-prop between floor and roof.

Although the length of stroke of each cutting tool is eighteen inches, the practical cutting length is sixteen inches, and, consequently, the three cutters jointly give a total effective depth of four feet at each stroke of the machine, finishing the work as it goes along. The mechanism employed consists of a hydraulic reciprocating engine, adjustable to any height and angle, having a self-acting valve motion. The cylinder is four and a half inches diameter, and lined with brass, and the piston made tight with ordinary hydraulic leathers, which can easily be renewed. Within the piston rod is attached the cutter-bar of steel, carrying the tools or cutters. These can be varied in number to suit the depth to be holed at one operation. The cutting tools are of double sheer steel, can be easily made, and are very strong, and can be removed and replaced in a few moments; they can be readily sharpened on an ordinary grindstone. The cutter-bar is also moveable, when transporting the machine from place to place, for which purpose the main cylinder is, for the time being, placed longitudinally with the rails. (*See dotted lines in Fig.* 1.)

The machine is about three horse-power, and weighs one ton, and will work either right or left. (*See dotted lines on ground plan.*) It is self-acting in all movements, and will ascend steep gradients; being simple in all its parts, it is not liable to get out of order, and is easily managed by an ordinary miner, and can be transported from place to place, on the ordinary rails, about the mine,

The machine undercuts "holes," or "kirves," with a man and boy as attendants, and completes the work with once going over, at the rate of fifteen yards per hour, and at any angle and height from floor rails, being suitable for either "dip" or "rise" workings, and is capable of cutting the thinnest seams. The pressure of water which actuates this apparatus can be obtained either from the stand pipes in the pits, or from pumps attached to any existing engine, or from an engine and pumps specially made for the purpose. The quantity necessary is only what is sufficient to fill the circuit of the pipes, using it over again when desirable, as in the Bramah press.

Each machine uses thirty gallons per minute, at about 300 pounds pressure, according to the hardness of the coal or mineral to be operated upon. In cutting the shale of the Cleveland ironstone band, a somewhat greater pressure is found to be necessary.

There is no limit to the pressure of water that may be used, nor the distance it may be forced without loss of power, beyond that due to its friction along the pipes. The same water pressure is also applicable to work pumps and rotary engines for hauling, &c., and other requirements in the mine, at a distance from the engine power.

In cases where there is a fall of water, say of 100 pounds pressure, it can be "intensified" by a self-acting machine to 400 pounds pressure, to work the coal-cutter, but sacrificing three-fourths of its bulk, which is set free.

In arranging the engine and pumps required to make a "continuous stream" of water pressure for working these machines, it is preferable to have two steam cylinders, so that there be no dead center. They are constructed to work one, two, or four machines. Pipes, if for one machine, are of 2-inch bore, wrought iron, a superior quality of gas pipes strong enough to stand 500 pounds pressure, and are supplied at 3*s.* 6*d.* per yard. These pipes are screwed together in the ordinary manner, and adapt themselves readily to the irregularities of the floor of the mine. A flexible pipe 1½-inch bore, suitable for the same pressure, allows the machine to traverse.

The cost of each self-acting coal-cutting machine as here described, without its anchor-prop, traverse chain, or pipes, is £125.

This self-acting, hydraulic, coal-cutting machine, or "iron man," which has now been two years at work, does not dispense with the labor of the miner, but performs for him the undercutting, which is a most laborious operation, either in the end or face of coal, and in a more efficient and economic manner than he can do it himself. The coal so operated on by the machine does not fall forward when becoming detached from the roof, but settles on the lower bed, thereby avoiding serious accidents. It is claimed that the saving in coal alone more than pays for the outlay;

and that it is practicable to cut with the most perfect ease into the floor of the mine, thus preventing all waste of coal whatever.

The size of the coal is improved, the amount of slack is considerably reduced, and a single seam, it is said, will yield more by one thousand tons of coal per acre than when worked by hand labor in the usual manner.

COAL-CUTTING MACHINE OF MESSRS. JONES AND LEVICK.

This machine may be described as a contrivance for holding and swinging a miner's pick so as to undercut a coal-seam nearly as it is done by hand. It is actuated by compressed air, and is mounted on a carriage or truck with four wheels, with an extended cast-iron platform in the rear for the man who works the machine. A crank-pin on a fly-wheel actuates two bevel-wheels for moving the machine back or forward on the rails of the gallery.

The handling of this machine is very simple. The workman on the platform turns a wheel so as to bring the pick into the proper direction; he then opens a cock admitting compressed air into the cylinder by working the slide with a lever. The machine being thus set in motion, it is merely requisite to move it forward to follow up the work done by the pick. The air, on leaving the cylinder, escapes freely into the gallery.

We subjoin the reported results of experiments made by this machine in two mines in England:

In the High Royd colliery, in a hard coal, and in a gallery in which the rails were in a bad state, with an air pressure of from 2 to 2½ atmospheres and 70 to 80 blows per minute, the average hour's work of the machine was a channel from $8^m.20$ to $9^m.15$ long and from $0^m.90$ to $1^m.00$ deep, including stoppages. The width at the bottom was $0^m.037$, and on the face $0^m.08$. During 10 hours' consecutive work the work produced by this machine was equal to that of 20 miners during the same time; and it appears that the consumption of air is equal to about 3 horse-power.

FIRTH'S PATENT COAL-CUTTING MACHINE.

This is also a percussive machine, and is worked by compressed air. It is mounted upon wheels which run upon rails on the floor of the mine. A pick is attached at the forward end of the machine to the lower end of a vertical shaft, and a horizontal swing or sweep is given to it by means of arms and levers connected with the piston-rod. In its form and mode of operation, this machine somewhat resembles the preceding. Some improvements in this machine have been reported recently. It is stated to be working in the seam known as the "Little Coal," which is 2 feet 8 inches thick, and to have under cut a face of 500 yards in length to a depth of 3 feet, using a new form of the pick which removes the dirt as it proceeds.

Mr. Firth has also recently invented a method of fitting picks with movable cutting points. It is the general custom to work picks with points solid; that is, the point and pick in one piece. By this arrangement it becomes necessary to take the whole pick out of the pit whenever blunted, in order that it may be sharpened. The improvement consists in making a boss on that part of the pick nearest the point. In this boss is a socket of any suitable shape, by preference a circular taper socket, the loose point being cottered into the socket against a piece of

India-rubber, or other suitable substance, at the bottom of the socket or around the outer edge of the socket, so that when the blow is given some part of the strain is taken off the point. The edge of the socket is brought as close as possible to the point, for as the socket must enter the groove made in the coal, and must be clear of the top and bottom of the groove, and as in some cases the groove is not more than one and three-quarter inches in height, it will be readily seen that the closer the socket is to the point the greater the resisting strength of the point.

HURD'S COAL-CUTTING MACHINE.

Mr. F. Hurd, of Rochdale, England, has invented another form of coal-cutting machine, in which a number of steel cutters or teeth are placed on an endless chain or band moving longitudinally around a long arm. The invention is claimed to consist* in cutting horizontal, longitudinal, radial, and diagonal grooves in the coal or other mineral to be excavated, by means of a series of link stocks containing the cutters, which are jointed together in such a manner that no rivets or connecting pins are required. This series of cutters passes round a pulley mounted in a radial arm, and around a toothed wheel fixed to a shaft which fits in a telescope frame, to increase or reduce its length; the radial arm is provided with grooves which support the back of the cutter stocks, and prevent them from being drawn out of the groove in the radial arm. The toothed wheel may be driven to give motion to the cutters by an improved motive-power engine, or it may be driven in any other convenient manner.

The position of the radial arm is changed so as to give the required cut by a worm fixed to the outer shell of the telescope shaft, and a cam fixed to the driving wheel; this cam, by a lever and catch, turns the worm at intervals, and thus advances the cutters to the extent required. The engine consists of an oscillating cylinder to which the compressed air or other elastic fluid is admitted, and from which it is exhausted through two or more ports, the oscillation of the cylinder causing the ports to be opened and closed at the proper times without the aid of eccentrics or valves for giving the requisite to-and-fro motion to the piston and piston rod, which latter is connected to the crank pin in the fly-wheel. The engine can be reversed by two double taps placed in the passages leading to and from the ports, which taps are connected and worked simultaneously by levers or gearing. The cutting apparatus, and the engine by which it is driven, are connected to a bracket which fits on a screwed pillar, and it is raised or lowered by gearing connected to the engine, and which gearing reverses the direction of motion up or down by changing the position of the wheels. The bracket also supports two shafts with two eccentrics for acting on surface clips, one to secure the bracket in the position required, and the other to secure the radial arm. An apparatus for compressing air is also included in the invention. It consists of a series of pump barrels, the pistons of which are worked by a diagonal disk or other equivalent; this disk, or its equivalent, is driven by steam or other power, and the pump barrels are all united to the air receiver. As the pressure increases in the receiver, the piston rods are disconnected in succession from the driving disk, or its equivalent, until the final compression is obtained by the last pump barrel. The pumping apparatus is placed in a water course to keep the barrels cool.

An idea of the form and operation of the cutting machine may be ob-

* Described with drawings complete in the Colliery Guardian, November 19, 1869.

tained from the annexed figures, showing a machine designed for working in very narrow seams. The first is a plan, and shows the principal

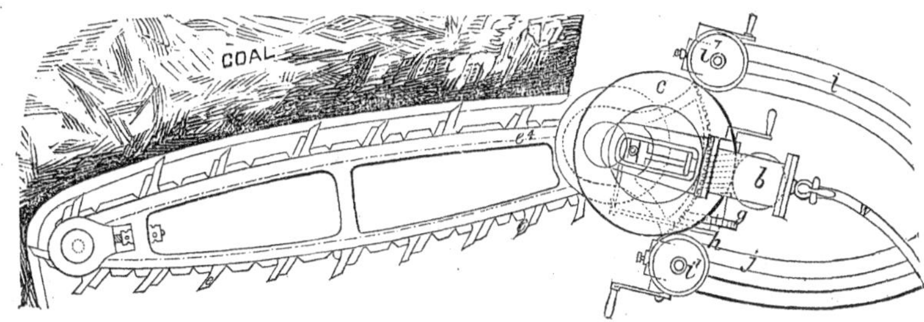

Hurd's Coal-cutting machine.

part of the frame *j j* of the machine with its long arm e^4 reaching forward and carying the cutters *e e*, by which the groove is cut in the coal. Steam or compressed air is admitted through the pipe *w* to the cylinder *b*, in which a piston moves back and forth and gives motion to the fly-wheel *c*.

The arm is controlled by a tangent screw working in a segment of a wheel, the outlines of which are shown between *i* and i'. By means of this screw, moved by a crank at the side of the cylinder *b*, the arm can be thrown to one side or the other. It has a horizontal sweep of three feet or more, carrying the cutters with it, as shown in the figure, each tooth in succession cutting or scraping off a little of the coal. Alternate teeth are different, one cutting a double groove and leaving a little ridge or tongue which the next tooth cuts away. The cutter stocks, into which the cutters *e e* are set and held by a screw, are linked together in a peculiar manner without rivets or pins, as indicated in the figure, which shows only two of the teeth in the sockets. One socket, by means of the hook-like or curved connections, holds to the next, and thus form a chain which slides in the groove of the arm. The figure also shows a portion of one side of the end of the arm, holding the pulley upon which the chain of cutters turns. By means of a screw and lock-nut this pulley may be thrown outward to take up the slack of the chain.

This apparatus is reported to be working in a 20-inch seam, and making a semi-circular sweep of 6 feet 6 inches in four minutes, with only 25 pounds pressure on a 6-inch cylinder with six inches stroke, cutting a groove of 1¼ inch. The weight of the machine is nearly four hundred pounds. Mr. Hurd has also made a machine to be worked by hand, which is much lighter.

BREAKING DOWN COAL BY HYDRAULIC PRESSURE.

As it is exceedingly difficult, if not impossible, to secure perfect ventilation in all parts of coal mines so as to effectually dilute the combustible gases and render them inexplosive, it becomes very important to dispense with the use of gunpowder, the explosion of which not only fills the workings with smoke and vitiates the air, but frequently ignites the fire-damp. It is the opinion of one of the inspectors of mines in England that half the explosions of fire-damp are traceable to firing shots, and that a vast number of accidents from falls of roof are caused by the shattered condition of shale-roofs, after blasting to the extent now practiced. In dangerous coal-seams it is clearly wrong to use gunpowder, and it is perhaps a mistake under any circumstances. The exceptions are thought to be rare, while the accounts of fatal accidents are numerous.* Wherever much powder is used in getting down the coal, the value of the coal is much lessened. It is a well-known fact in England that the least capable men in any colliery use the most powder, and as a consequence the coal which they mine is less valuable than that thrown down with less consumption of powder, by skillful and experienced miners. Again, in some cases, coal-seams themselves have been ignited by the use of powder.

All these objections to the use of powder have rendered a substitute very desirable. Mr. Samuel P. Bidder, jr., of England, proposes to use the force of a hydraulic press, and has experimented with a machine constructed for the purpose. The machine that he exhibited in model at the Institution of Civil Engineers is described as follows:†

The principal machine consists of a small hydraulic press, weighing about 60 lbs., and of 15 tons power. To this press is attached a pair of steel tension straps, bent in the form of a tuning-fork, and which are connected with the press by a collar. At the end of these straps is first placed a clearance box, about 4 inches long, and upon each side of the straps expanding pieces, (also made of steel,) which exert a pressure at the sides of the hole, and are 15 inches long. The points of a pair of twin wedges, 15 inches by 3 inches, constituting one wedge, are then inserted in the expanding piece, and the machine is fixed in the hole. The hydraulic press, (having been already charged with about three pints of water, which may be used over and over again without loss,) is then worked by a man by means of a small handle, and the ram from the cylinder is forced out, thus driving up the pair of wedges between the expanding pieces, giving a lateral extension of about 3 inches. This not being in all cases sufficient to bring down the coal, the press is withdrawn, and the relief-valve opened, thereby allowing the water to return to the reservoir. A second wedge is then inserted between the two twin wedges by means of a small rod, five-eighths of an inch in diameter, and, the press being again connected, this wedge is driven home in the manner before described. By this means an additional expansion of 3 inches is obtained, making a total expansion of 6 inches, which in most cases is found sufficient; but a third wedge can be applied, if necessary, and the expansion thus increased to any reasonable extent. In this manner as much as 10 or 12 cwts. of coal have been brought down in ten minutes.

The drilling apparatus, the principal part of the machine, consists of a screw 4 feet by 1½ inches in diameter, to the end of which is attached the drill. The fulcrum for taking the resistance of the screw is obtained by inserting a bar of iron in the coal at the side of the place selected for the hole which the machine has to drill. This small aperture is made by punching with the ordinary instrument a hole 10 inches deep and 1 inch in diameter, and the time occupied in making this preparation is usually about four minutes. The small bar for taking the resistance of the screw is then inserted, and it may either be fixed at the side or in the face of the coal, as the case may require. The screw is then adjusted to this bar, and the drill driven in the coal by a man turning the handle at the end of the screw. The time occupied in drilling this hole for the machine, 3 inches in diameter and 3 feet 6 inches deep, is from 10 to 15 minutes, according to the hardness of the strata; and if it is necessary to drill the hole in such a position that the rotary motion of the handle by which the screw is propelled cannot be obtained, a ratchet may be used, so that, under any circumstances, no difficulty can be felt in procuring the required motion.

---

*Another sad illustration of the carelessness of some miners, notwithstanding the knowledge they have of the perils to which they are subjected in the pursuit of their daily avocations, is furnished by a shocking calamity which occurred at the Astley Deep Pit, Dukinfield, on Thursday evening last week, and the cause of which has since been ascertained. Certain parts of the pit are known to be strongly charged with gas, and the colliery regulations very properly prohibited blasting in consequence. In spite of the rule, however, and well knowing, as they must have done, the awful risk to which they were subjecting both themselves and their fellow-workmen, two miners fired a shot in one of the highly dangerous "brows." They have paid the penalty of their hardihood and recklessness by the loss of their own lives; but along with them seven others have also been hurried into eternity. One of these men had been warned before the magistrates of the consequence of neglecting the precautions prescribed in the rules only a few months ago. The inquest was on Saturday formally opened and adjourned.—*Colliery Guardian, March* 11, 1870.

† Mining Journal, June 12, 1869.

The first trial of the machine was made at a pit belonging to the North Staffordshire Coal and Iron Company, (Limited,) at Talke-o'-th'-Hill, in a heading in what is called the Eight-feet Banbury seam of coal, at a depth of 350 yards from the surface, and under ordinary working circumstances, so far as the place selected was concerned.

Considerable difficulty is always found in fairly testing a machine under such circumstances as these, but, notwithstanding every disadvantage, the hole for the machine was drilled and about 4 tons of coal brought down in 25 minutes. Mr. Higson asked a workman in charge of the place how long it would have taken him to have drilled the hole and fired the shot according to the present system of blasting, and he considered that an hour would be required for the purpose, and a pound of gunpowder used, at a cost of 5*d.* The superiority of the machine was, therefore, evidenced by the saving of 35 minutes in time and 5*d.*, the cost of powder, and the work was done without the smallest danger to any one. Two further trials of the machine were made in other parts of the workings, in both the Seven and Eight-feet seams, with results equally satisfactory. The mode of using the machine in the working of coal would be to provide each set of colliers with a pair of steel tension straps, and the machine could easily be carried about by a man like a double-barrelled gun under his arm from place to place. It would thus be necessary to have only one press for a large number of these places; the entire cost of the machinery is very small.

SECTION III.—TRANSPORTATION, VENTILATION, ETC.

CHAPTER VIII.

TRAMWAYS AND WAGONS.

As mines increase in depth and extent, the cost of sinking and maintaining shafts is much increased, and it is no longer economically possible to keep several hoisting-shafts in operation. It is therefore necessary to confine the hoisting to one central shaft, which thus becomes the only outlet of a constantly extending system of underground tramways, over which the minerals or débris are conveyed to the shaft in order that they may be raised to the surface. As the work of extraction of the ore or coal progresses, the distance of the mineral from the shaft, especially in collieries, is constantly increasing, being in some of the European collieries as much as 4,500 feet or more, and it is thus become a very important item in the expense of mining to move the mineral to the shaft.

So, also, when, as is common in California and Nevada, veins are reached by long tunnels, the tramming or underground transportation forms a serious item of the cost of getting the mineral to the surface, and it is important to determine the best forms and sizes of the wagons and tracks to be used.

TRAMMING AND TRAM WAGONS IN CALIFORNIA.

Very little attention has been given in the mines of the west to this subject of tramming. The forms of wagons, or "cars," as they are usually called, are almost as numerous as the mines in which they are used. In general, they are made of wood (there are some of iron) banded with iron, and are supported upon small cast-iron wheels, running upon axles of the simplest form. The size varies with the size of the tunnels, but is never larger than a man can manage with ease when loaded, except when, as at the Mount Diablo coal mines in California, horses are employed for the haulage. These coal mines perhaps present the best examples of underground tramming upon the Pacific slope.

The average distance of underground hauling at these coal mines, is now perhaps not far from one-third of a mile. This distance varies, of course, in the different mines, and in different parts of the same mine. The maximum distance of underground haulage is in the old or upper Black Diamond gangway, which, from its face to the mouth of the tunnel, is now about 4,200 feet. This tunnel is about 400 feet long, before reaching the coal, and extends for the remainder of the distance on the coal and is constantly being worked further. The haulage upon the horizontal tramways is done by horses at an average cost of not less than fifteen cents, and probably as great as twenty cents, per ton per mile.

The sizes of cars, tracks, &c., vary considerably in the different mines, but the tracks are all alike in their construction, being made by spiking a tight strap-iron rail upon wooden stringers supported on wood cross-ties. A light I-rail would be a decided improvement. The cars at most of the mines have to be made so that they can be used not only on a horizontal roadway, but also upon an incline. They are therefore built higher behind than in front, in order to prevent the coal from falling back out of the full cars as they ascend the slope. At the Mount Hope slope, leading to the lowest level of the Black Diamond mines, and pitching at an angle of 37° 15′ to the south, the cars, built of wood and sometimes of sheet-iron, have the following interior dimensions: Length, 6 feet 6 inches; width, 2 feet 5 inches; depth in front, 2 feet 5 inches; depth at rear end, 2 feet 11 inches. The width of track is about 36 inches. These cars hold about a ton of coal and they are drawn up the slope by a steam winding engine. Some details concerning this hoisting will be given beyond.

TRAMMING UPON THE COMSTOCK LODE.

The annexed figure, drawn to one-twentieth of the full size, shows the construction of a dumping car, made of wood, designed to run equally well on a horizontal track, upon a steep incline, or upon the surface. It is the form used some years since at the Ophir mine, on the Comstock lode. The body of the car is supported a little forward of its center upon the extreme end of a strong frame which turns upon a central pivot and rests upon a lower frame or truck, carrying the low wheels. This arrangement for turning the car upon a pivot allows its load to be dumped on either side of the raised track at the dump-pile of ore, or at the attle-heap. The forward end is closed by a flap-door opening outward, suspended on an iron rod, extending from one side of the car to the other. The back end of the car and half its length on top are closed with planks, secured by strong iron straps.

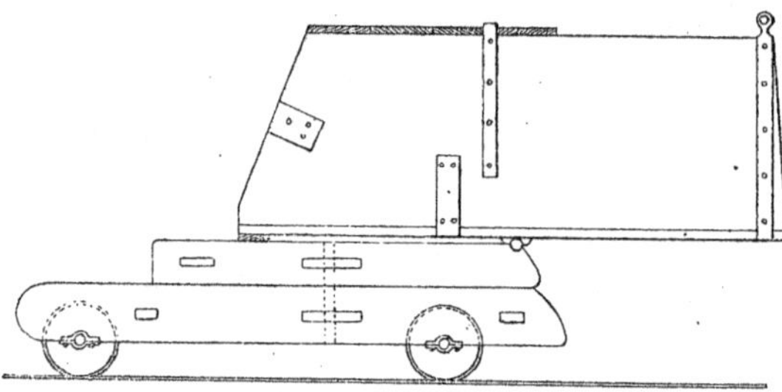

Dumping Car for inclined shaft or gallery.

UNDERGROUND TRAMMING ABROAD.

The next figure represents the tunnel car used at Freiberg, Saxony. The load is sustained upon the axles by a timber extending longitudinally in the center, under the car.

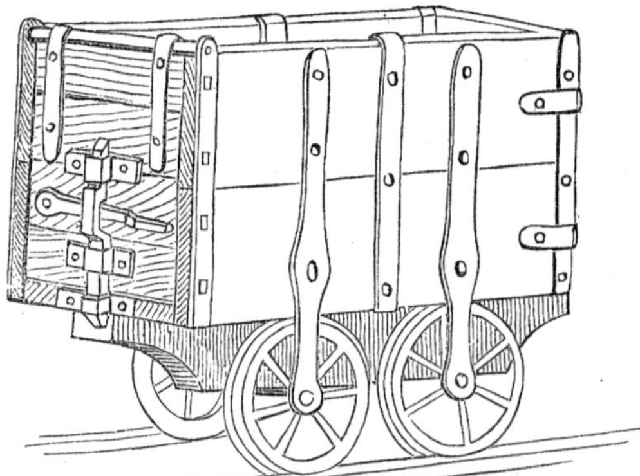

The wheels are of good size, and the outer ends of their axles are supported by the heavy iron bands depending from the side of the box.

The next figure will recall to the minds of those who have visited the Freiberg mines the "hund," or dog, so commonly employed in that district. It is of wood, bound with iron, and constructed of such a size as to be managed, when loaded, by a single man. The axles are fixed, and the car is turned, when necessary, by tilting it so as to lift the forward axle and leave the weight resting on the two larger wheels only. These dogs are particularly useful in mines where tracks have not been laid. Their broad wheels enable them to go through ordinary galleries, or over the inequalities of the surface. They are generally, however, run on strips of boards, or ways otherwise prepared, to diminish the labor of the miners propelling them.

The rapidly increasing production of the coal mines of Great Britain and the Continent has necessitated great improvements in the methods of transportation underground. The wagons used for the purpose and their running gear are no longer roughly and rudely constructed, but are made with great care. The wheels are accurately made, well bored, and fitted with carefully turned axles, and these are kept well lubricated by grease-boxes, so as to prevent loss of power, wear, and friction.

In France and Belgium a few years since a plain flat rail, set on edge and tightly wedged into the cross-ties or chairs, was preferred to any other. The size of the iron depended upon the weight to be sustained. For cars carrying 500 kilogrammes, 0 .055 by $0^{m}.011$ was sufficient; but if the track was to be used for a long time, heavier iron was preferred. The width of track was, and is, in general, from $0^{m}.60$ to $0^{m}.80$. At the Blanzy collieries, where the cars carry about 1,000 kilogrammes, (one ton,) the width is $0^{m}.80$, and the flat-bar rails measure $0^{m}.07$ by $0^{m}.02$.

At the Anzin collieries it is found advantageous to use iron cross-ties, with chairs welded or riveted to the ends, in preference to cross-ties of wood. Rails with a rounded summit, and thicker at the base than the top, were in use there in preference to the square-edged rail, but these have in turn given place to a light I-rail. It was calculated by Burat in 1861 that the tramways at Anzin, $0^{m}.60$ wide, and with cross-ties of iron at distances of $0^{m}.80$, did not cost over five francs per lineal metre.

But great improvements have been made since that time, and in the Supplément au Matériel des Houillères, Professor Burat states that the conclusions arrived at, after very careful investigations of the methods, are: 1. That the narrow-gauge tracks, those, for example, of $0^{m}.50$, are the most desirable. 2. That the flat rails and bar rails on edge should be abandoned for rails presenting at least two centimetres of bearing surface to the wheels. 3. That the charges for the cars should not be greater than 400 kilogrammes, net weight, in order that the attendant may easily turn the car on curves of short radius, or put it upon the track in case of its running off. Light I-rails are in use in some of the collieries, as well as the method of oiling known as Évrard's, by means of an oil-box placed in a hollow axle.

SELF-LUBRICATING AXLES.

Évrard's contrivance is described in the reports upon the Paris Exposition. It is designed to supply oil in moderate and regular quantities to the journals or bearings of the wheels of wagons for underground tramming, and for excluding all grit and dirt from the bearing surfaces. The wheels are supported by journals J J, working in a hollow cylinder or box *a* extending across the bottom of the car. This cylinder is calibered at each end, for one-third of its length, for the reception of the journal. The middle third of the cylinder is left rough, and receives an oil-box, which may be filled through a hole in the cylinder, closed by a screw *s*, with a conical point, which enters the oil-box and nearly closes the hole in it, leaving only a small opening, through which oil can exude in small quantities whenever a bubble of air enters. The journals are retained in their places by caps *c c*, fixed to the truck and fitting over the ends of the cylinder and catching upon a shoulder left upon the journal.

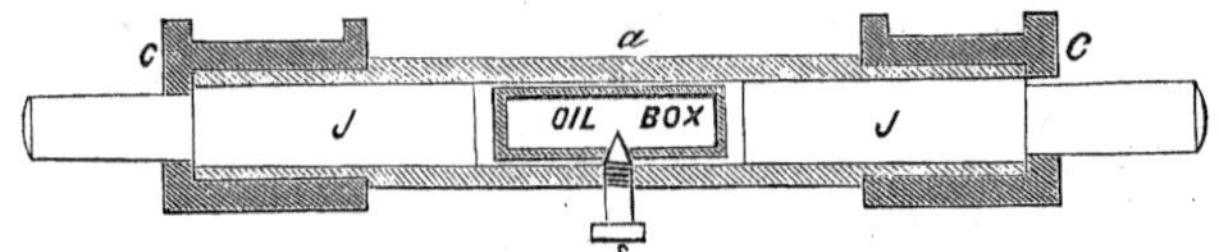

Évrard's Self-lubricating Axle.

Axles of this kind used upon wagons at the mines of the Vicoigne Company consume a decilitre of oil in running an aggregate distance of 150 kilometres—about 62 miles. Oil is renewed every fortnight.

M. Évrard, in his description in detail,* states that a car with its two axles did not consume more than three decilitres of oil in 22 days' running, the total distance run having been 448 kilometres.

Since the Exposition of 1867 a commission of mining engineers has been organized in Belgium for the purpose of studying the different forms of cars and tramways in use in the coal basins of the north of France and in Belgium. The car designed by M. Parent has been introduced in many of the mines of the Anzin company, and appears to give great satisfaction. The body is rectangular, $1^m.10$ long, $0^m.778$ wide, and $0^m.57$ deep; capacity, five hectolitres. The body is made of iron, two millimetres thick for the sides and four milimetres for the bottom. The total weight of the car, with wheels of wrought iron, is 190 kilogrammes, and with cast-iron wheels, 210 kilogrammes. They cost 96

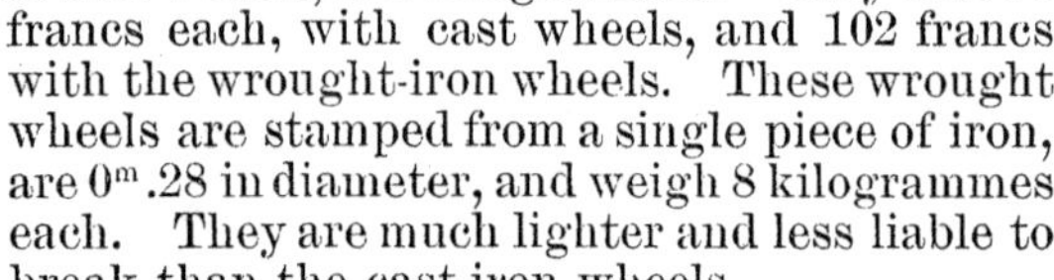
francs each, with cast wheels, and 102 francs with the wrought-iron wheels. These wrought wheels are stamped from a single piece of iron, are $0^m.28$ in diameter, and weigh 8 kilogrammes each. They are much lighter and less liable to break than the cast-iron wheels.

At the Chazotte collieries, M. Max Évrard has adopted the Pagat wheel and axle. This is a broad-faced wheel of small diameter, the form and construction of which may be best understood by reference to the annexed figure, which is a section through the center, showing the end of the axle and the oil-box. This oil-box appears to be the chief merit of this wheel. The end of the axle protrudes within it, and the wheel is held in place by a simple spring linchpin inserted through one of the large holes made in the hub to permit the introduction of the grease from time to time. These two openings are closed by corks *c c* only. A

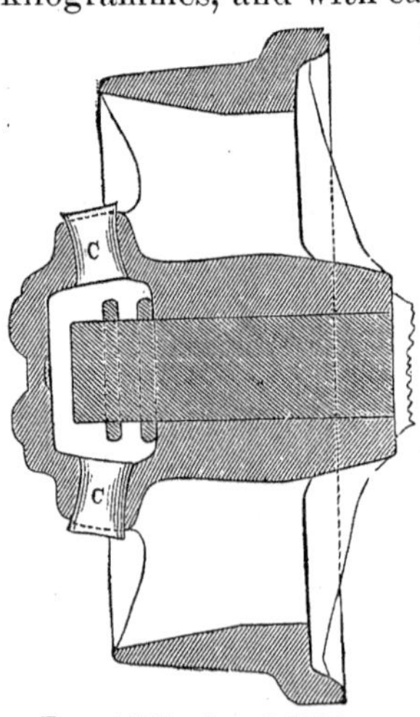

Pagat Wheel and Oil-box.

* In Burat's Matériel des Houillères—supplément, 1865, pp. 12–14.

hard grease or tallow is used, and is inserted by means of an injector. When by movement of the wheel the axle warms a little, the grease slowly melts and runs into the bearing so gradually that it need not be renewed oftener than twice a week.

According to M. Évrard this box once filled with grease is sufficient for running a distance of sixteen kilometres. It holds 128 grammes; the grease costs 52 francs per 100 kilogrammes, and the expense per ton, per kilometre, is, consequently, for the four wheels of a car, 0 fr.0455. These wheels are used under an oval tub car, the capacity of which is limited to 340 kilogrammes.

At Blanzy, the cars are rectangular, expanded over the wheels; carry a charge of 600 kilogrammes and weigh 230 kilogrammes. The wheels turn upon the axles, and the axles turn in boxes fixed to the body of the car.

USE OF SMALL TRAM-WAGONS.

In South Wales it has been argued that small tram-wagons are more economical than large ones, since they permit less height of the drifts, less cost of tramways, and the use of ponies and boys instead of horses. At a meeting of the Institute of Engineers it was stated that at a colliery in the Aberdare Valley there had been effected, by the introduction of small trams, a saving of 1*s.* a ton. The vein was 3 feet 8 inches thick, and the old principle was to cut as much as 6 feet 6 inches for head-way and horse road. But upon the introduction of the small trams the whole depth to be cut was 4 feet 6 inches; and, consequently, there was a saving of two feet in top or bottom—the top being a hard cliff. In getting out 150 tons a day with the large tram, fourteen horses were employed, at a cost of £4 12*s.* 8*d.*; with small trams, the same amount of horse work was done for £1 11*s.* 8*d.*—that was the cost of ponies, boys, and jiggermen—so that there was a saving of nearly 6*d.* a ton on that item alone.

On the other hand, it was asserted that it is certainly possible to devise a large tram with a smaller tare in proportion to the load than would attend a tram with a capacity of only six or ten hundred-weight; and further, that it is very doubtful whether a saving of one-third could be made in the cost of hauling by the use of ponies rather than horses.

The following figures were given as showing the comparative cost of working with large and small trams in the same colliery—No. 3 vein, which varied from 2 feet 6 inches to 3 feet 6 inches or 3 feet 9 inches.

	Tram of one ton.			Tram of ten hundred weight.		
	s.	*d.*		*s.*	*d.*	
Cost of cutting coal	2	0	per ton.	2	0	per ton.
Cutting bottom for horse height	0	3	per ton.	0	1½	per ton.
Hauling underground	0	4½	per ton.	0	3½	per ton.
Carting coal in stalls	0	2	per ton.	nil.		per ton.
Banking, screening, &c	0	1½	per ton.	0	1	per ton.
Total	2	11		2	6	

Showing a saving of 5*d.* per ton in favor of the small tram. But it was admitted that with a thick vein these items might be altered materially.

This is a matter upon which no general rule can be established; the miner will of necessity be governed in the choice of the form and size of wagons by the peculiar local conditions of the colliery.

PORTABLE TRAMWAYS.

In coal cutting or drilling by machinery, or in any mining work where rapid advances are made, it becomes important to be able to quickly extend the tramway or track so as to keep the machine well up to the face. To facilitate this, Mr. Firth, of England, who has made and patented several improvements in coal-cutting machines, proposes to make the ties or sleepers in such a form that the rails can be twisted or sprung into them. His plan is described in an English journal as follows:

It is the present custom in fixing the railroad for coal-cutting machines, to use rails about four yards in length, having one sleeper for each joint and one or more intermediate sleepers for each pair of rails. The kind of sleeper hitherto used has been of such a form that the intermediate sleepers have to be hammered on and off each time the road has to be removed nearer to the face of the coal. The improvement consists in making the intermediate sleepers of such a form that rails can be twisted out of and into them, instead of hammering the sleepers off and on to the rails, which improvement tends to a great saving of labor and time in making the railroad for coal-cutting machines, and subsequently in taking it to pieces and putting it together again whenever it has to be removed. At the outer end of the sleeper is a lug under which the outer flange or edge of the foot of the rail enters, and the foot of the rail then drops below a stop on the sleeper, which prevents the rail escaping laterally until its inner edge is intentionally raised. The same form, or a modification of the same form, can be applied to the tramroads of mines generally, also to sidings and railroads of other descriptions, and by this means no wooden wedges or keys are required to keep the rails in their places.

TRAMMING BY STATIONARY ENGINES.

In Belgium the formations through which the galleries of the mines are cut are so soft, and undergo such continual change by swelling, that it is not practicable, except in rare cases, to establish a system of hauling the coal by stationary steam power such as has been successfully introduced in the English collieries.

In most of the coal mines of England the regularity of the strata is such that a shaft may be used for a long time for the extraction of an enormous amount of coal brought to the shaft from great horizontal distances below. It is not unusual to see in Great Britain shafts from which 600, 1,000, 1,200, and even 1,500 or 1,600 tons are extracted in twenty-four hours. Such an amount of work, extending over great periods of time, requires all the parts of the shaft to be constructed in a solid and permanent manner.

For the conveyance of such immense quantities of coal to the shafts it is necessary to use power greater than is afforded by men trundling the wagons in the usual way. The coal is loaded into wagons containing from 350 to 450 kilogrammes each, and five or six of these wagons are then formed into trains, which are drawn by horses to the main tramways, which vary in length from a few hundred yards to even a mile.

Tramways may be divided into three classes: first, those in which the slope toward the shaft is sufficient for trains to descend by their own gravity, and, in descending, to draw up the empty trains; second, those in which the grade is reversed, and sufficient to permit the empty trains to descend from the shaft to the end of the road by their own gravity; third, those in which the bed or grade is horizontal, or nearly so, necessitating power for the movement of the trains either way.

In the second class the loaded trains are usually drawn up toward the shaft by means of a cable wound upon a drum by a steam engine, while the empty cars are lowered by a cable unwinding from the same drum.

In the third class an endless rope or cable, which traverses the gallery along the track between the rails, is moved by an engine, and the trains are coupled to this moving rope and so carried to their destination. A few details upon this third class of tram roads may be desirable. It is understood that a double track is laid on the levels where this method of moving the trains is used. The general arrangement of the cables, the engine, &c., are shown by the figure in plan showing two tracks, the engine, &c.

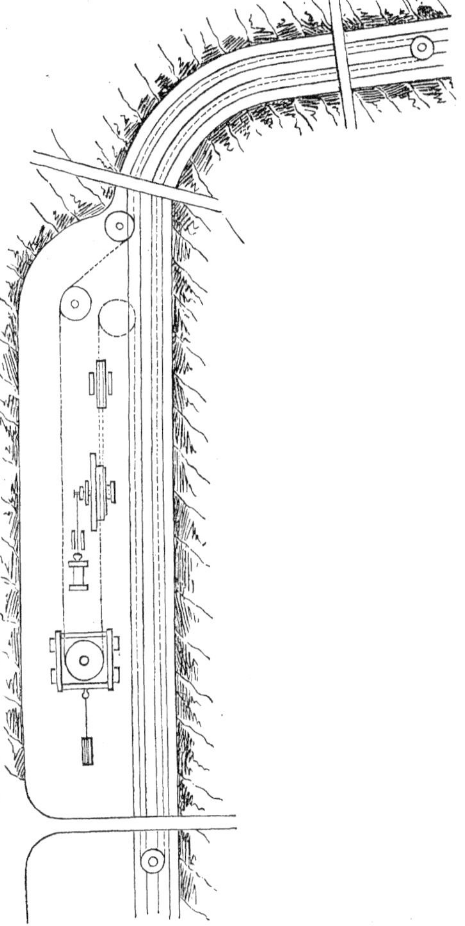

Tramming by steam-power underground.

The driving engine is generally placed in a recess cut at one side of the gallery, and near an air-shaft, by which the smoke from the furnaces can escape. The cable is wound upon a drum, and is supported throughout its course by horizontal rollers, and in the curves is guided by vertical rollers. At the ends of the route the cable turns upon drums placed between the tracks, the diameter of which is equal to the distance from center to center of the roads. In some cases the cables run for a part of the distance underground. In order to secure a proper tension of the cable, it is passed over a pulley upon a movable frame, counterpoised in such a way as to take up the slack of the cable and give a constant tension. The cable travels constantly in one direction, and thus moves opposite ways upon the two tracks. Trains of twenty or thirty wagons can be moved by this arrangement.

Formerly in some mines the engine was established at the surface, and the cable was guided to the bottom by pulleys and sheaves; this was the first plan adopted, but it occasions too much friction and wear of the rope, and now the engine is always placed underground.

To start or stop the trains it is not necessary to stop the cables. There is a conductor in the first wagon of each train. When he wants to put the train in motion he lifts up the cable with a hook, makes it pass along a wooden block fixed under the wagon, and by means of a lever he brings forward a wooden wedge, which squeezes the cable against the wooden block. Cable and wagon, being then connected, move together. By maneuvering his lever the other way, the conductor disconnects the rope and stops the train. When the train arrives opposite the machipe, or where the cable runs under ground, the conductor loosens the rope and the train runs alone. The momentum carries the train up to the point where the cable reappears; the conductor then again connects the rope to the train as before.

In the coal mines of Pelton the principal road is 1,500 metres in length. It is partly horizontal and partly on a slope of five degrees. The driving cable is $0^{m}.022$ in diameter, its running speed is $6^{m}.00$ per second, and it carries a train of 30 wagons; the width of the rail is $0^{m}.60$; the strength of the motive power is 40 horse-power; and the cable transports 52 trains in 12 hours, representing a duty of 560 tons of coal.

	Francs.
The labor costs	13.50
Coal (refuse) for fuel, 6 tons at 3 francs	18.00
Repairs, interest, &c	76.50
Total	108.00

Which represents a cost of 0.137 franc per ton per kilometre. Under the most favorable conditions transportation by horses costs 0.21 franc per ton, and by trammers, 0.67 franc.

GRIP PULLEYS.

In hauling heavy loads up inclines in mines or elsewhere, the grip pulleys may be used with great advantage. Mr. A. S. Hallidie, of San Francisco, has recently invented a pulley of this description, which is noticed as follows in the Scientific Press of that city:

> Its novelty consists in so arranging the two gripping jaws or clips, that they will be operated by the strain upon the rope, without the necessity of bolts, rivets, screws, or other device for holding them in place. The rim of the wheel is made in two parts, one of which is formed solid with an arm, and of only half the desired thickness of the rim, so that it forms a shoulder. This is then bolted or riveted to the other part, thus forming a rim of the required thickness. The flanges, between which the gripping jaws or clips are placed, are simply spread apart in the ordinary manner of forming the groove in pulleys. At intervals around the entire grooved periphery of the wheel are cavities or recesses, placed opposite one another in the two flanges. These are made widest at the lower part. The clips or jaws are made with spreading arms, so as to admit the rope easily, and the corners extend into the cavities just mentioned, thus preventing their dropping out, while allowing of a slight motion to and from one another. A groove or space is made just below the point of meeting of the clips, so that when the strain comes on the rope or chain, which rests on the bottom of the groove between the two jaws, the central part of each clip will be depressed, thus causing the jaws to grip the rope and prevent its slipping, while the strain is on, but as soon as this is removed, the jaws will work freely in their sockets and allow the rope to open them, and thus free itself from the pulley. This invention, in which the jaws are operated automatically by the strain on the rope and their own weight, is exceedingly simple and effective, has no complicated parts to get out of order or break, and is cheaper than other kinds.

TRAMMING BY MINING LOCOMOTIVES.

Many efforts have been made to substitute small locomotive engines for animal power in underground haulage, especially where the amount to be moved is constant and large. In some of the Pennsylvania collieries such locomotives are now successfully employed. The first machine of this kind was built for the Lehigh Coal and Navigation Company by Messrs. Grice & Long, of Philadelphia. It is a locomotive of peculiar construction, measuring 12 feet in length by about 4 feet 4 inches in width, and 6 feet in height from rail to top of stack or roof. It weighs 11,000 pounds, with water and fuel. The wheels are about 2 feet diameter, are four in number, and are all drivers. Distance between the wheels, 5 feet 6 inches; gauge of track, 3 feet 6 inches; rails, 40 pounds per yard.

The work to be done is to draw the wagons or "cars" from a "coal breaker" into the mine, a distance of about 7,500 feet, 5,500 feet of which is in what is known as No. 5 Tunnel, near Summit Hill. A great part of the road is in a gangway in the coal of a seam overlaying that worked. As the coal is a hard anthracite, there is no danger to be feared from fire.

The working expenses of the engine for two months are known with accuracy. In order to compare them with the cost of doing the same amount of work by mules, we will assume the mine to be working to its full capacity, 600 tons of clean coal per day. To do this work with mules would require the handling of 300 "cars" of two tons each (99 cubic feet) per day, and about 40 cars of "slate," "waste," etc. To haul these over 7,500 feet of road, requires three teams of seven mules each, drawing 20 cars in a train; there are needed, therefore, three sidings to pass trains on, and 60 cars are on the road at a time; there will at the same time be 20 in the mines, and 20 outside; in all, 100 cars will be required to do the work. The wear of the roads by mules, requires the constant work of one man to keep them in repair.

To do the same amount of work with the locomotive requires but 50 cars, since the engine takes in a train of 15 cars in less than half the time required by the mules; 15 cars in the mine and 15 outside, or say 50 in all, suffice to "handle" 600 tons of coal per day. There is but one "siding" required by the engine; it is at the end of the road, and is arranged with an air shaft to carry off the steam and gases from the combustion of the coal.

The engine has abundantly proved itself capable of drawing 15 to 18 cars, the road being so graded as to make the work of drawing the loaded wagons out, no greater than that of taking the light ones in. Its maximum speed is 9 miles per hour, though it does not run at that rate "underground"—it draws a train with ease round a curve of 75 feet radius.

The following comparison of the expenses attending working with the locomotive and by mules has been made:*

Locomotive per day.		*Mules per day.*	
1 engineer	$3 50	21 mules, at $1 per day	$21 00
1 boy	1 25	3 drivers	6 30
Repairs, oil, fuel, &c	1 55	Extra cost of keeping road in repair	2 00
Total	6 30	Total	29 30

Leaving a balance of $23 per day in favor of the locomotive.

The men are sent in to their work on the wagons. When these are drawn in by the engine, there is a saving of 15 minutes, morning and evening; and as one miner cuts, on an average, 14 tons of coal (clean and prepared for market) per day, and has one laborer to load the same, it will effect a saving of 30 minutes a day for eighty-six men, or four days, at $2=$8 per day, by using the engine for this work. The average of 14 tons per day is above that performed by the miners, generally, throughout the anthracite mines, owing to the high inclination and great thickness—from 20 to 50 feet—of the seams in the Panther Creek Valley. In the Wyoming coal-fields, the average amount of coal mined per man per day, is about 10 tons.

If we consider the first cost of the motors referred to, we find:

Locomotive	$3,000	21 mules, at $200	$4,200
50 mine wagons	6,250	100 mine cars, at $125	12,500
1 siding, say	1,000	3 "sidings" for passing trains	3,000
Total	10,250	Total	19,700

Showing a balance of $9,450 in favor of the engine.

* R. P. Rothwell, mining engineer, in the American Journal of Mining.

Taking the interest on the above at 10 per cent., and allowing 200 working days per year, since these mines are not worked during the winter, and counting twenty cents per day for keeping each mule 100 days in winter, we obtain a total saving of $7,565 per annum, or more than six cents a ton upon the coal mined, effected by the introduction of the locomotive.

The constructors state that this comparison of a few of the principal items of cost and working expenses may be accepted as substantially correct for the location referred to. The actual working of the locomotive justifies the conclusions deduced, yet its introduction is still too recent to warrant a very positive assertion that the results will always show so large a balance in its favor.

Since the data were obtained for the foregoing estimates, another and an improved mining locomotive has been put into the mines, and the manager of the colliery reports that both have proved eminently successful. Two more have since been added to the list, and the saving effected by their substitution for mules is so great that it will soon cover the first cost of the machines.

The general appearance of these locomotives is shown by the figure. They are built very low and compact, so as to pass through the galleries of the mines, and to suit any required gauge from 2 feet 6 inches upward. The height sometimes does not exceed 5 feet from the track to the top of the smoke-stack. It is of course desirable, where there is head room, to give a greater height to the stack. These locomotives will haul from 50 to 120 tons, gross load, the capacity of the engine being controlled by the gauge of track and the head-room. The mine-locomotives weigh from 9,000 to 12,000 pounds each, and work well upon a 28-pound rail. For outside work, taking the coal to the breakers and returning the empty cars; at bituminous coal pits for conveying the coal to the point of shipment; air furnaces, quarries, &c., they are built from four to nine tons in weight, each size increasing by one ton.

Mining Locomotive.

All these engines are remarkably open and accessible for cleaning and repairs, there being no part that cannot be readily reached. Considering the very limited space afforded by the mine gangways, the constructors of these locomotives have been remarkably successful in combining the boiler and machinery so as to effectually meet the requirements of the work.

SURFACE TRANSPORTATION.

At most of the mines in California and Nevada, the cars used in the mine are taken to the surface and used there also to convey their load to the dump-pile or into the mill. But when the point of delivery is far removed from the mouth of the mine, the mineral is either thrown into enormous wagons, to be hauled by horses over the common roads, or into larger cars, running upon rail.

The two most notable examples of mining railways in California are the road at the Pine Tree and Josephine mines, in Mariposa County, and the railway leading from the Mount Diablo mines to the point of shipment of the coal at Antioch, upon the San Joaquin River. The road at the former place is built from the mouth of the mines to the mill on the Merced River, and has a zigzag course along the almost precipitous slopes of Hell's Hollow. The cars, loaded with quartz, are formed into trains and descend by gravity along the steep incline, the speed of movement being controlled by brakes; the empty cars are drawn up by mules.

On the road from the Mount Diablo collieries, the haulage of the cars is effected by locomotives of peculiar construction, very compact and small, so as to pass readily through a low and narrow tunnel. These engines work on a grade of 275 feet to the mile for one and a half miles, and on an eight-degree curve, carrying 30 tons, at the rate of twelve miles per hour. They are coal-burning; cylinders 14 by 18 inches; six driving-wheels, three feet in diameter; and each locomotive weighs 25 tons.

These, the first mining locomotives built in California, were designed and constructed at the Union Iron Works, San Francisco, by H. J. Booth & Co.

In Nevada, a road has recently been built from Virginia city, upon the Comstock lode, to the Truckee River.

In the annual report of the Gould and Curry Mining Company, President Bull alludes to the advantages, present and prospective, of this Virginia and Truckee railroad, toward which the trustees had advancd $40,000. In a previous report, it was estimated that these advantages would result in a saving of 34 per cent. in the annual expenses of the mine. Though the railroad was at that time not yet completed, there had been already a marked reduction in the cost of wood and timber. There had also been a considerable saving in the amount of supplies necessary to be on hand. At the close of 1868, the supplies at the mine amounted to over $80,000. To have provided for such supplies for the winter of 1869–'70 would have rendered an assessment of $7 per share necessary. The railroad will permit the company to draw their supplies as needed throughout the year, and hence the value of the supplies at present on hand aggregates only about $30,000. Instead of paying $15 per cord for wood, the price has been reduced to $11 50, while for spring delivery contracts were offered at $9 per cord.

At the mines of the Red Mountain Company, Silver Peak, Nevada, there is a fine surface railway, about a mile and a half long, and remarkable for the boldness of its curves and grades. The loaded cars descend upon it by gravity, and the empty cars are drawn up by mules. The road winds along the mountain side, "heading" the numerous cañons, until it arrives at a point above the larger dumps, where the ore is to be deposited to be removed in wagons. The remaining descent to the dumps could not be traversed by the road, even with such curves as had been employed above, except by enormously expensive trestle-work or masonry. The only practicable route required an acute angle in the road, and this was in fact introduced, by means of a back switch, the suggestion, I believe, of Mr. J. E. Clayton, the superintendent. The track runs past the point of turning, and, for a few yards, up hill. The car, rapidly descending, shoots by the switch, and its velocity is diminished by the up grade. It is stopped with the brakes, the switch is changed, the brakes are opened, and the car starts again by gravity, and runs back to the switch, where it is deflected upon the next descent at an acute angle to the last. The whole operation is performed in a few moments by one man. By the use of such back switches, a surface tramway may surmount great difficulties of ground at small cost and trouble. The dumps of this company are like those of the Comstock mines. The ore is taken from them by large "back-action" wagons, and hauled six and a half miles further, to the mill, over an excellent wagon road, constructed at great expense, and presenting so uniform a down grade that fifteen or twenty tons or upwards can be hauled on it by a team of eight or ten mules. It is my impression that the wagon-road cost about $20,000, and the railroad about $15,000.

TRANSPORTATION UPON WIRE ROPE.

Mr. Charles Hodgson is the author of a system of transporting by suspending the load upon a moving endless wire rope. This rope is supported on pulleys sustained by posts about seventy yards apart on the average, passes around a clip-drum at the end, and is worked by an ordinary portable engine. The rope moves at a speed of about five or six miles an hour, and the boxes suspended from it carry from one to five hundred-weight each. They are so attached that they pass the pulleys with ease. The full boxes hang on one side of the supports, and the empty ones on the other side. About thirty-five miles of line have been completed, and about one hundred miles in length are constructing. The cost of a line capable of transporting one hundred tons a day is about £400 per mile, and the average cost of transportation, including maintenance, is about twopence per ton per mile.

TRAMMING UPON A FIXED ROPE.

An interesting example of transportation upon a stationary wire rope, used as a track, stretched tightly upon posts, is found at the Brown mine, Colorado. This mine is on a steep mountain slope, about sixteen hundred feet from the mill below it, and the rope is used to convey the ore from the mouth of the mine to the mill. Two one-and-a-quarter inch wire cables are stretched between the two points, one for the descent of the loaded cars, the other for the ascent of the empty cars. The cable is sustained upon the projecting end of a horizontal beam, *d*, tipped with an iron bar, *e e*, as shown in the annexed figure. Its upper surface thus forms an unbroken track. The cars *f* are suspended upon it by means of a curved frame-work of iron, *g*, in which there are two wheels, with hollow faces to fit the curvature of the cable.

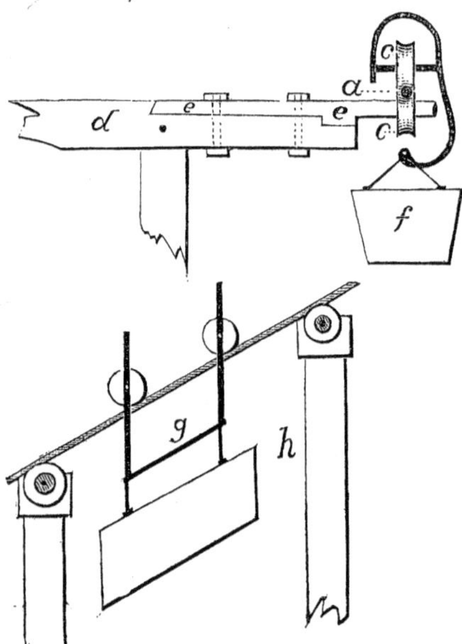

Transportation of ores upon Wire Rope.

The descent of the loaded car, draws up the empty ones on the other track by means of a small iron rope, half an inch in diameter, by which also the speed is regulated.

AUTOMATIC DUMPING.

At the Mount Diablo mines, California, there is, at the Hope colliery, an automatic arrangement by which the mine cars empty themselves into the bunkers. The forward end of each car is closed by a flap-door, hung upon a rod at the top in the usual manner, and secured by a latch. As the cars come to the surface, each one is switched off upon a separate branch track, leading to a little platform at the head of the screen, over which the coal runs from the cars into the bunkers. This platform is just wide and long enough to receive and hold one car, and is hung upon trunnions at the side of the track, and about two feet higher than the rails. The T-rail is used upon the platform, and at the front end of the latter the rails are curved upward and backward for eighteen inches or two feet, so as to fit and receive the forward wheels of the car, and hold it upon the platform while the whole tips forward. As the loaded car runs on the platform the wheels strike the curve of the rails, and the car is stopped; but as the centre of gravity of the loaded car is somewhat higher than the trunnions of the platform, the momentum tips the platform and car forward and the load is discharged. As the car tips forward, the latch strikes against a bar of iron and is withdrawn, so that the door drops open. The larger cars, in which the coal is transported to the vessels at the river, are discharged by a similar device, except that the platform is tipped by a hand crank and gearing. The arrangement of the small cars for automatic dumping is similar to that at Blanzy, except that there the rail is re-curved backwards far enough to include both wheels, and the forward wheel, instead of striking the rail, abuts upon a piece of timber by which the shock is deadened. The trunnions are bolted to a vertical plate of iron, which supports the track below, and is prolonged above so as to overhang the body of the car, and help to retain it when inverted.

OILING THE AXLES OF TRAM WAGONS.

A contrivance, known as Halliday's, for oiling the axles of tram wagons or cars, which has been in use for some time at Mesne Lea colliery, England, consists of an open vat, or tub, placed under the track and fitted with a small force pump in the center. This pump has two spouts or jets, drawn to a point like the tube of an oiling cup, and then rising to the level of the axle-bearings. Oil being placed in the vat, and the car having been run over it into the proper position, so that the jets are opposite the bearings, the attendant presses with his foot upon a lever, which moves the piston of the pump and throws the oil into the bearings. The excess drips back into the vat, and is not wasted upon the ground, as is ordinarily the case.

CHAPTER IX.

HOISTING MACHINERY AND APPARATUS.

The simplest form of hoisting apparatus is the common hand-windlass, with a bucket made of the half of a barrel, familiar to every miner. In Mexico, and frequently in Arizona and Nevada, the bucket is represented by a rawhide sack, which has the great advantage of being light, strong, durable, and cheap. There are no hoops to fall off when it is dry, and it cannot be stove by falling down the shaft.

Experiments have been made with the windlass in Great Britain and on the continent. Weisbach says that two men can raise a weight of 17 pounds 2.4 feet per second in a pit 120 feet deep throughout a period of eight hours. This is equal to about 8 tons 12 hundred-weight per day. Mr. Walker, in England, supposes two men raising coal from a depth of 150 feet. One man can exert a force of 12 pounds at a speed of 220 feet per minute. To convert into foot-pounds, we have: $12 \times 220 = 2,640$ foot-pounds. Then, $2,640 \times 60$ minutes $\times 8$ hours $\times 2$ men $\times 150$ feet $= 7$ tons 10 hundred-weight 96 pounds, raised by the two men in a day. This shows theoretically what *can* be done. Practically, such results are not attained.

As the depth of the pit or shaft increases, a horse-whim is substituted for the windlass, and this in turn is displaced by water-power or a steam engine and hoisting gear, with horizontal winding drums. Horse-whims of good construction have drums from eight to twelve feet in diameter, but they are often larger. The arms attached just below the drum are from 30 to 36 feet in length. In Mexico whims of enormous dimensions are constructed for hoisting from the large and deep shafts, and they require ten or twelve horses. As the strength of the hoisting apparatus is increased, the size and weight of the buckets are made to correspond, and iron is substituted for wood, or the tubs are made of plank and are heavily ironed.

KIBBLES.

Probably the best form of mining bucket, and one which is more or less in use in California, is the Cornish kibble, a cylindro-conical vessel, made of iron, in plates one-quarter of an inch thick, and strongly riveted together, as shown in the figure. A kibble of medium size weighs three hundred-weight, and has the following dimensions: height, 34 inches; diameter at the top, 22 inches; at the bulge, 24 inches; at the bottom, 15 inches. The charge is seven hundred-weight. But this weight is too great for horse-whims; and for these the kibbles are made smaller, weighing from one to one and three-quarters hundred-weight, and holding a mean charge of two hundred-weight.

At Drakewell's, Cornwall, some years ago, kibbles were in use weighing $4\frac{1}{2}$ hundred-weight; charge 15 hundred-weight; height, 36 inches; diameter, 33 inches.

Cornish Kibble.

When a loaded kibble is brought to the surface it is inverted and discharged by inserting a hook, at the end of a hanging chain, in the loop at the bottom; the kibble is then lowered and becomes suspended by the bottom while the load falls out.

SKIPS.

Kibbles or buckets swinging freely in the air can only be used in large and vertical shafts, where there is room for them to ascend and descend without striking the sides. In narrow shafts, and particularly in those which for a part of the way are not perpendicular, but inclined, it becomes necessary to confine the buckets to a certain path, and this is done by means of guides placed along the sides of the shaft. Buckets or boxes so guided are known as *skips*, and have been much used in Cornwall and in some of the gold mines of California. The annexed drawing of a skip used at the Princeton mine, Mariposa Estate, will serve to show the construction. It consisted of a rectangular box, made of boiler-iron, one-quarter of an inch thick, and strongly riveted with angle-irons in the corners. It was 5 feet 5 inches in its greatest length, and two feet square in section. The wheels, one foot in diameter, ran upon short axles bolted to the side of the box, and served to support it when passing along the inclines, and to keep it in place when rising between the vertical guides. These guides were of wood, 5 by 6 inches square, and faced with a strap-rail. Short bars of iron, or "rubbers," projecting from the skip behind these guides, together with the wheels in front, served to keep the skip in position. The bottom was made inclined, at an angle of about 45 degrees, as shown in the figure, and the load was discharged through a flap-door, secured by massive hinges in front. On rising to the top of the shaft, it throws open two oaken trap-doors, which fall back and close the opening as the skip passes, and in the descent of the skip for dumping, its inclined bottom rests upon one of these doors, inclined at a similar angle. The door serves also as a chute to direct the load into a car placed to receive it below.

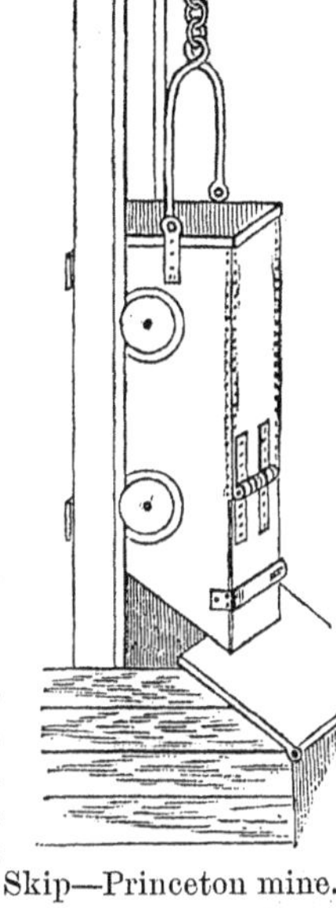
Skip—Princeton mine.

When the Princeton mine was in its best condition, and worked with most vigor, the hoisting was effected through three shafts, all within a distance of about 500 feet, and with three engines. They took out an average of 180 tons a day, working one shift of eight hours only, for a long period, and sometimes 200 tons a day, hoisting in skips, a ton at a time in one, and 900 pounds in the other. The main shaft, where the largest amount was hoisted, was at that time 330 feet in depth.

The skips in Cornwall weigh from 6 cwt. to 9½ cwt., and the charge varies from 11 cwt. to 12½ cwt. Skips are applicable, especially in mines with inclined or crooked shafts, where for a part of the course the hoisting is upon a slope and in another portion is vertical. At the Amador mine, (Hayward's,) instead of skips, cylindrical iron tubs, guided along the slope of the shaft by two strong stringers of timber faced with iron, were in use for several years. The cylindrical form of the tubs permitted them to rest in the angle between the two guides, and a rounded rim at the top and projection at the bottom were the only points of contact with the guides; the body of the tub was thus kept from wearing. These tubs were about six feet long and twenty inches internal diameter. By this arrangement of the two tubs, one descending while the other was ascending, both the ore and water of the mine were brought to the surface. Pumps have since been introduced for raising the water, but I believe the ore is hoisted as before.

COST OF HOISTING IN CORNWALL.

Some interesting data in detail have been published by Mons. M. L. Moissenet* in regard to the cost of hoisting at several of the most prominent mines of Cornwall, England. He finds it to range from one shilling and twopence to one shilling and elevenpence per ton for depths ranging from 150 to 250 fathoms. Four examples are cited: Dolcoath, where the hoisting is by kibbles and chains in inclined and elbowed shafts; United mines, where skips with flat ropes work in a vertical shaft; Levant, where skips, with flat and wire ropes, work in an elbowed shaft; and Carnbrea, where kibbles, with chains and skips, with

* De l' Extraction dans les mines du Cornwall, etc., par M. L. Moissenet, Ingenieur des mines. Annales des Mines; II, 1862.

flat and wire ropes, work in various kinds of shafts. The particulars in each case extend over a period of twelve months, and tables are given for each mine, showing the quantity hoisted and the cost of materials used, not only in the shaft but at the engines, and in filling and landing.

From the various tables I have compiled the following, showing the mean depth, the quantity extracted in tons, the cost per ton, and the cost per ton per 100 metres at the four different mines.

Name of mine.	Mean depth.	Quantity extracted, tons.	Cost per ton.	Cost per ton per 100 metres.
	Fathoms. Metres. *m.*	*Tons.*	*s. d. Francs.*	*Francs.*
Dolcoath	250 = 457.19	20,166	1 11 = 2.3981	0.5212
United Mines	240 = 438.96	19,200	1 7 = 1.9440	0.4418
Levant	190 = 350.00	16,800	1 2 = 1.4313	0.4089
Carnbrea	150 = 274.00	36,000	1 6¾ = 1.8857	0.6977

At Dolcoath a little over 42 per cent. of the cost was in the shaft, 37 per cent. at the engine, and 21 per cent. (nearly) for filling and landing.

HOISTING MACHINERY IN CALIFORNIA AND NEVADA.

The simplest form of steam hoist, and the one usually employed in California and Nevada, for depths of a few hundred feet, especially if used in connection with pumps, is a steam engine with eight to ten inches diameter of cylinder and sixteen inches stroke, with or without link-motion to the valves, the engine only requiring to run one way. Upon the crank shaft is a pinion, grooved generally with a large V, the inner faces having an inclination toward each other of 60 to 90 degrees. This pinion gears by friction into a large V-wheel, proportioned to the size of the other, so as to hoist in the shaft from 200 to 300 feet per minute.

This large V-wheel usually forms one flange of the winding drum, and upon the opposite end of the drum is a second flange of the same diameter as the V-wheel, but with its periphery broadly recessed to receive a friction strap. The winding drum is made of boiler-iron, and is riveted securely to a projecting rim cast on the inner side of each of these wheels. The dimensions of this drum are usually 2 feet 6 inches diameter by 2 feet 6 inches long. The diameter of the large-friction V-wheel is 4 feet, and of the brake-wheel the same. The whole is keyed upon a shaft 3½ to 4 inches in diameter, and is mounted upon a wooden frame swinging upon a hinge. By means of a lever the large V-wheel is pressed firmly into contact with the fixed pinion on the engine shaft while hoisting. While lowering, it is thrown out of contact, and being perfectly detached from the engine, is free to unwind, its movement being controlled by the application of the friction band. The motion of the engine is controlled by the throttle-valve, and continues all the time in one direction, it being used only during the hoisting.

This construction for a hoisting engine is simple, durable, and comparatively safe for small loads and shafts that do not exceed two or three hundred feet in depth. For deeper mines and heavier work the drum-shaft is supported upon a frame which slides upon a secure bed, and can be pressed up to the V-pinion by levers, and the friction surface is increased by making several V-grooves instead of one, and giving them an acute angle. Where two or more shafts are to be worked from the same engine, a man is placed at each brake. Some engines drive as many as four winding drums from one crank-shaft. One of the disadvantages of this method is the unequal wear of the V-wheels, which require turning off as often as twice a year, and sometimes once in two months.

Hoisting gear of the kind just described is manufactured by the Union Iron Works. By means of long levers the engineer can control the engine while standing at the mouth of the shaft. The piston of the engine has two-feet stroke, and the fly-wheel is eight feet in diameter. The winding drum is three feet in diameter and three feet in length. This construction is characterized by extreme simplicity and great strength.

Another form of hoist much in use for the mines of the west is the common link-motion engine, with a light fly-wheel fitted with a good

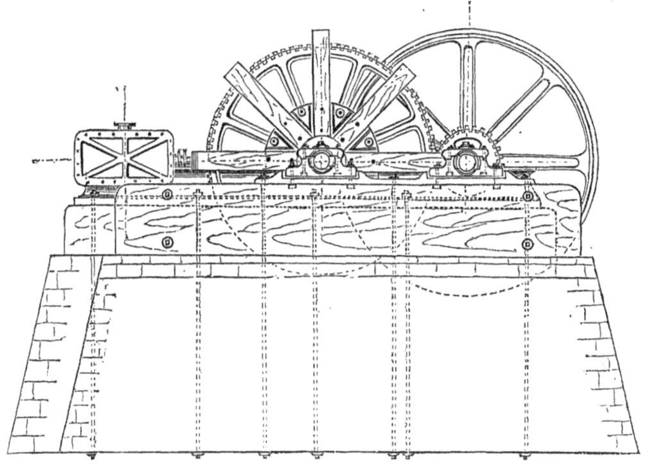

Booth & Co.'s Hoisting apparatus—elevation.

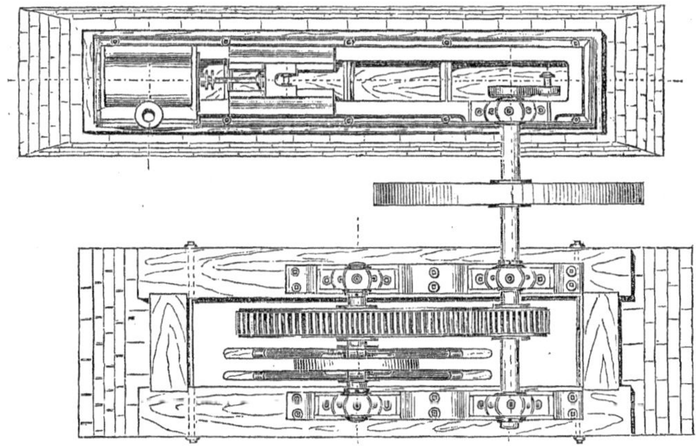

Booth & Co.'s Hoisting apparatus—plan.

brake, and a strong flanged pinion upon the end of the crank shaft. This pinion gears into a spur-wheel, keyed upon the shaft of the winding drum or reel. With this construction the engine and the winding drum can be turned either way, and if two skips or cages are worked at the same time and from the same level in the mine, the cables are wound so that one unwinds while the other is winding up, one thus balancing the other. But where the points of departure in the hoisting change, one reel or drum is made with a hub-flange or clutch, so that it can be easily adjusted to wind from a greater or less depth, as required. In mining requiring a sudden change of distance of hoisting, (from either an upper or a lower level,) each reel and wheel should run independently and have a separate friction band. The pinions on the crank-shaft are fitted with a clutch, which can be thrown in or out of gear when required to lower. The engine is under the control of one man, and each brake and reel under the control of another. When the bell strikes for either reel to hoist, the engine-man slows the engine to allow the clutch of the pinion to be put into gear. The brakeman then releases the brake and the hoisting commences. For stopping, the clutch is thrown out and the reel is held by the friction brake. In this way two or four shafts can be worked from one engine, and to any number of levels.

The above-described form of hoisting apparatus is illustrated by the annexed cut, giving a vertical and a side view of the machine with its foundation, as made by H. J. Booth & Co. It is here shown with a single bobbin for a flat cable; the spokes of this bobbin are of wood, and are not joined together by iron segments.

HOISTING AT THE MOUNT DIABLO COAL MINES.

At the Mount Diablo collieries the coal is hoisted in cars up a slope of 37° and 327 feet long, by an engine with a 14 by 30-inch cylinder. The crank-shaft carries a fly-wheel 12 feet in diameter, and a pinion 2 feet in diameter, geared into a spur-wheel 6 feet in diameter, which forms the end or flange of the winding drum. There are two drums, so connected by a clutch gearing that they can be easily disconnected at any time if desired. These drums are of iron, covered with wood, and are about 19 feet in circumference. A powerful brake, worked by the foot of the engineer, is fitted to the circumference of the fly-wheel, and is capable of stopping the engine very quickly. The engine makes 120 double strokes in a minute, and the usual time of hoisting a car carrying about one ton of coal is thirty seconds. Only one car is hoisted at one time, and about 200 are drawn up in the course of ten hours. But this is not the limit of the working capacity. As many as 270 have been taken out in that time, and the number could be exceeded if desired. Round iron wire rope, ¾ of an inch in diameter, is used, and passes over rollers about 3 feet in diameter. In some of the pits a flat wire rope, winding upon a reel, has been substituted.

At the Pacific Coal Mining Company's mines, near Mount Diablo, a very well constructed shaft was sunk vertically to a depth of 400 feet, and was provided with excellent hoisting works from the establishment of H. J. Booth & Co. The engine of 75-horse power was geared to a bobbin-shaft. There were two bobbins, winding inversely; flat iron cable, balanced; a link motion, and an ordinary brake, operated by the foot of the engineer. The pumping was performed by a separate engine of 150-horse power, 15-inch plungers, and a lift-pump.

HOISTING UPON THE COMSTOCK LODE.

Upon the Comstock lode, in Nevada, preference is given to one heavy, short-stroke engine, with balance valves and link motion; a pinion upon the crank-shaft; heavy spur-wheel, and flat winding cable.

The mines on the Comstock lode which have large hoisting works and wire cables include the Chollar-Potosi, Empire, Gould & Curry, Hale & Norcross, Imperial, Lady Bryan, Savage, and Sierra Nevada. An engine recently put up by the Risdon Iron and Locomotive Works, of San Francisco, has a 20-inch cylinder with 40-inch stroke, with 3 feet 6 inch pinion, 12-feet spur-wheel, 14-inch face by 3½-inch pitch, a single winding reel for flat cable, 5 feet in diameter, sheave, or shaft pulley, 8 feet in diameter. With this it is intended to work from a depth of 2,000 feet.

HOISTING IN GUIDED CAGES.

In each of the methods described the mineral, having been taken to the shaft, is either dumped in a pile and then shoveled into the bucket or skip, or is dumped through a chute directly into the skip, and the empty car is returned to the face. But this necessitates a rehandling of the mineral, which, when it reaches the surface, must be again dumped into a car or wagon, by which it can be delivered at the proper point away from the shaft.

These and other considerations have led to hoisting the car and load together to the mouth of the shaft. This effects a great saving in time, labor, and wear and tear of apparatus. It is the method adopted in the mines upon the Comstock lode, and in all well-appointed vertical shafts of any considerable depth elsewhere. To effect this, a compartment of the shaft is fitted with vertical stringers, or "guides" of wood or iron, extending from the top to the bottom, which serve to guide the movement of a platform cage, into which the car can be placed. The platform is fitted with rails of the same gauge as the track, and the car is rolled upon these and secured by bolts. The platform is a little smaller than the compartment of the shaft, and forms the bottom of a framework of iron, by which it is suspended. The frame rises above it on each side and connects with a cross-piece above the car, to which the hoisting cable is attached. The platform and the framework together form the "cage." By means of projecting ears or bars of iron or steel rubbers on each side, at the top and bottom, which partly embrace the guides, it is kept from contact with the sides of the shaft, and thus glides freely up and down. The only friction is between the rubbers and the guides, and this friction, in truly vertical shafts, is very slight. The shaft becomes, in fact, a vertical railway, and is a continuation of the tramways below, uniting them with the distributing tracks above. Tramming and hoisting thus become a connected and continuous operation. A carload of mineral is rolled to the bottom of the shaft and placed upon the platform, the signal is given to the engineman above, and the load starts upon its vertical journey.

Most of the mines at Virginia City and Gold Hill, upon the Comstock lode, and in other parts of Nevada, and the principal deep mines in California, with vertical shafts, now use the cage. It is single, large enough for one car only, but the hoisting is very rapid, from 500 to 1,200 feet per minute, (8 ft. to 20 ft. per second,) and with heavy loads weighing from 5,000 to 8,000 pounds.

The construction of the cage, as I have remarked, is very simple, being usually a square plank platform with a track, upon which the car stands, and suspended by a kind of stirrup-frame of iron at each side to an arched cross-bar of iron at the top, through the center of which the rod of suspension passes freely, and is firmly bolted just below to a

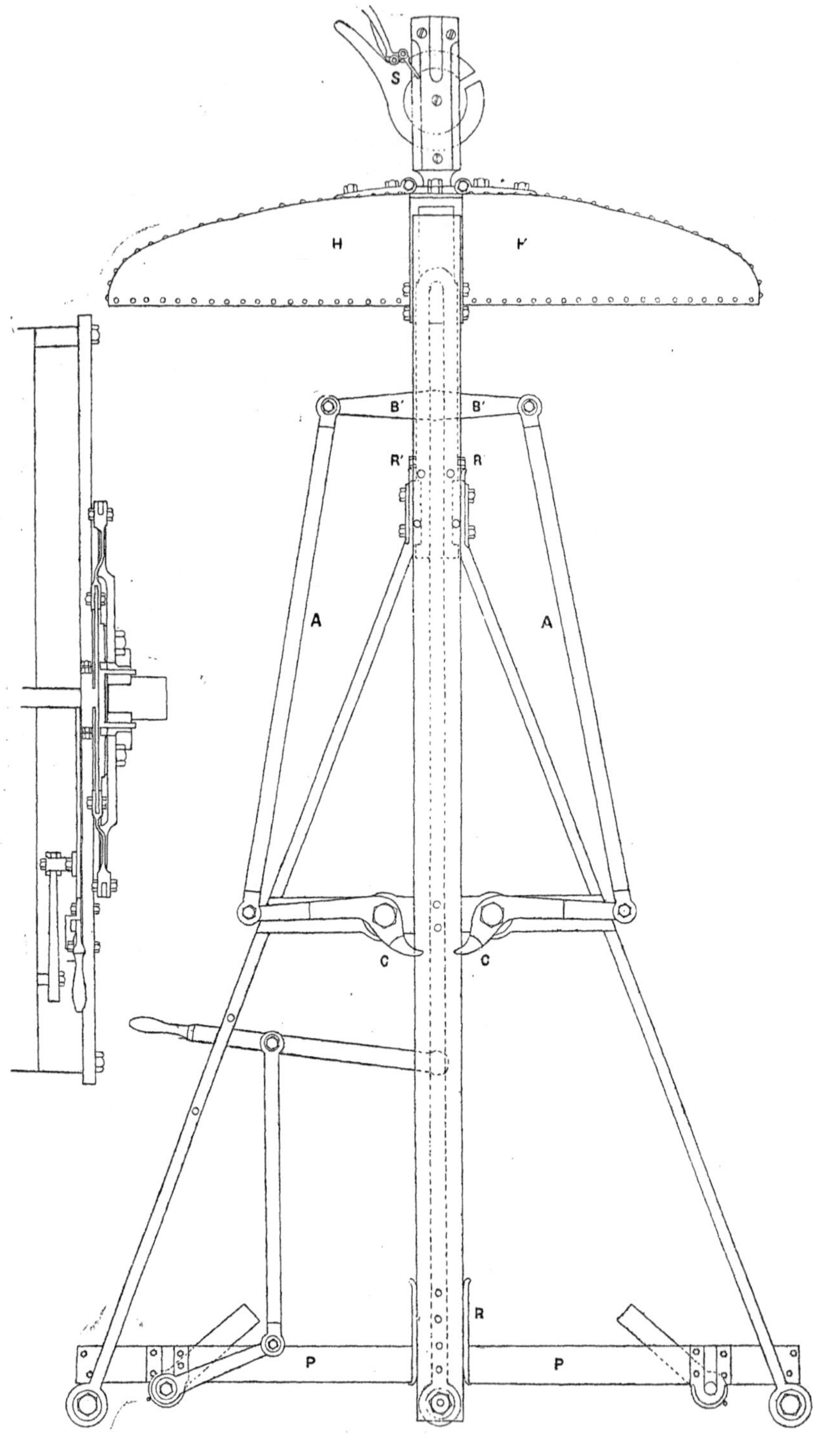

Side view and plan of one end of the Safety Cage in use in Nevada.

second iron cross-bar, free to move up and down in slots made in the frame on each side. This second cross-bar is connected at its two ends by arms on the outer side of the frame with the lever ends of dog-clamps or safety catches. The construction will be more readily understood by reference to the figure, giving a side view of the most approved

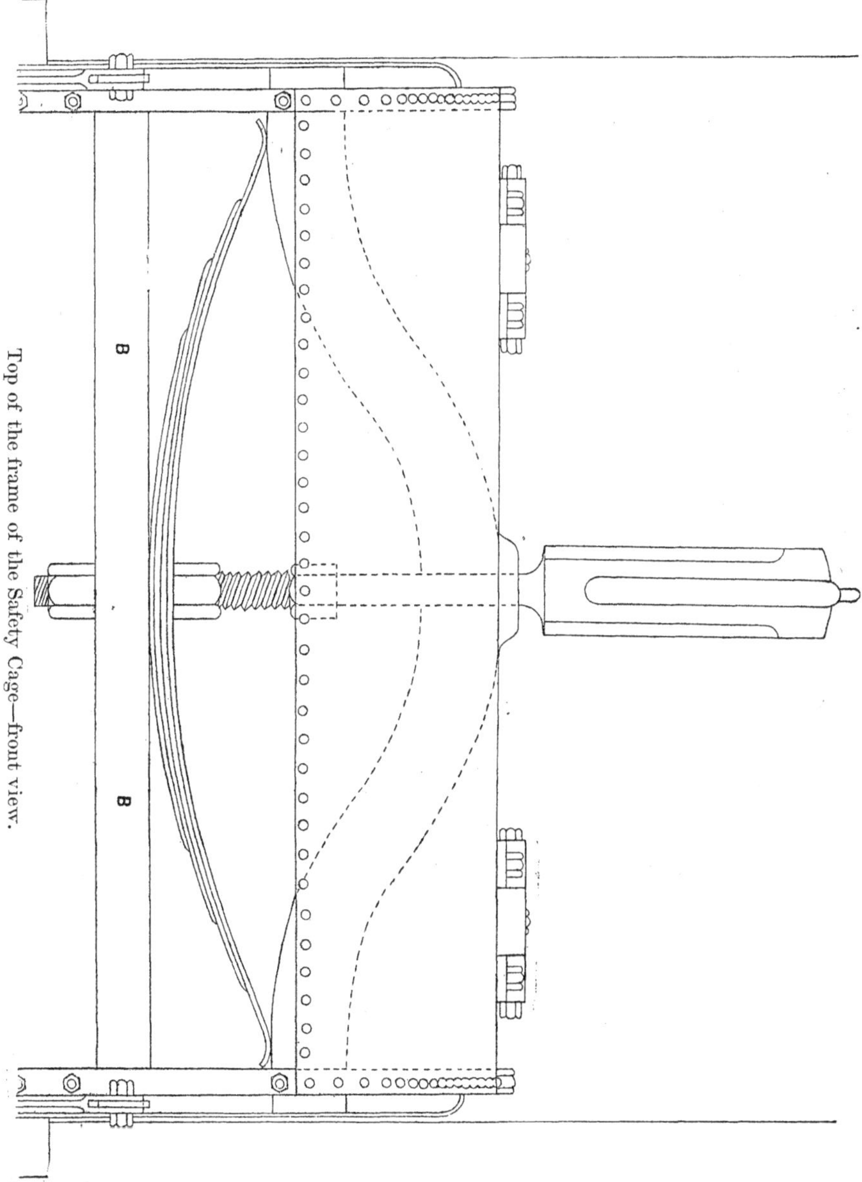

Top of the frame of the Safety Cage—front view.

form of the cage and catch, now in use in the mines of the Comstock lode. The platform P P is five feet long and three feet eight inches wide. It is surmounted by a hood, H H, of boiler-iron, firmly secured by hinges to the top of the frame, and designed to protect the miners from falling bodies. The height of the cage from the top of this hood to the bottom of the platform is eight feet. The ends of the rubbers are seen at R R and R′ R′; the clamps, or safety catches, at C C; and the arms A A, connecting these with a cross-piece above, B′ B′. A safety hook, S, for detaching the cage in case of overwinding, is placed at the top and turns in the head of the suspending rod. When the cage is at rest at the bottom of the shaft, or whenever it is not suspended by the winding cable, the cross-bar B B, and cross-piece B′ B′, are pressed downward by a long and powerful steel plate spring, and this throws the points of the catches C C into the *sides* of the guide-timber, and not into the face, as is the case with Fontaine's and other safety catches. The construction of the upper part of the cage, including the spring and the suspension rod, is not shown in the side view of the cage, but will be seen in the second figure, giving a front view.

During hoisting or lowering the spring is compressed, and this serves to relieve the cage and load from the shock which attends a sudden commencement of hoisting.

The hand-lever just above the platform controls iron rods which rise through the floor of the cage and hold the cars securely in place during the ascent and descent of the cage.

The whole construction is light and simple, and has given general satisfaction. It is not closed in at the top and sides as closely as in the foreign mining cages, and is high enough to allow miners to stand upright as they ascend and descend. The hood is hinged to prevent the imprisonment of miners in case of accident, or drowning, if, as sometimes happens, the cage is lowered into water.

EUROPEAN GUIDED CAGES.

In Europe cages are made in a much more substantial and cumbrous manner, and they are generally arranged to receive several cars, either one above another upon separate platforms or, when the shaft is wide enough, two or three abreast. At Mons, in shaft No. 12 of Grand Hornu, eight wagons have been put into one cage of four stories. When the wagons are large, as, for example, those of twelve hectolitres at Blanzy, the cages are only two stories high.

They are usually made of iron, on account of both lightness and strength; and the angle irons and T-irons are found to be well adapted to the purpose. The cage of four stories was the form in use a few years since at Anzin. It is made of angle iron, strongly riveted, and weighs as follows:

	Kilogrammes.
Plate and angle irons	655
Sheet iron	220
Cast iron	32
The safety catch, (parachute)	218
Total weight of the cage	1,125

This cage will carry 2,000 kilogrammes of coal in the four wagons, which themselves weigh 720 kilogrammes, thus making the dead weight as much as 1,845 kilogrammes.

The cage used at Charleroi holds four wagons, like those at Anzin;

but they are here placed end to end upon two floors only, and the cage weighs 900, the four wagons 780, and the charge 1,600 kilogrammes.

At the Paris Exposition of 1867 Nicholas Libotte, constructor, of Silly, near Charleroi, exhibited some cages intended for the collieries of Charleroi, Belgium. These cages are remarkable for their extreme lightness and strength, and for the perfection of the forging. They are made of *steel*, are intended for a narrow shaft, and are capable of taking six wagons, one above another. The cage weighed as follows:

	Kilogrammes.
Cage	1,434
Parachute	128
Total	1,562

Another cage, similarly constructed, was made in two stages only, but was also designed to receive six wagons, three on each stage:

	Kilogrammes.
Weight of cage	1,268
Weight of parachute	164
Total	1,432

This cage was made for a shaft near Liege, Belgium.

In order to diminish the shock which results from the sudden descent of a cage upon the platform at the bottom of a shaft, especially when the cage is used for the descent of miners, caoutchouc springs have been placed under a false platform or landing, so as to prevent violent concussions when the motion of the cage is not sufficiently arrested in season to avoid a shock. So also, in order to avoid the sudden shock at the commencement of hoisting, spiral springs have been placed between the end of the cable and the top of the cage, so that the spring would be compressed before the cage began to move. But such springs require to be very strong and heavy to be of any service where such great weights are to be lifted; and this has led to the plan of placing large steel plate springs under the axle bearings of the great pulleys at the top of the shaft. But it is also desirable to have an elastic form of attachment to the cages; and this is secured to a certain extent by the use of the safety-catch, which requires a spring.

CABLES, WIRE ROPE, WINDING DRUMS, &c.

The leading mines upon the Comstock lode extend from 1,000 to 1,300 feet below the surface. In nearly every one the companies have changed their hoisting works several times, increasing their power and improving their construction to suit the increased duty of winding from constantly augmenting depths. Hemp cables have given way in part to round wire ropes, and these in turn to flat wire cables, some of them made of steel wire. The dimensions of these flat cables are 3 by ½ inch to 6 by 1½ inches for iron, and 2½ by ½ inch to 4 by ½ inch for steel. The length is usually 1,500 feet.

The manufacture of wire cordage and flat winding cables for mines is carried on in San Francisco upon an extensive scale at the works of A. S. Hallidie, erected in 1857. Their capacity of production is now over 1,200 tons of rope and cable annually. Their manufactures embrace every description of wire cordage, from the delicate bell and signal cord to those of a single piece 3,000 feet long and weighing nearly 40,000 pounds. Most of the hoisting works upon the Comstock lode have been supplied with winding cables from this establishment.

This firm has recently made a cable for the Imperial mine 1,600 feet long, 6 inches wide, and ½ inch thick, weighing 8,400 pounds. This cable is wound upon a 6-foot drum, but as generally several layers of the cable remain on the drum, not being unwound, the diameter is increased to 6½ to 7 feet. The sheaves for flat cables are usually only 7 feet in diameter, but this is too small; they should not be less than 12 feet.

DIAMETER OF WINDING DRUMS.

It is a common defect in all the hoisting works of California and Nevada that the winding drums and pulleys are too small. In Europe the diameter of winding drums has been greatly increased, and there are many examples of drums 20 feet in diameter. At the Casimir Perier colliery at Somain the round wire rope is used upon a drum with a diameter of $7^{m}.14$, or 25 feet. Twenty-five turns of this drum winds up 600 metres of cable. The weight of cable is four kilograms per metre.

These large drums are particularly desirable for wire ropes, which are destroyed very fast by a short bend. On these large cirumferences the turns are fewer, and the cable need not be coiled several times over itself, which causes great wear and destruction of the strands. Each turn of a drum 22 feet in diameter represents 66 feet of length of cable, and 25 rounds will reach 1,650 feet deep. With a rope one and a half inch thick the drum would have to be a little over three feet in length. In such a case the radius of the drum in winding would remain the same when wire rope is used; but this is not the case with hemp rope, which has a much greater diameter, and when winding up around the drum it must coil upon itself several times, and thus increase considerably the radius of the drum, and, on the other hand, in unwinding or lowering into the shaft the radius of the drum is rapidly reduced.

The difference of radius is insufficient to compensate for the weight of the unwound cable, and such an arrangement requires powerful engines to lift up the dead weight of cable at the start. From that moment less and less power is required until the two buckets or cages meet in the shaft; then the descending cable gradually takes the advantage of the ascending one, and the steam-engine, instead of driving, is soon driven with an increased velocity by the increasing weight of the descending cable. To avoid these inconveniences a system of counterpoises is used. Ropes carrying a counterpoise are wound around sheaves placed on the shaft of the drum; these counterpoises play up and down the shaft for about fifty or sixty metres; the cable unrolls as it goes down, and the radius of the sheaves diminishes. It is so arranged that when the entire cable is paid out and the counterpoise is down the two buckets or cages pass each other in the shaft. At that time the strain upon the hoisting drum changes, as also the action of the counterpoise. The rotary motion of the hoisting drum continues in the same direction, as also that of the sheave, which now winds up the rope of the counterpoise in the opposite direction. The force required to raise up this counterpoise counterbalances the weight of the descending cable. Another way, which gives better results, consists in using a very heavy cast-iron chain as a counterpoise.

M. Quillacq, a Belgian engineer, after having visited the hoisting works of England, and examined the system of counterpoises used there, proposed to place the winding bobbin directly over the shaft, and thus to dispense with the sheaves. Drums seven metres in diameter are placed on the top of the shaft, instead of the sheaves, and are driven directly by a double-cylinder engine. This system, which is fully described in "*Le Matériel des Houillères*," by Professor A. Burat, has not been entirely successful so far; but it has shown, however, that an economy of fifty per cent. can be realized on the wear and tear of cables.

Although difficult to do away entirely with the sheaves, it is quite easy to increase their diameter so as to avoid giving a short bend to the cables. It has been suggested that a series of rollers or small sheaves, placed on a curve of large radius, might advantageously be used instead of very large sheaves.

STEEL-WIRE CABLES—WEIGHT AND STRENGTH OF CABLES.

The use of cables made of steel-wire has been highly recommended on account of their superior strength and lightness. In practice abroad the high hopes entertained of the value of these cables have not been realized. The wire undergoes rapid changes, and has been found after five or six months' use to become brittle, so that the cable could no longer be relied upon. Some of the flat cables now in use in Nevada are made of steel; but no data regarding their weight and wear have been received.

The following table exhibits the size in inches of flat cables, their weight in pounds per fathom, their working load and breaking strain.* I have added also a valuable table which has recently been published, giving the comparative strength of iron, steel, copper, and hemp cables, expressed in dimensions and weights of the metric system.†

* From Hunt's edition of Ure's Dictionary.

† From Etudes sur les Arts Textiles, &c., per Michel Alcan, p. 34.

Approximate dimensions, weight, and strength of round and flat cables of iron, steel, copper, and hemp.

ROUND CABLES.									FLAT CABLES.									STRANDS.								
	Iron.		Steel.		Copper.		Breaking strain of hemp cables of the same diameter.			Iron.		Steel		Copper.		Breaking strain and weight of hemp cables of the same dimensions.			Iron.		Steel.		Copper.		Breaking strain and weight of hemp strand of the same diameter.	
Diameter.	Weight per linear metre.	Breaking strain.	Weight per linear metre.	Breaking strain.	Weight per linear metre.	Breaking strain.	Breaking strain.	Weight.	Breadth and thickness.	Weight per linear metre.	Breaking strain.	Weight per linear metre.	Breaking strain.	Weight per linear metre.	Breaking strain.	Breaking strain.	Weight.	Diameter of the strand.	Weight per linear metre of each strand.	Breaking strain of each strand.	Weight per linear metre of each strand.	Breaking strain of each strand.	Weight per linear metre of each strand.	Breaking strain of each strand.	Breaking strain.	Weight.
m.	*k. g.*	*k.*	*k. g.*	*k.*	*k. g.*	*k.*	*k.*	*k. g.*	*m.*	*k. g.*	*k.*	*k. g.*	*k.*	*k. g.*	*k.*	*k.*	*k. g.*	*m.*	*k. g.*	*k.*	*k. g.*	*k.*	*k. g.*	*k.*	*k.*	*k. g.*
0. 005	0. 072	502	0. 073	832	0. 082	420	70	0. 017	......	......	......	......	......	......	......	......	......	0. 0015	0. 011	82	0. 011	137	0. 012	69	8	0. 004
0. 0054	0. 104	724	0. 105	1, 199	0. 118	606	101	0. 025	0. 056	......	......	......	......	......	......	......	......	0. 0018	0. 016	119	0. 016	198	0. 018	99	12	0. 006
0. 0063	0. 142	985	0. 142	1, 631	0. 160	723	137	0. 034	0. 012	2. 603	17, 811	2. 613	29, 687	2. 962	14, 855	2, 710	0. 678	0. 0021	0. 021	161	0. 021	269	0. 024	135	15	0. 008
0. 0072	0. 185	1, 286	0. 186	2, 131	0. 210	1, 075	179	0. 045	0. 058	......	......	......	......	......	......	......	......	0. 0024	0. 028	211	0. 028	352	0. 032	176	20	0. 010
0. 0081	0. 234	1, 628	0. 235	2, 697	0. 265	1, 361	227	0. 057	0. 0125	3. 004	20, 266	3. 016	33, 778	3. 418	16, 889	2, 915	0. 734	0. 0027	0. 035	267	0. 035	445	0. 040	223	25	0. 012
0. 0090	0. 289	2, 010	0. 290	3, 330	0. 328	1, 680	280	0. 070	0. 063	......	......	......	......	......	......	......	......	0. 0030	0. 043	330	0. 043	550	0. 049	275	31	0. 015
0. 0099	0. 350	2, 432	0. 351	4, 029	0. 396	2, 033	339	0. 085	0. 013	3. 807	25, 650	3. 823	42, 751	4. 333	21 375	3, 548	0. 887	0. 0033	0. 052	399	0. 053	665	0. 060	333	38	0. 019
0. 0108	0. 417	2, 894	0. 418	4, 794	0. 472	2, 420	403	0. 101	0. 072	......	......	......	......	......	......	......	......	0. 0036	0. 062	475	0. 063	792	0. 071	396	45	0. 022
0. 0117	0. 489	3, 397	0. 491	5, 627	0. 566	2. 840	473	0. 118	0. 014	4. 711	31, 666	4. 729	52. 779	5. 362	26, 389	4, 466	1. 116	0. 0039	0. 073	557	0. 073	929	0. 083	464	52	0. 026
0. 0126	0. 567	3, 940	0. 569	6, 526	0. 642	3, 294	549	0. 137	0. 080	......	......	......	......	......	......	......	......	0. 0042	0. 085	646	0. 085	1, 077	0. 097	539	61	0. 030
0. 0135	0. 651	4, 423	0. 653	7, 492	0. 737	3, 784	630	0. 157	0. 016	5. 717	38, 316	5. 739	63, 862	6. 508	31, 931	5, 667	1. 417	0. 0045	0. 097	742	0. 098	1, 237	0. 111	619	70	0. 035
0. 0144	0. 741	5, 146	0. 743	8, 524	0. 839	4, 302	717	0. 179	0. 085	......	......	......	......	......	......	......	......	0. 0048	0. 111	844	0. 111	1, 407	0. 126	704	80	0. 040
0. 0162	0. 938	6, 513	0. 941	10, 788	1. 062	5, 445	907	0. 227	0 ·017	6. 877	45, 630	6. 903	76, 001	7. 831	38, 001	6. 373	1. 593	0. 0054	0. 140	1, 069	0. 141	1, 781	0. 160	891	101	0. 050
0. 0180	1. 158	8, 041	1. 162	13, 319	1. 311	6, 722	1. 121	0. 280	0. 098	......	......	......	......	......	......	......	......	0. 0060	0. 173	1, 319	0. 174	2, 199	0. 198	1, 099	124	0. 062
0. 0198	1. 401	9, 729	1. 406	16, 116	1. 586	8, 133	1, 355	0. 339	0. 019	8. 735	57, 713	8. 768	96, 187	9. 942	48, 094	8, 193	2. 048	0. 0066	0. 210	1, 596	0. 211	2, 661	0. 239	1, 330	159	0. 075
0. 0216	1. 667	11, 579	1. 673	19, 179	1. 888	9, 679	1, 612	0. 403	0. 108	......	......	......	......	......	......	......	......	0. 0072	0. 250	1, 900	0. 251	3, 167	0. 285	1, 583	179	0. 089
0. 0243	2. 110	14, 655	2. 117	24, 274	2. 389	12, 250	2, 041	0. 510	0. 0215	10. 888	71, 250	10. 930	118, 752	12. 393	59, 376	10, 165	2. 566	0. 0081	0. 316	2, 405	0. 317	4, 008	0. 360	2, 004	227	0. 113
0. 0270	2. 605	18, 092	2. 614	29, 968	2. 950	15, 124	2, 519	0. 630	0. 121	......	......	......	......	......	......	......	......	0. 0090	0. 390	2, 969	0. 392	4, 948	0. 445	2, 474	280	0. 140
0. 0306	3. 345	23, 239	3. 358	38, 492	3. 789	19, 426	3, 226	0. 809	0. 0235	14. 098	91, 518	14. 152	152, 530	16. 047	76, 265	12, 511	3. 128	0. 0102	0. 501	3, 813	0. 503	6, 356	0. 571	3, 178	359	0. 180
0. 0351	4. 402	30, 576	4. 418	50, 646	4. 985	25, 559	4, 257	1. 064	......	......	......	......	......	......	......	......	......	0. 0117	0. 659	5, 017	0. 662	8, 362	0. 752	4, 181	433	0. 236
0. 0396	5. 603	38, 919	5. 623	64, 464	6. 346	32, 533	5, 419	1. 355	......	......	......	......	......	......	......	......	......	0. 0132	0. 839	6, 386	0. 842	10, 644	0. 957	5, 222	602	0. 301
0. 0441	6. 948	48, 267	6. 974	79, 948	7. 870	40, 347	6, 721	1. 680	......	......	......	......	......	......	......	......	......	0. 0147	1. 041	7, 920	1. 045	13, 200	1. 187	6, 600	747	0. 373
0. 0486	8. 439	58, 620	8. 470	97, 096	9. 558	49, 001	8, 162	2, 040	......	......	......	......	......	......	......	......	......	0. 0162	1. 264	9, 619	1. 269	16, 031	1. 441	8, 016	907	0. 453
0. 0531	10. 074	69, 979	10. 111	115, 909	11. 410	58, 496	9, 744	2. 436	......	......	......	......	......	......	......	......	......	0. 0177	1. 509	11, 483	1. 515	19, 138	1. 720	9, 569	1, 083	0. 541

The dimensions in this table are stated in fractions of a metre; the weights in kilogrammes and grammes, and the breaking strain in kilogrammes.

Table showing the size, weight, and strength of flat cables for mining purposes of hemp, iron, and steel.

HEMP.		IRON.		STEEL.		EQUIVALENT STRENGTH.	
Size in inches.	Pounds weight per fathom.	Size in inches.	Pounds weight per fathom.	Size in inches.	Pounds weight per fathom.	Working load.	Breaking strain.
						Cwt.	*Tons.*
4 by 1⅛	20	2¼ by ½	11	....	....	44	20
5 by 1¼	24	2½ by —	13	....	....	52	23
5½ by 1⅜	26	2¾ by ⅝	15	....	....	60	27
5¾ by 1½	28	3 by —	16	2 by ½	10	64	28
6 by 1½	30	3¼ by —	18	2¼ by ½	11	72	32
7 by 1⅞	36	3½ by —	20	— by —	12	80	36
8¼ by 2⅛	40	3¾ by 11-16	22	2½ by ½	13	88	40
8½ by 2¼	45	4 by —	25	2¾ by ⅜	15	110	45
9 by 2⅓	50	4¼ by ⅔	28	3 by —	16	112	50
9½ by 2⅗	55	4½ by —	32	3¼ by —	18	128	56
10 by 2½	60	4⅝ by —	34	3½ by —	20	136	60

PRECAUTIONS IN USING WIRE-ROPE.

In winding with round wire rope upon conical drums, it is important to make sure that the angle of inclination of the surface of the drum is not too great, as otherwise the coils of the rope are apt to slip off and cause serious accidents. Several fatal accidents have occurred in England from this cause. They are mentioned beyond in connection with the notice of the various forms of safety cages. Mr. Wales, a government mining inspector, (Great Britain,) in his examination upon the cause of one of the accidents referred to, said:

"In his opinion, what most affected the proper and safe working of the spiral drum was the angle which the rope formed between the pulley over the shaft and certain portions of the drum. In the present case the angle was fifteen degrees, and in his opinion the accident was principally due to that fact, and not to any defect in the rope, which was broken by the jerk caused by the rope falling from the drum. In conclusion he remarked that in erecting spiral drums care should be taken to have the rope at as easy an angle as possible, and in no case ought it to exceed from ten to eleven degrees."

Professor Warrington Smyth, of the British Royal School of Mines, in one of his lectures directs attention to the precautions necessary in the use of conical drums. He mentions the case of a very serious accident a few years ago, by which the lives of a number of men were sacrificed, simply, he believes, in consequence of the cage having been wound up at too great a velocity, and then allowed to slacken too suddenly, the result being that the laps got loose, some part slipped off, the rope went over the edge of the drum, and was snapped. Mr. Smyth then points out how this danger may be obviated by an ingenious contrivance of M. Lemielle, which consists of an endless rope passed down the shaft, and over a pulley at each extremity. The rope is thus kept constantly stretched out, and motion is communicated to it by a direct-acting cylinder, which sets one of the pulleys in motion.

It is found to be very dangerous to allow wire ropes to wind over any inequality or projection by which the wires are subjected to repeated bending back and forth. At the Cannock Chase Colliery, England, in 1867, the flat-wire cable suddenly snapped and precipitated eight men and boys to the bottom of the shaft, killing five. The inspector found that at the point of fracture the cable had been covered for about eighteen inches with hemp, which had become hard and solid, and formed a bolster or projection on both sides of the cable, three-fourths of an inch thick. The object of placing this hemp upon the cable was to show the engine man when the cage was opposite a certain drift, where it had to stop. In passing to and fro over a pulley five feet in diameter, and under a drum of the same diameter, the constant bending broke off the wires. This effect was probably gradual, since it appeared on examination that only twenty-five or twenty-six wires, one-seventh of the number in the cable, were whole when the cable finally parted. The covering also prevented the condition of the cable from being known, and it was believed that the breaking of the wires had been going on for three weeks or a month before the accident.

EXAMPLES OF HOISTING WORKS ABROAD.

As the depth of our mines increases the importance of improving our hoisting works becomes more and more apparent, and it will, therefore, be appropriate to notice in detail some of the best specimens of hoisting engines now in use abroad, particularly at the collieries of Belgium, France, and Great Britain, where we find the most perfect types and exhibitions of mining upon the most extended scale. At present our best hoisting works are only approximations in construction and in magnitude to those abroad. The extent of our mines has not required us to carry our machinery to such a degree of perfection; but the day is not distant when for the Comstock lode alone we shall not only have to avail ourselves of the fruits of experience in deep mining in foreign countries, but even to improve upon their most admirable and beautiful machines.

There is nothing to prevent, indeed there is much to encourage, us to push our explorations of the Comstock lode to a depth of 3,000 feet or more; and for this purpose very powerful engines and hoisting apparatus will be required. The wise provision which should characterize all large undertakings, especially in mining, requires us to take this subject into careful consideration. The engineers of Belgium and France have for some years past been discussing the best methods of carrying the exploitation of their coal beds to a depth of at least 1,000 metres; and some of the opinions expressed upon this subject will be mentioned at the close of this division of the report, after some details concerning the existing conditions of hoisting have been given.

There are two principal types of hoisting apparatus: the single engine, acting upon the drum or bobbin-shaft, through the medium of gearing, and the double engine, acting directly upon the bobbin-shaft by cranks set at right angles with each other. Of these two types, the double direct-acting engines are preferred for large collieries, where rapid hoisting is essential.

Professor Burat, in remarking upon the use of engines acting directly upon the shaft of the winding drum, states substantially that whenever the conditions of hoisting do not require a greater force than 80 horse-power, gearing should be used; and that the direct-acting engines with two cylinders should actually exert at least 100 horse-power. If the cages are not required to move with a velocity of at least four to five metres a second the gearing is evidently preferable to placing the winding drums upon the crank-shaft. This opinion is confirmed by comparisons between the consumption of coal in hoisting works upon the two plans, which are in favor of the machines with gearing. For hoisting with great rapidity, the direct-acting machines are the best, and are now generally used.

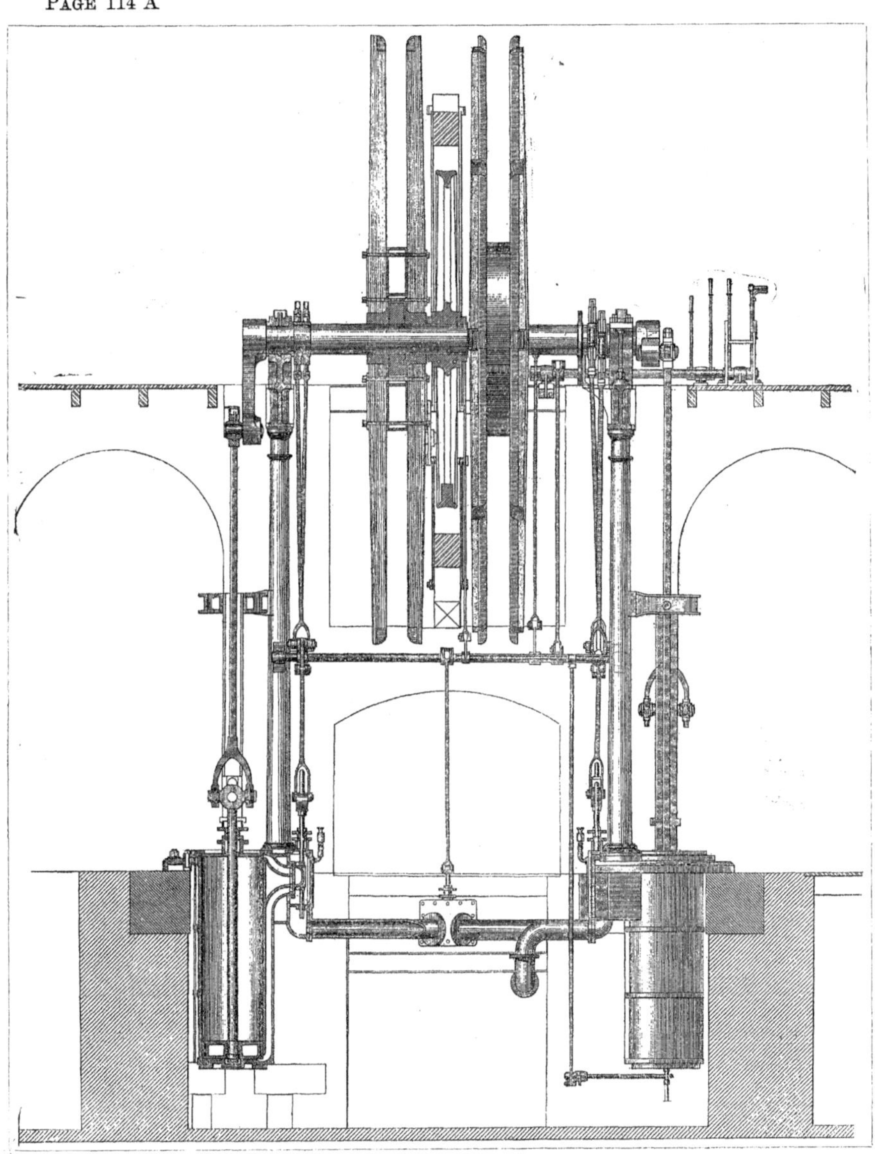

VERTICAL HOISTING ENGINE—QUILLACQ'S CONSTRUCTION.

Many establishments, and especially those of Haine-Saint Pierre, of Couillet, and of Seriang, in Belgium, and of Quillacq, at Anzin, have produced hoisting apparatus of this type which appear to leave little to be desired. Such machines are made either vertical or horizontal. In the former the winding reels are raised high in the air, and the only advantage appears to be that the inclination of the cable is lessened, so that the angle it makes with the surface of the sheave is increased. A disadvantage is the instability of the machine, owing to the little breadth of foundation, and to its great height. The horizontal engines are much more firm and substantial.

The accompanying illustration, printed upon a separate sheet and inserted, (page 114 A,) represents an engine of Quillacq's construction of the vertical type. This figure is reduced by Bien's photo-relief process from one of the beautifully engraved plates in Burat's Atlas. It does not require much explanation. One cylinder is shown in section with the piston at the lower end. The brake-wheel is between the two bobbins. The engineer stands upon an elevated platform on a level with the bobbin-shaft, and controls the valves by means of levers. Three inches and three-eighths of an inch upon this reduced drawing represents a distance of about five metres.

In all of these modern engines a very great improvement has been made by the addition of a powerful brake, worked by steam. Instead of the attendant exerting a large part of his strength upon the lever of a brake, it is now only necessary for him to open a valve by a hand lever, and thus admit steam to one side of a piston in a short cylinder, and the brake is instantly applied with greater force than a man could possibly exert. For such powerful engines as are now in use, and worked as they are at a high rate of speed, a brake of this kind is indispensable.

Mr. Quillacq, constructing mechanical engineer at Anzin, appears to have been a pioneer in the construction of large direct-acting double-hoisting engines. He published a description of one of these engines in 1859.*

The cylinders were each $0^{m}.600$ in diameter, and the pistons had a stroke of $1^{m}.800$; bobbin-shaft $3^{m}.400$ long and $0^{m}.290$ in diameter; two bobbins $6^{m}.500$ in diameter; Stephenson slide motion; a steam brake, with the cylinder $0^{m}.350$ in diameter, drawing the two brakes of wood powerfully upon the periphery of a wheel $3^{m}.300$ in diameter. This machine was provided with signal indicators, and apparatus for arresting the motion of the engines and cages after the cages passed a certain point above the mouth of the shaft. The whole machine, with feed-pumps and fixtures, weighed 42,000 kilogrammes and cost less than 40,000 francs.

The same constructor exhibited a very beautiful hoisting apparatus at the Paris Exposition in 1867. It was a double engine of about 200 horse-power. The cylinders were vertical and connected directly with the bobbin-shaft, supported high in the air above the engines. Cylinders about 3 feet in diameter and 6 feet stroke. Link motion upon both. Bobbins for flat wire or hemp cable, and 22 feet in diameter. Steam brake, signal indicators, and apparatus for preventing overwinding were all included in this beautiful machine, for 38,000 francs. It appears from a bulletin that from 1856 to March, 1867, inclusive, the firm had supplied 67 machines of 7,012 horse-power in the aggregate, varying from 6 to 500 horse-power, the latter for pumping.

In a machine exhibited by A. Audry, engineer of the establishment of Mr. F. Dorzee, near Mons, the bobbin-shaft is placed below on a

* Annales des Mines.

level with the floor, and the cylinders rise vertically above it and act downward, instead of upward, as in the engine by Quillacq. The cylinders of this machine are $0^{m}.90$ in diameter and the stroke $1^{m}.40$. Five machines have been made upon this model at different times from 1853 to 1867, varying in capacity from 80 to 150 horse-power.

A very beautiful machine of the direct-acting horizontal type was exhibited at Paris in 1867, by the establishment of M. M. Schneider & Co., of Creuzot. Its strength, proportions, and convenient arrangement of the various parts were admirable. The cylinders, 2^{m} long and $0^{m}.550$ in diameter, are placed $5^{m}.60$ apart, from centre to centre. The rods are connected directly with cranks of 1^{m}, placed at right angles upon the opposite ends of a main shaft, $0^{m}.3$ in diameter, which carries the two bobbins and the friction-wheel, to which the brakes are applied by means of steam, acting upon a piston in a small cylinder below the floor of the engine-room. The diameter of this wheel is 3^{m}, and the length of each of the two wooden blocks which bear upon its periphery is $1^{m}.2$. The diameter of the drum of the bobbins is $2^{m}.04$, and total diameter along the arms is about $5^{m}.5$. The arms of the bobbins are of wood, and the extremities are not connected by segments, as in many of the Belgian and French machines. The length of the lever controlling the brakes is $1^{m}.9$, the diameter of the cylinder $0^{m}.34$, the length $0^{m}.47$.

The engineer stands midway between the forward ends of the cylinders, with both the bobbins in full view, and by means of conveniently placed levers and hand-wheels controls the movements of the engine and the operation of the steam-brake.

The details of construction of a portion of this engine are shown by the accompanying figure, reduced by the photo-relief process from the larger working drawings published in the *Portefeuille des Ingénieurs*, by the Messrs. Armengaud. The figure gives a longitudinal elevation of the bobbin, the brake-wheel, and brakes, together with the steam cylinder for operating the brake, and the levers by which the engineer controls the movements of the engine. The cylinders of the horizontal engines and their valves are not shown. B is the bobbin-shaft, carrying the bobbin with wooden spokes D D D and a cast-iron brake-wheel P P. The spokes, eight in number, are not united by segmental rims at their extremities, as in some machines, but are disconnected, the cable winding truly between the two opposite sets of spokes without catching upon their ends. These spokes are firmly bolted by their inner ends to a cast-iron socket plate, $2^{m}.040$ in diameter. This plate and the brake-wheel P P are securely keyed to the shaft B. An arm, K, $1^{m}.90$ in length, works loosely upon the shaft B, and by means of the connecting rods J J controls the brake pieces I I, faced with blocks of wood $1^{m}.20$ long, which fit into the hollow face of the brake-wheel P P. The brake-pieces, as will be seen, are supported in an upright position 3 .230 apart by the prolongation of their frames to the foundation below, to which they are united by hinge joints. The undue separation of these brake-pieces is prevented by set screws placed behind each, and their approximation and pressure upon the brake-wheel is controlled by means of the rod K, extending from the end of the arm K to the steam cylinder M. By means of the hand-lever O N steam can be instantly admitted to one side or the other of the piston in M, and thus operate the brakes with great force.

The engineer stands upon a platform just above the steam cylinder M, and controls the link-motion by means of the horizontal hand-wheel R. The dimensions and distances of the most important parts are indicated upon the figure in metres and in fractions of a metre.

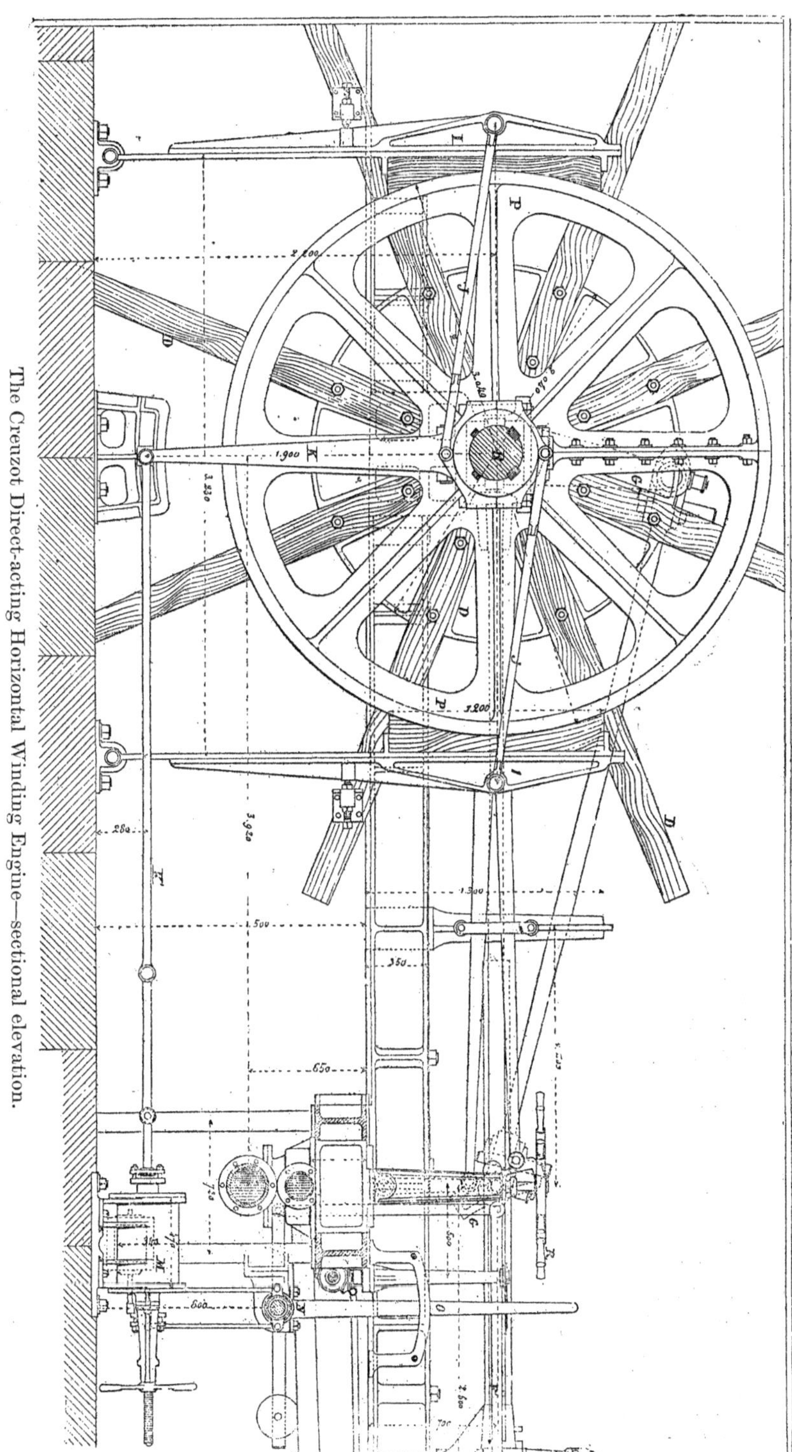

The Creuzot Direct-acting Horizontal Winding Engine—sectional elevation.

At the mines of Sainte-Barbe, at Bezenet, the extraction from a depth of 161^m to 185^m is effected by a double horizontal engine, the two cylinders being connected directly with the bobbin-shaft. The pistons are $0^m.7$ in diameter, and $1^m.9$ stroke. The drum or center of the bobbins is $3^m.5$ in diameter, and the minimum radius of winding space is therefore $1^m.75$ for one of the bobbins, and greater for the other, which winds from the greatest depth. The brake is controlled by a separate steam-cylinder. A contrivance for preventing accidents in case of over-winding closes the throttle-valve of the engine and puts on the steam-brake. This apparatus once prevented a very serious accident, by arresting the cage before it reached the sheaves.

The cages weigh 1,900 kilogrammes, ($1{,}600^k$ iron, and 300^k of wood,) and are made to receive six cars. Four sheet-iron cars weigh, when empty, 960 kilogrammes, and contain 20 hectolitres of coal, weighing 1,600 kilogrammes. The dead weight is therefore $1{,}900 + 960 = 2{,}860$ kilogrammes. In ordinary working the time of ascension of the cage and load is 27 seconds. The landing and returning the cars require a mean of 18 seconds; total time, 45 seconds. Practically, they take out four cars a minute, or 240 cars per hour, and 2,400 in ten hours of effective work. Experience has shown that they can extract regularly 2,000 cars, containing 10,000 hectolitres, in ten hours. The two cables are adjusted to hoist from two levels, 24^m apart. The drainage is effected with a single trip, and occupies only a part of the night. The quantity of water extracted varies between 6,000 and 10,000 hectolitres. The cables are 23 centimetres wide and 42 millimetres thick, made of iron wire covered with hemp.*

As an example of the dimensions and cost of modern hoisting engines in Saxony, the following from the notes of W. Fairley, mining engineer and surveyor, is interesting: The mine is at Zwickau, the Brückenberg colliery, 444 English fathoms in depth. The shaft is rectangular in section, 28 feet long by 8 feet broad; one-half of it is used for winding with two cages, the other half for a ladder-shaft and return air. The ventilation is effected by a Guibal's ventilator, measuring 7^m by 3^m, and driven by a 50-horse engine. The hoisting works consist of a pair of horizontal engines, built at the Wilhelm's Hütte, Sprottan, Schleswig, at a cost of £2,850. The cylinders are 42 inches diameter, stroke 8 feet, winding-drum for flat ropes 12 feet diameter, ropes tapered. The time required for hoisting from the 444 fathom level is two and a half minutes, a speed of about 20 feet, on an average, per second. The cage carries two wagons of 10 hundred-weight side by side, and is furnished with a safety apparatus for its arrest in case of the breakage of the rope.

GENERAL OBSERVATIONS UPON HOISTING ENGINES.

In all these engines for collieries, where coal is so abundant and cheap, very little attention has been given to the question of economy of fuel, a very important one for regions like that of the Comstock, dependent upon wood brought from a distance at considerable expense. Condensing engines are too complex for hoisting purposes, where it is so often necessary to reverse the motion; and the only direction in which it appears possible to effect a great saving of steam is in working it expansively as much as possible by the use of suitable cut-off valves. The Exposition of 1867 contained a double engine on Woolf's plan, and consequently with four cylinders, which could be used advantageously as a

* From data supplied by MM. Lan and Baure to Professor Burat, 1867.

hoisting-engine, if the necessary apparatus for changing the direction of rotation were supplied.

It is an interesting fact that English colliery owners find it for their advantage to contract for their hoisting-engines and machinery with the French constructor Quillacq, at Anzin. This eminent maker astonished the British members of the international jury by the statement that he had supplied both pumping and winding engines to an important Newcastle colliery. It is admitted by the British reporter upon that class in the exposition, that the order was given to the French manufacturer simply in consequence of his lower price and better finish, as compared with the tenders from English houses; and he observes: "Here we have, then, one of our Newcastle mines actually working by means of French-made machinery, fairly brought in, by open competition, to the midst of our machine shops and foundries; and when we look at the inland position of Anzin, and the unquestionable disadvantages which have to be combatted in a district where coal and iron are comparatively dear, I cannot but think these results redound to the credit of French engineering, and inculcate on ourselves an important lesson."

Opinions upon the relative value of the two methods of mounting hoisting works, whether they should be vertical or horizontal, are still divided. The English generally prefer the vertical form. There is not only the advantage in regard to the inclination of the cables upon the pulleys, a very considerable advantage when one of the cables is wound on the lower surface of the bobbin, but the engineer can be placed much nearer to the landing-place of the cages, and thus, having their movements directly under his eye, will avoid many accidents that would otherwise happen, notwithstanding any system of signals. It has been supposed that the vertical machines are much more costly than the horizontal; but M. Parent, director of the Anzin works, who has used both, holds an opposite opinion. There is so much doubt in regard to this matter that the Anzin company, having two shafts to provide with hoisting works, decided, in 1868, to place a vertical engine over one shaft, (Haveluy,) and a horizontal one over the other, (St. Mark.) The question of the relative advantages is still undecided; but it is agreed that in all cases it is best to place the engineer as near to the landing of the cages as possible; and to secure this, the position of the horizontal engine has been changed. The engine has been turned end for end, so as to place the cylinders toward the shaft, and bring the engineer within five or six metres of it.

In order further to illustrate the general form of large hoisting works abroad, one of the engraved plates in Burat's Atlas has been reduced, and is printed upon a separate sheet to accompany this chapter. It represents the construction at the colliery of Bezenet, and shows not only the large derrick supporting the great pulleys over the shaft, but the two-story iron cages, the cars, and the arrangement for automatic lowering of the loaded cars to a track upon the general level while the empty cars are hoisted. The engine-house and engine, with the large bobbin for flat cable is seen at the right-hand end of the plate. A rod with an ram projecting over the cage is so arranged as to stop the engine in case of over-winding. The boilers are set outside of the building upon the extreme right.

HOISTING FROM GREAT DEPTHS.

The Academy of Sciences of Brussels in 1856 proposed the subjoined question for discussion, and the minister of public works offered a special prize for a satisfactory answer: [Translation.] "Indicate a complete practicable method for extending the exploitation of collieries to a depth of at least 1,000 metres, without sensibly increasing the cost of working beyond that in Belgium at the present time."

Among the most remarkable of the memoirs presented was that of M. Devillez, professor of mechanics at the school of mines of Hainault. He concludes that, without any new invention, but with a judicious use of the best means of exploitation then employed, it was quite possible to succeed in working at such great depths. He proposes to use, instead of hemp, flat cables of iron wire, weighing, on an average, $7^{k}.33$ per running metre, or a total for each of 733 kilogrammes. Cables of the same length of hemp would weigh more than 9,000 kilogrammes. With such wire cables, he could raise, at a mean velocity of six metres per second eight wagons containing together 2,700 kilogrammes of coal. The dead-weight of the cage and wagons would reach 2,150 kilogrammes. The whole could be brought to the surface in three or four minutes, and he thinks that a 200 horse-power engine would be sufficient for the service. The initial radius of the bobbins, according to calculation, should be $0^{m}.72$ for tapering cables of iron wire and $1^{m}.00$ for those made of hemp.

Another method proposed for hoisting from great depths, and already put to a test in practice, deserves mention. It is the contrivance of the engineer, M. Mehu, and was experimented with in one of the shafts at Anzin. It consists of two vertical oscillating rods moving up and down in the shaft, as in the man engine, and attached to the extremities of a hydraulic balance. One rod raised the full wagons, and the other carried down the empty wagons. But after being tried successively at the mines of Anzin and of Bonchamp it has been abandoned.

TURNING OR STARTING GEAR.

An apparatus has recently been constructed and applied in England for rendering uniform the driving power of single cylinder steam-engines used for winding or other purposes. It is well known that the driving power of single engines is far from being uniform throughout the revolutions of the crank. At the end of the stroke dead-centers exist, and there is no tangential pressure at all; and from these points the pressure upon the crank pin in the direction of its motion gradually reaches a maximum at about the middle part of the stroke, and as gradually diminishes to nothing. The object of the apparatus, which the inventors* call "turning-gear," is to enable single engines to be started, reversed, or to work with the facility and regularity of double engines, with their cranks at right angles to each other. The advantages claimed for the apparatus over double engines are its great cheapness and the possibility of its application to existing engines as well as to new ones. It consists of a small supplemental oscillating steam cylinder, placed below and a little back of the main crank, and connected with it by the middle of a jointed connecting rod, one end of which turns upon a fixed bearing in the foundation. A toggle-joint is thus formed, and the piston connects at the joint. This toggle is so placed as to operate tangentially upon the crank when near its dead-points. The inventor claims that by such means the engine possesses equal driving power during every part of the crank's revolution, so that upon the dead-centers all the work is done by the turning gear, but during the rest of the revolution it is done by the crank alone, or in combination with the turning gear. With this transfer of pressure from one part of the revolution to

* William Macgeorge, London, and Arthur Rigg, Chester.

another no steam is consumed; there is no loss of power, except the mere friction of the apparatus; neither is there any direct gain.

He says:

For winding purposes at collieries or mines, single engines are objectionable, although frequently used, and double engines are preferable on account of their handiness and safety from overwinding and the uniformity of their power at every part of their revolution. Now, as this turning gear gives to single engines all the advantages belonging to double engines, there is manifestly a saving in first cost, and to this must be added less expensive foundations and a smaller engine-house. It is equally applicable wherever the use of a fly-wheel is inconvenient, and has been applied to a compound marine screw engine of 100-horse power. With its use there is not the slightest hesitation or uncertainty in starting or reversing, and the engine can either revolve at full speed or be made to crawl slowly round, with the regularity of clock-work. It would be almost superfluous to point out the peculiar advantages of this latter capability in doing pit work at collieries.

The inventor claims to accomplish the same result for engines which revolve in one direction only, by placing a large double cam upon the end of the crank shaft, in such a position with respect to the position of the crank that it is acted upon by a roller forming the head of a short piston, working in a cylinder directly under the shaft. This is a very simple and cheap form and can be applied to any engine. Drawings of this apparatus accompany the Colliery Guardian for January 28, 1870.

CHAPTER X.

SAFETY-CATCHES, OR PARACHUTES.

The great depths to which mining operations are now carried; the increased rapidity of movement of the cages, (often as great as thirty and forty feet in a second,) and the paramount obligation to protect the lives of the miners who often ascend and descend by the cages, has led to the adoption of a variety of contrivances for arresting the fall of cages in the event of the breakage of the cables by which they are suspended. Such contrivances are known as *parachutes* or safety catches.

The great velocity of hoisting requires the cages to be guided in the shafts by vertical tracks, which are commonly constructed of wood, though of late they are being replaced by iron and steel; these tracks, called *guides*, being continuous and equidistant along the path of the cage, furnish a foundation upon which the various parachutes can act to sustain the cage in the event of breakage.

A large number of patents relating to this important and indispensable apparatus have been taken out, but it may be said that there are only three types, and that these originate from the same principle—levers drawn up and away from the guide by the traction of the cable, and in an opposite direction by the tension of a spring which tends to throw the levers outward upon the guides, so as to press upon or into them with a force capable of stopping the fall of the cage in case of the rupture of the cable.

One of the forms of safety catch now in use in the Savage silver mine upon the Comstock lode has already been described and shown by a figure in connection with the description of the ordinary form of cage. This description and figures will be found upon pages 576, and 571.

In 1845 M. Machecourt published a description of a parachute which he had applied to the cages in the shaft of a coal mine at Decize. This parachute consisted of two pointed bars or arms of iron crossed and turning upon a rod like the two blades of a pair of shears. While the cage remained suspended by the cable the points of these arms were drawn inward, away from the sides of the shaft, but in the event of the rupture of the cable, the arms were thrown outward and downward by springs, and penetrating the timbers of the shaft, held the cage suspended.

In 1849 M. Fontaine, of Anzin, constructed a parachute for the Tinchon shaft upon this principle, but in a better form, and at the time of the publication of Professor Burat's Matériel des Houillères, in 1861, the form most in favor and indeed the only form with which sufficient experience had been acquired to justify a recommendation of its general use, was the Fontaine parachute, then in use in more than fifty shafts in France and Belgium. It is considered as having originated with the Anzin company, and owes its introduction and success to the careful attention with which all its details were studied and modified by long experience.

All parachutes combined and constructed on this principle have given satisfactory results, and it may be said that, if the security obtained is not complete and absolute, they have, nevertheless, rendered such great services that their application has become a question of humanity, which cannot be ignored. The following figures will speak in a stronger and more peremptory manner than any description to persuade miners and engineers to adopt parachutes in their mines. At the mines of Anzin, from 1851 to 1859, in fourteen shafts supplied with parachutes, twenty-nine cable ruptures occurred, and the parachutes saved the lives of one hundred and fifty men. What can be more eloquent and more persuasive than this fact?

At the mines of Blanzy the experience has been similar, and it is probable that if an account had been taken of all the accidents by the rupture of cables in Europe since parachutes came into use, it would show that the men who have been saved from certain death by parachutes can be numbered by thousands.

In order that a parachute should act well, it is necessary that the strength of the spring should be equal to 150 kilogrammes, (300 pounds,) and then the weight of the cage makes the rest; and the heavier that weight the more energetic is the grasp on the guides.

The three types are—

1. *The parachute with claws*, which acts by a pressure exerted upon the guides tending to penetrate them longitudinally.

2. *The parachute with eccentrics*, which acts by a pressure exerted laterally on the sides of the guides, and perpendicularly to the plane which passes through both of their axes.

3. *The wedge parachute*, which acts by means of a set of metallic jaws taking hold of the guide, which is made wedge-shaped. This parachute gives a lateral pressure exercised upon the faces of each guide, and perpendicularly to the plane of the parachute.

These several types will be considered one after the other.

FONTAINE'S CLAW PARACHUTE.

The annexed figure represents Fontaine's parachute with claws. It is the oldest, and was constructed and put in use at the mines of Anzin, and may be said to have originated with this company, At first this parachute was supplied with only one spring, but two are now used, as shown by the drawing. It was the type exhibited upon the two-story cage sent by the company of Anzin to the Paris Exposition, in 1867.

The two stout diagonally placed arms in the drawing are armed with sharp steel points, and are so placed in the frame of the head of the cage that when it is suspended in the shaft by the cable, these claws

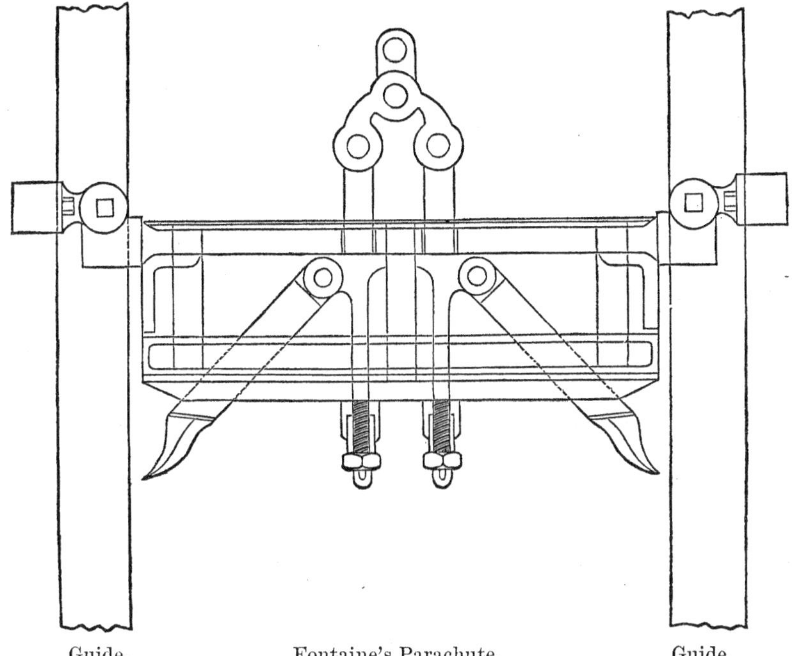

Guide. Fontaine's Parachute. Guide.

are drawn up so as not to touch the guides. Two strong, spiral springs, replaced in some parachutes by steel elliptic springs, are placed below, and in the event of the breaking of the cable they draw down the upper ends of the claws, and the lower and steel-armed ends are forced outward into contact with the wooden guides, penetrating and sometimes splitting them. The cage is thus arrested in its fall, and is sustained entirely by the wedging of these claws against the guides and timbers of the shaft. Each claw can work independently, the double hook at the top permitting either one or both to be thrown out together or to different distances, so that inequalities in the size of the shaft or of the distance between the guides may not prevent a perfect contact of both arms. The projections beyond the guides upon each side are intended to represent a part of the framework at a point where the guides are perforated for the reception of a bolt intended to prevent the cage from being hoisted prematurely. This is a contrivance introduced by the engineer Cabany, and is placed at the bottom of the shaft.

The Fontaine parachute has given satisfactory results in saving the lives of men, but the claws injure or destroy the guides. It also necessitates the use of very heavy timbers for the guides and their supports, inasmuch as pressure from the claws is exerted in one direction, and if the guides should yield or bend outward the effect would be lost. The first cost of such heavy guides and timbering is very great, and any accident, by destroying a portion of the guides, requires a great expenditure for repairs.

AUDEMAR'S PARACHUTE.

In order to avoid these difficulties other constructions have been devised. One by Mr. Audemar, engineer in the service of the mining company at Blanzy, is shown by the annexed figures. It consists of four

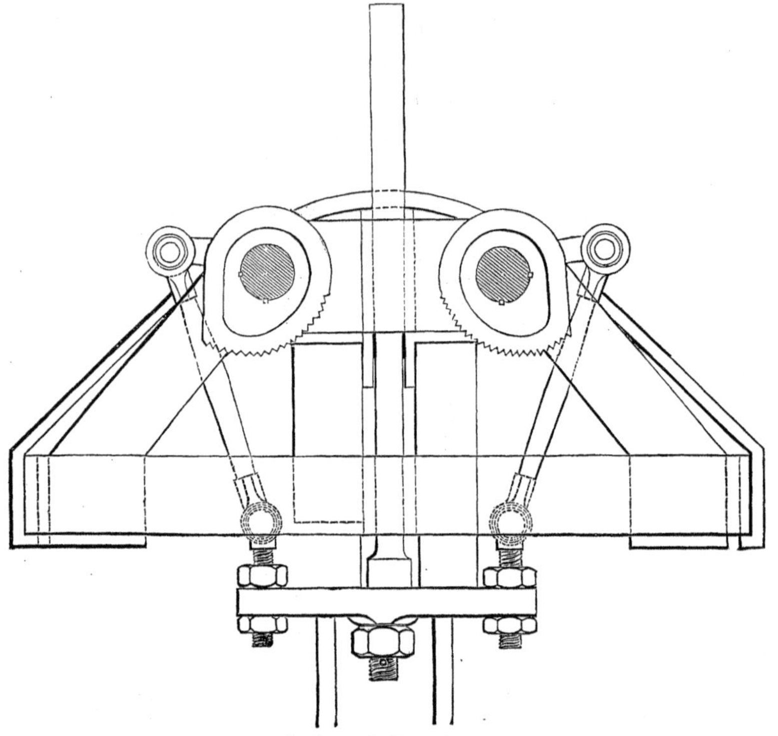

Audemar's Parachute.

eccentric wedges, two on each side, and placed on opposite sides of the guides; the release of the springs by the breaking of the cable causes these eccentrics to turn and to powerfully squeeze the guides and thus stop the descent of the cage. This parachute is as certain in its action as that of Fontaine, and does not split the guides. The guides and the framework may also be made much lighter, for there is no outward thrust or pressure tending to bend or break the timber.

It will be noted that the action of the "dog-clamp" safety catch upon the cage used in Nevada (see p. 56) is similar to that of this eccentric catch. The *sides* not the face of the guide are acted on in both cases.

The spiral springs used by Mr. Audemar are made of steel wire $0^{m}.01$ in diameter. When fully expanded they are $0^{m}.39$ long, (nearly 10 inches,) and they may be condensed to a length of $0^{m}.25$; but in order to preserve their full elasticity the springs are condensed from $0^{m}.09$ to $0^{m}.11$ only. A compression of $0^{m}.09$ is sufficient, and this gives a resistance of 180 kilogrammes, (about 360 pounds.) Motion is communicated from the springs to the eccentrics by means of arms and levers, as shown in the figures. The first figure shows the position of these arms and the eccentrics when the cage is suspended by the cable; and the second their position when the strain from the cable is released and the springs are expanded. The spiral springs are contained in cylindrical boxes, one part sliding over the other. One of these boxes and the spring are shown in section in the second figure.

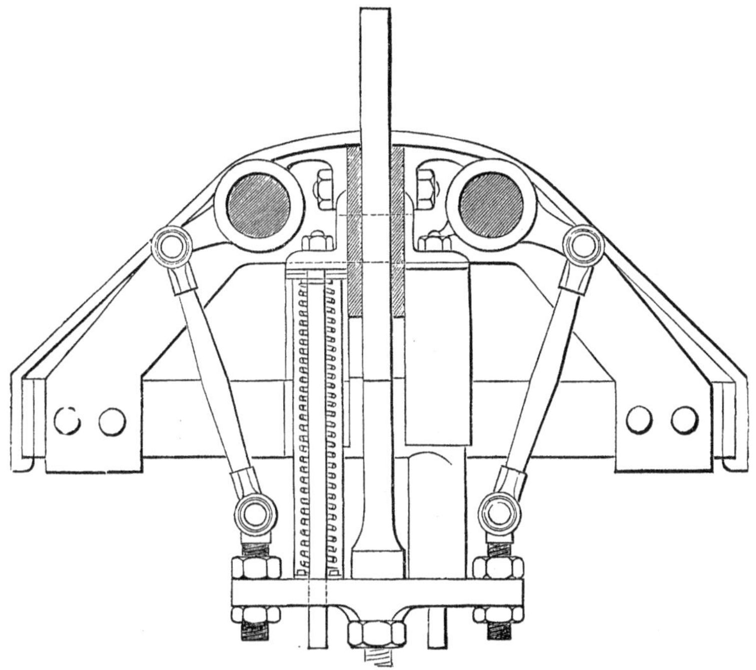

Audemar's Parachute—section showing one of the springs.

The experience of more than fourteen years with parachutes of this type has been most satisfactory. In this construction the springs are kept in constant use by being compressed and they thus relieve the shock when the cage is started.

MICHAT'S PARACHUTE.

A variety of the same type as the Blanzy construction, designed by Mr. Michat, is shown with sufficient clearness by the appended figure, and a description is unnecessary. It is evident that it does not differ essentially from the parachute just described.

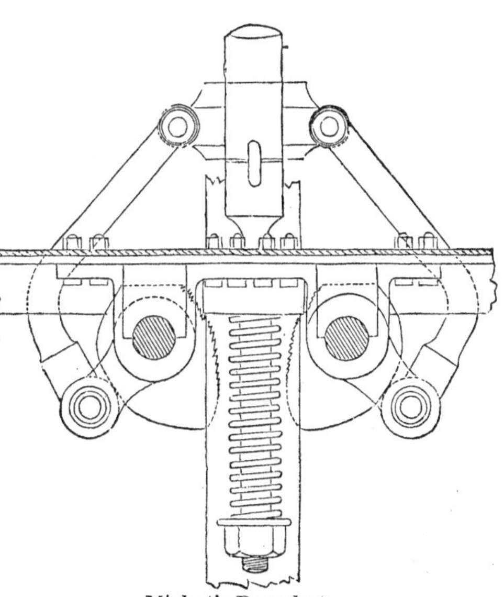

Michat's Parachute.

BRAUNE'S PARACHUTE.

This is a third variety of the same type, but it differs from the others by its extreme simplicity and the nature of the spring. This form originated with Mr. Braune, chief engineer of the mines of the

Vieille Montagne Company. A simple India-rubber band spring is all that is used to draw the eccentrics in upon the guides. It is said to have given satisfaction for a period of three years or more; but it is doubtful if a spring of this nature can long remain active and reliable when under constant tension.

PARACHUTE WITH WEDGES.

The third type of parachute is known as Nyst's, and is constructed to act like a wedge. It has arms like a parachute with claws, but the latter are replaced by a metallic jaw, in the form of a hollow wedge, fitting to the form of the guide, which is made wedge-shaped. When the parachute with the cage is sustained by the cable, the jaw moves along the guide without touching it; but if a rupture occurs, it then presses upon the guide and wedges powerfully, so as to arrest the descent of the cage within a distance of only $0^{m}.25$ or $0^{m}.30$. The action is thus very prompt, but it is so gradual that there is no perceptible shock.

Braune's Parachute.

This construction does not injure the guides, and it has the advantage over the parachutes of the second type that iron guides may be used, the reduced size of which is much less cumbersome in shafts than heavy timbers. It, however, requires the guides to be made with great accuracy, and uniform in size and angle of the wedge, and the difficulty of obtaining them has prevented this parachute from coming into general use.

THE VALUE OF SAFETY-CATCHES IN SAVING LIFE.

Although the construction of parachutes has not by any means reached perfection, there being some difficulties attending their use, they have rendered the greatest service in mining operations, repeatedly preventing great losses of life and property; and no excuse can be received for allowing a single mining cage to be without one wherever miners are permitted to ascend and descend in it. Accidents from the unaccountable breaking of the strongest cables are not infrequent; and when it is well known to mining engineers that parachutes of the proper construction have repeatedly been the means of saving life, it is strange that there should be any hesitation in adopting them. Even while writing this chapter the report of a recent accident (January, 1870) at one of the shafts of the Dowlais Company has been handed to me, and a condensed account of it is inserted as appropriate in this connection:

A fatal accident happened at the Deep Pit, Vochrhiw, the property of the Dowlais Company, on Saturday afternoon, about 5 o'clock, by which five persons lost their lives. It appears five men were ascending the pit, and when within 27 yards of the top the rope broke and the poor fellows were precipitated to the bottom, a depth of 500 yards. The bodies were smashed to pieces, and death must have been instantaneous. This is the same pit where a similar accident occurred a month ago, when two men lost their lives. It happened in the same manner as the one on Saturday, and apparently from the same cause. The Vochrhiw pit is a very large colliery, employing about 600 hands. It is 400 yards deep, and is worked by two shafts, Nos. 1 and 2; the No. 2 being the shaft generally used for the passage up and down of men and horses, the other shaft being reserved for mineral alone. But, as these accidents show, the rule adopted by the company has not been kept by their men

The pits are worked by spiral drum—an invention which has called forth on several occasions the approval of the government inspector, as they enable the engines to raise heavy weights as well as the cage and rope of a pit 400 yards deep with ease, and without any extra power. But then safety depends chiefly, we may say, upon the angle formed between the rope and the pulley above the shaft with certain portions of the drum. It ought not to exceed ten or eleven degrees, though the angle at the time of the first accident was as much as fifteen degrees, and to that Mr. Wales ascribed the accident, as it produced the overlap of coil which led to the accident. On that occasion the coil overlapped when the men were two hundred and fifty yards from the bottom, and the jerk caused by its falling into its place snapped the rope and precipitated the cage to the bottom. On Saturday night the No. 2 pit was busy between 6 and 7 o'clock in bringing out the colliers, and there were then at the bottom of the No. 1 shaft four hitchers and the overman of the pit. In their anxiety to get out without walking through the workings to the other shaft, it is conjectured the whole of them got into the cage of No. 1 shaft, and signaled to the banksman to set the engine in motion. The engine started, and the cage was brought to within 27 yards of the bank when the fatal overlap of coil again occurred, and the jerk which followed snapped the rope and brought about the dreadful catastrophe.

Here we have the particulars of two fatal accidents from the same cause, and in the same mine, within about a month; and it does not appear that any effort was made after the first accident to prevent a second, nor does it appear that the cage in either case was provided with any form of safety-catch. At the inquest after the first accident at Dowlais, it was testified by the engineer's foreman that a similar accident, but to an empty cage, had previously occurred in the same pit.

In the Colliery Guardian of September 16, 1869, there is an account of a shocking accident which occurred at the Kirkless colliery, Wigan. The men were leaving the pit early in the afternoon, and while eight of the number were being drawn to the surface the wire rope on one side of the drum slipped as it was being wound on, the loose coils fell over the flange at the end, became entangled in the eccentrics at the side, and, weakened by the chaffing which it had received by being pressed between those revolving parts, parted by the sudden jerk given by the cage as it took out the slack in descending. The cage, containing eight persons, fell, of course, to the bottom of the shaft, a distance of 270 yards, and several men were instantly dashed to pieces. At the inquest upon the bodies, the government inspector said the drum was rather too conical, and, in his opinion, some slight deflection of the pulley had caused the rope to coil back, and so led to the slip. A drum of that shape required the nicest management and care in keeping the pulleys straight.

Here is another account, of an accident in Pennsylvania, reported in the daily papers since this chapter was written:

SHENANDOAH CITY, SCHUYLKILL COUNTY, *March* 29, 1870.

A terrible accident occurred at the coal mine of Richard Hecksher, a few miles from this place, at an early hour this morning. While four men were descending the shaft to commence the day's work, the rope broke, precipitating them to the bottom, over 60 feet. All were instantly killed.

There appears to be great opposition on the part of English miners to the introduction of any form of the parachute. In some observations by a "miner," upon the above-described accidents, the following passages occur:

Are any of the safety-cages, which have from time to time been invented, really suitable and efficient; and, if so, why are they not adopted? Now, the fact is, a really suitable and efficient safety-cage has still to be discovered; all that have yet been brought forward being objectionable for one reason or another. That many of the contrivances are highly ingenious cannot be questioned, but in practice they have, without exception, been found wanting; either they are too fragile, damage the guides, or require such continual attention to keep them in order that it is dangerous to place reliance upon them; and it is generally felt that if reliance be placed upon an apparatus of the failure of which there is a remote probability, it is better to depend upon the rope alone. The various safety-cages which have been proposed are readily referable to two classes, and the great question is, which class is the best? One class of catch—for really the safety-cage is merely a safety-catch applied to an ordinary cage—is so arranged that it is brought into play at the end of each journey up and down the pit, the object being to prevent the apparatus becoming worthless from disuse. The idea is doubtless good, but the objection is, that the wear and tear are so great that the apparatus is worn out and useless before it is required to avert calamity, the consequence being that when the accident happens it is fatal, as usual. In the other class the apparatus is never brought into play until the accident occurs, the object being to avoid the dangers inseparable from the former; the wear and tear are, of course, prevented, but frequently, when the accident happens, it is found that the whole concern has become fixed from disuse.

Perhaps the only arrangements not open to these objections are those somewhat like Aytoun's and Nyst's, each of which depends for its safety upon the mere change of position of a metal fork, or its equivalent, so as to become fixed against the guide-rods. Both of these catches are extremely simple, have no springs, or similar contrivances, to get out of order, and would not cost more than a few shillings to apply them. It has been said that they knock the guide-rods to pieces when they are brought into action, but as the damage can only occur when an accident has happened, and a calamity been averted, surely this should not prevent their adoption. As neither are protected by patent, every colliery proprietor can have them made by his own smith. It is a very common opinion among practical men that the use of safety apparatus begets carelessness on the part of those engaged about the shaft, but perhaps the ground for this complaint is more apparent than real, and as the cage is without question as safe with the apparatus as without it, it might be desirable to accept reliance on the catch as more than equal to the diminished attention of the men.

The last paragraph of this extract is a good answer to the general drift of the opinion expressed by the British jury upon the safety-cages exhibited in the International Exhibition of 1862: "The jury gave careful attention to all the varieties of this apparatus, and were strongly impressed with the merits of several of them, and with the desirableness of enlisting in this cause the interest of the intelligent mechanician. But they share in the repugnance of colliery viewers to trust to the action of a spring on which most of them depend, and which, of whatever substance it is made, is sure by degrees to lose its elasticity, and is thus liable, unless frequently looked after, to fail at the moment when required. They are also aware that a great inconvenience, not to say danger, has been introduced by all those hitherto employed, in consequence of the apparatus being brought into play by a plunge during the rapid descent of the cage, and that hence several of these inventions, after being fairly tried for one, two, or three years, have been ultimately removed. Nor is it too much to say, although an insufficient argument if taken alone, that the employment of this apparatus has a tendency to make people careless about the examination and renewal of ropes."*

In view of the very satisfactory experience with parachutes in the large collieries upon the continent, and, above all, the fact that they have repeatedly saved many lives, the writer trusts that their use will not be neglected in the mines of the West; and it is gratifying to know that they are now attached to most of the cages in the mines upon the Comstock lode.

It would not be difficult to collect many accounts of fatal accidents in those mines, which probably could have been avoided if properly constructed parachutes had been used. There is one remarkable case on record, showing the usefulness of another precaution, though it providentially failed to be another of the terrible warnings which call for the use of parachutes: A cage in the Hale and Norcross Mine was precipitated to the fifth level, a distance of 230 feet, without breaking any bones of a man who was upon it. The entire steel-wire cable fell down the shaft and coiled upon the roof of the cage. The roof protected the miner from being crushed by the cable; and this shows the importance

* Reports of the British jury, Exhibition of 1862.

of placing a hood upon every cage in which miners are conveyed. The form of such a hood is of some consequence. There is a case on record in England of a miner, standing in a drift near the bottom of a shaft, being killed by a pebble which, falling from the surface upon the dome-shaped roof of the cage, glanced off and struck him.

Examples are not wanting of the utility of safety attachments to cages in mines upon the Comstock lode. In February, 1869, a steel-wire cable was broken in the Imperial-Empire shaft; but, owing to the safety attachment to the cage, no other damage was done. The Mining and Scientific Press of San Francisco, in September, 1865, reports that in one of the mines (the Sierra Nevada, it was believed) a safety cage, heavily laden with ore, had nearly reached the top of the shaft when the rope parted. The safety catch prevented a free fall, but the load was so heavy that the descent of the cage was not completely checked, and it went to the bottom so slowly that not a bolt or timber was broken. Frequent experiments made in the Comstock mines, by cutting the cable above a loaded cage suspended in the shaft, have proved the efficiency of the parachute.

SAFETY HOOKS.

With the modern powerful and rapidly winding engines, the least inattention on the part of the engineer as the cage nears the surface may permit it to ascend to the sheaves and produce great destruction. Numerous and fatal accidents from this cause are reported in the mining journals. Even while this report is printing, accounts of an accident at a colliery near Wigan* show the fearful results of over-winding, and the importance of some means of prevention. Various contrivances have been proposed and adopted to prevent this over-winding. Safety-hooks, which open and leave the cage free to rest upon spring-catches below it, are the most common; but it would seem that the best contrivance of all is the very simple one of placing one arm of a lever, a bent bar of iron, in the path of the cage, so that if it passes that point the supply of steam to the engine is shut off, and the valve of the steam-brake is opened. Thus, by one blow upon this bent lever, the engine is stopped, the brakes are applied, and the winding of course ceases. This has been rendered possible by the addition of the powerful brakes operated by steam.

Among the many forms of detaching-hooks which have been pro-

***Extraordinary colliery accident near Wigan.*—Shortly before 10 o'clock on Tuesday night a shocking colliery accident, by which one man was killed and four others received injuries more or less serious, occurred at Messrs. Blundell's No. 1 Sinking Pit, situated in the township of Pemberton, near Wigan. The shaft has been in course of construction for nearly a couple of years; it is of more than the ordinary diameter, and the work has hitherto progressed without serious impediment. The men employed work in eight-hour "shifts," and at a quarter to 10 on Tuesday preparations were made for bringing one of these working parties to bank. Four men entered the hoppett to ascend, and they were drawn to the surface; but here the engineer, Thomas Ackers, found he was unable to reverse the engine or to apply the brake, owing to some derangement of the machinery. The consequence was that the hoppett was drawn at great speed over the pulley, and then through the roof of the engine-house into the building itself, which was a perfect wreck in a few seconds. Two of the men, fearing, from the speed at which they approached the surface, that they were about to be "pulleyed," made a desperate leap for life as they reached the bank, and one of them escaped, comparatively speaking, uninjured, while the other, fearfully shaken, was falling into the pit-shaft, when he was saved by the banksman. A third, named Butler, kept his place until the hoppett arrived at the engine-house, when he was flung a distance of forty yards over the building, and he, too, escaped with his life; but the fourth was not so fortunate, as he was dragged into the house and killed instantaneously. The engine tender was also seriously hurt by the falling débris.—*From the Colliery Guardian, March 11, 1870.*

posed, there is one which is advertised in the English journals as extensively used in collieries. Its construction will be seen from the figure. It consists of two plates, placed face to face, and turning upon a central bolt. It forms a part (a link) of the winding cable or chain, and is so made that if drawn up through a hole in a cross-beam, bushed with a heavy cast iron lining, E, E, the expanded wedge-shaped sides, H, H, are pressed together, by contact with E, E, so as to liberate the bolts of the cable, A and B, at D and D. At the same time a square shoulder upon each plate of the link catches upon the upper edge of the hole, and sustains the weight of the cage. This is said to be extensively used. A form of safety-hook used in Nevada is shown upon a previous page, in the drawing of the cage now in use upon the Comstock lode.

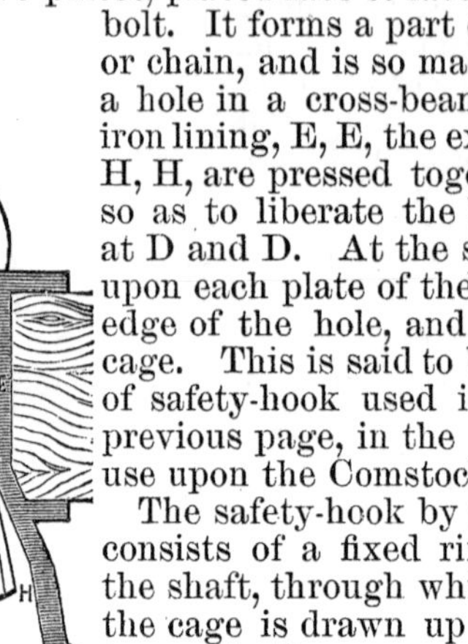

Safety Detaching-hook.

The safety-hook by S. Bailey, proposed in 1860, consists of a fixed ring between the guides over the shaft, through which the cable passes. When the cage is drawn up too far this ring acts upon two projecting arms, which detach the cable, while, at same time, hooks are thrown outward over the ring, and by these the cage or kibble remains suspended.*

SIGNAL INDICATORS.

Carefully made indicators are now attached to winding engines, in such a manner that the position of the cage in the shaft is shown to the engineer by the movement of an index or pointer along a horizontal scale, and as the cage approaches the top a bell is sounded once or twice, and if it ascends too far the apparatus shuts off the steam and stops the engine.

CHAPTER XI.

RAISING WATER.

It is unnecessary here to do more than mention the very common method of raising water from mines of small extent by means of the tub and windlass, precisely as ore is raised, or by a barrel fitted with a large valve in the bottom, which opens and allows the barrel to fill automatically when it reaches the sump. This method was in use at the Amador mine to a depth of at least eleven hundred feet, the buckets being of iron and cylindrical, like the tubs for ore, and sliding like them upon the guides along the inclined shaft. Guided skips fitted with valves are similarly used.

In Virginia City, Nevada, along the Comstock lode, many of the shafts were kept drained by these simple means, and the only apparatus worthy of further note was the method of delivery of the water into movable launders. When the barrel of water reached the surface, a launder, running upon rails laid on each side of the shaft, was pushed under it. The barrel was then allowed to descend and rest upon cross-bars, and, by raising the valve, the water was discharged into the head of

* Jour. Mining, 1860, and Rev. Universelle, May and June, 1860, p. 511.

the launder and conveyed away without the necessity of moving the barrel out of the line of the shaft.

Cylindrical water-tubs have been used to a considerable extent in the French collieries. They are usually made with a capacity of 20 hectolitres, equal to five hundred and twenty-eight gallons, and weigh about 700 kilogrammes. The water enters by a large valve at the bottom, and is discharged through a side orifice. With this form of apparatus for hoisting water, it is necessary, in order to avoid loss of time, to provide guides in the shaft, so that the tub may be drawn up and lowered rapidly. It has also been found highly advantageous to commence discharging the water as soon as the tub reaches a sufficient height above the pit, without bringing it to rest. An arrangement for this purpose is shown by the accompanying plate, reduced from a figure given by Burat in his atlas of *Le Matériel des Houillères*. Instead of bringing the tub of water to a complete rest upon catches at the top of the shaft, it is kept slowly ascending, and strikes a movable knocker or

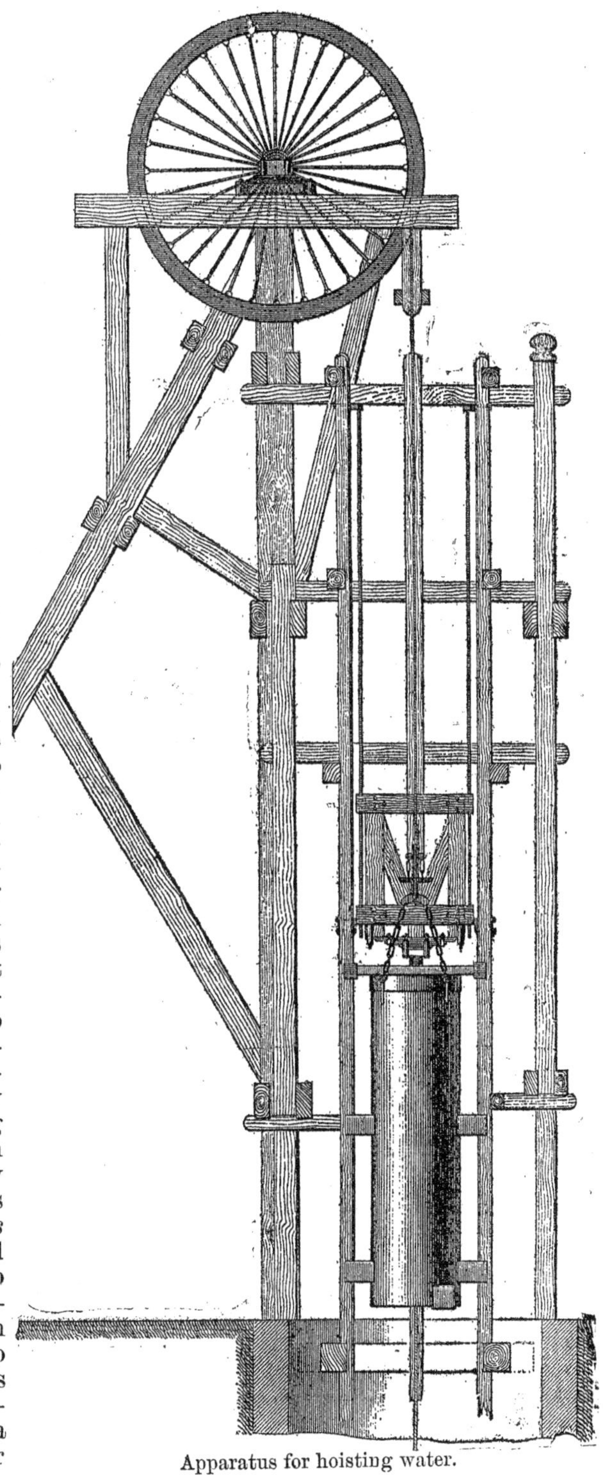

Apparatus for hoisting water.

frame-work, which throws open the discharge valve and lets the water escape. The motion may be stopped as soon as the valve is open, and as soon as the tub is emptied it may be lowered without any loss of time. The practical value of this improvement is shown by the results obtained with it at the Lucy pits, near Montceau-des-Mines. At these shafts, 200 metres in depth, 30 tubs of water, containing 25 hectolitres each, were raised per hour, being a total of 750 hectolitres of water; but this being insufficient, the automatic discharge apparatus was added, and the number of deliveries of tubs of water at the surface was easily increased to 50 or 60, discharging from 1,200 to 1,500 hectolitres per hour.

The lift and plunger pumps used in California and Nevada are generally of small size, and have no special peculiarities. They are generally connected with either the engine used for hoisting or with that for running the mill.

CHINESE PUMP.

In placer mining the "Chinese pump" is much used for draining the pits where the water does not require to be raised to a great distance. This is essentially a chain-pump. A continuous belt of canvas 5 or 6 inches wide has cleats of wood firmly secured to it at intervals, and is made to pass continuously through a rectangular box, the lower end of which is fitted with a roller over which the belt passes, and is inserted in the water to be raised from the pit. The upper end delivers the water into a launder or trough, by which it is conducted away. The belt passes over a wheel at the top, and motion is given either by the hand or by a belt from a water-wheel near by.

DRAINAGE BY SIPHONS.

The siphon has often been brought into use for draining in mines, pits, and quarries, where it was not necessary to raise the water to a great height, and where the necessary fall for the delivery end could be conveniently had. There has been a notable example of the successful use of a siphon on a large scale during the past year at a deep placer claim in Gravel Range, Tuolumne County, California, where Mr. George A. Treadwell employed one a little over 1,000 feet long and 4 inches in diameter. This pipe was made of No. 24 galvanized iron, in joints 30 inches long, riveted and soldered together. The water was raised 18 feet, and the discharge end had a fall of 40 feet, so that the delivery was 22 feet lower than the receiving end, or shorter leg of the siphon. The two ends of the pipe were furnished with large 4-inch brass cocks, which were closed when the siphon was to be filled. The filling was easily accomplished in about two hours by means of a 3-inch Douglas force-pump, throwing water in at the highest point through a vent-cock, through which, also, smaller quantities of water could be supplied from time to time to displace air that gradually accumulated through leaks. An air-chamber at the bend was projected, but was not made, inasmuch as it was found to be but little trouble by shutting the 4-inch cocks at each end to fill up the siphon with the pump in a short time when the men were at their meals.

The flow at both ends was easily controlled by the cocks, the lower or delivery cock being usually left fully open, while the receiving cock was partly closed. The velocity of the current was sufficient to carry out tons of coarse sand and gravel, some of the latter as coarse as English walnuts; and sluice-boxes set at the usual slope were kept half fulof water. There was no trouble in keeping the water within 2 inches of the receiving end, and this was plunged to within 5 inches of the bottom of the shaft.

PUMPING ENGINES IN THE EUROPEAN MINES.

There are three principal types of pumping engines for mines:

1. The single-acting balance-beam engine, known as the Cornish engine.
2. The single-acting engine, working the pump-rods direct, without a balance beam.
3. The double-acting engines placed in the interior of mines.

As explanatory of the construction and working of the first type, I insert a very clear and interesting description of a Cornish engine of the largest class: *

CORNISH PUMPING ENGINE.

The engine called Taylor's engine was erected in the year 1840, at the United Mines in Gwennap, now included in the Clifford Amalgamated Mines, and is worked with high-pressure steam, with expansion and condensation. It is single acting; that is, the steam is only employed for lifting the pump-rods and filling the pump-barrels in the shaft; the return stroke, which drives the water out of the pump-barrels into the rising pipes being effected by the fall of the shaft rod, as soon as an equilibrium is established in the cylinder, by opening a communication between the two faces of the piston. The steam piston moves vertically in a cylinder formed of two concentric tubes, the inner one forming the cylinder, and the outer one a protecting case, or jacket; the small annular space between the two is constantly filled with steam at the maximum pressure produced in the boilers, in order to keep the walls of the inner cylinder at a uniform temperature. In practice, it is customary to surround the cylinder with other non-conducting envelopes; thus, a shell of brickwork inclosing an air space is first placed round the jacket, which is further inclosed with coatings of felt, lagged with wood. These outer envelopes are not shown in the model. The piston-rod is attached by Watt's parallel motion to the end of a beam oscillating about a horizontal axis, whose bearings are carried on the outer wall of the engine-house. The beam is formed of two parallel cast-iron plates bolted together, the two plates being kept a fixed distance apart by wrought-iron pins. The two arms of the beam are of unequal length; the steam piston and mechanism for working the valves are attached to the longer arm, which works within the engine-house; the main pump-rod and rods of the air and feed-pumps are attached to the shorter arm, which works in the open air; a gallery projecting from the wall of the engine-house gives access to the bearings on the out-door side of the beam.

The engine has four valves for the distribution of the steam; three of these are placed near the top of the cylinder, and the other one is at the bottom. One of them is a plain disk valve, with a single conical beating face, and is independent of the engine; the other three are of the kind known as the double beat, or Hornblower's valve, a construction in which the bearing faces opposed to the pressure of the steam are reduced to a pair of narrow conical rings, the valve and its seat being

---

* This description is extracted from Bauerman's Descriptive Catalogue of the Mining Models, &c., in the Museum of Practical Geology, attached to the London School of Mines.

so formed as to present a very large steam passage when open. Of the three upper valves, that on the right-hand side (as seen when facing the cylinder from the outside) is the governor, or regulator valve. It is a plain disk valve, which is maintained at a fixed opening by means of the setting screws on the rod attached to the right-hand pillar of the valve gear framing. By this valve the steam is admitted from the main steam-pipe through the large hollow column on the right into the top steam-chest. The central valve is the admission valve; it commands the passage whereby the steam at full pressure enters and leaves the cylinder above the piston, and is governed by a system of levers attached to the uppermost of the three horizontal shafts, which are attached to the two vertical pillars or standards in front of the valve cases. The left-hand upper valve is the equilibrium valve; it is placed at the top of a hollow column, through which the steam passes from the upper to the lower face of the piston, in order to establish an equality of pressure at the end of the steam-stroke; the movement of this valve is effected by the central arbor. The bottom, or exhaust, valve, which controls the passage of the exhaust steam from the cylinder to the condenser, is attached to the lower horizontal arbor.

The valves are opened by falling weights, and closed by the action of tappets on the plug-rod, acting on curved handles projecting from the front of the horizontal shafts. The sector-shaped cams and catch levers outside the bearings of the horizontal arbors keep the valves locked in position during the repose of the engine.

The engine is intermittent in its action, a pause being made after the descent of the main rod in the shaft, varying in duration according to the amount of water to be lifted; this is effected by a simple hydraulic regulator, known as the cataract. The cataract, which is placed in the well below the floor of the engine-house, is a square wooden plunger box, open above and closed at the bottom, with the exception of a small conical hole, which can be stopped by a plug attached to a vertical rod; the plunger moves in a square cistern of water, a little larger than itself, and is attached to a vertical rod passing through a collar projecting from the right-hand frame pillar; it is further attached by a chain rolling on a sector-head to a double-armed lever, which oscillates about a horizontal axis; the shorter arm of this lever is pressed down by a roller at the lower end of the plug-rod, during the upstroke of the engine, a balance weight being fixed to the end of the opposite arm, which raises the shorter arm when the pressure of the rod is taken off. The action of the cataract is as follows: When the in-door side of the beam makes its down stroke, during the lifting of the main rod in the shaft, the cataract plunger is driven down in its cistern, displacing the water in bottom of the latter, which consequently rises above the open top of the plunger box and fills it up; this water afterward flows out through the small hole in the bottom of the box with more or less rapidity, according to the position of the conical plug; and during this time the valves are closed and locked by their catches, the steam piston is at the top of its stroke with a slightly compressed cushion of steam above it, and the expanded steam of the preceding stroke below it. As soon as sufficient water has flowed out of the cataract plunger to establish the preponderance of the balance weight on the longer horizontal arm of the lever, the box rises, and the rod attached to it opens the exhaust valve by striking against the catch lever and releasing the balance weight. The steam below the piston flows away to the condenser, and a vacuum is formed in the cylinder. The catch on the steam valve is formed by the vertical arm of an angle lever, whose horizontal arm is parallel to the exhaust-valve catch, and is connected to it by a parallel bar with a slotted link at the top, which works on a pin at the end of the horizontal arm of the upper catch.

When the bottom of the link strikes the pin, the steam valve is opened in a similar manner to that already described for the exhaust valve. The piston descends under the full pressure of the steam in the cylinder until the link frame at the back of the plug-rod closes the valve, by pressing against the handle which projects from the top arbor, the sector on the arbor, in turning, gradually lifting the catch lever, which falls into its place as soon as the end of the cam has passed the notch. The steam is now cut off, and the remainder of the stroke is effected by the expansion of the steam already in the cylinder. The length of the full steam stroke is determined by the position of the link frame on the plug-rod; the proportion of expansion is diminished or increased by raising or lowering the link by the setting screw on the front of the rod.

The exhaust valve is closed by the plug on the right-hand side of the rod shortly after the closing of the steam valve. The equilibrium valve is opened at the end of the stroke by its balance weight; this establishes a communication between the upper and lower faces of the piston, equalizing the pressure on both sides, when the piston is drawn up in the cylinder by the excess weight on the outer side of the beam. The equilibrium valve is closed by the left-hand plug during the rise of the rod. This confines a small quantity of steam above the piston, which forms a cushion by compression, and brings the moving mass to a state of rest.

The condenser and air pump are connected with the out-door side of the beam. The latter is surmounted by an open hot well of large capacity. The feed pump draws its supply directly from the hot well, and forces the water through a double U tube, passing four times through the exhaust pipe, where it is heated by the waste steam on its passage from the cylinder to the condenser. The feed water is further heated by circulation through a system of horizontal pipes in a flue at the back of the boilers. The steam from the six boilers is collected in a cylindrical steam chest, with hemispherical ends, cast in two pieces, which are united by a wrought-iron expansion joint. The main steam-pipe passes from the chest under the floor of the engine-house, and terminates in the right-hand vertical column, at the top of which the governor valve is placed. The main rod which works the pumps in the shaft is formed of two square balks of timber placed side by side, and united by wrought-iron fish plates and bolts. The excess weight of the rod above that necessary to drive the water out of the pump barrels is balanced off by five balance bobs, of which three are placed under ground and two are at the surface. The latter are cast-iron beams, constructed in a similar manner to the beam of the engine, one end being connected by a wooden rod with the main rod on the shaft; the other carries a wooden box, which is loaded with masses of rock, acting as a counterbalance. Catch pieces, or stops, are fixed to either side of the beam to prevent it going beyond its proper distance in case of breakage on either side. The in-door catch is formed by an iron cross-piece fixed above the beam which is received on a pair of spring beams carried on horizontal balks crossing the upper part of the engine-house. The out-door catch is formed by two pieces of timber strapped on to the front of the main rod. The lower ends of these beams, which are of the same size as the main rod, are caught by a mass of timber formed of horizontal balks piled one above another in the shaft. This bed of timber is not shown in the model.

The large capstan and shear frame over the shaft lead the rope by which the pump barrels, &c., are lowered in the shaft. It is worked by manual power.

The following are the dimensions of the more important parts of the engine:

Diameter of steam cylinder	85 inches.
Length of stroke of piston	132 inches.
Diameter of regulator valve	10.8 inches.
Diameter of admission valve	15.0 inches.
Diameter of equilibrium valve	18.5 inches.
Diameter of exhaust valve	25.0 inches.
Diameter of main steam pipe	18.0 inches.
Diameter of exhaust pipe	24.0 inches.
Diameter of condenser	30.0 inches.
Diameter of air-pump piston	37.0 inches.
Diameter of air-pump valve	30.0 inches.
Diameter of hot well	55.5 inches.
Diameter of feed pump	6.0 inches.
Length of main beam	34 feet 2½ inches.
Height of main beam at centre	7 feet 1½ inches.
Length of beam, steam side	17 feet 10½ inches.
Length of beam, out-door side	16 feet 4 inches.
Length from centre of beam to point of attachment of air-pump rod	9 feet 7½ inches.
Length of feed-pump rod	6 feet 8 inches.
Length of stroke of main rod	10 feet.
Section stroke of main rod { breadth	24 inches.
Section stroke of main rod { depth	12 inches.
Diameter of piston rod	7½ inches.
Diameter air-pump rod	3½ inches.
Diameter of feed-pump rod	2½ inches.
Diameter of axis of main beam	20 inches.
Diameter of journals	16 inches.

Boilers:

4 of 30 feet length, 5 feet diameter of outer shell.
3 feet 4 inches diameter of inner tube.
2 of 34 feet length, 5 feet 10 inches external diameter.
Steam chest, 30 inches diameter.
Feed-pipe, 5½ inches diameter.

The engine was started in December, 1840; its performance was continuously reported in "Lean's Engine Reporter" up to the end of 1851. The most economical condition of working was reported in September, 1842. The mine was then 201.2 fathoms deep; the load on the piston amounted to 75,362 pounds, or 12.05 pounds per square inch of surface. The engine, making five strokes per minute, developed a quantity of work equal to 114.2 horse-power. The quantity of fuel consumed showed an effect of 107,494,580 foot pounds per bushel of coal of 94 pounds, equal to 1.74 pounds per horse-power per hour.

The last return, in December, 1851, shows a duty of 62,000,000 of foot pounds per bushel, or 2.9 pounds per horse-power per hour. The depth had increased to 239 fathoms; the load per square inch to 15.8 pounds, giving a duty of 165 horse-power, at a speed of 5.5 strokes per minute. The greatest working speed attained appears to have been in December, 1849, when the engine made 7.5 strokes per minute, showing

221 horse-power, with a consumption of 2.4 pounds per horse-power per hour. The method by which the above duties is computed consists in comparing the amount of coal burned with the theoretical volume of water discharged by the pumps during the period of observation. The actual volume is, however, somewhat smaller, the discharge of the best mining pumps being from 2¼ to 2½ per cent. less than the theoretical amount for each lift.

DIRECT-ACTING PUMPING ENGINES.

The models earliest imported from England, or constructed in France or Belgium, were all of the first type; but they were gradually replaced by those of the second, or the direct-acting engines, so that the use of the beam engine became exceptional. The two types, though so different in form, do not differ much in the details of construction. They are both single-acting and are provided with the same kind of apparatus for the distribution of the steam; and the Hornblower valves, used in both, are controlled by one or two cataracts.

In some cases, where there is very little space in which to place an engine, they are made without the condenser, and the cylinder is placed over the shaft, the piston-rod being connected directly with the pump-rod. This is the simplest and least costly form of pumping engine to erect, but the expenses of working with it are of course much greater than with condensing engines. Instead of the consumption of one and a half kilogramme of coal per horse-power per hour, as in the Cornish engine, the high-pressure engines consume four to five kilogrammes. For this reason condensing engines of the Cornish type are generally used, and of these the direct acting form has been generally preferred, but with the addition of the beam, for the purpose of counterbalancing the rods and for working the condenser.

Burat, in his *Matériel des Houillères*, sums up the relative advantages of the two types of construction, the balance-beam engines and the direct-acting engines, substantially as follows: The balance-beam engines are especially adapted to pumping where great diameters of cylinder are required, because they do not obstruct the mouth of the shaft; because their foundations, being at some distance beyond the sides of the shaft, are much firmer and more secure; and because the different parts of the apparatus are more accessible for cleansing and repairing.

The direct-acting machines are the best, when the cylinders do not exceed 1^{m}. 50 in diameter and the pumps, 0^{m}. 45. Their installation is more simple; they occupy less space, and can, in most cases, be placed over one compartment of a shaft used for hoisting, and without a special building; and the conditions throughout are much more simple than can be secured with the other type.

A failure to obtain as great an economy of steam in many of the French and Belgian engines as is claimed for the Cornish engines has led their engineers to think that the statements of the performance of the latter are exaggerated. In reality the average consumption in Cornwall is 1^{kil}.50 of good coal per hour per horse-power. It is but rarely that the consumption has been reduced to one kilogramme, when every part of the apparatus is in the most favorable conditon, depending upon the depth and diameter of the column, the size of the rods, and the proper relation of the force to the work to be done.

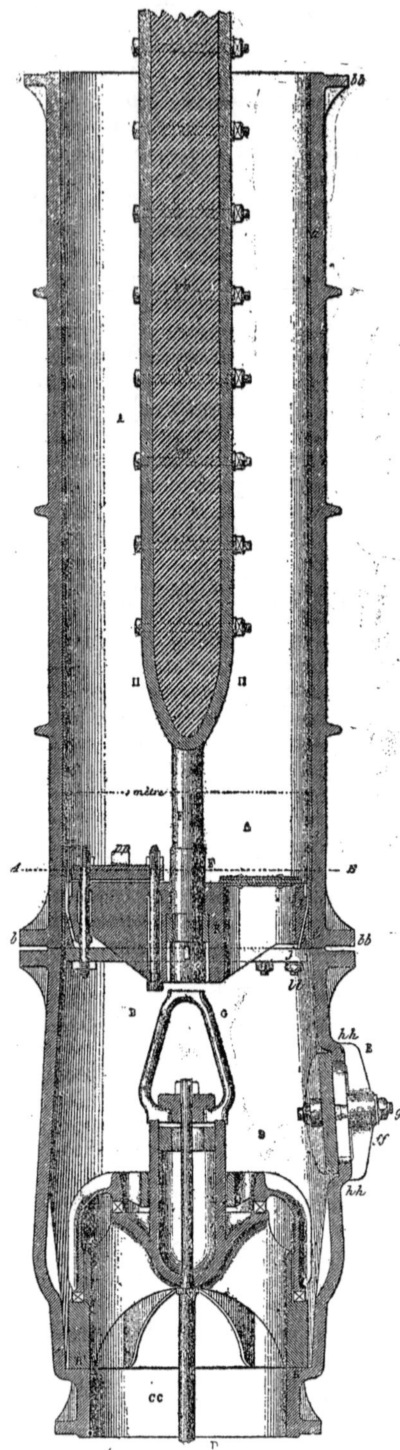

Bleiberg Lifting Pump.

BLEIBERG LIFTING PUMP.

The annexed figure reduced by the photo-relief process from Plate LXII of the Atlas of Burat's Matériel des Houillères, gives a sectional view of the pump barrel and the two vales of a lifting pump at Bleiberg. It is one metre in diameter, and is made for a height of column of 22 metres. The piston can carry a charge of 17,000 kilogrammes. The valve chamber B B is provided with a manhole E, securely closed by a cast plate held in position by a bolt and nut *g g*, passing through the cross-bar *f f.* The barrel of the pump is lined with bronze. It is $3^{m}.45$ high, and the piston has a stroke of $2^{m}.85$. The piston is pierced with eight triangular openings. The packing consists of a circle leather firmly secured to the piston by a ring of iron *j*. The lower valve is one of Hornblower's construction.

EXPERIMENTS AT BLEIBERG.

In the year 1850 a commission was formed to investigate the performance of the pumping machinery at the mines of lead and zinc at Bleiberg in Belgium. Engines of great power had just been erected, and the engineers of the establishments of Seriang had exerted themselves to produce the most perfect specimens, with all the latest improvements of the best Cornish engines.

The steam-cylinder of the engine at Bleiberg was $2^{m}.67$ in diameter; (surface, $5^{m2}.5990$;) the mean stroke $^{m}3.65$; the relation of the arms of the beam 6.4: 5; the stroke of the pump-rods $2^{m}.85$. The steam being at a pressure of 2.90 atmospheres in the boilers, the initial pressure in the cylinders was 2.42 atmospheres. The steam was cut off at $0^{m}.70$ of the stroke, and the remainder of the movement was performed by the expansion and the condenser, so that at the end of the stroke the steam occupied a space equal to five times its primitive volume.

The commission continued the observations from the 9th to the 15th of January, and reported them in detail.* The engine having worked during 127 hours 15 minutes, gave 50,043 pulsations, and 43,118 kilogrammes of coal were consumed. This coal was the stone-coal of Seriang, broken to the size used in Cornwall. The stroke of the pumps was maintained uniformly at $2^{m}.85$, and the effective height of the column of water at $71^{m}.50$. The result of these figures was that the machine gave a mean useful effect of 234 horse-power, and the consumption of coal per horse-power per hour was an average of $1^{kil}.448$. Burat finds the relation of the force exerted to the effect produced to be as 377:234=1:0.621; and observes that this remarkable economy of fuel in a work which is far from being advantageous to the motor, since at each stroke it must overcome the inertia of an enormous mass, results from a series of favorable conditions in which the machines are established and work. These favorable conditions may be summed up as follows: 1. Generation of steam in boilers with large heating surfaces; good coal and good raking. 2. A steam chest of great capacity, and pipes and openings of large diameter for the admission and emission of steam. 3. Condensation as perfect as possible. 4. Expansion developed as much as possible, favored by the conditions of single action and the inequality of speed of the piston, which are coincident with the best conditions of movement for a column of water.

PUMPING ENGINE AT GRAND HORNU.

The great pumping engine of Grand Hornu was constructed at the works of Seriang, for a shaft 460 metres deep. It works a series of eight plunger-pumps and two lifting-pumps of $0^{m}.50$ in diameter, and four metres stroke. These pumps are placed one above the other, at distances varying from 30 to 60 metres. The upper plunger-pump, 60 metres from the surface, is worked by a double rod, each arm having a square section of $0^{m}.484 \times 0^{m}.242$, and being formed by the juxtaposition of two pieces of $0\ ^{2}.242$. These rods are completely enveloped in iron $0^{m}.024$ thick. The double rods gradually diminish in size toward the bottom of the shaft, but in each section the weight exceeds that of the column of water to be thrown out. The total weight to be counterpoised is 200,000 kilogrammes; and this is effected by two balance beams mounted upon opposite sides of the master-rod, directly below the engine.

The engine is direct-acting, the cylinder being mounted directly over the shaft. It has three floors or stages: 1. The cylinder; 2. The condensers, with their air-pumps; 3. The balance beams. The cylinder is jacketed to prevent condensation. It is $0^{m}.05$ thick and is made in two pieces, each $1^{m}.60$ high. There are three valves: the admission valve, $0^{m}.42$ in diameter and rising $0^{m}.06$; the equilibrium valve, $0^{m}.51$ in diameter and rising $0^{m}.08$; the exhaustion valve, $0^{m}.60$ in diameter and rising $0^{m}.85$. The condensers have a diameter of $1^{m}.20$, and are $2^{m}.50$ high. The air-pumps are $0^{m}.95$ in diameter, and have a stroke of $2^{m}.10$. The balance beams are $11^{m}.40$ long, and each carries 90,000 kilogrammes of counter-weights, formed of plates of cast iron.

QUILLACQ'S PUMPING ENGINE.

At the Paris Exposition of 1867, M. Quillacq, who has already been mentioned as the constructing engineer of hoisting machines, exhibited the drawings of a very perfect specimen of pumping engine recently

* Proces-Verbaux de la Commission contradictoire.

erected by him at the mines of Fiennes, in the Boulonnais, France. This was a single, direct-action engine, without the beam, as in the Cornish type. The cylinder is provided with a jacket of cast iron, inclosing a space in which steam circulates. The distribution is made by three valves of admission, equilibrium, and exhaustion, controlled by a double-acting cataract, which determines the time of rest at each extremity of the stroke. The cylinder, $2^m.65$ in diameter, is 4^m long, and supported by two wrought-iron girders $1^m.35$ high, placed in the walls of the building.

The steam is admitted in the cylinder under a pressure of 3.75 atmospheres, and is cut off at half-stroke.

The condenser has two air-pumps of $0^m.90$ diameter, and 2^m stroke. The water is injected through two valves, one of which opens at the same time with the introduction of the steam, and the other at the same time with the escape-valve, so that at the beginning of the stroke the two valves are open, while at the end one of them is closed.

This machine is designed to raise water from a depth of 400 metres, by means of six plunger-pumps, and a lift-pump at the bottom. The diameter of the pumps is $0^m.60$ and the stroke $4^m.00$. The principal rod which transmits the movement to the pumps is of iron and weighs 200,000 kilogrammes. The following are the weights of some of the principal parts of the engine in kilogrammes:

Steam-cylinder	40,000
Iron girders	12,000
Piston-rod	4,000
Cross-head	1,600
Two equilibrium balances	40,000

The total weight of the engine and fixtures, without the counterpoise, is 175,000 kilogrammes.

The other elements are—

Six plunger-pumps	70,000
One lift-pump	7,500
Main rod	200,000
Counterpoise attached to the rod	75,000
Counterpoise attached to counterbalances	140,000

The total weight of the masses put in motion, including the piston and the beams, is 465,000 kilogrammes.

DOUBLE-ACTING PUMPING ENGINES—STEAM PUMPS.

The double-acting pumping engines placed in the interior of mines have been applied at depths of 100 to 150 metres, and for quantities of water reaching 10,000 hectolitres a day. The Blanzy coal companies have applied this system in their mines. They have erected a 300 horse-power engine at a depth of 340 metres, to throw 25,000 hectolitres of water to the surface daily. The drawings of this engine were exhibited at Paris, in 1867. The apparatus consists of two horizontal steam-cylinders, working four horizontal plunger-pumps, which force the water into an air-chamber with which the delivery column, 300 metres high, is connected. The apparatus is placed 40 metres above the bottom of the mine, and the water is lifted to that point by four lift-pumps, so that in case of accident or stoppage the pumps will not be covered with water.

There are many different forms of the double-acting steam pumps in the United States, and some of them have been successfully used in mines upon the Pacific slope. It is not possible here to describe all of the varieties offered to the public, and to discuss their relative merits. To single out one or two for description would not be just to the many inventors who have carried these pumps to great perfection.

PUMPING AT THE SAXON COLLIERIES.

The following is cited from the notes of Mr. W. Fairley, as an example of pumping at the Saxon collieries:

The Pumping Engine Company at Zwickau, which drains the water from the Bockwa Manor, is worthy of notice. This manor is about 180 acker, or about 190 English acres area, and the company pumps the water for the different coal companies for the payment of a tax of $2\frac{1}{2}$ groschen per 10 centner, or 6d. per ton English, of coal worked. The water does not exceed altogether more than 200 cubic feet per minute, and for lifting this they have two engines, one 84 inches (Saxon) diameter, 11 feet in the cylinder, and 9 feet stroke in the pump, working seven strokes per minute as the maximum. The pumps are two 23 inches diameter, forcing 250 feet long each, and one 23 inches diameter, lifting 100 feet long; the other engine is direct-acting, 68 inches (Saxon) diameter, with 10-feet stroke, working a $17\frac{1}{2}$-inch set. For supplying these engines with steam, there are seven egg-ended boilers, each 7 feet diameter and 40 feet long.

WATER-PRESSURE ENGINES FOR MINES.

In mountainous regions, where water under a considerable head or pressure can be had, it may be advantageously utilized for pumping, hoisting, or other mining operations requiring power, by means of hydraulic engines and surface or underground wheels. There are many places on the Pacific coast where such engines can be introduced with advantage. They are usually constructed for pumping only, and are single-acting, with long cylinders placed vertically over the pump shaft, the pump-rod being simply a prolongation of the piston-rod. The water is admitted to the under side of the piston, and when it has run its upward stroke the water is allowed to flow out and the piston descends.

The absence of any sensible elasticity in water renders the motions resulting from its use under pressure in engines susceptible of perfect control; but the same inelasticity causes sudden shocks and blows to the moving parts if the inlets and outlets are made as in engines operated by the elastic fluids, steam or air. It is therefore necessary to use valves of peculiar construction, by which the flow of the water may be gradually increased or slackened, and to provide other means for preventing impact and securing smoothness of action.

Many such engines have been constructed for pumping mines abroad, and have operated successfully for long periods with very little expense or attention. One was erected by the engineer Trevithick at the Alport mines, in the year 1803, and worked continuously for forty-seven years, until 1850, when work upon the mines ceased. In this engine the water was admitted first upon one face of the piston and then upon the other, alternately, and the inlets and outlets were opened and closed by two pistons at the side.

An engine erected by Mr. Darlington at these mines had a cylinder 50 inches in diameter and a stroke of 10 feet. The cylinder was placed directly over the shaft and the piston and pump-rod were continuous. The column of water was 132 feet high and gave a pressure upon the piston of about 58 pounds to the square inch, or more than fifty tons upon its area. Water was raised from a depth of 22 fathoms by means of a plunger 42 inches in diameter, and when the mine was very wet, nearly 5,000 gallons of water per minute were discharged into the adit. The water under pressure was admitted under the piston only; cylindrical valves admitted a full flow for seven-eighths of the stroke only, and then commenced closing, while a small valve opened and allowed enough water to pass in to complete the stroke.

The largest engine erected by Mr. Darlington was similar in its general construction to that just described. It had a cylinder 35 inches in diameter; stroke 10 feet; pressure column 227 feet high. Its average speed was 80 feet per minute, and its greatest speed 140 feet per minute. The pressure of the water was 98 pounds per square inch, giving a total weight of 40 tons upon the piston. This engine was automatic, the motion was certain and regular, and the cost of maintenance was trifling.

Sir William Armstrong has made use of water pressure obtained from natural falls to produce rotary motion by means of a pair of cylinders and pistons, with slide valves, in some degree resembling those of high-pressure steam-engines, but provided also with relief valves. Water-pressure engines of this description were erected at the lead mines at Allenheads, in Northumberland, and are used for the various operations of crushing the ores, hoisting, pumping, and driving the machinery of the concentrating works. Small streams of water which flowed down the slopes of adjoining hills were conducted into reservoirs at elevations of about 200 feet, and from thence by pipes to the engines.

In a mining district upon the river Allen, in England, where the fall of the water is not sufficient to work water-pressure engines, overshot wheels have been used to force water into accumulators, from which it could be conveyed in pipes to the required points.

Table showing the locality, engineers, and dimensions of some of the principal water-pressure engines.

[From Ure's Dictionary, edited by Robert Hunt.]

Locality.	Engineer.	Diam'r of cylinder.	Length of stroke.	Speed per minute.
		In's.	*Feet.*	*Rev's.*
Northumberland	Westgarth	10	......	.....
Ems	Unknown	13½	4	8
Bleiberg	Unknown	7	6½	100
Chemnitz	Unknown	11	8	48
Ebensee, Salzsburg	Unknown	9½	1 5-12	17
Clausthal	Unknown	16½	6	48
Alte Mordgrube, Saxony	Unknown	18	8	64
Alport mines, Derbyshire	Trevithick	25*	10	120
Do	Fairbairn	36	5	70
Do	Darlington	50	10	140
Do	do	18	7	154
Do	do	24†	10	120
Do	do	24†	10	120
Lisburn	do	20†	6	96
Cwmystwyth	do	24†	10	140
Talargoch	do	50	10	140
Minera	do	35	10	140
Wildberg	do	3	5	80
South Helton colliery	Armstrong	3 ‡	12	200
Allenheads	do	6	18	180

* Double. † Two cylinders. ‡ Four cylinders.

Underground water-wheels are used in various parts of Germany, when the circumstances permit. Where a system of mines is drained through a deep adit, the water can be transferred from one mine to another, and its fall utilized by such wheels, until it finally reaches the level of the adit by which it escapes. Instances of this may be observed in the district of Freiberg, Saxony.

WATER-WORKS AT WHITE PINE.

There is a very interesting exhibition of hydraulic engineering at the White Pine mines, due to the skill and enterprise of the distinguished engineer A. Von Schmidt. Water is there pumped a height of 900 feet in round numbers, in two lifts of 450 feet each. There are four large steam engines, two at each station, and each engine of 177 horse-power. The cylinders are 22 inches in diameter and they have a stroke of five feet. They can be worked together or independently. The water is forced through 12-inch pipes of boiler iron, and the capacity of the works is reported as 2,500,000 gallons daily.

CHAPTER XII.

RAISING AND LOWERING MINERS.

The ascent and descent of miners in the mines of the West, when of depths not exceeding 200 feet, is usually by ladders in one compartment of the hoisting shaft; but in all guided shafts where cages are used it is customary to descend and ascend in these cages. This is not only dangerous, but it interferes with the work of hoisting ore; and in all deep mines, especially in vertical shafts, it becomes important to provide some other safe and rapid means of hoisting and lowering the men.

This necessity has been met abroad, and in some of our mines upon Lake Superior, by the introduction of the man-engine, known in Germany as the *Fahrkunst* and in France as *echelles mobiles.* They are all alike in principle, and consist essentially of two strong beams or rods hung side by side in the shaft of a mine. Each beam has platforms or landings large enough for a man to stand upon placed at equal distances from the top to the bottom. Handles to be grasped by the hands of the men are attached at a convenient height above each platform.

They are not a modern invention, having been known in Germany during the last century; but they did not become generally used, and were almost forgotten, until about forty years ago. Since then they have been used extensively in Germany, Belgium, and Cornwall.

In the year 1833, when the deep George adit was opened in the mines of the Harz, two water-wheels were thrown out of work, and the idea was suggested of using the pump-rods attached to them for the ascent and descent of the miners. The experiment was tried. The rods were strengthened, stages or platforms were attached at suitable distances, and a regular alternate up-and-down motion was given to them by means of the wheels. It was a great success; the miners were relieved from most of the arduous labor of climbing, and even invalids, who before could not reach the lower parts of the mine, were enabled to resume their work.

The principle of the man-engine will be made more clear by reference to the annexed diagram. R R and R′ R′ represent portions of two heavy rods or beams, extending from the top to the bottom of a shaft, and suitably guided and supported throughout their length. To these rods, and at equal distances, small stages or platforms, A B C, and A′ B′ C′, are securely fixed.

An alternate upward and downward movement is given to each of these rods; while the rod R, with its stages, is ascending, the opposite rod R′ is descending. This movement brings the platform A on the rod

R opposite to the platform B′ on rod R′, and the platform B opposite the platform C′. The motion is then arrested for a moment, and is immediately afterward reversed, and the platforms return to their original position. If miners are standing upon the platforms of R, they will all be raised by the upward movement a distance equal to half the distance between the platforms. At this point, the motion ceasing, the miners step from the platforms of the rod R to those upon the rod R′, and by the next movement are again lifted, when they step across as before, and so on until the top of the shaft is reached. The descent is similarly accomplished.

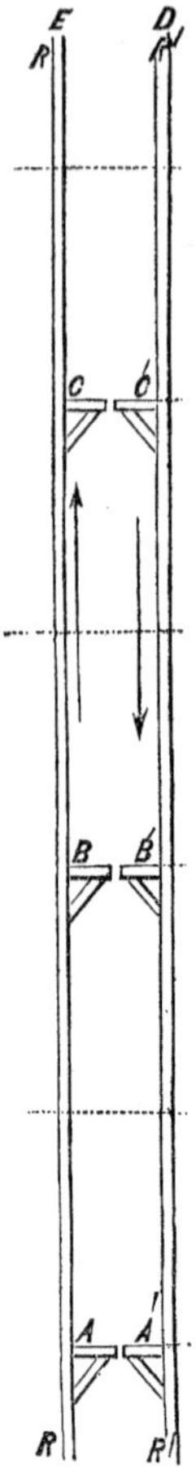

In some mines only one of the rods moves, and the other remains stationary, or rather the second rod is omitted, and stages are fixed to the side of the shaft in the rock itself; in such cases the single rod has to move the whole distance between two stages instead of half that distance, as when two rods are used.

When a single rod is used in connection with fixed stages, the miners pass alternately from the stage on the rod to the stage fixed in the rock. They then wait until the half-stroke brings a fresh stage opposite to them, on which they place themselves, and so on.

The distance between two stages on the same rod generally varies from $4^{m}.50$ to $8^{m}.00$. The stroke of the apparatus with two movable rods is always half the distance between the stages, consequently it varies from $2^{m}.25$ to $4^{m}.00$. There are from four to eight double strokes per minute.

The single-rod man-engine is the one most used in Cornwall. It makes three strokes of 12 feet each per minute. The rods are generally about seven or eight inches square, decreasing in size toward the bottom. The weight is counterbalanced by levers or by balance-bobs, attached at different levels.

Motion is imparted to the rods of the man-engine by means of water-wheels with cranks, steam-engines with crank-motion, or direct-acting steam-engines, the two rods being connected by balance-beams in such a way that their motion, though inverse, is equal and simultaneous. M. Warocqué substituted for the cumbrous balance-beams a column of water, contained between the pistons of two cylinders side by side, and connecting freely below the pistons, and made other improvements so important that the *echelles mobiles* are described in some publications as *Warocquères*.

The crank motion is particularly well suited to the movement of the man-engine, inasmuch as the velocity of the movement decreases gradually at the beginning and end, and becomes almost nothing as the crank passes the centre, thus giving time for the miner to step from one beam to the other, or from the beam to the stage fixed to the side of the shaft.

When direct-acting engines are used, there is a stoppage after each stroke to give the miners time to pass from one stand to the other. This stop varies from two to eight seconds, which is ample, as the passage from one stand to the other does not take more than one second. This would be a very good system if the stop were always rigorously the same. But all who have worked the machine with direct single action and cataract know that it is impossible to obtain this regularity. The irregularity may indeed cause accidents. The miner, relying on the normal time of the stoppage, may be surprised in the midst of the movement he is making, and as the single-action engine starts suddenly, and very quickly acquires a great velocity, he may have one leg roughly taken up while the other remains on the stage which rapidly goes down.

When the man-engines receive their reciprocal motion from a crank on a revolving shaft, there is, so to speak, no stoppage. The stages which approach each other are hardly on the same level when they separate again; but by taking care to have the machines provided with regulators and heavy fly-wheels, the movement is regular, and there is no change to surprise the miner at the moment of his passage from one stage to the other.

It must not be forgotten that the movement of the machine being uniform, that of the connecting-rod which commands the man-engine is variable. It is very slow at the commencement of its stroke, is accelerated at the middle of the stroke, and becomes slow at the end. The miner, thanks to the regularity of the movement and the slowness of speed, when the stages approach the same level and separate from each other, can begin his passage from one rod to the other a little before the stroke, and continue it a little after.

Experience proves that this second method is the safest. The persons who go down for the first time on these machines do not experience any disagreeable sensation. It is not so with the single-acting machines; when, after the stoppage, the stage lifts or lowers a person suddenly who is not accustomed to them, he experiences a disagreeable sensation, (a sinking at the stomach,) which is increased by the sudden stop at the end of the stroke. This feeling is similar to that experienced when one is lowered or "dropped" suddenly in a cage; and, with some persons, produces sickness and fainting. In the Saxon mines, at Freiberg, the movement is given by water-wheels and cranks; and there is nothing about it unpleasant or awkward to any one accustomed to life underground. The writer, after watching the movement of the rods for a few moments in one of the shafts, stepped upon and used them without difficulty. There is always this advantage to one unaccustomed to them, that if, from any cause, the step from one stage to the other is not taken in time, it is perfectly safe to remain upon the rod and be lowered and hoisted again.

Man-engines worked by direct-acting engines, in order to raise the same number of men in a given time, must move more rapidly than when the motion is communicated by a crank.

Let us suppose two man-engines, worked by these different engines, having a stroke of $3^{m}.00$ and making 6 double strokes per minute. The speed per minute is equal to $3^{m} \times 12$ strokes single $= 36^{m}$. Therefore, while the crank machine will take 60 seconds to go over these $36^{m}.00$, or a mean velocity of $0^{m}.60$, the single-acting engine will take 60 seconds diminished by 12 stoppages, which are generally of $2\frac{1}{2}$ seconds $= 30$ seconds; its speed must then be double—$1^{m}.20$. The diagrams annexed clearly indicate the difference that exists between the working of these two methods.

In these curves the abscisses represent the number of seconds from the beginning of an oscillation, and the ordinates the corresponding spaces passed over by a stage.

The machine with single action predominates in Belgium, while the crank machine is more used in Germany and England. The single-acting machines are generally placed directly over the shaft.

These engines are composed of two steam cylinders joined together;

the piston-rods are attached directly to the man-engine. The steam acts directly and alternately underneath or above one or the other of the pistons.

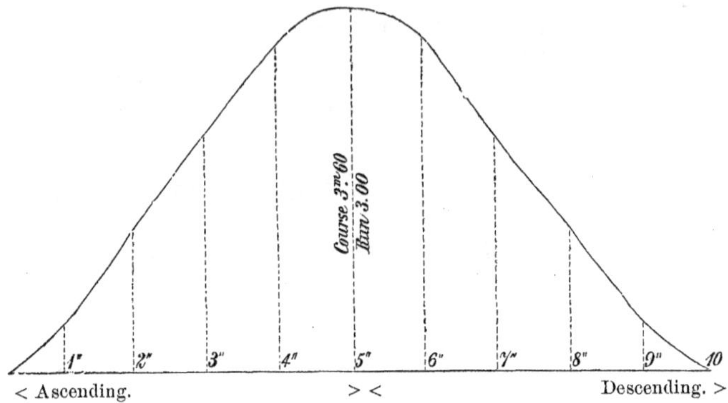

Working curve of the stage of a Man-engine when actuated by a double-acting engine.

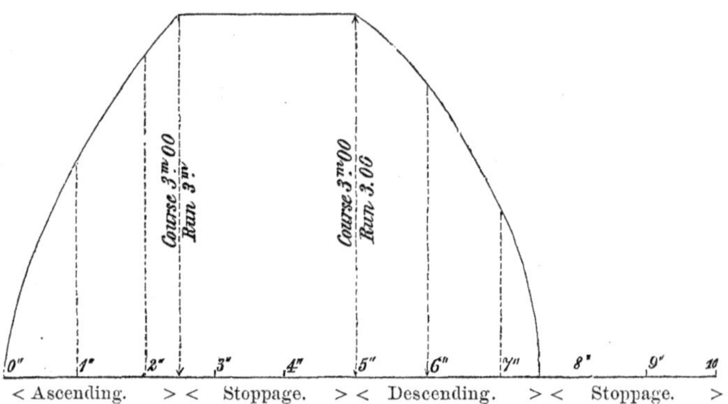

Working curve of the stage of a Single-acting engine.

But there is an important condition to be observed, which complicates this arrangement a little. The platforms of the man-engines must have exactly the same velocity, and the strokes must terminate at exactly the same moment, so that both sets of platforms will be connected. This problem has been solved in two principal ways.

One method, designed by M. Hanrez, is to connect the rods by a pinion, as shown in the annexed figure.*

A strong rack is placed on each rod, and these work into opposite sides of the same pinion, steadied by an intermediate guide-rod. Uniformity of motion has thus been secured, for it is evident that when one rod descends the other must move simultaneously and equally. Every precaution has been taken by the constructor to prevent breakage. The teeth of the pinion and the racks are strong and carefully cut; and very few accidents have occurred.

The other method consists in extending the piston-rods through the upper cover of the cylinders, so that these two rods may be connected by a chain working over a pulley. They then necessarily move simultaneously. As a pulley working between the cylinders would have too

* From Plate L, *Matériel des Houillères*, Burat.

small a diameter, two leading pulleys are placed over the cylinders surmounted by a larger one.

M. Hanrez has also proposed to do away with the racks and pinion by the substitution of two balance-beams connected with a third and central balance. The plan of rolling up and unrolling chains over pulleys is credited to M. Colson.

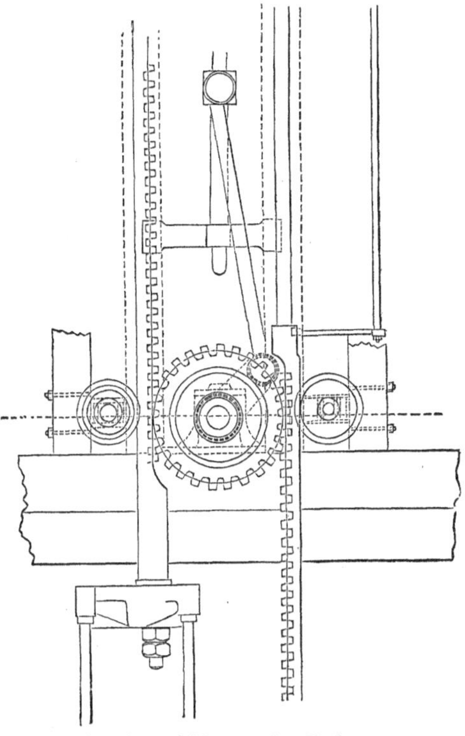

Gearing of Man-engine Rods.

When the motion is imparted, not by a direct-acting engine, as we have just been considering, but from the rotation of a crank, it is also necessary that the two rods should be connected together in order to secure an equal amplitude and speed of movement. Some of the principal methods will be briefly noticed. In general, balance-beams and varlets are worked together by a connecting rod, moved by another connecting rod, taking its motion from a gearing, the pinion of which is placed on the main shaft of the steam-engine.

The annexed figure will give an idea of this arrangement. To avoid the great expense incurred by these balances, Mr. Garffin suspends the rods to flat cables, which pass over leading pulleys, and are attached to the two extremities of a wagon rolling on rails and worked by a connecting rod moved by the engine.

An ingenious arrangement by Messrs. Vaux and Guibal has been tried, but its utility has not yet been established by practice; but it is, nevertheless, worthy of being noticed.

Two cylinders are placed above the rods, as in the direct-acting engines. The engine gives motion to a strong pump without valves, which alternately forces and draws water from the cylinders over the shaft of the mine, thus alternately raising and lowering the pistons attached to the rods of the man-engine. The result is an alternate and opposed action of the rods. This plan would be excellent if the loss of water could be prevented.

M. Colson, at one of the reunions of engineers at Hainault, Mons, described some improvements which he had made in the form and construction of the rods.*

Instead of making the rods of a continuous piece for the whole depth of the mine shaft, which requires them to be strong enough at the top to carry the whole weight of the apparatus, M. Colson divides them into a certain number of small shafts, suspended by chains to pulleys, balancing themselves two and two. These isolated rods are much lighter than in the other construction. The principal rod, extending down the

* Burat : *Matériel des Houillères.*

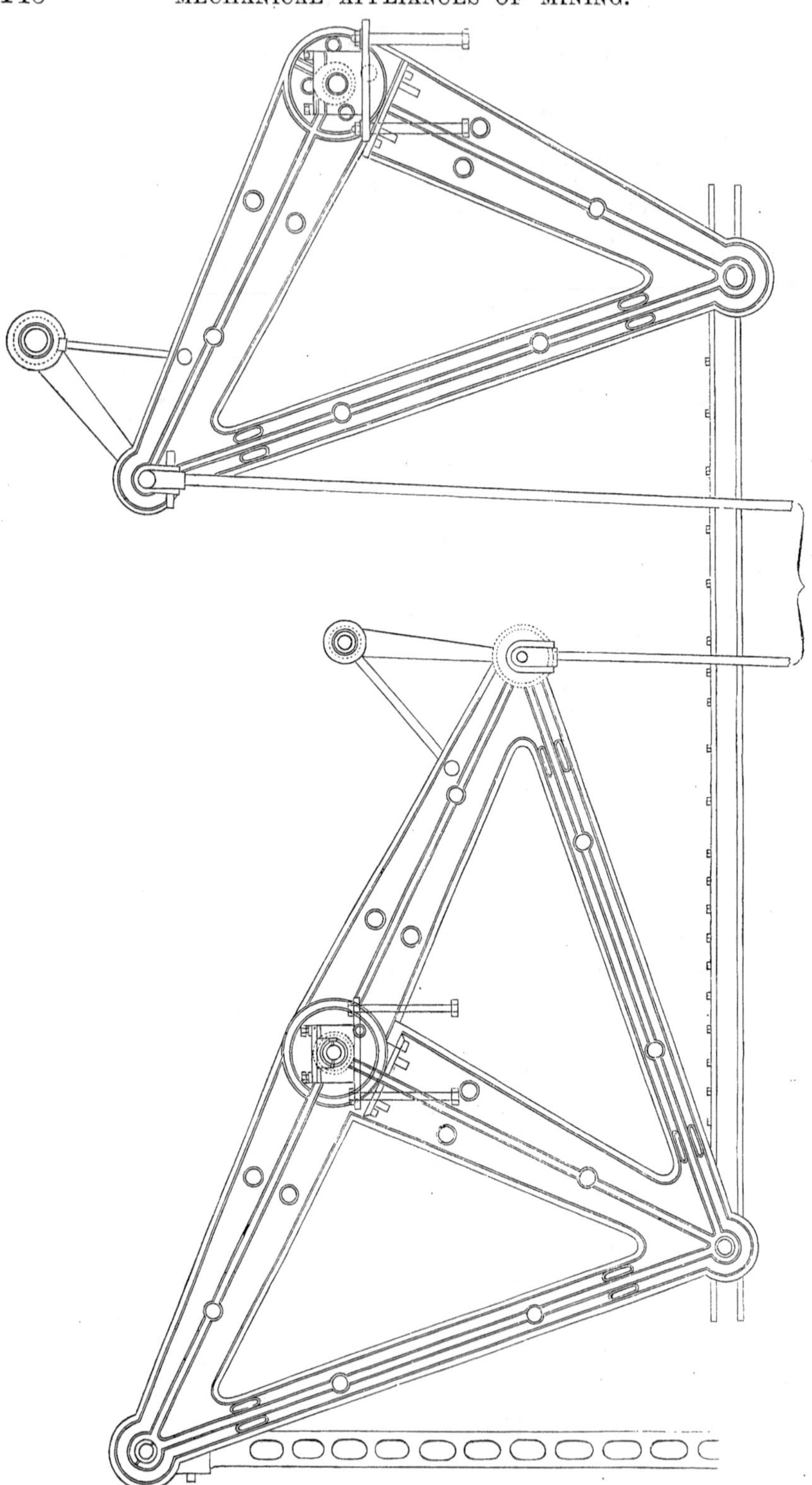

Arrangement for communicating motion to the rods of a Man-engine.

whole depth of the mine, binds the small shafts together without supporting them; therefore its strength must be proportioned only to the strain it has to overcome, which is very little compared with the strain in the man-engines with continuous rods. M. Colson gives a stroke of 10 metres, which he obtains by the alternate winding and unwinding of two cables.

The velocity of movement until now, except in the Colson machine, has never exceeded 50 metres per minute. The cost of construction varies considerably according to the construction, and, above all, according to the price of materials and labor in different countries. It varies between 75 to 200 francs a metre for a depth of 200 to 500 metres. The engines made recently are nearer the lesser price, and hardly exceed the sum of 100 francs per metre.

The power required for the movement of the man-engine varies from ten to fourteen horse-power for 100 metres of height. The amplitude of motion, as already stated, varies from $2^{m}.25$ to $4^{m}.00$, but in Colson's form it is from $10^{m}.00$ to $15^{m}.00$. In Cornwall, it is about twelve feet.

The rods.—The rods are either made of wood or of iron. Iron is lighter, with the same power of resistance, and requires less room.

Whether the rods are made of wood or of iron, they are all made with a decreasing section from the top to the bottom of the apparatus. The wooden rods are made in two ways—either of beams adjusted end to end, like the rods of lifting pumps, or they are made with planks, the ends of which are stepped together, as indicated in the annexed figure. Gradually, as the load to be carried allows of it, a plank is left out so as to reduce the weight as much as possible, and yet retain all the necessary solidity.

Iron rods have been made in various forms, but generally in the shape of angle iron. The round or flat iron has the inconvenience of allowing too much vibration, especially at the bottom.

The number of rods for each side of the man-engine may be one, two, three, or four. The single rod is generally used in the inclined shafts. It is composed of a piece of wood running on rollers at about six or eight metres apart. These rollers of wood or cast-iron are laid on sills of wood fixed in the rock.

The stages or platforms are made of planks large enough to receive both feet, and are firmly supported by iron brackets below; iron handles are securely fixed by bolts to the rods, at a height of about $1^{m}.00$ to $1^{m}.30$ above each stage, to enable the miner to keep his balance.

Where the rods are separated by fixed ladders, as in some instances, the distance required to pass over from one stage to the other varies from $0^{m}.65$ to $0^{m}.75$, which renders the apparatus incommodious and even dangerous. The stages are sometimes made large enough to carry two men at once, which permits the miners to pass each other with ease in going up and down, some ascending while others are descending; but in Freiberg the miners pass each other without much difficulty on the small and single stages.

The landing places or stages.—The stages are made of the lightest wood possible, and their dimensions vary according to the space at command; they should not be less than $0^{m}.50$ to $0^{m}.60$ square; but some are made which are only $0^{m}.40$.

But with these small dimensions they are dangerous. These stages are generally put in iron frames, which serve at the same time to bind the rods. When two stages, one on the ascending, the other on the descending rod, are level with each other, the distance which separates them varies from 0m.03 to 0m.25, and even to 0m.30.

When the space is wide, there is danger in crossing from one stage to the other, for the miner may step into the empty space and be precipitated to the bottom. But if, on the contrary, the space is very narrow, the passage is very easy, but there is danger that the miner may imprudently let his head or his shoulder project beyond the stage on which he is, so as to be struck or caught by the stage of the opposite rod during the movement.

This difficulty is avoided in two ways—either by making the stage in two pieces, one fixed and the other hinged, so that it rises when it meets with an obstacle, or in fixing under each stage inclined planks, well dressed and smoothed, which push against an obstacle and force it back within the limits of the opposite stage. This last plan can only be used where the movement of the man-engine is not too rapid; if the motion is rapid, the first is preferable.

The hinges of the stages are made either of copper or of very strong leather to avoid oxidation. In the mines of Freiberg, Saxony, the stages are not placed opposite each other, but side by side.

Balance weights and pulleys.—The rods and stages work in guides at distances which vary from twenty to fifty metres from each other. But this is not sufficient. It would not be prudent to leave such a mass, 200 to 500 metres long, suspended without any other support.

The whole weight is therefore balanced by what are called balance pulleys. They are placed two and two alongside the rods. The opposite rods are then connected by chains, which pass over these pulleys and thus sustain a part of the weight of the rods. The weight of one rod also counterbalances the weight of the other. Adjusting screw rods at the ends of the chains give the means of changing the length of the chain so as to secure the proper strain on each support or pulley. The arrangement of the rods, the central ladder-way, and the balance pulleys and chains, are shown in the annexed figure.

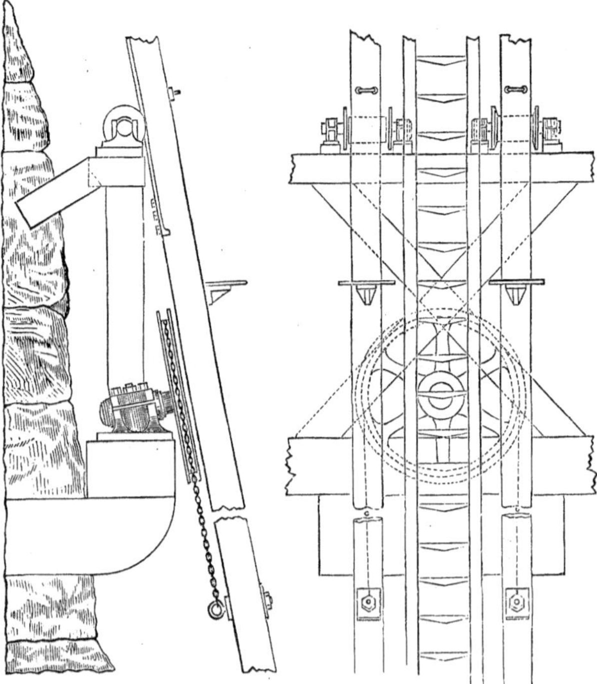

Support of the rods of the Man-engine in an inclined shaft.

The hydraulic balance has been tried for the same purpose. It is composed of two pistons: one is placed on the first set of rods, the other on the second. To these pistons two pump-barrels correspond, connected with each other by a pipe giving free communication. The descending set of rods, taking the piston with it, forces the water into the other pump-barrel, and as the water has no outlet, it forces up the other piston, lifting the other set of rods with it.

The hydraulic balance would be very good if the packing of the piston could be kept tight. Unfortunately it cannot; water is lost, and then the descending piston does not transmit its pressure to the rising piston before some part of the stroke is lost, so that the balance is disturbed. It has been abandoned for this reason. When the man-engine is single-acting—that is to say, where there is not more than one rod and the other rod is replaced by a line of fixed stages—the rod must be balanced to prevent the shock it would receive at the bottom by the impetus gained during its descent. This balance can be obtained by chains attached at different heights of the lift, passing them over pulleys attached to the rock and attaching to their ends counterpoises of sufficient weight. Such an arrangement is very dangerous from the liability of the chains to breakage.

In England such pulleys are replaced by beams carrying balance weights; but although this arrangement is safer, it is much more expensive. The stroke, always a long one with a man-engine, requires beams of large dimensions, and they cannot be lodged in the shaft without making very large excavations in the rock, which are very expensive.

Hydraulic regulators.—To regulate the descent, a hydraulic regulator or brake is also used. It is a pump furnished with a suction-valve, and the outlet of the pump is furnished with a tap. The piston of this pump is fixed to the shaft of the lift; when this latter rises the pump fills with water; when the piston falls the water can only escape by the small opening, and the issue can be regulated by the tap. The rapidity of descent may thus be varied at will.

Operation of the man-engine.—We may now compare the different methods for the ascent and descent of miners, and note the great saving of time and strength resulting from the use of the man-engine.*

To go down 100 metres of ladder requires about 15 minutes, (900 seconds,) equal to 9 seconds per metre. If we suppose that the men follow each other at 2 metres distance, after the first man has arrived at the bottom of the shaft it will be 18 seconds before the second man gets to the bottom, and so on; so that, if the shift is composed of 200 men, it will require 900 seconds + (200 × 18 seconds) = 900 + 3,600 seconds = 4,500 seconds, or 1 hour 15 minutes, for them all to descend to the bottom.

If the shaft is 400 metres deep, 15 minutes per 100 metres must be added for the descent of the first man, which makes altogether 2 hours for 200 men. With this basis for calculation it is easy to find the time required for the descent of any number of men to any given depth.

The ascent of 100 metres of ladder requires about twice as much time as the descent; then, if we take the depth of 400 metres, and the number of men 200, we have for the descent by ladders 2 hours, and for the ascent 4 hours—in all 6 hours, which, added to 8 hours' work per shift, makes 14 hours, during 6 hours of which the work in ascending and descending is much harder than the actual mining.

It is impossible for men to continue to perform such labor, so that in most mines over 250 metres deep the hours of real work are shortened and the balance of the time is set apart for the work of ascending and descending.

* This comparison as well as other details respecting the man-engine are taken from the Exposition reports.

The Polytechnic Society of Cornwall, in comparing the rate of mortality among men working at different depths, (accidents deducted,) estimates that in works of 400 to 500 metres in depth, where ladders are used, the lives of the men are shortened by twenty years. However this may be, it is certain that the prolonged use of ladders gives rise to serious derangements of the organs of respiration, and renders a certain number of men unfit for work before they are thirty years old.

The time required for lowering and raising a shift of men by cables is not as easy to estimate as that required where ladders alone are used. It depends, in fact, on two variable elements—the rate of speed, and the number of men that can be lifted at each time.

The rate of speed varies according to the importance of the workings; in shafts without guides it is often from one to two metres per second; in shafts provided with guides and cages, it is from three to twelve metres per second; but when the men are taken up and down in the cages, the speed is often slackened, keeping it about three to six metres per second. The number of men carried at once is from two to three in the small workings, and sixteen to twenty, or more, in mines of greater extent.

A comparison of the time required for the descent by ladders and by lowering in cages may be made as follows: Assuming that there are 200 men in a shift and that the depth is 400 metres, the rate of speed, averaging, say five metres, and that eight men are carried at once—at five metres per second, to ascend or descend 400 metres requires $\frac{400}{5}=80$ seconds. To this must be added about two minutes (120 seconds) for the stepping in and out of the men, and the starting and stopping of the engine, which makes altogether $120+80=200$ seconds. Lowering 8 men at once, we have $\frac{200}{8}=25$ journeys in all for the shift; the time will therefore be 25×200 seconds $=5,000$ seconds $=1$ hour 24 minutes. Doubling this for the entire time in going into and out of the mine, will be 2 hours 48 minutes, which is half the time taken for the ascent and descent of the same number of men by ladders. But these figures are not absolute; they may vary widely, either more or less, according to the extent of the workings.

The advantages and disadvantages of the rope are inversely to those of the ladders; the health of the men does not suffer, but there is less security, and accidents are much more serious.

Accidents by ropes and by ladders are as 3 to 2; but this ratio is still increased by the fact that of 100 accidents to men, 94 are killed and 6 injured.

These deplorable consequences from this method of transportation of miners caused the Prussian government to prohibit the lowering or raising of men by the cages in the mines of Prussia.

In order to estimate the time required for the ascent and descent of miners by the man-engine, let us take our standard example, 400 metres of depth, and 200 men to send down or lift up for each shift.

Allowing the stages to be 6 metres distant from each other, and the man-engine to make 6 double strokes per minute, in one minute a man will then have passed upon and from 6 stages; he will then have been lifted $6^{m}.00 \times 6=36^{m}.00$, and consequently will rise the 400 metres; in $\frac{400}{36}=12$ minutes, in round numbers. Each double stroke thereafter will deliver another man at the surface, or, which is the same thing, the machine will lift 6 men per minute; the 200 men will therefore arrive at the surface in $\frac{200}{6}=34$ minutes in round numbers, which, added to the 12 minutes required for the whole ascent of the first man on the stages, gives in all 46 minutes; doubling this for the lowering and lifting of one shift of men, and we have 92 minutes (1 hour and 32 minutes) for the whole, and that without either danger or fatigue. So that for 200 men and 400 metres of depth, the ascent by ladders requires 6 hours; by hoisting, varying from 1 to 4 hours; by the man-engine, only 1½ hour.

The fitting up of a man-engine is doubtless a considerable expense, but it is soon repaid by the time saved, and the prevention of muscular fatigue of the miner.

For further details respecting the construction and working of man-engines reference may be made to the following-named works, from which a part of the information here presented has been compiled: Burat's Matériel des Houillères; Portefeuille de Cockerill; Zeitschrift des œsterreichischen Ingenieur-Vereins, 10ter Jahrgang; Annales des Travaux Publics de Belgique, vols. 4 and 6; Annales des Mines de France, 5me, vol. xv; Revue Universelle, vols. iv, v, vi, xiv, xvi.

CHAPTER XIII.

VENTILATION.

Very few of the mines of the West are so deep and extensive as to require any elaborate and extensive contrivances for their proper ventilation. In most cases, their position and construction are such that a current of air circulates spontaneously through them by reason of one of the openings being at a greater altitude than some other, as, for example, one or more shafts with tunnels leading to them from the hill-side. If the air in the mine is warmer than that outside, it rises in the shaft, and is replaced by the influx of the colder air through the tunnel. But the conditions essential to ventilation in this way are not always found, and it becomes necessary to resort to artificial means to supply the miners at the extreme points of the mine with fresh air. In driving long tunnels, especially where powder is used, the air is rapidly vitiated, and soon becomes unfit to breathe.

There are two ways in which ventilation may be effected, either by *drawing* the impure air out, or by *forcing* pure air in. A good example of the first-named method was presented at the Latrobe tunnel, Virginia City, which was driven for the greater part of the distance without a ventilating shaft, one only having been sunk not far from the entrance. Tin pipes were first used to convey the air and were placed along the top of the tunnel extending from a few yards back of the face to the bottom of the air-shaft. But it was found difficult to maintain a good draught, and the metal pipe was replaced with one of wood, made of boards about eight inches wide, and rabbeted so as to form tight joints. With this arrangement no difficulty was experienced; the heated air at the end of the tunnel escaped constantly through this tube and rose in the shaft, while the pure air from the outside flowing in at the mouth of the tunnel took its place. In this instance it was evident that the non-conducting quality of the wood prevented the air from becoming cooled in its passage before it reached the shaft.

The method of producing a draught by means of a fire or by connecting the ventilating pipes with the ash pit of the furnace fires is well known and is often resorted to on a small scale in California.

The only example of mechanical ventilation worthy of special mention which came under the writer's observation in California was at the Princeton gold mine, Mariposa Estate. Foul air was generated to such an extent in the southern part of the mine that it could not be entered. A simple centrifugal fan-wheel, about ten feet in diameter and two feet wide, was erected over the nearest shaft. This fan-wheel was not inclosed, but revolved between two vertical temporary walls of boards, thus leaving the arms and fans fully exposed to view. The mouth of the shaft was tightly closed, excepting two openings connected by box tubes with large openings in the walls of boards, around the axis of the fan-wheel. When this wheel was put in motion by a band from the engine, it produced a strong current of air up the shaft, and cleared the workings of foul air in a short time. It was evident that a much smaller blower would have answered the purpose.

For *forcing* pure air into tunnels and drifts of slight extent an ordinary wind-sail or a fan-wheel driven by hand or attached to the horse-whim is usually employed; but these, of course, from their want of forcing power, are not very effective. The object in using them in most cases is not so much to supply pure air as to give a cooling current or blast of air near the workmen.

In several of the mines upon the Comstock lode, the "Indiana Blower," Root's rotary compression blower, is used with great success in ventilating. Mr. James G. Fair, superintendent of the Hale and Norcross Silver Mining Company in March, 1869, had the blower in constant use, day and night, since its adoption by the company in August, 1868. Although of only medium size, it supplied sufficient air to enable them by the use of branch pipes and dampers to prospect simultaneously at different depths, and at considerable distances apart upon the same level. It furnished air to two gangs of miners in separate drifts on the 1,030-foot level, and partially ventilated the level 100 feet above that, and with but a portion of the power the blower could have utilized.

The Potosi Company have had a No. 2 blower for ventilating the levels below the 900-foot station; and they have been successfully used upon the Yellow Jacket mine since the great fire. Mr. Winters, the superintendent, in August last, in a letter to the agents, said, "I have great pleasure in stating that they work admirably. If we had been without them, it would have been quite impossible to work our mine since the great fire in this and the adjoining mines."

This blower gives a "positive" or force-blast, taking in and forcing forward a definite quantity of air at each revolution. Its construction is shown by the figures annexed.

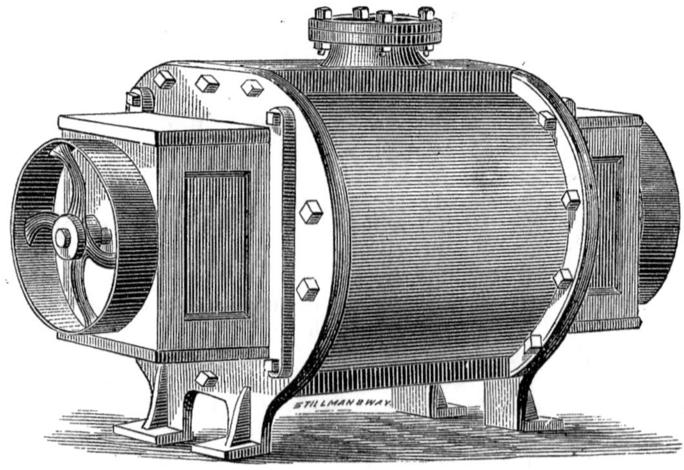

Root's Rotary Compression Blower—exterior.

The first figure shows the external form of the case, and pulleys at each end for the reception of driving-belts. The cross-section of the interior shows the inlet and outlet and the form of the arms or wings. The case is usually made of cast-iron, with the cylindrical parts bored out, and the head-plates faced off truly upon a boring-mill, arranged for the purpose. The friction is confined to the journals and cog-wheels. The arms or wings do not touch in running, but move as closely together as possible without being actually in contact. They are about two feet long and make from 100 to 300 revolutions a minute. A machine exhibited at the Paris Exposition was said to produce a pressure equal to one-third of an atmosphere, or five pounds to the square inch, when driven at the rate of 250 turns per minute.

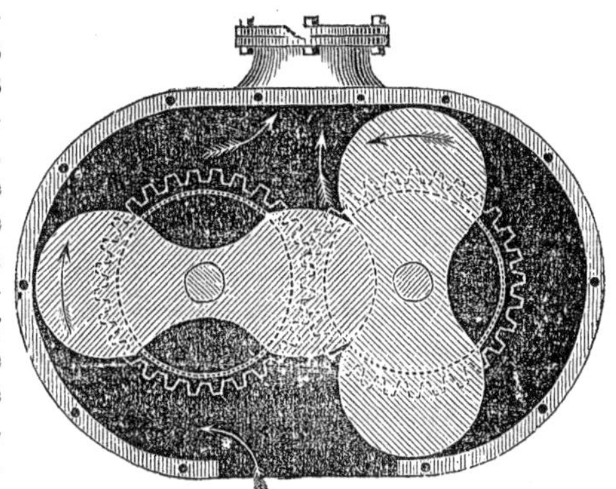

Root's Blower—cross section.

In the coal mines of Pennsylvania more and more attention is now given to ventilation, as not only the ordinary difficulties of working, but also the liability to accumulations of dangerous gases increase with the depth of the mines. The different systems of natural and artificial ventilation, including the use of the furnace, steam-jet, and blower, have been vigorously discussed during the past year or two by Messrs. Rothwell and Harden, mining engineers of Wilkesbarre, in the columns of the New York Engineering and Mining Journal. The latter gentleman seems to esteem the furnace more highly than the former, who in most cases prefers fans. The arguments on both sides were interesting and valuable; and those directed against the furnace were emphasized shortly afterward by the terrible catastrophe at Avondale, where apparatus of this kind set fire to a column of gas and burned the brattice of the shaft and the breaker over it, closing the only entrance to the mine and sacrificing a large number of lives. A fan has been substituted for the furnace at Avondale; yet under some circumstances a fan is inferior. For instance, when a fan is disabled or interrupted its effect ceases at once. Thus, at some critical moment in a mine, or in some very fiery mine, where every moment is a critical one, the fan ventilation might instantly and totally cease, while a furnace, though neglected or interrupted, would continue to act, though with diminishing effect, for hours. The precaution of maintaining a duplicate fan always in reserve is calculated to remove the objection.

MECHANICAL VENTILATION OF MINES ABROAD.

For the extensive collieries of Great Britain and the continent of Europe powerful means of ventilation are required, and the subject receives great attention among mining engineers and constructors. The miners not only have to contend with the air vitiated by their own respiration, by the animals employed, and by the lamps, but the coal beds themselves give off large volumes of deleterious gases, and the dreaded fire-damp, the collier's great destroyer. Coal mines therefore require more elaborate and costly preparations for ventilation than any other.

The mean depth of the English coal mines is 180 metres; of those in Belgium, at Charleroi, 360 metres; at Centre, 350 metres; and at Mons, 416 metres.

A few years ago nearly all the important collieries of England were ventilated by means of furnaces placed near or at the bottom of ventilating shafts, by which the air was rarefied and made to ascend. In such furnaces, from ten to twenty tons of coal were burned daily. This required large furnaces and costly excavations, and galleries of large size for the air-courses. In Belgium and France mechanical ventilation has been carried to a great degree of perfection. This system is said to be well established by experience as much cheaper and less dangerous than the use of furnaces, and is gradually replacing the furnace ventilation.

Mechanical ventilators may be grouped in three classes: 1, centrifugal ventilators, or fans; 2, rotary pumps, or force-blowers; 3, piston machines, with reciprocating motion.

Ventilators of the first class are of great dimensions, capable of delivering immense volumes of air. They have been in use for about thirty years, and have undergone many changes and improvements. Like most other ventilators, they act by aspiration, producing to a certain extent throughout the mine a lower barometric pressure than is found in the external air. This depression varies in general from five to seven centimetres of water.

Guibal's ventilator.—Guibal's ventilator, after having undergone many

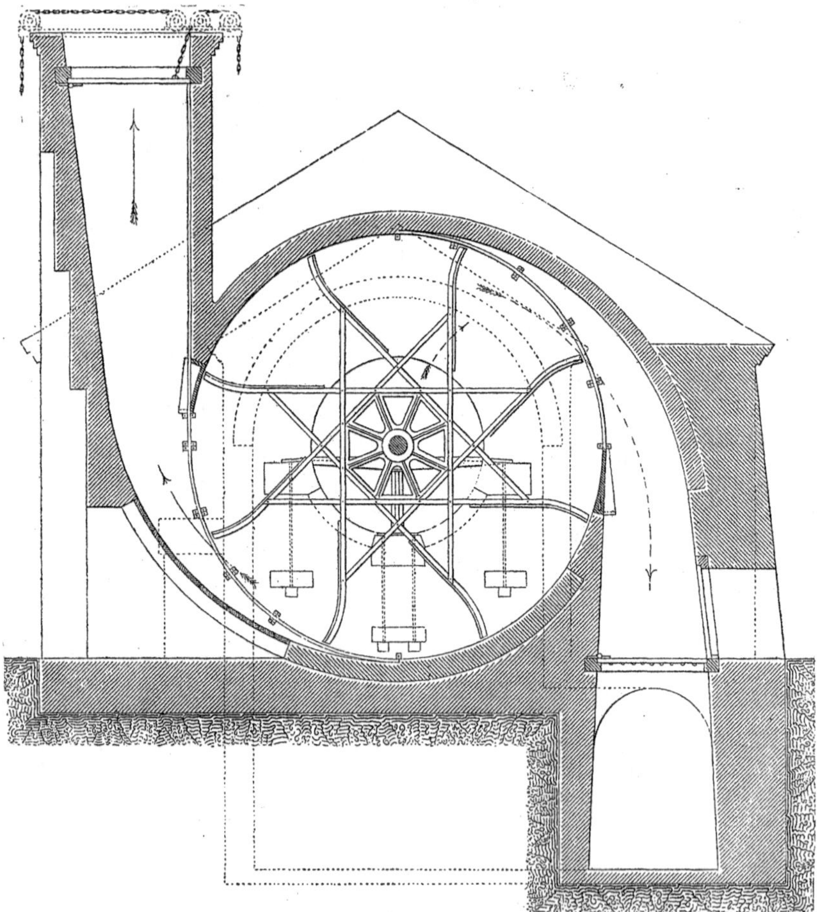

Guibal's Ventilator—section.

changes and improvements through a series of years, is now most in favor. It is made with a diameter of 7 to 9 metres, and is inclosed for three quarters of its circumference. The other quarter has a movable valve, so that the size of the delivery opening can be varied at will. The air of the mine is received by a central opening, of which the diameter is equal to that of the shaft, and it is thrown out through a vertical chimney, the sectional area of which increases as it ascends, in order that the current may enter the outer air with a progressively reduced velocity. These ventilators are also used to throw air into the mine by reversing the current.

The construction shown in the section is that of the ventilator established by M. Guibal at the Blanzy mines. It has two chimneys, one for delivering the air from the mine upward, and the other for a reverse movement when it is required to take the air from the surface and force it downward into the mine. In this case a valve or door at the top of the chimney closes the opening, and when the fan is used to throw the air out of the mine the reversed chimney is closed by a similar door. This form of ventilator was formerly made open without an envelope or outer case; but it was soon found that much of the power was lost by re-entering currents of air.

In 1862, M. Guibal sent to the London Exhibition the plan of a ventilator capable of displacing 100 cubic metres of air per second. This required a fan nine metres in diameter and four metres wide.

The engineers of the Blanzy mines, guided by a long experience with Duvergier's ventilator, have adopted a machine with the axis vertical. The fan turns in a pit lined with masonry and covered over. The air is drawn in from below and is thrown out through an opening to a chimney at the side. It is about 30 feet in diameter, and is known as the Audemar ventilator.

FAN-BLOWERS.

To this same class of ventilators belong the great variety of the ordinary fan-blowers, and it will be sufficient for the objects of this notice to mention only one or two of these, which have been used to some extent in mining.

Lloyd's noiseless fan.—Lloyd's noiseless fan, an end view of which is shown in the figure, consists of a hollow drum, made of two cones of thin metal, and divided radially by curved partitions, extending from

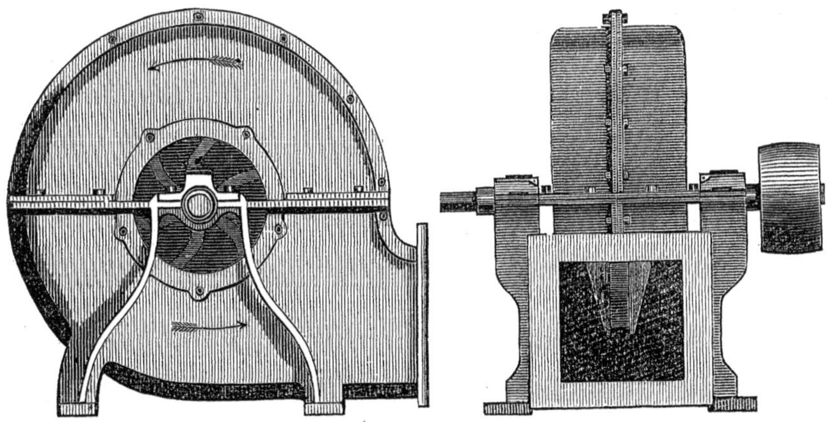

Lloyd's Noiseless Fan.

the axis of revolution to the periphery. Its construction much resembles that of Appold's pump. The air is taken in by openings at the centre around the shaft, and discharged between the partitions at the circumference. It is made of various sizes, from thirteen inches to four feet in diameter; the smallest are run with the velocity of 1,800 to 2,000 feet per minute, and the largest 800 or 1,000. When used as an aspirator in mines, the surrounding box is not required.

Schiele's fan.—Schiele's compound blowing fan consists of two fans resembling Lloyd's, and acting successively upon the same air. The first fan drives it into a chamber between the fans at a pressure of about six ounces; the second compresses the air still more, so that at the delivery pipe it has a pressure of about twelve ounces per square inch. A ventilator upon this principle was used in the ventilation of the Exposition building at Paris, 1867.

It is well to note here that for the purposes of aspiration of air from mines, where great volumes of air are to be moved at a low velocity, and through large galleries and drifts, the large centrifugal blowers or fans are well adapted; but for forcing air in through narrow pipes or conduits, where large volumes cannot pass, velocity and pressure are required, and for this purpose the compression or force-blowers of the second class are preferable.

ROTARY COMPRESSION VENTILATORS ABROAD.

Of the second class, the rotary compression ventilators, Fabry's and Lemielle's appear to be the most used. Fabry's consists of two interlocking wheels, with three arms, the extremities of which are in the form of a cross, with epicycloidal arcs, the surfaces of which, coming in close proximity or contact with each other, carry forward a volume of air equal to the inclosed spaces at each revolution. These ventilators are generally $1^{m}.70$ in diameter, and from $2^{m}.00$ to $3^{m}.00$ long.

Lemielle's ventilator.—Lemielle's ventilator revolves horizontally. For 20 to 25 revolutions per minute, and a delivery of 30 to 40 cubic metres of air a second, the diameter should be 7 metres and the height 5 metres.

Cooke's ventilator.—Mr. Cooke, of England, has recently proposed a ventilator of the same class. It is described in "Engineering," from which I condense the following description:

The machine is of a size suitable for a 1,000-feet pit, and it is intended to yield, per minute, 180,000 cubic feet of air, with an exhaustion equal to 3 inches of water; or 150,000 cubic feet, with an exhaustion of 4 inches; or 120,000 cubic feet if the drag is increased to 5 inches of water.

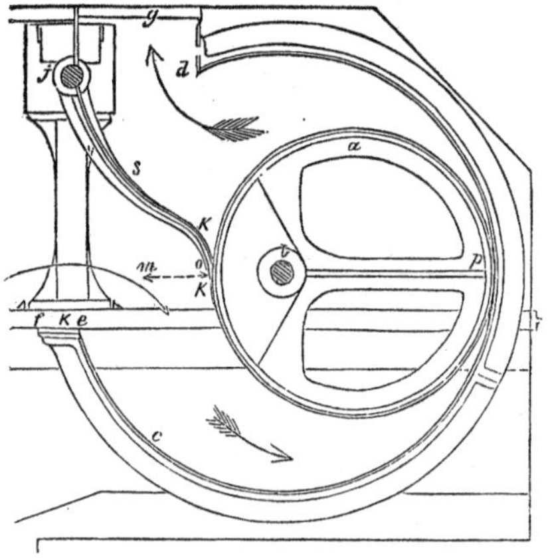

Cooke's Ventilator.

It consists of two drums, *a*, each 8 feet in diameter and 16 feet in length, these drums being mounted eccentrically on the shafts *l*. The amount of eccentricity of each drum is 2 feet, and each as it revolves thus moves in contact—or almost in contact—with a cylindrical casing, *c*, of 6 feet radius. The casings, *c*, are closed at the ends by the brick walls which form the side of the apparatus, these walls being coated with plaster over those portions against which the ends of the drums, *a*, work, and being connected at the top by the covering. The casings are not complete cylinders, each being open for a portion of its circumference, *d e*. The air from the mine is led to the apparatus by the shaft, which communicates with the space surrounding the casings, and it is drawn into these casings, and finally discharged at openings by the action of the revolving drums, *a*, in a manner which we shall now proceed to explain.

The portion of the casing left often is closed by a vibrating arm or "shutter," *s*, hung by the upper edge at *j*, and the lower edge of which is kept closely in contact with the surface of the revolving eccentric cylinder by means of an arm keyed upon a prolongation of the shaft *j*, beyond the side of the machine.

Each arm is 6 feet long between centers, this length corresponding to the distance between the center of the shaft, *j*, and the center, *m*, from which the curve of the lower part of the shutter, *j k*, is struck. In fact the center of each arm agrees exactly in position with the center, *m*, to which it corresponds. On one end of each of the main axles, *b*, is fixed a crank, each crank having a 2-foot throw, and the center of its crank-pin exactly corresponding in position with the center of the eccentric drum on the same shaft. Each of these cranks is connected by a link to the end of the corresponding rocking arm, and as the length of this link is equal to the radius of the drum, *a*, added to the radius *m o*, of the lower part of the corresponding shutter, *j k*, it follows that each shutter is kept in constant contact with the drum to which it belongs. The lower edge, *k*, of each shutter sweeps over a curved surface of plaster, *e f*, this plaster, which is held in a hollow casting as shown, enabling a sufficiently tight joint to be made very readily.

The action of the apparatus, which we can best describe by considering the motion of one drum only, is as follows: When the moving parts are in the position directly opposite to that shown in the section, the communication between the interior of the casing, *c*, and the space surrounding it is closed by the shutter, *j k'*; but as the drum, *a*, moves round in the direction of the arrows, the lower end of the shutter, *j k*, gradually approaches the shaft, *b*, and a space is thus opened between its lower edge, *k*, and the edge, *e*, through which the air can enter the casing, *c*, this opening reaching its maximum area when the parts are in the positions shown. As the drum continues its motion, the shutter, *j k*, returns again toward the position, *j k'*, and the air which has entered the casing is swept round to the discharge opening, *g*. The curved surface, *e f*, is made of such length that the lower edge, *k*, of the shutter keeps in contact with it during the time that the point, *p*, of the drum, *a*, (the point of greatest eccentricity,) is passing between the points *d* and *e* of the circumference of the casing—and in fact somewhat longer—thus preventing any back leakage.

The two drums, *a*, are so connected to the engine as to be moving always in contrary directions. One reason for this is, that the air contained between each drum and the interior of its cylinder is nearly a complete crescent, and consequently much smaller at the horns than in the middle. By having a second drum working at the horns when the first is working at the middle of its crescent of air, the two drums are made together to give an equable stream of air in the shaft. A second reason for adopting this plan is, that convenient sizes for mine ventilators are apt to be too long, and if the weight is to be divided this plan admits of the convenient disposition of the engine, while, at the same time, doubling the bearings of the machine. A third reason is, that although the drums are perfectly balanced as respects their own rotation, there remains the reciprocation of the shutters and their levers and connecting rods, which, instead of introducing vibration into the machine, are by this means made to compensate each other through the girders upon which they respectively act. A fourth reason, not unimportant in large machines, is, that the shutter as adopted in the plan (the small weight of this shutter being as much as possible concentrated near the axis, so as to assist its pendulous action, and diminish as much as possible the travel of its center of oscillation) has the pressure of the air on one side only, and consequently puts a certain strain upon its connecting rod, which, by this duplicate arrangement, exactly counterbalances that upon the connecting rod of the other machine, the strain of course passing through the side rods from one drum to the other. When the machine is not duplicated it is proposed to place a balance weight near the axis of the shutter, at the same time partially balancing the pressure of the air, and making the shutter vibrate more in harmony with the revolutions of the drum. The next thing to be observed is that the opening on the top of each machine is equal to the extreme opening of the shutter into the cylinder internally. The machine whose shutter is in this position is at its greatest work while the shutter of the other machine is closed, and consequently no work is for a moment going on there. It will also be noticed that the openings which have been spoken of are much greater than half the area of the shaft to which the machine is applied. This is to avoid giving the air a higher average velocity in any part of its passage through the machine than that prevailing in the shaft. The machine acting on the thick part of the crescent doing much more than half the whole work then going on, the opening has been proportioned, so as to realize the required velocity.

The shafts, *b*, are provided at one end with cranks, which are coupled to a crank of equal throw fixed at the end of the crank shaft of a horizontal engine placed by the side of the apparatus. The motion is thus communicated from the engine to the drums in the same manner as the coupled wheels of a locomotive are driven, a simple arrangement which will no doubt be found to work well. The arrangement also allows either drum to be disconnected, when it requires to be stopped, without necessitating the continued stoppage of the other. This advantage is sufficient in fiery mines, at least, to justify the precaution.

We think that the particulars we have given of Mr. Cooke's ventilator will show that the machine possesses many features that render it entitled to the careful attention of those interested in mine ventilation. The apparatus consists of but few parts, and those are all of simple construction, and are subjected to nothing more than very ordinary wear and tear. The eccentric drums are of sheet iron, $\frac{3}{32}$-inch thick, supported by cast-iron eccentrics, which also form the balance weights. The casings in which the drums work are also of sheet iron $\frac{1}{8}$-inch thick, stiffened by ribs; while the side walls of the apparatus are of brick, and have cast-iron columns built into them to support the plummer blocks. As the drums revolve barely in contact with the casing and flaps they will be subjected to little or no wear so long as the bearings of the shafts, &c., are kept properly adjusted, and these bearings being all fully exposed to view there is no reason why they should be neglected. Indeed, one of the great practical advantages of the arrangement is that all the wearing parts are completely open for inspection.

Upon the performance of this blower in model, "Engineering" remarks:

This model represented, to the scale of 1 inch to the foot, the ventilator we illustrate, and it was tested against a 25-inch Lloyd's fan, by employing an engine to drive the model and fan alternately, full steam being admitted to the engine and the boiler being kept blowing off in each case. Under these circumstances the maximum pressure against which the fan was found to deliver air was equal to 9⅝ inches of water, while Mr. Cooke's ventilator blew well against a pressure of 22 inches, beyond which the engine power was insufficient to drive it. In another experiment the model, although driven through a belt and gearing, was found to utilize 78 per cent. of the indicated power of engine when exhausting against a drag of 6 inches of water. This is a very high duty, all things considered, but at the same time we see no reason—judging from the construction of the apparatus—why an equally good result should not be obtained from the trial of the machine on a large scale. The fans which have been applied for ventilating purposes have been found to yield an effective duty of from 40 to 55, or in some cases nearly 60 per cent. of the power applied; but the efficiency, even of the best fans, varies very materially at different speeds and under different circumstances, and, moreover, unless used on the duplex system—that is, one for receiving and condensing the air delivered by another—they cannot be conveniently worked against high pressures. Mr. Cooke's ventilator, on the other hand, appears well adapted for working against much higher pressures than are ever wanted for mine ventilation, and we believe that in a slightly modified form it might be advantageously employed for supplying blast to cupola furnaces and for similar purposes.

Root's compression blower.—Root's compression rotary blowers, in use in our mines, and already described, belong to this class, and for simplicity and effectiveness compare favorably with either of the above.

Evrard's blower.—Evrard's compression blower may also be noticed here. It is constructed upon the same principle as the rotary steam-engine of Breval. Two cylinders of equal length, and whose radii are as two to one, revolve in contact, one rolling upon the other, except where two cycloidal indents in the smaller cylinder receive in succession each of four projections or pallets upon the larger.

Thirion's hydraulic pressure blower.—Of the third class—machines with a reciprocating movement—Thirion's hydraulic pressure blower is worthy of special mention; and this notice I extract from the report of President Barnard: *

Still a third compression ventilator appeared in the Exposition, which, for its simplicity and its originality, seems to merit notice. It is called by the exhibitor, Mr. Thirion, of Mirecourt, France, a *machine soufflante à colonne d'eau*, but the water referred to in the name served no other purpose but to pack the moving parts and prevent friction. The figure annexed will serve to render the construction intelligible.

Three cylinders are here seen, side by side. The two lateral ones are the compressors, and the middle one the regulator. One of the compressors is shown in section. A is a cylinder of wood or sheet metal, as may be convenient, bolted to the base which sustains the whole. Within this is another cylinder, and between the two is an annular space which may be filled to any level desired with water. The water level in the figure is shown at O. Between these two cylinders is suspended an inverted cylinder,

* Machinery and Processes of the Industrial Arts, pp. 193–196.

or cylinder open downward but closed at top, which enters the annular space between the two cylinders first named, without touching either. In the top of this suspended cylinder are two valves, E and E, which open inward. A cap is placed on the central

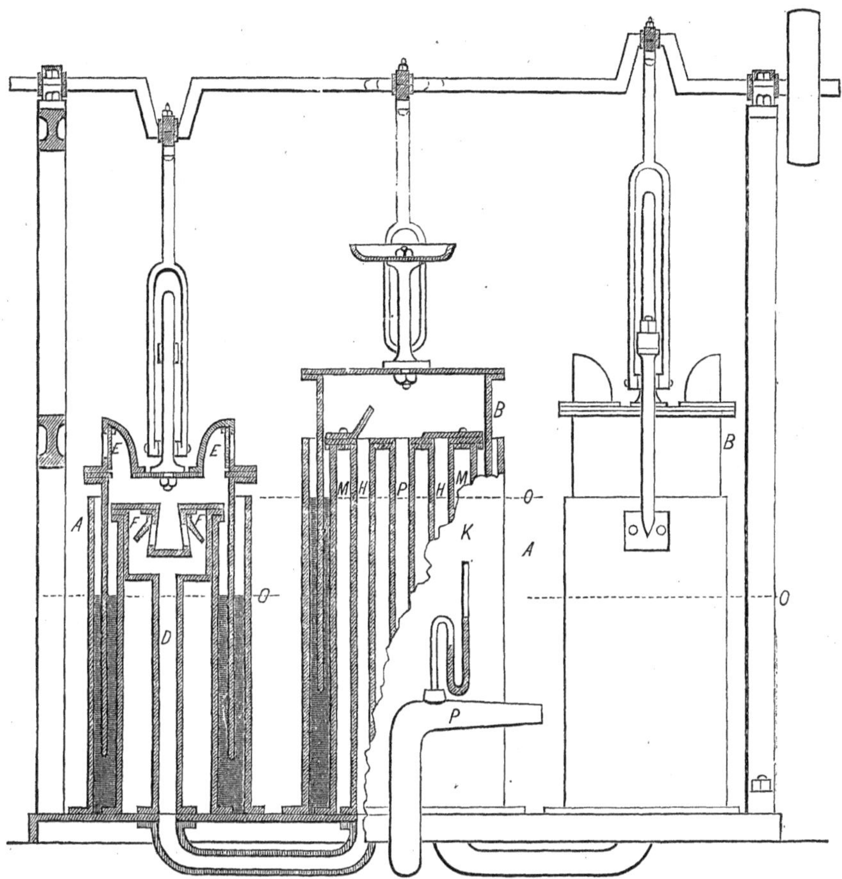

Thirion's Hydraulic Pressure Blower.

cylinder within, and in a valve-box beneath this are two other valves, F and F, which open outward as shown. From the closed space into which these valves open descends a pipe D, which communicates beneath the base by means of the recurved and rising tube H, with the regulator. The action of the machine will now be easily understood, it being observed that the regulator is constructed on the plan of the compressor so far as that the cylinder B, which is closed above and open below, descends into an annular space containing water, like the suspended cylinder of the compressor. The cylinder B, however, is not suspended, but is simply kept in an upright position by a guiding rod proceeding from the centre of its crown. It has also a scale pan above it to receive pressure weights, and should have a safety valve, though none is shown in the figure. The movable cylinder of the compressor is suspended from a crank or eccentric on the driving shaft of a prime mover. As in the revolution of the shaft the cylinder is lifted, air enters by the valves E, which spontaneously open. As the cylinder descends the valves E close, and the valves F are opened by the pressure of the contained air which is condensed by the force of the motor. The condensed air then finds an escape through D and enters the regulator through H. At the top of H is a valve which is represented as raised by the entering currents. The cylinder B rises to give room for the entering air, the pressure remaining constant and being dependent on the weight with which the scale pan is loaded. The second compressor acts alternately with the first; so that a stream of air is constantly entering the reservoir from one or the other. A tube P, from the centre of the regulator, descending below the base, conducts the blast to the point where it is needed, and where it is delivered through a tuyere, P. A siphon gauge, attached to this tuyere shows the pressure of the air at the efflux. Of course, as the pressure is increased, the level of the water within and without the movable cylinders, both of the compressors and of the regulator, will become unequal; and the maximum pressure attainable will be only equal to the vertical height between the top of the fixed cylinder A and the bottom of the movable cylinder when at its highest point. If the water in A is in too great quantity to admit of such a pressure it will run over until the pressure is attained. If it is in deficiency, the maximum cannot be attained, but the air at some pressure inferior to the maximum will begin to escape from beneath the bell. These statements are founded on the supposition that the suspended cylinder, or bell, divides the annular space into which it enters equally. Greater pressure may be obtained by the use of a liquid heavier than water; and, for powerful blasts Mr. Thirion proposes to employ mercury. With water he obtains a pressure of ninety-five centimetres, (about three feet,) or say a pound and a half to the square inch. Substituting mercury, there might be obtained, with half the difference of level, two-thirds of an atmosphere. The pressure of a pound and a half, however, is about four times that which is furnished by a good ventilating fan, and higher than is commonly used in cupola furnaces.

This machine has four very decided recommendations. It works almost without friction or leakage; the deterioration by wear is inappreciable; the perfect and exact regulation of the pressure is easy; and finally, the excellence of its performance depends in no degree upon precision of workmanship. It is a machine, therefore, which is especially adapted to the exigencies of furnaces in new countries and among the mountains, since it can be easily constructed on the spot, and will give no trouble in consequence of derangements.

CHAPTER XIV.

SAFETY LAMPS, AND FIRES IN MINES.

As connected with the subject of ventilation, the following notices of the principles upon which safety lamps depend for their efficacy, and of the construction of those most used, have been prepared:

In the common Davy lamp the flame is surrounded by a cylinder of black iron-wire gauze, with 28 apertures to the linear inch. This cylinder is firmly set in a brass ring which screws upon the top of the oil vessel. The weight of this oil vessel is held by three stout upright wires, outside of the gauze cylinder, and brought together at the top for the reception of the ring by which the whole can be carried. The upper portion of the wire-gauze cylinder is made double to secure greater dubility under the corroding effects of the air on the hot wire.

The two Davy lamps first used in a coal mine are still in existence in the collection of the Museum of Practical Geology, London, and are described as of small size, with cylindrical oil-vessels of copper. The wire-gauze envelopes or cylinders are of very fine brass wire, and the mesh is very small. Three iron-wire standards extend from the oil vessel below to a flat brass cap or roof, to which the carrying ring is attached by a swivel joint. The original safety lamp of Sir Humphrey Davy is in the possession of the Royal Institution.

Various modifications of the Davy lamp have been made from time to time, and there is a great variety of lamps in use, but those best known, beside the simple Davy, are the Stephenson, Clanny, Mueseler, and Boty.

Stephenson's safety lamp was invented by the celebrated engineer George Stephenson, at about the same time that Davy designed his. In this lamp the wire-gauze cylinder is lined with a close-fitting glass chimney. The air is admitted below, through a number of small holes in the brass ring. It has a cap of perforated sheet copper. It is considered safer than the common Davy lamp, since the gauze, being kept from contact with the flame by the glass lining, cannot become red hot.

The Miners' safety lamp, invented by Struve, of Swansea, which has been extensively introduced in the fiery collieries of South Wales, is similar to the Davy lamp, differing chiefly in this, that the wire-gauze cylinder is expanded at the bottom and made longer, so as to reach half-way down the sides of the oil box and include half of it. This enlargement of the gauze cylinder at the base gives it a conical form and a much broader surface than at the top. The advantages of the construction are the free admission of air through the numerous meshes of the enlarged base, the greater cooling surface of the gauze, and less obstruction to the diffusion of the light downward and in other directions.

In the Clanny lamp a part of the cylinder of wire gauze is replaced by a cylinder of thick glass, the object being to secure more light from the flame than can pass through the wire gauze in the usual construction. The glass cylinder has a larger diameter than the gauze cylinder, and is supported in a frame made of two brass rings, one above and the other below, and united by six vertical wires. The wire-gauze cylinder is secured to the upper ring, and the air for the supply of the combustion enters through the gauze above the glass, and has to descend to the wick. This construction does not give much more light than a common Davy lamp, owing to the absorption of the light by the thick glass.

Mueseler's safety lamp also has a thick glass cylinder over the light, with a conical gauze chimney above it. It is so constructed that the feed-air is made to descend along the inner surface of the glass, keeping it cool, before being deflected upon the flame. This lamp is much used in the collieries of Belgium and the north of France.

Eloin's lamp has a short, thick glass cylinder around the flame, and the outer surface is curved, so as to diffuse the light. Instead of a wire-gauze chimney, there is a brass tube covered with wire gauze at the top. The air enters through a short vertical wire-gauze cylinder, and is distributed upon the flame by an argand cap.

Boty's lamp also has a short glass cylinder, but above it there is an ordinary gauze chimney. The air is admitted through a perforated copper ring placed a little below the level of the flame.

ILLUMINATING POWER OF SAFETY LAMPS.

All safety lamps differ greatly in their illuminating power, owing to their various forms and the positions of the parts, and to the varied conditions under which the air for the support of the flame is admitted. It is estimated that it requires eight lamps of Davy's construction to give out as much light as a wax candle, six to the pound. Taking such a candle as a standard for comparison, the illuminating power of some of the principal lamps is indicated by the figures which follow, showing the number of lamps required to produce a light in each case equal to one candle.*

Davy's lamp, with gauze	8.00
Stephenson's lamp	18.50
Upton and Roberts	24.50
Dr. Clanny's, (glass)	4.25
Mueseler's, (glass)	3.50
Parish's lamp, with gauze	2.75
Davy's lamp, without gauze	2.50
Common miner's candle, 30 to the pound	2.00

* From Hunt's edition of Ure's Dictionary.

In order to prevent miners from opening their lamps, and thus bringing the naked flame in direct contact with the combustible gases, various plans have been devised, the most common being to lock the lamp by means of a screw attached to the body of the lamp, the point of which may be made to enter and hold the brass ring by which the gauze cylinder is held to the oil vessel. This is done by a key which fits the square head of the screw. Lamps are also so made that the light is extinguished as soon as they are unscrewed, and before the body of the lamp and the protecting gauze are completely separated. Dubrulles' self-extinguishing lamp is contrived so that the wick is turned down within the tube as soon as the lamp and the wire-gauze cylinder are disconnected.

LAMP UNLOCKED BY MAGNETISM.

One of the methods recently proposed for so locking the wire-gauze cylinder to the body of the lamp that the miners cannot disconnect the two parts, consists in placing a spring bolt or catch in the interior, without any opening or other means of reaching it from the outside. When the two parts are put together they cannot be separated by mechanical means without cutting into the outer casing. But these spring bolts may be withdrawn by the attraction of a powerful magnet applied to the outside of the lamp.

The efficacy of all safety lamps depends, as is generally known, upon the resistance offered by wire gauze to the passage of flame due to the cooling of the gases. Combustible gases pass freely through the meshes, and may ignite and burn inside of the gauze-cylinder, but ordinarily the temperature of the gauze does not become sufficiently raised to permit the flame to ignite the gas on the outside. Under some conditions, however, the gauze becomes red-hot, and the flame will then pass through.* It has also been found by experiment (September, 1867) that nearly every lamp in use will explode a mixture of carburetted hydrogen gas and atmospheric air, if placed in a current of this mixture.

In these experiments the gas was taken from a 9-inch pipe at the Oaks Colliery, England, where a current of gas flows upward at the rate of three and a quarter miles per hour. An ordinary Davy lamp, with the sheath outside, exploded in 31 seconds, and again in 7 seconds. With the sheath inside it fired the gas in 63 seconds. The Clanny exploded in 13 seconds; a Belgian lamp (Meuseler?) had the glass broken at the end of 55 seconds; several Stephenson lamps gave different results: the flame was extinguished in a few seconds, or continued burning for over a minute. Three of Morrison's lamps were tested, and were extinguished in 7, 5½, and 60 seconds, respectively, the velocity of the current of gas passing at the time being, according to an anemometer, 700 feet per minute.

These experiments, or the reports of them, are very unsatisfactory, inasmuch as the composition of the gas is not stated, nor are details given of the manner in which the lamps were exposed to its action. But similar experiments have been continued, from time to time, and one of the latest reports of them is herewith presented. The results will be seen at a glance by examining the table:†

---

*It is the opinion of Robert Hunt, F. R. S., that the hypothesis of cooling will not explain the phenomenon of non-transmission of the flame. He conceives the "impermeability of wire gauze to flame to be due to a repulsive power established between the hot metal and the ignited gas, similar in character, although differing in condition, to that which prevails between water and a white-hot metal."

† From the London Mining Journal, December 4, 1869.

Experiments with mining lamps at Eppleton Colliery, November 25, 1869.

No.	Lamp used.	Velocity of current in feet per second.	Duration of experiment in seconds.	Result.
1	Davy	8	4½	Exploded.
2	Davy	8	3	Exploded.
3	Stephenson's, (original)	8	2	Went out.*
4	Stephenson's S. W. C., (solid tube)	8	9	Went out.†
5	Stephenson's S. W. C., (perforated)	8	2	Went out.
6	Stephenson's, (original)	8	2	Exploded.‡
7	Stephenson's S. W. C., (perforated)	8	3	Went out.
8	Stephenson's, (original)	8	5	Went out. §
9	Stephenson's, (original)	8	3	Went out.
1	Davy	11. 3	2	Exploded.
2	Stephenson's, (original)	11. 3	10	Went out.
3	Stephenson's S. W. C., (solid)	11. 3	....	Still burning.
4	Stephenson's S. W. C., (perforated)	11. 3	....	Still burning.
5	Stephenson's S. W. C., (perforated)	11. 3	30	Out.
6	Stephenson's S. W. C., (solid)	11. 3	4	Out.
7	Stephenson's S. W. C., (perforated)	11. 3	3	Out.
8	Davy	11. 3	3	Exploded.
9	Stephenson's, (original)	11. 3	5	Out.
10	Stephenson's, (ordinary)	11. 3	5	Out.
11	Stephenson's S. W. C., (solid)	11. 3	6	Out.
12	Stephenson's, (ordinary)	11. 3	8	Exploded.
13	Stephenson's S. W. C., (perforated)	11. 3	10	Out.
14	Stephenson's S. W. C., (solid)	11. 3	30	Out.
15	Davy	11. 3	9	Exploded.
16	Stephenson's S. W. C., (perforated)	11. 3	9	Out.
17	Stephenson's S. W. C., (perforated)	11. 3	3	Exploded.‖
18	Stephenson's S. W. C., (perforated)	11. 3	4	Exploded.¶
19	Stephenson's S. W. C., (solid)	11. 3	3	Out.
20	Stephenson's S. W. C., (perforated)	11. 3	5	Out.
1	Davy	14. 3	2	Exploded.
2	Stephenson's S. W. C., (solid)	14. 3	18	Went out.
3	Stephenson's S. W. C., (perforated)	14. 3	7½	Went out.
4	Stephenson's, (original)	14. 3	6	Went out.
5	Stephenson's S. W. C., (solid)	14. 3	36	Went out.
6	Stephenson's, (original)	14. 3	60	Went out.
7	Stephenson's S. W. C., (solid)	14. 3	2	Exploded.**
8	Stephenson's S. W. C., (solid)	14. 3	17	Went out.
9	Stephenson's, (solid)	14. 3	20	Went out.
10	Stephenson's, (solid)	14. 3	60	Went out.
1	Davy	23	1	Exploded.
2	Stephenson's S. W. C., (solid)	23	60	Went out.
3	Stephenson's S. W. C., (perforated)	23	7	Went out.
4	Stephenson's S. W. C., (original)	23	19	Went out.

* This lamp was used in the years 1815 to 1835.
† Made after the same principle as the above lamp.
‡ Exploded through gauze not being in its place.
§ Glass cracked.
‖ This is the lamp left with Mr. Hann on September 30, and which was very much out of order.
¶ Not a distinct explosion—a double report.
** Exploded through a broken glass.

The results of the experiments will be found to correspond very nearly with those obtained on September 30 last, (see Mining Journal, Oct. 16,) the Davy lamp having exploded, as before, with a speed of 8 feet per second. It will be seen that only the Davy and Stephenson lamps were tried, but the Stephenson lamps tried are divided into four classes :

1. The original Stephenson lamp, which was in use from the year 1815 up to the year 1835.

2. The improved Stephenson lamp then introduced. This lamp was only improved in order to make it more portable, the weight being considerably reduced, and perhaps a little more light got, but it was not intended to alter the principle of the lamp in any respect. It appears, however, that this was done unintentionally to a certain extent, as a close examination of the two lamps, and a careful study of these valuable experiments, will clearly show. The original Stephenson lamp tried in the last experiments has a very short copper tube on the top of the glass, and this tube is only perforated at the *top*, and not at the *sides*, while the improved Stephenson has a tube

rather longer than that of the old lamp, and this tube is perforated both at the top and sides; and this slight difference in construction has been shown by these experiments to be of some importance.

3. The Stephenson lamp was tried with a tube not perforated at the sides, thus restoring the lamp very nearly to its present state. And,

4. The lamp which was left with Mr. Hann, described as an ordinary Stephenson, and stated to be very much out of order.

It will be seen that in the first series of experiments shown in the table the speed of the inflammable current was 8 feet per second, and the Davy lamp was readily exploded, but the other lamps were extinguished with one exception when the gauze exploded, "through the gauze not being in its place."

In the second series of experiments a speed of 11.3 feet per second was used, when the Davy, of course, exploded, and the Stephenson lamps stood the test, and, what is remarkable, were not extinguished, but remained burning in some cases. But there is one exception to this, as the lamp described as the ordinary Stephenson (experiments No. 12 and No. 17) exploded, although the other Stephenson stood the test, and the cause of this apparent anomaly appears to be obvious enough.

In the third series of experiments a speed of 14.3 feet per second was used, and the trials varied from 2 up to 60 seconds, the results being that the Stephenson lamps were extinguished with one exception, where "the lamp exploded through a broken glass."

In the fourth series of experiments the speed employed was 23 feet per second, and the three Stephenson lamps experimented upon were simply extinguished. These were the original Stephenson lamp, and the improved lamp, one with a solid tube on the top of the glass, and another with a tube perforated at the sides as well as at the top.

The experiments, on the whole, must be regarded as very satisfactory, as they confirm in every essential particular those formerly made on September 30, and the result ought to inspire the public with confidence as to the safety of the Stephenson lamp under any circumstances likely to occur in mines. The experiments, however, show that great caution and care ought to be used in the construction of those lamps, as a very slight variation in the form may interfere with the principle of the lamp. The copper tube referred to, which is placed on the top of the glass, requires great care, and there is no doubt that it ought only to be perforated at the *top;* and it (the copper tube) ought also to be very carefully fitted to the sides of the wire gauze and the top of the same, so as to prevent any current passing between the glass cylinder and the wire gauze.

From these and other well-known facts, it will be seen that safety lamps, in mines containing explosive gases, afford a relative security only. This was, perhaps, never more strikingly (and harmlessly) shown than in an incident which occurred some years ago, in Zwickau, Saxony.

A lecturer* had been explaining the principle of the safety lamp to a considerable audience, and proposed to illustrate his remarks with an experiment. For this purpose he had prepared a simple apparatus, consisting of a large glass jar and a rubber pipe with a glass elbow at one end. The other end of the pipe was connected with a gas fixture; a safety lamp was set inside the jar, and the bent glass nozzle was introduced to the bottom of the lamp. The lecturer remarked, that, upon turning on the gas, an explosive mixture of carburetted hydrogen and common air would be formed in the jar; the flame of the lamp would be elongated, and a long blue tip would be seen; then the whole interior of the wire-gauze cylinder would be filled with flame; but, though the gauze might become red hot, the flame could not, in any case, strike through to the outside—all of which phenomena, positive and negative, would be clearly visible through the transparent jar. The gas-cock was thereupon opened, but instead of the peaceful demonstration looked for, a prompt contradiction of the theory was the result. The flame was communicated almost instantly to the gas outside of the lamp. In some confusion, the lecturer repeated the experiment, but with the same result; and he finally gave it up, confessing his inability to explain the disappointment, except on the hypothesis of some unknown imperfection in the lamp. The occurrence made a good deal of stir, particularly as there are many coal mines in the Zwickau district troubled with fiery

* Mr. A. Mezger, mining engineer.

gases, and at that time recent accidents had been occasioned by explosions in spite of safety lamps. The test was therefore repeated, still more publicly, upon some sixty lamps of various patterns, and it was found that only the old-fashioned Davy, and one other, the name of which escapes us, would retain the flame. Those lamps were found to be particularly dangerous which possessed separate openings below for the admission of air to support the flame.

These experiments indicate the same conclusion as was lately arrived at by English investigators, namely, that the strength of the draught of inflammable gases through a safety lamp has much to do with the degree of its security. The Zwickau lamp may have been unusually faulty in construction, rather than principle; but this fact, though it might lessen the importance of these special experiments, could not alter the general bearing of both practice and theory on the question of the safety of all lamps. The principle involved is that of the rapid conduction and radiation of heat by the wire of the gauze surrounding the flame. Before the burning gas can pass through the meshes, it is said, so much of its heat will have been abstracted, and radiated away in all directions, that it will fall below the temperature of ignition or explosion. Now, this depends upon the amount of heat communicated to the wire in a given time. The wire may get hot faster than it can grow cool again, and if this increase of temperature is carried to a white heat, the gas outside will be set on fire. But the amount of heat given to the wire in a certain time depends again on the amount of burning gas that passes through it in that time, and hence it is clear that a strong current of gas may overheat the wire and cause an explosion. The Davy lamp is not constructed to favor a strong current. Indeed, one complaint of it has been the feebleness of the light, from insufficient air. It appears, however, that attempts to remedy this deficiency are fraught with peril.

We desire to call the attention of engineers to the great simplicity and conclusiveness of the test above described, and to urge that it be at once applied to the lamps of every mine. There can be no harm in knowing whether the lamps will do what is claimed for them. It is true that common illuminating gas forms with common air a more explosive mixture than does the fire-damp of mines; but the severity of this test ought to be nothing against it, so long as any lamp can be found to bear it.

In the general dissatisfaction with the use of safety lamps, which spread through the Zwickau district after the experiments alluded to, a new and bold plan was suggested, and has been carried out in several cases with the best success. This was nothing more nor less than *to burn naked lights in great numbers* wherever inflammable gases made their appearance. Some of the workings presented, under this system, an unwonted appearance. In one case, the fire-damp could be heard streaming out of the fissures of the coal, with that peculiar humming sound which the miners know so well and fear so greatly; the innumerable lights carried each a long blue tip—the usual signal of danger—yet no harm occurred. The gases were quietly consumed as fast as they entered the mine, and the illumination was carefully kept up, night and day, Sundays and between shifts, that no opportunity was given for an accumulation of explosive material.

The great difficulty of this plan is its direct injurious effect on ventilation. The stationary lights with which the mine is crowded, in addition to those carried by the workmen themselves, must necessarily use up a good deal of oxygen, and produce a good deal of carbonic acid. But this is an evil which can be combated in other ways and, at all events, it is preferable to the danger of explosion. Perhaps it might be an improvement to use safety lamps instead of naked lights, hanging them in great numbers along the walls, so as to secure the complete, quiet combustion of the gas. But it must be confessed that, even under circumstances of the greatest danger, the naked lights have done very well, and no accident, so far as we are aware, has ever resulted from their use in this way.

Propositions have been made to explode the accumulated gas in workings before the workmen are allowed to enter it. In a rude way, this has frequently been done in fiery mines; and to remove all personal danger, it is now suggested that the explosion be effected by means of a battery. But this whole system of allowing the fire-damp to accumulate while the workmen are absent, and then firing it off all at once, strikes us as much inferior to the simple expedient of burning it gradually, as above described.

FIRES IN MINES, AND THE MEANS OF EXTINGUISHING THEM.

In spite of all precautions in the way of proper ventilation and the careful use of safety lamps, fires will sometimes occur, as many mining communities have had terrible opportunities of knowing. The methods employed for extinguishing them are therefore worthy of notice. On this subject I cannot do better than quote the excellent essay of Mr. R. P. Rothwell, of Wilkesbarre, Pennsylvania, which appeared last summer in the New York Engineering and Mining Journal:

Taking account of the nature of the mineral, we are not surprised that fires should be much more frequent and dangerous in coal than in ore mines; they are, however, by no means confined to coal or lignite deposits, but may and do occur in all kinds of underground workings where timber is used. In the great majority of cases fires originate, below as above ground, through carelessness or imprudence. A miner will lean his lighted candle or lamp in such a position that it can ignite a prop or other piece of timber. Such appears to have been the case in the recent disastrous fire in the Crown Point, Kentuck, and Yellow Jacket mines. The careless or imprudent hanging of a grate or fire-pot near the coal at the foot of our downcast shafts or slopes (where it is placed in winter to prevent the pumps and rods from being covered with ice) has been the cause of fires in several of our anthracite mines. Ignorance of, or inattention to, the proper manner of constructing ventilating furnaces has also been a frequent cause of fires in coal mines, but probably the most fruitful cause of these disasters is the ignition of fire-damp, or carbureted hydrogen in coal mines; the ignition first produces explosion, and in mines yielding an inflammable coal it frequently ignites the fine particles blown about in a burning atmosphere, and these communicate the fire to the solid coal of the pillars; or the gas may continue to burn at some "blower" till it has ignited the coal in which the fissure or vent occurs. These so-called "accidents" are generally due to carelessness in the use of "open" lights, or in the opening of safety lamps in places where the gas exists in quantity. The practice of blasting in coal mines, which produces large quantities of the dangerous gas, has also caused a great number of deplorable explosions and fires; and the question of substituting some other agent, such as water, wedges, &c., for powder in mines of this kind, is now receiving much attention among European mining engineers. "Fiery" mines, such as those in the Richmond (Virginia) bituminous basin, would be greatly benefited by the successful substitution of a safer agent for the powder now used, where rock or hard coal has to be mined. In our anthracite mines the hardness of the coal would render the use of powder more necessary, while the smaller quantity of fire-damp found in it would, at the same time, make the substitution of a safer agent less desirable. The exercise of greater vigilance in the inspection and use of safety lamps would, doubtless, greatly diminish the number of explosions and fires in coal mines.

Many bituminous coals, and bituminous shales which are found among the coal beds, are, under certain circumstances, subject to "spontaneous combustion." This always occurs where the coal or shale is crushed in a confined space with an exceedingly feeble ventilation; indeed, spontaneous heating of the coal, accompanied as it is by an abundant production of carbonic-acid gas, was generally attributed to the decomposition of iron pyrites (sulphuret of iron) under the influence of the moisture in the air, and a circulation of air so languid as not to dissipate the heat generated, while sufficient to supply the oxygen necessary to support combustion. It has, however, been observed that the coals producing the greatest quantity of pyrites are not always the most subject to heat spontaneously, while it has also been noticed that the most inflammable coals are those containing the largest proportions of oxygen; it has, consequently, been suggested that the more probable cause of spontaneous combustion may be the combination of oxygen with the carbon, under the influence of moisture, and which is accompanied by the generation of carbonic acid and a considerable amount of heat. In the coal mines of Silesia, where cases of spontaneous combustion are of frequent occurrence, numerous observations have demonstrated that this class of accidents need not be feared where the "roof" of the vein is either sandstone or conglomerate, nor near the outcrop, whatever the nature of the top rock may be; on the other hand, beds worked at a considerable depth, or even when moderately near the surface, but covered by a shale capable of being softened by moisture, are the most liable to spontaneous combustion.

It was long considered in Silesia that the only means of preventing fires from this cause, consisted in sending all the fine coal, "waste," or "gob," out to the surface. This was often impracticable, expensive, and not always effectual; hence other means of attaining the same end were sought for. Since it is well known that combustion cannot exist when deprived of oxygen or air, one means of preventing spontaneous combustion consisted in isolating the working places, or goaf, by means of a heavy dry wall, or by two parallel walls filled in between with clay or other material packed hard, and sometimes a heavy pillar of coal was left for the same purpose. In each case, however, the weight of the superincumbent rocks almost invariably crushes the walls or pillars, and produces cracks or fissures, through which air, sufficient to sustain the slow combustion of the coal, can pass. This method has been employed with greater or less success in some of the mines in the centre of France, and in the thick seam of Staffordshire. It is evident that when used the greatest possible care must be taken to keep the fissures closed, which are found from time to time, so as to seal hermetically the space inclosed. But besides the practical difficulty in effecting this, the fact that these inclosed spaces generally fill with fire-damp, and therefore form veritable magazines of a substance far more dangerous than powder, and which, through the crushing of a wall or pillar, or the fall of a portion of the roof, may at any moment be brought in contact with the lights of the men working in fancied security in the neighboring roads or chambers, is a sufficient reason for condemning so dangerous a system as that of isolation of the "goaves" by "pack walls."

The spontaneous heating of coal is so slow a process that the increment of temperature is easily carried off by a moderately rapid current of air; we can thus prevent the temperature from ever rising to the point of ignition, by simply ventilating the "goaves;" this, then, is the exact opposite of the last method, and though much safer and fully as practical, yet very serious objections can be made to it. It is all but impossible, owing to falls, &c., to keep the "goaves" sufficiently open to maintain the necessary circulation of air, and the expense of clearing up falls and opening the old workings, where obstructed, is so great as to render this method impracticable in many cases. The system is, however, more or less successfully used in many mining districts in England, Silesia, &c. There now remains but one other method to describe, and it is by far the safest and most efficient in the prevention of danger by spontaneous combustion. It consists in filling or packing with earth and other material sent down from the surface the spaces from which the coal has been removed, and which the waste of the mine does not fill. This method, though somewhat expensive in large seams which make but little waste, is assuredly the most effectual remedy, since it not only prevents the admission of air to the old workings, and therefore does away with the expense of ventilating them, but it prevents the falls of the roof, in which "blowers" are frequently opened, and renders impossible any accumulation of fire-damp, which is the great source of danger in the method of isolation by pack-walls, &c. Thus this method not only procures perfect immunity from danger by spontaneous combustion, but the system of mining of which it is the principal feature enables us to obtain all the coal of the vein. It is, therefore, not only the safest, but also, as regards the amount of coal obtained, the most economical, method now in use, and it is deservedly popular in Europe, and more especially in France, Belgium, and Germany, where it has been employed for a number of years, and has now taken the place of every other system in most of the coal mines.

Whatever precautions may have been taken to prevent fires, yet the carelessness, ignorance, and sometimes the malice of men are causes which cannot always be effectually guarded against; hence we must be prepared to meet the danger of fire when it occurs, and to apply *promptly* the most suitable means for its extinction.

When a fire originates in coal or timber, every effort should be *immediately* made to extinguish it by throwing water on it either with buckets, or, better, with a fire engine; or where practicable, by tapping the column-pipe of the pump and leading the water through hose to the seat of the conflagration. In some cases the use of portable "fire extinguishers," (which generate carbonic acid gas,) such as are now found in every village of the land, may prove of great service. If the fire originates by the ignition of a blower of fire-damp, efforts should be made with wet cloth, water, &c., to put out the flame; in some cases where these means failed, the flame has been extinguished by the concussion of the air, caused by discharging a cannon in the gallery where the fire exists. When the coal surrounding the "blower" has already become ignited it will immediately re-ignite the fire-damp; so that this method can only be applied either where the blower is in rock or where it has not had time to thoroughly ignite the coal. While these means are being applied, preparation should be made for erecting stoppings or dams, in view of the failure to extinguish the fire by the direct means; yet these should not be abandoned till there is no further possibility of success. When it is no longer possible to approach the fire near enough to throw water on it—that is, when the fire can no longer be kept under control—it becomes necessary to resort to other methods of extinction, viz:

By isolating the part of the mine on fire, and then applying extinguishing agents to the part inclosed. When this fails or becomes impracticable, there remains but one other method, viz:

By closing the entire mine, and applying the same extinguishing agents.

These agents are water, carbonic acid, and nitrogen gases, steam, or any other gas incapable of sustaining combustion; those mentioned being adopted on account of their effectiveness and small cost.

The isolation of a fire in a mine is effected by constructing walls or stoppings across all the galleries or other openings which connect this portion with the remainder of the mine. These stoppings are sometimes walls of brick or masonry, varying in thickness from twelve inches to six or eight feet; at other times two lighter parallel walls are built, and a current of air allowed to circulate between them in order to keep the inner wall cool, or else the space between the walls is filled in with clay and mine-waste; while still another method is to make a stopping, several yards in thickness, entirely of clay, waste, &c. In cases where it can be done without danger, a timber stopping or even a simple board bratticing can be adopted; the kind of stopping as well as its strength will depend on the position of the fire, its extent, the presence or absence of fire-damp, whether the stopping is intended to dam back water or not, and such like considerations, which under the enunciations of fixed dimension, are impracticable. The *essential* in every case is that the stopping should be *air-tight*, and that it should be constructed with the least possible delay, and at such a distance from the fire as to allow time for its completion, before the smoke and irrespirable gases produced by the fire can prevent the men from working.

Notwithstanding that the ventilation of the part on fire has been reduced to a minimum by the erection of temporary bratticing, &c., yet the combustion of the coal and wood produces such enormous volumes of irrespirable gases that the work of building the stoppings is one of great difficulty and danger, more particularly in mines producing fire-damp, where the danger from explosion is still greater than that from the gaseous products of combustion.

It is evident that the stoppings can be constructed with least difficulty by commencing with those on the "outside" of the fire, or the side from which the air *proceeds to* the fire, and afterward building those "inside" the fire, or where the air *comes from* the fire; yet in mines yielding fire-damp this method of proceeding is attended with great danger; the fire-damp mixing with the air confined between the stopping and the fire makes an explosive compound, which is carried forward toward the fire, where it ignites, and though it may not cause a fatal accident, yet it almost invariably throws down the stoppings by which it was sought to isolate the fires. As from one-tenth to one-seventh of its volume of carbonic acid, added to an explosive mixture of air and fire-damp, renders the latter entirely inexplosive, (a larger quantity renders it incapable of sustaining combustion,) and as the products of combustion are carbonic acid and nitrogen, it follows that by closing first the galleries on the side toward which the air from the fire goes, we prevent the danger of explosion by mixing carbonic acid with the air contained between the stopping and the fire, and by throwing the smoke and irrespirable gases back on the fire, we go far toward extinguishing it. It is true it is a matter of great danger and difficulty to build stoppings between a fire and the "returns," but by the use of temporary bratticing and by commencing at a sufficient distance from the fire, it is often practicable, and it is always desirable. Where it is impossible to build the stoppings in this order then, when practicable, it would be advantageous to inject carbonic acid gas, or choke-damp, (through a pipe in the stopping,) from the moment the latter comes near completion, so that the air contained between the stopping and the fire may not become explosive. We speak, of course, of mines yielding fire-damp. Where carbonic acid is not available, it will sometimes be possible to inject steam, which will not only deaden the fire, but will, at least, diminish the intensity of the explosions.

The stoppings completed—and where there is no danger from explosion or need of inundating with water the part on fire, there is no necessity for making them heavy—we proceed to fill the part inclosed with carbonic acid gas, with choke-damp, with steam, or with water. In the first case the carbonic acid can be manufactured either

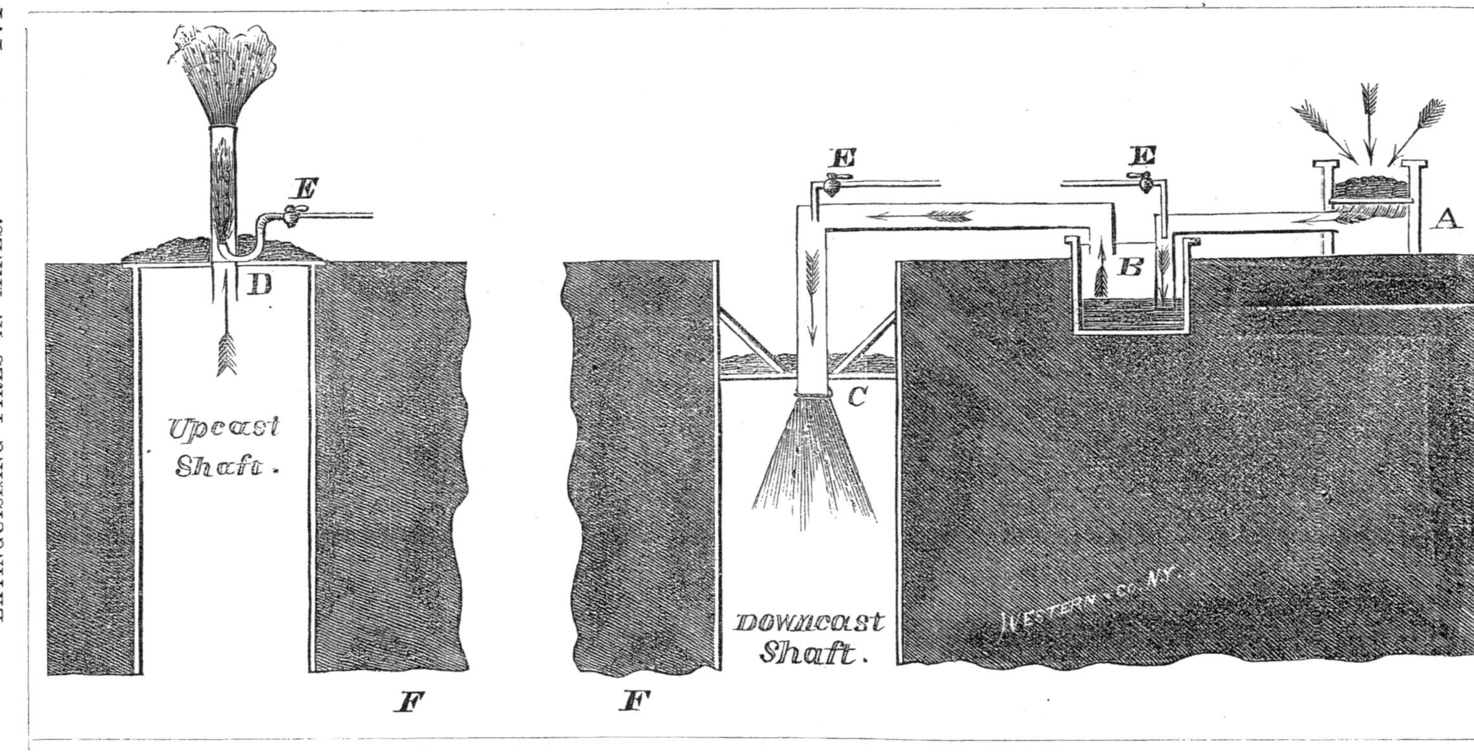

Goldsworthy Gurney's apparatus for manufacturing After-damp, 1849.

A.—Furnace. B.—Water-tank. C.—Downcast stopping. D.—Upcast stopping. E, E, E.—Three steam jets. F, F.—Galleries from shaft to shaft.

pure, or nearly so, by the use of any strong acid, such as sulphuric or muriatic acid and chalk, or limestone, or any of the carbonates of low price and easily decomposed. This gas is easiest prepared in a lead vessel, which is not attacked by the acid. Where the space to be filled is not great, some of the numerous patent fire-extinguishers might be found of service, as being quickly and easily brought into action. These methods have the advantage of supplying the gas at a low temperature, and thereby facilitating the cooling of the rocks after the flame is extinguished. If the circumstances are such as to make the use of choke-damp—that is, a mixture of carbonic acid and nitrogen—advisable, it can be produced in one of the furnaces of which drawings and particulars are given below. In either case, as carbonic acid and choke-damp are both heavier than air, it follows that the tube through which we admit these gases should be at the lowest, and that through which the air from the inclosed space is allowed exit should be at the highest attainable point of the isolated workings, and the admission of the gases should be continued till it is evident they have completely filled these works. This is easily proved by their instantly extinguishing lamps, burning tow, &c., at the outlet tube. The tubes should then be closed, leaving only a siphon or water-gauge to mark the difference in pressure between the inside and outside of the stoppings, and a place for the introduction of a thermometer used to note the variations in temperature, so as to know when it will be safe to open the stoppings. The greatest care should be taken to keep the stoppings air-tight; they should be frequently inspected, and where from any reason it is found desirable to "drown out" or inundate the part on fire, they should have a thickness proportionate to the head of water they will have to retain.

When the fire has assumed greater dimensions, or when its position is such that it becomes dangerous or impossible to confine it by stoppings such as we have described, it becomes necessary to abandon the entire mine and to resort to closing the shafts.

Even when it is decided to inundate the mine, it is always advisable to close the pit, whether the mine produce carburetted hydrogen (fire-damp) or not, since by so doing we deaden, at least, the combustion, and prevent, in a great measure, the damage always caused by the high temperature produced by a rapid combustion. The shaft should, therefore, be immediately closed hermetically, provision being made for openings through which a registering thermometer can be introduced, and a bent pipe, or siphon, containing water, to show the pressure behind the stopping, and prevent its becoming excessive, while at the same time it prevents the admission of fresh air.

The closing of the shaft may be effected by hanging heavy pieces of timber, by means of chains, some distance down the shaft. On the platform thus made clay is thrown, and packs itself by the force of the fall, thus rendering the stopping perfectly air-tight. The tubes above mentioned should be inserted, and one siphon should be so arranged as to allow the water to flow down the shaft, instead of accumulating above the stopping. Where the pit is divided into a number of compartments, it becomes difficult to close it perfectly in this way. The mouth of the pit is then covered over with planks or iron doors, and clay, sand, &c., packed on this, every crevice being carefully closed. Great attention must be paid to this, more particularly in the case where it is desired to "smother out" the fire without the injection of steam or carbonic acid, otherwise a quantity of air may enter, which, though insufficient to maintain an active combustion, may yet suffice to support a slow fire, or, at least, greatly increase the time necessary for its complete extinction.

Where the mine does not produce fire-damp, there is no great danger in closing the pit, but if that gas is given off in any considerable quantity, the closing of the pit is sometimes attended with great danger, there being a certain time after the closing when the quantity of atmospheric air is sufficient to make an explosive mixture with the gas from the mine. After a time, the quantity of air, or rather oxygen, is diminished by that consumed by the fire itself, and the incombustible gases produced by the combustion, mixing with the fire and fire-damp, soon render the compound inexplosive. In such mines it is highly desirable to inject steam alone, or, better, steam and carbonic acid, into the downcast from the earliest practicable moment, so as thereby to diminish, as far as possible, the chance of explosion during the operation of closing; and it should continue to be injected after the stopping is made till the mine is completely filled, which can be known by the air issuing from the upcast extinguishing a lighted lamp, &c. It is almost needless to add, that great care should be taken, and no open lights allowed near the shaft when there is any possibility of fire-damp existing in dangerous quantity. If the mine does not produce that gas, the immediate admission of choke damp is not so necessary, though it is always desirable as checking the spreading of the fire.

As the majority of fires occur from explosions of fire-damp, it follows that in most cases the air doors, bratticing, and other divisions necessary to guide the air current through the mine, are destroyed. It is then difficult to ascertain if the carbonic acid has gone into every part of the mine, or whether a large amount of air may not yet remain in the workings; this should be carefully considered in deciding on the means to be adopted to extinguish the fire, and also in fixing on the time for reopening the pit. Not a few of our fatal accidents occurring from explosions were caused by reopening the mine too soon, or before the coal had time to cool down below the temperature at which it will ignite. In some cases, it may even be considered safest and most economical to fill the mine with water. This decision must be taken only after a careful consideration of the position of the fire, the amount of water needed to fill the works to the depth required, the time necessary to pump in that water, the nature of the roof and coal in the works, and the effect which a longer or shorter inundation would have on them, the facility for getting the water out, &c. The inundation of a mine is always an expensive expedient, and should only be adopted as a last resort; yet there are cases where it is undoubtedly the best method to adopt. Each case requires a special study, and the method which might be the most suitable in one may not be adapted to another. The great sources of expense in inundating a mine are the damage caused by the water remaining for any length of time in the works (with certain kinds of rocks—some slates and fire-clays especially,) the falls of roof, causing delay and expense, and the delay and cost of filling with and pumping out the water. And in coal subject to spontaneous combustion it not unfrequently happens that when the water has been pumped out, the wetting of the "gob," or "waste," causes it to heat, and even to ignite, before the ventilation can be fully re-established. Every other means should in general be tried before inundating the mine, and the most efficient of these various means are the introduction of steam, carbonic acid, (choke-damp,) and after-damp, which is a mixture of nitrogen and carbonic acid. Steam is available at almost every mine, and is easily applied; it should be carried in pipes, and discharged as near the seat of the fire as possible, in order to prevent its condensation; it is a very efficient extinguishing agent, and from the facility with which it can be employed, it is now commencing to be much used; in many cases, a rubber hose, made especially for a steam hose, is all that is required to carry it for several hundred feet, and it will last as long as the occasion requires in most cases. The greatest disadvantage in the use of steam is its energetic action on some rocks, causing them to disintegrate and "fall;" but where the roof is such that it is not materially injured by steam, this is one of the most convenient, and it is always one of the most effective extinguishing agents we can use. Its action is limited to the expulsion of the air, and as it maintains a high temperature we are generally obliged to inject water, in order to cool the rocks sufficiently to allow the men to work, and also to prevent any possibility of reignition. The following example of its application will prove instructive: In 1857, at the St. Mathew mine, near St. Etienne, France, steam was injected after the mine had been on fire for eight days; this was continued for seventy hours, after which cold water was injected for three days, in order to cool the sides of the shaft, galleries, &c., previous to descending into the mine. The pit was then opened, and a current of air circulated while the men went down. After two days, however, the mine again caught fire, and it became again necessary to close the pit. Steam was then injected during twenty-four hours, and, after an intermission of eighteen hours, cold water was injected for twelve hours. The fire broke out a third time, and steam was admitted for eleven hours, then cold water, after which the men were enabled to enter, and extinguish the fire completely by throwing water on it. I believe the same process was employed at the Yellow Jacket and Kentuck mines, on the Comstock lode, which were on fire a few months ago.

The application of carbonic acid or choke-damp and after-damp is more complicated than that of steam, since the materials for its manufacture are not often on hand. The most usual method of manufacturing carbonic acid is by means of chalk or limestone, or any cheap carbonate easily decomposed, treated with one of the cheaper acids—as sulphuric, nitric, or hydrochloric. The gas produced in this way has the advantage of possessing a low temperature; it not only extinguishes the fire but tends to cool the rocks to a point below the temperature necessary for ignition. Portable machines, known as "fire extinguishers," are convenient means of manufacturing this gas where the quantity required is not very great, and they are to be found everywhere, at a small cost, and are always ready for use. Where the quantity of gas required is very large, as, for example, in filling a mine, one of the cheapest and most convenient methods of producing it is by the combustion of coke or charcoal in a furnace of suitable form, and, as it was the means adopted in the first application of "after-damp" or carbonic acid to the extinguishing of fires in mines, we will devote some space to it, especially as the credit of the invention is commonly misapplied. The first application was made by M. Jules Letoret, in Belgium, in the year 1844. Five years later (1849) we find the same principle applied in England by Goldsworthy Gurney, who takes credit himself for the invention, and is even at the present time credited with it by nearly all the English engineers. It is scarcely possible that Mr. Gurney could have been ignorant of M. Letoret's invention, for we find him perfectly "posted" on the application of his steam jet in the Belgian mines, about the same time.

On the 15th of February, 1844, a fire occurred from an explosion of fire-damp in the No. 2 shaft, Agrappe colliery, near Mons, in Belgium; the pit was 1,171 feet deep, three veins at different levels being worked. Efforts were made to extinguish the fire by throwing water on it; but it had already made too great progress, the frequent explosions of fire-damp having become very dangerous. It was then decided to reverse the ventilating current in order to prevent the fire from destroying the pumps. M. Jules Letoret then prepared to introduce carbonic acid into the works, that gas having, as we have already stated, the property of rendering harmless an explosive mixture of carbureted hydrogen and air, if only added to it in the proportion of one-tenth to one-seventh. Several experiments were made for the manufacture and introduction of this gas—the first on the 17th of February, 1844. The effect of the gas was to reduce the number and violence of the explosions, but the fire still continued to burn at the foot of the shaft; the pit was not perfectly closed at the time. On the 23d of February M. Letoret built a furnace, intended to produce carbonic acid, in a continuous manner, from the combustion of coke; the shaft was closed hermetically, leaving only openings for the introduction and outlet of the products of combustion. This apparatus is shown in the accompanying figure, and is of so simple a construction as to require but little explanation. The furnace was charged with burning coke and charcoal to the depth of 17 inches, that depth being found sufficient to consume all the oxygen in the air passing through the fire, and to produce carbonic acid and nitrogen, (a greater depth of fire will produce at the same time carbonic oxide;) and as this gas issued from the furnace at a high temperature the reservoir of water, *h*, was inserted through the stopping, so that the gases might be cooled and prevent any chance of igniting the woodwork of the shaft. When the apparatus was set to work on the 24th of February, the fire was visible at the foot of the shaft; on the 25th the flames and explosions had ceased; the introduction of "after-damp" was then stopped, and fresh air was allowed to enter the mine; but on descending into the mine a large fire was discovered, quite red, but with little flame. The work of clearing out the gallery leading to it was commenced, in order to be able to throw water on the fire; but the barometer indicating a diminishing atmospheric pressure, the fear of fresh discharges of carbureted hydrogen induced the abandonment of the mine, into which carbonic acid was again introduced. On the 26th, the flame and explosions having again ceased, fresh air was readmitted, and on entering the mine water was thrown on the fire by means of fire-engines; timbers were set, though with difficulty, on account of the high temperature, and because the rocks, decomposed by heat, disintegrated and fell when water was applied. This work was continued to the 3d of March, when the fire was entirely extinguished and the rocks cooled down. The roof had fallen to the depth of 22 feet. Thus a fire which had threatened to destroy the mine, or at least to prevent its working for months or years, was completely extinguished in the course of ten days.

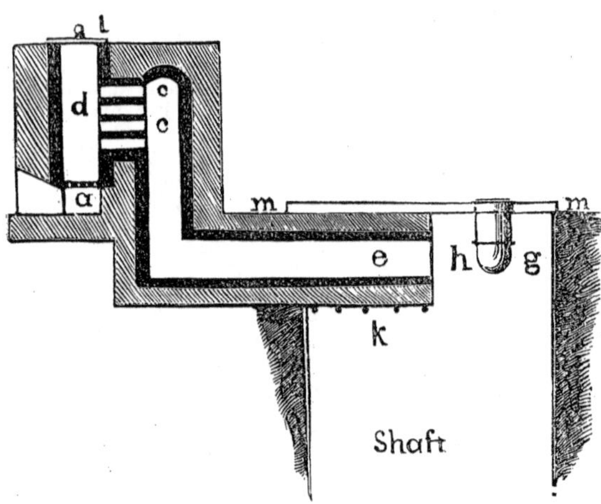

Letoret's Furnace for manufacturing After-damp, 1844.

a.—Ash-pit. *d.*—Fire-place. *c.*—Pipes carrying off the flame. *e.*—Pipe carrying gas into the pit *f.* *g.*—Pipe admitting water. *k.*—Iron bars supporting *e.* *m.*—Iron flooring covered with soil.

The above particulars, taken from a "Memoire" by M. Jottrand, in the "Annales des Travaux Publiques de Belgique," though very brief, are yet sufficient to show the manner of operating in such cases, and to establish M. Letoret's claim of invention of this method of extinguishing fires in mines.

I shall now describe Mr. Gurney's furnace and manner of operating. The full particulars are given in a parliamentary report on accidents in coal mines, 1849.

The drawing on page 641 shows the arrangement of the apparatus. The furnace was four feet square, the ash-pit air-tight, and the pipe leading from it thirteen inches in diameter. This pipe plunged into a tank of water, B. In order to cool the gas before entering the mine the air was drawn through the fire and forced into the pit by means of three steam jets, E E E, working with a pressure of from thirty to forty pounds of steam in the boilers.

The fire which called this apparatus into use occurred in the Astley pit, (390 feet deep,) near Manchester, England, on the 2d April, 1849. The mine being very fiery, there were great fears of an explosion. The engineer in charge, Mr. Darlington, wrote to Mr. Gurney—well known from his application of the steam jet to mine ventilation—to know if there was any means of "drawing fire-damp out of a closed mine without letting air in." Mr. Gurney, in his evidence before the parliamentary committee above referred to, says: "An idea struck me, (from experiments I had made in passing air through a closed vessel running through the fire, where I found the whole of the oxygen to be combined, and nothing going out but nitrogen and carbonic acid,) if we made a large furnace and connected with the ash-pit, perfectly air tight, a cylinder, and put a steam jet in the cylinder, we might draw air through the fire and drive nitrogen into the mine." Mr. Gurney found that passing air through a fire 18 inches deep would consume the whole of the oxygen of the air; M. Letoret found 17 inches sufficient. It is evidently desirable that the depth of the fire should not much exceed that necessary to effect the complete combustion of the oxygen and the formation of carbonic acid; for when it is increased a portion of the carbonic acid takes up another equivalent of carbon and forms carbonic oxide, a gas which, though incapable of sustaining combustion, being itself combustible, would not act as energetically as the carbonic acid or nitrogen in preventing explosion or combustion.

After injecting this after-damp (mixture of about four-fifths nitrogen and one-fifth carbonic acid) into the pit for two hours, a little white cloud coming out of the upcast showed that the mine was full, which fact was easily proved by the gas coming out of the pit extinguishing burning tow, &c. The quantity of gas injected was estimated at 6,000 cubic feet per minute, and the operation was continued for five or six hours after the gas commenced to come out of the upcast. The fire was then drawn and fresh air forced through the mine by the same pits. After two hours and twenty minutes the cloudy appearance at the upcast disappeared, and a lamp would burn in the gas coming out. The fire was found to be extinguished, though it had been burning for nearly two weeks before commencing this operation. The expense of the apparatus was estimated not to exceed five to ten pounds.

In a fire which occurred about two months later (June, 1849) in the same pit, Mr. Darlington applied carbonic acid made in the wet way—with limestone and sulphuric acid. The fire in this case was walled off and the generating apparatus placed in the lower gallery, and a quarter-inch steam jet placed in a pipe inserted through the stopping in a higher gallery. Mr. Darlington says: "We commenced injecting carbonic acid through the four-inch pipe at 2 a. m., and at 5 a. m. the men were at work." Of course the fire was a fresh one, or the rocks would not have had time to cool in that time. The expense was from £10 to £15, or more than that for filling the entire mine with after-damp in the previous case, where the gas was made with "charcoal, the waste coal round the pits, and a little limestone."

SECTION IV.—BREAKING, CRUSHING, AND GRINDING ORES.

CHAPTER XV.

BREAKING AND CRUSHING.

Ores which reach the surface in large solid blocks require to be broken into fragments that can be easily handled before they can be placed in machines for reducing them to still smaller fragments, or to powder.

The sledge is the simplest and most common tool for this purpose; and it is followed by spalling hammers, until none of the fragments are much larger than the fist. Until within a few years this was the common and only way of breaking up ore into sizes suitable to be fed into the mortars of stamp-batteries, and it is still used where only small quantities are to be broken, and the extent of the operations do not justify the expense of obtaining suitable machines for the purpose.

HEAVY STAMPS.

The first attempts upon the Pacific coast to substitute machine for hand labor in spalling ore were in the direction of stamps of unusual weight, raised by cams to a height of four feet, and allowed to drop upon the mass of rock to be broken. Stamps of this kind, either single or two in a battery, were placed at the superb mills erected near Aurora, at the Real del Monte, and at the Antelope. They weighed 2,000 pounds each. There were no mortars, but a solid bed or anvil was surrounded with massive grates, made of bar iron, through which the fragments could drop. Masses of ore, from one to two feet in diameter, could be rolled in and subjected to a succession of blows. The two heads could break up about two tons an hour, but with an enormous expenditure of power, as is evident when we consider that for each blow a ton weight of stamp was to be raised four feet, and also that the smaller the mass to be broken the greater was the force of the blow. Thus when a mass of quartz, say six inches in height, lay upon the anvil, the stamp fell upon it from a height of three feet six inches; but when a block two feet high, which needed a much harder blow, was upon the anvil, the stamp fell only two feet. Similar stamps were in use at Washoe and at Virginia, but were soon abandoned because of their manifest defects and cost.

BLAKE'S ROCK BREAKER.

The machine for breaking up rock now most in use is the invention of Mr. Eli Whitney Blake, of New Haven, Connecticut, and is generally known as Blake's Rock Breaker. It was designed at first to break up trap-rock into fragments for macadamizing roads. Its value for breaking ores into sizes suitable for feeding to stamps or jigs was quickly seen, and in 1861 it was introduced into California. Its first operation in the mines was at the Benton Mills upon the Merced River. The ore delivered there from the Pine-tree vein is noted for its hardness and massive character, and it required the constant labor of thirty Chinamen to spall enough to keep the stamps supplied. The same and a greater amount of work was better performed by the machine in a few hours, and effected a saving of seventy-five dollars a day, when sufficient rock was furnished to keep the machine running. From that time it has been extensively used, and is recognized as an indispensable adjunct to every well-appointed stamp mill.

The general construction of this machine has been rendered familiar by numerous figures and publications in the United States and in Europe. It consists, essentially, of a strong iron frame, supporting upright convergent iron jaws, actuated by a revolving shaft. The stones or masses of ore to be broken are dropped between these jaws, and a short reciprocating or vibratory motion being given to one or both of them, the stones are crushed, and drop lower and lower in the converging or wedge-shaped space, until they are sufficiently broken to drop out at the bottom. The size of the broken fragments may be regulated by increasing or diminishing the size of this opening between the jaws. But the construction and operation of the machine will be made more clear by the inspection of the annexed figure, accompanied by a description in detail of the various parts.

This figure is a sectional side view or elevation of the machine, representing the parts in place as they would be presented to view by removing one side of the frame. The parts of this figure which are shaded by diagonal lines are sections of those parts of the frame which connect its two sides, and which are supposed to be cut asunder in order to remove one side and present the other parts to view. The dotted circle D is a section of the fly-wheel shaft; and the circle E is a section of the crank. F is a pitman or connecting rod, which connects the crank with the lever G. This lever has its fulcrum on the

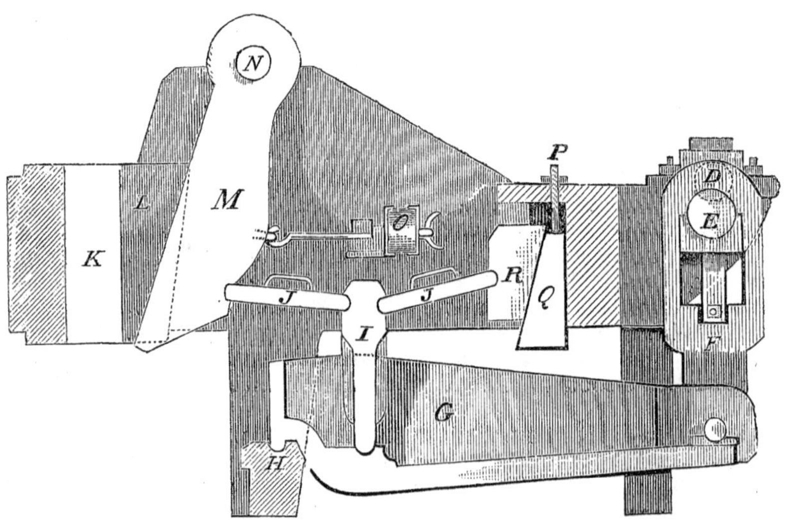

Blake's Rock Breaker—section.

frame at H. A vertical piece, I, stands upon the lever, against the top of which piece the toggles J J have their bearings, forming an elbow or toggle-joint. K is the fixed jaw against which the stones are crushed.

This is bedded in zinc against the end of the frame, and held back to its place by cheeks, L, that fit in recesses in the interior of the frame on each side. M is the movable jaw. This is supported by the round bar of iron N, which passes freely through it and forms the pivot upon which it vibrates. O is a spring of India-rubber, which is compressed by the forward movement of the jaw and aids its return.

Every revolution of the crank causes the lower end of the movable jaw to advance toward the fixed jaw about one-fourth of an inch and return. Hence, if a stone be dropped in between the convergent faces of the jaws, it will be broken by the next succeeding bite; the resulting fragments will then fall lower down and be broken again, and so on until they are made small enough to pass out at the bottom. The readiness with which the hardest stones yield at once to the influence of this gentle and quiet movement, and break down into small fragments, surprises and astonishes every one who witnesses the operation of the machine.

It will be seen that the distance between the jaws at the bottom limits the size of the fragments. This distance, and consequently the size of the fragments, may be regulated at pleasure. A variation to the extent of five-eighths of an inch may be made by turning the screw-nut P, which raises or lowers the wedge Q, and moves the toggle-block R forward or back. Further variations may be made by substituting for the toggles J J, or either of them, others that are longer or shorter; extra toggles of different lengths being furnished for this purpose.

Machines are made of various sizes. Each size will break any stone, one end of which can be entered into the opening between the jaws at the top. The size of the machine is designated by the size of this opening; thus, if the width of the jaws be 15 inches, and the distance between them at the top 9 inches, the size is called 15 by 9.

The product of these machines per hour, in cubic yards of fragments, will vary considerably with the character of the stone broken. Stone that is brittle, like quartz, granite, and most kinds of sandstone, will pass through more rapidly than that which is more tough. The kind of stone being the same, the product per hour will be in proportion to the width of the jaws, the distance between them at the *bottom*, and the speed. The proper speed is about 180 revolutions per minute; and to make good road metal from hard, compact stone, or to prepare ores for stamps, the jaws should be set from 1¼ to 1½ inches apart at the bottom. For softer and for granular stones they may be set wider.

The following table shows the several sizes of machines commonly made, the product per hour of broken stuff from the hardest materials, when run with a speed of 180; the power required to perform this duty; the whole weight of each size in round numbers, and the weight of the heaviest piece when separated for transportation.

Size.	Product per hour.	Power required.	Total weight.	Weight of frame and parts attached.
10 by 5	4 cubic yards.	6 horse.	6,600 pounds.	3,200 pounds.
10 by 7	4 cubic yards.	6 horse.	7,600 pounds.	4,100 pounds.
15 by 5	6 cubic yards.	9 horse.	9,100 pounds.	4,700 pounds.
15 by 7	6 cubic yards.	9 horse.	10,200 pounds.	5,600 pounds.
15 by 9	6 cubic yards.	9 horse.	11,600 pounds.	6,800 pounds.

The whole length of the machines to the back-side of the fly-wheels is from 8 to 8½ feet; height to top of fly-wheels, 5 feet; width, from 4 to 5 feet.

The machine may be driven by any power less than that given in the table, yielding a product per hour smaller in the same proportion.

Either of the sizes mentioned will break quartz enough in a few hours to feed a forty-stamp mill for one day. A machine of less capacity would of course have a smaller mouth and would not take large stones. It is usual therefore for mill-men to use the largest mouthed machine, and to run it a few hours each day. The rough quartz in blocks as it comes from the mine being ready on the platform near the mouth of the breaker, two men can feed it into the machine and break it up at the rate of five to ten tons per hour, according to the size of the machine.

Breakers have been made larger than any of the above for breaking very large blocks of ore. They are in use at Lake Superior, where they take in masses of ore eighteen inches in diameter by twenty-four in length, and crush them without difficulty. The fragments from these large breakers are received by two or three of the machines of the ordinary sizes and are broken again, so that the pieces will all pass through a two-inch ring. The metallic copper is readily picked out by hand from this broken ore. These large machines would be useful at many mines in California and Nevada, and would permit sledging to be dispensed with. The machine is made without the lever, and works very slowly, but without loss of power; since, when it is not crushing, the only power consumed is that required to overcome the friction, whereas with the heavy stamps, as we have seen, the greatest expenditure of power is when the least work is performed.

There are some modifications of the construction of this machine as here described. In England and France they are commonly made without the lever, the eccentric shaft being mounted on the top of the frame directly over the toggles. A pitman connects the eccentric shaft with

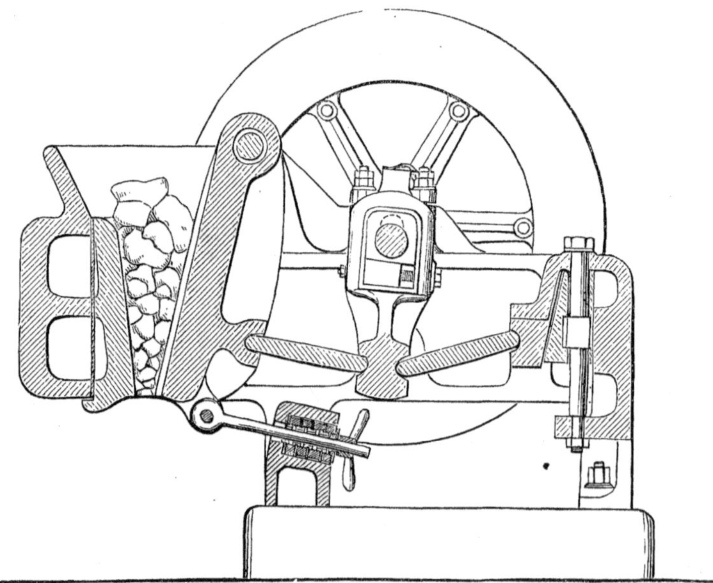

Blake's Rock Breaker, without the lever.

these toggles, and thus produces the oscillating motion of the jaw. This construction is shown by a sectional view as before, one-half of the frame being supposed to be removed. One only of the fly-wheels is represented. This is the form of the machine exhibited at the Paris Exhibition by the manufacturers under the patent in France. The mouth of this machine is expanded, hopper-like, so as to be more convenient for the reception of the masses to be broken. This may be a desirable addition in some cases, where comparatively small stuff is to be broken and is to be shoveled in from a floor lower than the mouth of the machine; but when the mouth is placed, as it should be, on a level with the floor of the dump pile, the hopper is not required.

The rock breaker may be successfully used instead of stamps to obtain either coarse or fine fragments suited to concentration. It has been attempted to increase the fineness of the product of the machine by placing an "obturator" or obstruction, such as a triangular bar of iron, under the outlet between the jaws, arranging it so that it can be raised or lowered by means of screws, in order to diminish or increase the size of the outlet for the delivery of the crushed stuff. The effect of this obstruction is to retain the stuff between the jaws until it is so much broken and comminuted that it will sift through the narrow slits left on each side of the bar. This method of operating may be successful with some materials but involves a considerable expenditure of power. It is also attended with some danger to the machine, since with materials that are easily impacted to a hard mass, the entire space between the jaws may become so tightly filled that some part of the machine must give way. The massive frame of a machine in California was broken asunder in this manner, simply by permitting the outlet between the jaws to become closed by the accumulation of a heap of broken stuff below it. Obturators have been tried; but the discharge from the machines is rendered so slow by them that they have been discarded as not practically valuable. A better way to accomplish the object is to first break the ores in an ordinary machine and then pass the fragments through a machine with a mouth 10 by 2 inches, the jaws of which move only about one-eighth of an inch and make 600 bites in a minute. Machines of this kind have been successfully used in preparing ores for jigs.

At the Churprinz mine, Freiberg, Saxony, two rock breakers are used to prepare the lead ores for the various concentrating machines. One breaker takes the rough ore as it comes from the mine and breaks it up into coarse fragments; these pass to a second breaker with the jaws set nearer together, so as to make fragments small enough for jigging. The finer portions of the first product are separated from the coarse by means of revolving screens.

The fragments of ores produced by rock breakers are better adapted in size and shape to the operation of concentration by jigging than the fragments made by rollers and stamps. When set coarse, for breaking quartz to be fed to stamps, the product consists of masses which do not exceed a certain size, and this permits a uniformity in the action of the stamps which cannot be obtained upon quartz broken up by hand, since in the latter case there is great irregularity in the size of the masses, and, as a general rule, the hardest and toughest are the largest. With self-feeding batteries, it is very important that the ore should be uniformly broken, and machine-broken rock is especially well adapted to automatic feeding. When the masses fed into batteries do not exceed a certain size, the wear and tear of grates is less than when the size is irregular. It is easy also with breakers to reduce the whole quantity of the ore to be stamped to fragments very much smaller than can be obtained by hand-breaking, unless by an expenditure of time far beyond what the economy of the breaking will permit. Quartz thus reduced greatly increases the product of a stamp-battery; the stamps have a greater and more effective blow, and mill-men often report that they can work from twenty to twenty-five per cent. more quartz with a breaker than without it, the battery being the same.

The jaws of the breaker are the only parts subjected to rapid wear, and in California and Nevada it is usual to provide the movable jaw with movable faces of hard white iron. These are made about four inches thick, and in such a form that they can be turned over or end for end, until they are too much worn to be longer used. They are secured to the jaw by means of conical bolts, and bedded in zinc or refuse type-metal, in order to have an equal and solid bearing. The forward or fixed jaw can also be reversed in its bed, and is held back to its place by wedge-shaped cheeks on each side. It is usual to make both jaws with vertical coarse corrugations or furrows, so that the ridges of one jaw are opposed to the depressions on the other, thus giving a zig-zag form to the aperture at the bottom. This tends to prevent long and thin pieces from slipping through without being broken; but it is not otherwise essential to the satisfactory operation of the machine, and plain jaws are frequently used.

CRUSHING BY ROLLERS.

Before the introduction of rock breakers, the most common method of crushing was by strong iron rollers, revolving slowly in close contact or pressed together by powerful weighted levers. The stuff was allowed to drop from a hopper between the rollers, and motion having been given to one by means of steam or water power the other roller was carried around by friction. This form of crusher is generally known as the Cornish crusher or rolls, and is much used at the metalliferous mines in Cornwall and elsewhere abroad. One was erected at the Keystone copper mine in Calaveras County, California, a few years ago for crushing copper ore preparatory to jigging.

The figure annexed will serve to give an idea of the general form of

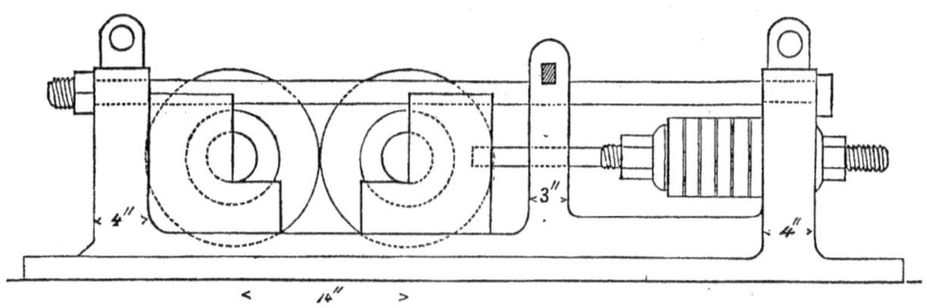

Rollers for crushing.

construction of the Cornish crusher. The rolls are supported by very strong bearings, in a frame strengthened by wrought-iron bolts. In the construction here shown, the rollers are kept in contact by India-rubber springs, or buffers, of great elastic force, one on each side of the frame. Each buffer is composed of six rubber disks, one inch thick, separated by a disk of iron one-quarter of an inch thick. The necessary initial pressure is obtained by means of two strongly-made screws in the axes of the buffers; and by screwing up or unscrewing the nuts on these screws the pressure may be increased or diminished, according to the necessities of the case. It is evident that it would not answer to rigidly fasten the rolls in contact. The accidental dropping of a steel tool, such as a drill or a hammer-head, between them would break the machine; and, moreover, they would not crush as fast and well without a certain amount of yielding to the materials carried through between them. But the use of rubber springs is a novel way of giving the necessary resistance. It is usually accomplished by means of weighted levers, the short arms of which being bent downward press upon a cylindrical bar or follower, which bears directly upon the back of one of the bearing blocks of the roll; or, what amounts to the same thing, the lever is made, by means of rods, to draw the bearing of one roll toward the other, thus keeping the surfaces of the rolls in contact. The amount of the pressure is determined by the extent to which the lever is weighted. This is the usual Cornish method; that by springs of rubber has been tried in Germany. The great advantages of springs are, that the machine occupies less space than when fitted with levers, and that the resistance or crushing pressure increases with the degree of separation of the rolls, whereas with the weighted levers the pressure is constant.

In practice it is found that the product of rolls geared together is greater than when one is carried around merely by the friction of the stuff crushed. It is also usual to have three or more rolls where the crushing is wholly done by rolling. The upper pair are set so as to take in large masses; and to increase the hold of the surface of the rollers upon the masses they are made fluted. The fragments falling from this first pair of rolls are divided between two pairs set below and pressed closely together.

The diameter of crushing rolls varies from 14 inches to 34 inches, (27 inches is a common diameter,) and the length or breadth of face from 12 inches to 22 inches. The rolls at the mine of Devon Great Consols in Cornwall are very large, having 34 inches diameter, and 22 inches face, and a pressing force on the rolls of 458 hundred-weight, revolving seven times per minute, and crushing 65 tons in 10 hours, at a cost of 2¼ pence per ton.

The annexed tabular statement of dimensions of rollers at various mines will give further details.*

---

* Extracted from Hunt's edition of Ure's Dictionary.

Dimensions and product of Cornish rollers at various mines.

Name of mine.	ROLLERS.				Total pressure on rolls.	SIFTER.				Diameter of raff wheel.	Horse power.	Quantity crushed in ten hours.	Cost of crushing per ton.
	Diameter.	Length.	Revolutions per minute.	Crushing area per minute.		Diameter.	Length.	Number of holes.	Revolutions per minute.				
	In.	*In.*		*Sq. In.*	*Cwt.*	*In.*	*In.*	*Sq.In.*		*Feet.*		*Tons.*	*Pence.*
Grassington mines	27	12	5½	5, 593	91	21	48	6¼	37	14	....	80	......
Minera	14	14	8	4, 920	73⅓	24	42	9	48	10 6-10	6	20	2½
Cwmystwith, No. 1	27	14	4	4, 748	78	20	33	9	24	16	....	32	2½
Cwmystwith, No. 2	27	14	4½	5, 341	85	24	36	9	24	16	....	35	2½
Goginan	30	14	5½	7, 254	39	20	39	9	36	16	....	30	2¾
Cwm Erfin	27	14	7½	8, 902	293	26	32	9	30	16	....	20	3
Lisburne, No. 1	27	15	6	7, 632	180	22	36	12¼	30	16	....	42	2½
Lisburne, No. 2	27	15	6	7, 632	224	22	36	12¼	30	16	....	42	2½
Derwent	27	14	7	8, 309	227	22	60	16	....	15	....	60	2¾
Goldscope*	14	18	14	11, 060	6	....	....	......	....	....	....	25	2½
East Darren	30	18	6	9, 996	207	24	36	16	45	16	....	25	2¾
Cefn Cwm Brwyno	20	13	5	4, 080	84	20	48	16	27½	14	....	20	2½
Lisburne, No. 3	18	16	8	6, 432	169	22	36	25	30	16	....	42	2½
Llandudno	18	15	15	12, 705	61	....	....	......	....	....	....	30	......
Wheal Friendship	23	12	10	8, 670	123	24	36	36	30	13	13	20	11½
Pontgibaud	25	12	12½	12, 075	36	22	44	36	60	15	15	17	2½
Devon Great Consols	34	22	7	16, 443	458	24†	84	64	21	....	....	65	3¾
Fabrica la Constante, Spain	24	15	10	11, 300	147	25	45	100	30	15	15	50	2¼
Fabrica la Constante, No. 2	27	15	10	12, 720	110	25	53	100	30	16	16	50	3¾
Fabrica la Constante, No. 3	24	12	16	14, 464	84	25	45	3, 600	38	(‡)	....	13-20	19
Fabrica la Constante, No. 4	27	15	15	19, 080	93	26	58	3, 600	45	(‡)	....	13-20	19′

* Goldscope has two sets of rolls, one fluted; the other plain.
† Two sifters, one 24 inches, the other 22 inches in diameter.
‡ Jacob's ladder, 192 feet.

WEAR OF ROLLS.

The surface of rollers soon becomes much worn; and when made of chilled iron, the irregularity of the chilling is soon made manifest by the unequal wearing away, the soft parts being hollowed out, while the harder remain in ridges or irregular bulges. It is therefore found preferable to use ordinary hard pig iron, or a mixture of hard white iron, similar to that used for the dies and shoes of stamps. The rolls are also made with an outer casing or shell, a short, hollow cylinder, that can be slipped upon the axis or core of the roll, and removed when too much worn. This is usually cast so as to make a firm lock-joint upon the core, or it is keyed by means of two or three keys or wedges slipped into recesses extending through from one side to the other at the line of junction, one-half of the hole being in the core and the other half in the shell.

The annexed figure shows a method of securing the facing upon rolls by tapering keys.* The outer cylinder C C can be slipped off and on the central conical cylinders without difficulty, and is secured in its place by six tapering or wedge-like keys, K K, placed at equal distances around the axis, and firmly held by the strong nuts at one side. This drawing is one-ninth full size. The roll has 14 inches diameter and 9 inches face. In all crushing machines of this description a large amount of the stuff must necessarily be passed through between the rolls several times; for it is evident that when a hard lump of ore passes through

* This figure is taken from the Jahrbuch fur den Berg-und-Hütten-Mann, 1867. Taf. ii.

and separates the rollers more than is usual, a considerable quantity of stuff drops through without being acted on. The result is the same when the rollers are fed too rapidly; they are kept asunder most of the time, and much coarse and uncrushed material passes through.

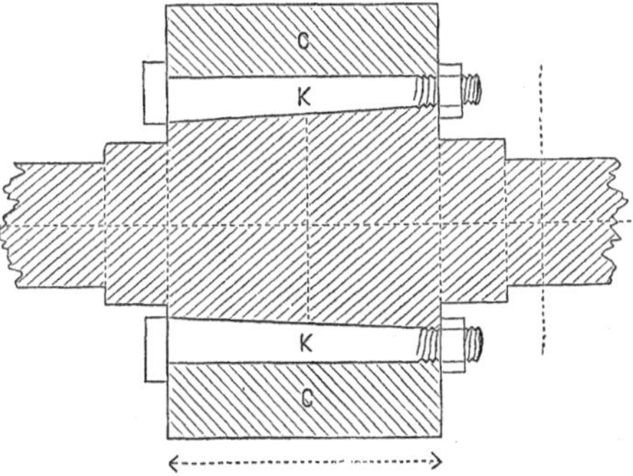

Roller—Freiberg, Saxony.

The crushed product is always received upon gratings or a revolving screen, by which all the fine or sufficiently broken portions are sifted out. The coarse fragments which require to be again crushed are dropped into a raff-wheel, or elevator, by which they are carried to the upper floor or platform and thrown out, ready to be shoveled into the hopper again. This raff-wheel is usually 15 feet in diameter, and resembles a water-wheel, but is made with the buckets turned inward. This forms a succession of box-like cavities, from which the ore falls out when, by the revolution of the wheel, they are carried to the top and inverted.

Rollers are usually driven by strong gearing, but at the Exposition in 1867 a set of rolls exhibited by Messrs. Huet & Geyler were driven by a belt, as is also a machine at Freiberg, in Saxony. M. Huet mentions rolls with as great a diameter as $1^{m}.20$; but the rollers in machines of their construction, driven by a belt upon a shaft carrying at the opposite end a small pinion, working into a large spur-wheel upon the end of the shaft of one of the rollers, did not exceed $0^{m}.09$ in diameter.

The hoppers of rollers for crushing large quantities of stuff are usually made large enough to hold a ton.

LUNDGREN'S PULVERIZING BARRELS.

An apparatus for fine crushing by means of rolling in a cylinder with a great number of small balls of hardened iron, was erected and used for a time at the Benton Mills, upon the Merced River, but was finally abandoned. The cylinder or barrel used was made of boiler iron, lined on the inside with shoes of hard iron, one inch thick. Its length was three feet and diameter five feet. The material, consisting of the battery sands, was screened and introduced in charges of 650 pounds. Some 2,000 pounds of chilled iron bullets, half an inch in diameter, were then added, and the whole made to revolve on its axis slowly, about 26 revolutions in a minute, for one and a quarter hours, at the end of which time the sand was reduced to a fine powder. The wear upon the balls is said to be very slight.

CRUSHING BY PERCUSSION—CENTRIFUGAL CRUSHERS.

For crushing minerals and other hard substances by projection from a revolving wheel or disk, an apparatus was devised and operated for a time by Messrs. Whelpley & Storer, in Boston, Massachusetts. To the part for coarse crushing they gave the name of *whirling table*. This is a saucer-shaped mass of metal, three and a half feet in diameter, weighing 800 or 1,200 pounds, and revolved horizontally with great velocity, as great as 1,025 times per minute. This table or disk forms the bottom of a circular cast-iron stationary tub, eighteen inches deep, the sides of which are perforated so as to allow small fragments to pass out. The table is so supported upon a vertical shaft, with a steel pivot resting in a cup of oil, that it revolves with but little friction, and the high velocity of rotation is maintained with but little expenditure of power. When any hard substance, such as a mass of quartz, is thrown into the cavity during the rapid rotation of the table, it is at once forcibly thrown outward against the grates, and, falling backward in fragments, these are in turn thrown rapidly outward again by the centrifugal force, and the operation is repeated until the fragments are small enough to pass through the perforations and escape to an outer chamber. If these perforations are half an inch in diameter, the fragments of the quartz will be like small gravel mixed with sand. It is claimed that one of these tables will reduce more than 200 tons of ordinary quartz in pieces from three or four inches in diameter to the size of coarse gravel in twenty-four hours. The inventors allow, in practice, an average of ten-horse power for the full working of one of these tables, and they rate the expenditure of power at about one and a half-horse power per hour for each ton of quartz. To obtain this result the velocity of the table must exceed 1,000 revolutions per minute. Blocks of hard white iron, such as Franklinite, are bolted upon the outer edge and face of the table. These, at high velocities of rotation, first strike the mass to be broken and splinter it before it reaches and wears the surface. With low velocities the machine is rapidly worn and injured, by the dragging of the stone over its surface. With the higher velocities only the edges of the hammers or iron blocks are worn, and these blocks last a much longer time in proportion to the amount of work done. The balance of this revolving table is regulated by bolting pieces of iron to its under side. This machine is not intended to be used as a *pulverizer*, but rather as a breaker, taking stuff three to six inches in diameter and reducing it to the condition of mixed sand and gravel, with a small percentage of dust. For carrying the reduction still further and gaining a product as fine as dust, another form of centrifugal apparatus, called the *pulverizer*, is used.

The pulverizer, as described by the same inventors, consists of four parts or elements: 1. An automatic feeding-mill, which furnishes a regular and constant supply of the material to be pulverized. 2. An iron drum or cylinder, containing an air-wheel, which converts the sand or gravel into dust, chiefly by the action of the particles upon themselves in the rotary currents of air created by the wheel. The material can be retained in the cylinder until it is completely reduced. 3. A fan-blower, by which the dust is drawn from the pulverizing drum as fast as it is generated. 4. The dust so drawn off is received and collected in a chamber or series of chambers.

The pulverizing cylinders, in use for two years or more, chiefly in crushing bones, were forty-two inches in diameter and eighteen inches in breadth. They had twenty-four paddles or arms of hard white iron, six inches long by three and a half in breadth. The revolution was in a vertical plane. It was found by experience that the proper velocity for economical results was about 1,025 turns in a minute. "This will require fifteen horse-power to produce 1,500 pounds of quartz powder, four-fifths of which should pass through a sieve of one hundred threads to the linear inch." The inventors further state that a very fair estimate of production allows one hundred pounds per hour of average dust to the horse power.

Efforts have been made in California to perfect a form of rotary crusher for dry crushing, and the mining public is indebted chiefly to Mr. Moore, of the Vulcan Foundry, for persistent efforts to solve the problem of a cheap and durable machine for dry crushing upon this principle. Much money was expended, and for a time it seemed as if success had been attained, but the practical difficulties inherent in this method proved insurmountable and the efforts to perfect the apparatus ceased. One of the chief difficulties was found to be the excessive vibration of the revolving disk at the required high velocity, the result of unequal wearing. The details of the experiments made at the Vulcan would form a very interesting and valuable contribution to mechanical engineering, and it is regretted that expected details on the subject have not been received in time for insertion here.

CHAPTER XVI.

STAMPS AND STAMP MILLS.

The stamp is the oldest, simplest, and most effective machine for crushing ores to powder. The breaker and Cornish rolls, already described, act by direct slow presure; while stamps in falling acquire momentum, and strike sharp, quick blows upon the mass to be broken.

The iron stamp batteries, now in use upon the Pacific coast, are made chiefly at San Francisco, and have been carried to a high degree of perfection by the joint efforts and experience of the mill-men and the metallurgical and mechanical engineers. It is but just to state that the stamp batteries made there are superior for gold and silver working to those in any other part of the world, and that they have become the type to be followed in the construction of batteries in Chicago, New York, and elsewhere.

It is now very rare in California to find the old-fashioned timber, square-stem stamp lifted by a wooden or iron cam set into a large shaft. Some that were erected in Grass Valley several years ago are still in existence; but the round stamps with cylindrical iron stems, free to rotate in the supports or guides, are now used almost exclusively in California and Nevada.

The whole stamp is composed of the following parts: the stem, the tappet, the stamp-head or socket, and the shoe. The mass of hardened iron on which it falls is called the die, and this is placed in the cast-iron box called the mortar.

The stem is usually made of 3-inch or 3½-inch round iron, from 10 to 12 feet in length, and turned off in a lathe and finished so as to be truly cylindrical, and equal in diameter in every part except for a few inches at the lower end, which is made tapering, so as to fit into a conical hole in the top of the head.

The tappet, or lifter, as it is sometimes called, is secured upon the upper part of the stem, and forms a projection three or four inches wide, under which the cam catches and lifts the stamp.

The first of the annexed figures is a vertical section of the tappet as it appears fixed upon the stem A; and the second an end view or plan, the contrivance for securing it to the stem being shown in both.

The tappet is made of cast iron, and weighs from 60 to 70 pounds. It is alike at both ends, so that when one becomes worn it can be reversed upon the stem. Formerly the tappets were attached to the stems by means of screw threads cut upon the latter, the tappet being screwed down as a nut upon a bolt; afterward key seats were cut to receive a transverse key; but these methods have been superseded by the much more simple and convenient device invented by Zenas Wheeler, of California, which has given his name to the tappet.

The tappet is cast with a rectangular recess in one side of the hole, for the stem. Into this recess a "gib," B, is placed. This is a rectangular block of wrought iron, flat on one side but hollowed on the other, so as to fit the curvature of the stem. Two transverse slots or openings at the back of the recess are provided for keys or wedges K K, by which the "gib" is wedged powerfully against the stem, so that the tappet is firmly secured at any desired place upon the stem. Thus no key seat or change of the form of the stem is required, and the tappet can at any time be removed without difficulty merely by driving out the keys.

Stamp Tappet—section.

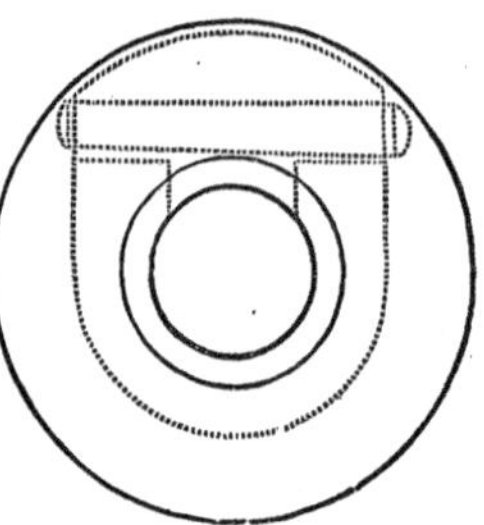

Stamp Tappet—plan.

The stamp-head or socket, as shown in the annexed figure, is cylindrical, and made of the toughest cast iron, strengthened with wrought iron hoops or bands, C C, C C, at the top and bottom, shrunk on while hot. It is cast with two conical openings, or sockets, one in each end, the upper being for the reception of the tapered end of the stem A, and the lower and larger opening, B, for the shank of the shoe. D D represent transverse rectangular openings, or key-ways, by means of which steel wedges can be inserted, so as to bear either against the end of the stamp-stem or against the end of the shank of the shoe, for the purpose of driving either out. This is often necessary for the shoe, when by wearing it has become too thin, and has to be replaced with another. The stamp-head is made in this form for the purpose of facilitating the removal of the shoe. With proper care the socket lasts for years, and after being once attached to the stem need not be removed; but the shoe wears out in a few weeks.

Stamp-head.

The form of the shoe is shown by S in the annexed figure, and the die by D. Both are round, in horizontal section, and are cast of the hardest and toughest white iron. The shoes are usually eight inches in diameter across the face, and six inches in length or height from the face to the shank. The die corresponds in diameter at the face, but they are often made with a broader face, sometimes square, and fitted into recesses in the bed of the mortar. They

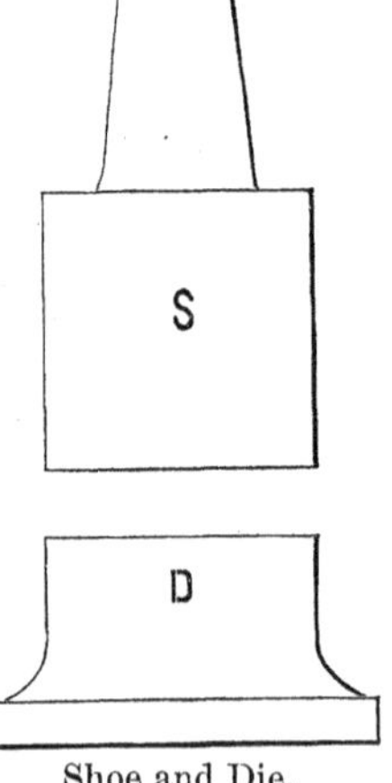

Shoe and Die.

are made of the same iron as the shoes, and are renewed as fast as worn out.

It is usual for the manufacturers to ship these different parts of the stamp disconnected, since their construction permits of their being united with ease, when they are to be placed in the battery. In order to fasten on the tappet, we have seen that it is only necessary to slip it on the stem and then wedge it fast by means of the keys and the gib. To attach the stamp-head it is only necessary to place the socket upon the die in the mortar, and let the tapered end of the stem drop vertically into it. A few blows with a hammer upon the upper end of the stem will wedge it firmly into the head, and it is made tighter by allowing it to drop, head and all, upon the die. This is regarded as a permanent connection; but with the shoe the case is different, and, to render it less difficult to remove this part when worn out, the shank, before being inserted into the socket, is covered with strips of pine, about one-quarter of an inch thick. These are held in place by a string, while the shoe is placed in its proper place upon the die, and the stamp-head is allowed to fall upon it. It becomes tightly wedged in the conical socket, and may be raised with the stamp. After dropping a few times upon the die, (protected by a bit of plank,) it is driven "home;" but there must be a little space left between the top of the shoe and the lower surface of the stamp-head. A stamp thus put together, with a three-inch stem and a 200-pound head, will weigh about 620 pounds, the tappet weighing 70 pounds and the shoe 95 pounds.

The smooth, round stem of the stamp permits it to revolve in rising or falling, so that all sides of the shoe are turned in succession toward the side where the quartz or ore is fed in, this being the side where the stamps with square stems are most rapidly worn away, because on this side the coarse material to be crushed is most abundant. By turning the stamp constantly in the battery this wear is equalized. Shoes should not be allowed to remain in the head until they are entirely worn out, as the wear will be partially upon the wrought iron band of the head, and thus weaken it. When no more than one inch, or three-quarters of an inch in thickness is left, the old shoe should be wedged out and a new one put in.

It is very important that shoes and dies should be equally hard throughout, so that they may wear away equally in all their exposed parts.

To manufacture shoes and dies of good quality for stamp batteries requires considerable judgment and experience. The proper selection and mixture of the iron is of first importance. Ordinary iron when chilled in iron molds is hard upon the outside, or to a slight depth, while within this hardened crust it is soft, and soon wears away, so that a shoe made in this manner becomes hollowed out like a saucer, as soon as the hard crust or chill of the face is cut through. A shoe made of hard white iron, weighing 95 pounds, will last for six weeks, sometimes longer; but ordinary iron will wear out in a month. A die four inches thick, and weighing 60 pounds, will last five or six weeks. A worn-out shoe and die will not together weigh more than 30 to 38 pounds.

This, however, depends upon the judgment of the mill superintendent. Some mill-men use the shoes and dies much longer than others. The above is the experience at the Princeton mill of 24 stamps, on the Mariposas estate. These stamps weighed about 500 pounds, and crushed about 45 tons of hard quartz in each twenty-four hours. The actual wear of shoes and dies was found to be about 1.54 pounds of the iron per ton of ore crushed. The wear of the shoe alone is generally estimated to be from one-half to one pound per ton of hard quartz crushed.

BATTERY MORTARS.

In the old-fashioned batteries, the mortar or coffer in which the stamps act is made of plank, bolted to a timber frame and lined with sheet-iron, and fitted with a cast-iron bed or shallow trough at the bottom, which serves as the die or anvil. But in working gold ores it becomes of the first importance to prevent all leakage in the batteries, especially where quicksilver is used. With wooden mortars this is next to impossible, particularly if they ever remain idle for a few days or weeks, and are allowed to dry. It moreover requires considerable time and skill to construct a mortar of wood in the most approved form, and in a region where time is so valuable as it is in all newly discovered gold and silver regions, it is a great advantage to have mortars already made, which only require to be set upon a suitable foundation to be complete. Cast-iron mortars fulfill all the required conditions, and they are now and have been for many years in general use in the mines of the West. They are made in many forms, and of various thickness and weight, by different establishments, but the following notices of the principal forms made by H. J. Booth & Co., at the Union Iron Works, San Franciso,* will suffice to show the general style of construction of all. They weigh from 2,000 to 4,000 pounds, and are cast in one piece, with the exception of the section mortar, intended for transportation in pieces in mountainous regions.

High mortar.—The mortar in common use upon the Pacific coast is known as the high mortar, and is here represented in cross-section and in front view.

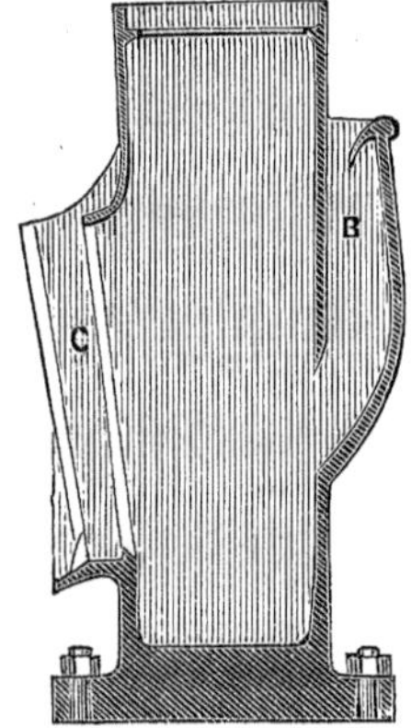

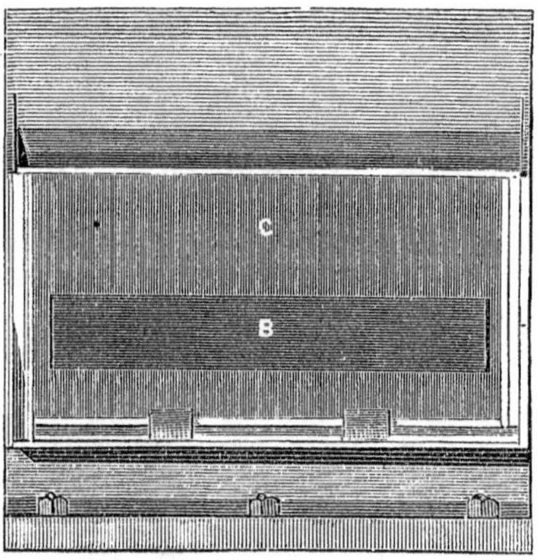

High Mortar.

It is four feet long, four feet high, and weighs about 3,000 pounds. They can be made for three, four, five, or six stamps; but five stamps to each mortar are found to work best. The ore to be stamped is fed through the longitudinal opening B at the back of the mortar, and falls upon the dies (not shown) ranged side by side in the bottom.

All the rock is supposed to have been made small enough by the breaker to pass through the narrow opening at the top. The large

*I am indebted to this firm for original working drawings from which the figures of batteries and stamps have been reduced.

opening in the front of the mortar is intended for the screen, made of Russian sheet iron, punched with fine holes. This is screwed or tacked securely to a wooden frame, which is slid into grooves C in the section, cast in each end of the frame, and is firmly secured there by long wedges of iron. Two lugs or ears of cast iron, placed at equal distances at the bottom of the opening in the front of the mortar, serve to sustain the screen-frame in front. The whole mortar is securely bolted down to the foundation through the heavy flanges cast upon the bottom.

Section mortars.—Mortars which have to be transported into places difficult of access are made in sections so that they can be taken apart and packed upon the backs of mules. These are called section mortars, and their construction is shown in the accompanying figures. This

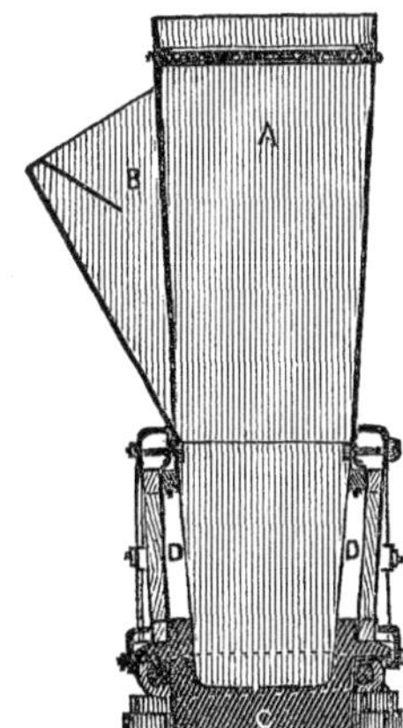

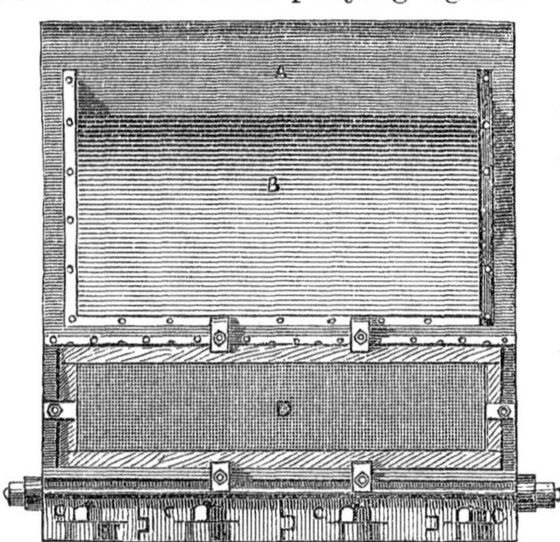

Section Mortar.

mortar, like the preceding, is for five stamps, and is four feet long The upper portions A A are made of boiler iron. The feed opening is shown at B. There are double screens D D, one on each side. The method of securing these screens to the openings by means of movable lugs or clamps, is also shown. The bottom is cast in sections c c c, and these are accurately fitted together with tongued and grooved joints, planed, and held by heavy iron bolts running through them from end to end, and secured by strong nuts upon the outside.

Donnell's mortar.—A form of mortar known as Donnell's is shown by

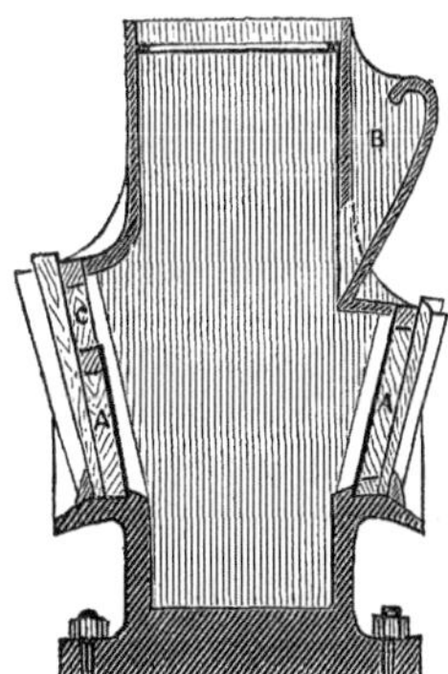

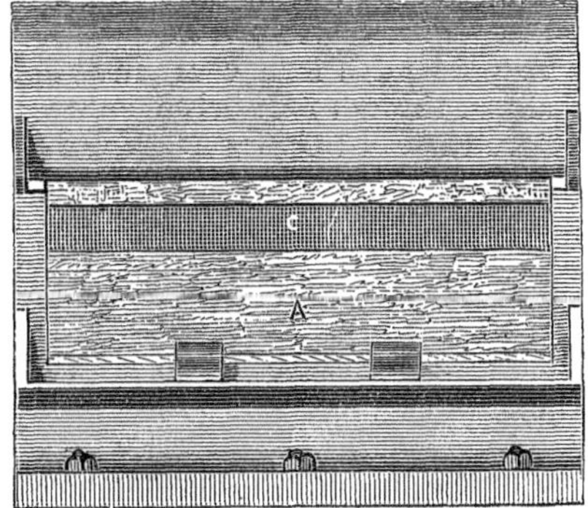

Donnell's Mortar.

the figures. The ore, as in the other mortars, is thrown in at the feed opening B, in the section, and the delivery is through one of the two openings in front and in the back. The screen C is narrow and is placed high above the dies, and occupies only a part of the opening in front. The lower portion of this opening and the opening in the back is closed by a door of wood A A, covered on the inside by a sheet of amalgamated copper which catches and retains the particles of gold. By removing the screen C, and making the door A higher, it may be used as a float mortar.

Dry mortars.—Wet stamping or crushing is general in California. Mortars for dry crushing are exceptional in that State; but the silver mills of Nevada, crushing ore which has to be subsequently roasted, require this form. Screens for the latter are placed higher and are made wider, and wire-cloth is substituted for perforated iron plates.

BATTERY SCREENS.

Screens for working ores wet are generally made of Russia sheet iron, of the softest and toughest quality, punched with fine round holes by means of a machine. The size of these holes varies from number nine of the common sewing needles to number one, the punches used being made of needles. Number one is thus the coarsest screen. The diameter of the holes of a No. 4 screen is one-twenty-fourth of an inch, and there are 144 holes in a square inch. In a No. 6 screen, the holes are one-fortieth of an inch in diameter, and there are 324 in a square inch. The screens vary in length from three to three and a half feet according to the length of the mortar, and are from ten to fifteen inches wide. When wooden frames are used, the punched screens are tacked on at the edges with common carpet tacks, a strip of baize or blanket being placed under the edge, to make a tighter joint and to facilitate the removal of the screen when worn out. The screens are also secured in iron frames, made with cross-bars so as to sustain them.

Sometimes the holes in the sheet iron are made in the form of narrow slits, about one-third of an inch long, with a view of increasing the rapidity of the discharge of the stamped stuff. For the same purpose, the screens are not placed vertically in the mortars but are inclined foward at the top, as indicated in the figures of mortars, by the recess for the reception of the screen frames.

CAMS AND CAM-SHAFTS.

The stamps of California batteries are lifted by iron cams, keyed upon iron shafts, and revolving at the side of the stamp stem under the tappet. Wooden shafts with iron cams inserted are now seldom used upon the Pacific slope, though formerly common, and used also in the gold region of the Carolinas and Georgia. The iron cams are made single, with one arm, and also double, with two; but the single cam is now generally preferred, as it permits the shaft to be brought very near to the stem and thus brings the commencement of the lifting surface of the cam nearly under the tappet. Cast iron is used; the bearing surface, about three inches wide, is made smooth by grinding; and the hubs are strengthened with wrought-iron bands. The proper form of the curvature of the cam is a modified involute of a circle, the radius of which is equal to the horizontal distance between the axis of the cam-shaft and the centre of the stamp-stem. The curvature should be increased or made greater than the regular involute, at each end of the cam. This is done so as to ease the contact, by allowing the cam to commence to act upon the tappet at the least practicable distance from the axis of the cam-shaft, where the concussion is least, and to prevent the outer end from scraping or tearing along the face of the tappet. This end is also cut out on one or both sides so as to prevent the corner from cutting the circular edge of the tappet. The face of the tappet should always be at right angles with the radius of the curvature of the cam at every part of its course. In practice it is usual to construct the cam-curve by means of a string and pencil. This string must be as long as the required lift or rise of the stamp, added to the distance between the axis of the cam-shaft and the axis of the stem. A circular disk of wood, with a radius equal to the last-mentioned distance, is provided, and, the string being fastened at the edge, is wound upon its periphery. It is placed upon a flat surface or sheet of paper; a pencil is fastened at the free end of the string, and the latter is unwound, being kept taut, while the point of the pencil traces a line upon the paper until the string becomes tangent to the circle at the point of attachment. This gives the involute with sufficient accuracy, and it is modified in practice as already mentioned. The cam-shaft is made of round iron, usually 4½ inches in diameter, turned and finished off, and having one and sometimes two key-seats cut in it longitudinally between the bearings for the purpose of fastening the cams in their places. One shaft is sometimes made to run fifteen or more stamps; but an independent cam-shaft for each 5-stamp battery is preferable. If there is a line of several batteries a counter-shaft is used. The stamps are held and guided in position in the mortar by guides above and below the tappet. These guides are, by preference, made of hard wood rather than metal. They are made in halves so that by dressing off the two opposing edges they may be readily refitted to the stem when they are too much worn away. Oak is preferred; but in its absence pine is substituted. The friction of metal guides is injurious to the stems. The guides for a battery of iron stem-stamps made in France in 1867, by Messrs. Huet & Geyler for the mines of Serena, Spain, were made of brass, like ordinary journal boxes, and the cams worked through a slot in the centre of the stem.

THE STAMP BATTERIES OF CALIFORNIA.

Having now described the various parts of a battery in some detail, it may be well to direct attention to their combination so as to form a complete stamp-battery such as is now in use in the best mills upon the Pacific slope. The annexed figure will serve to indicate the general appearance and arrangement of one of these batteries and the frame for its support.

This is a sectional elevation of a self-feeding stamp battery, as constructed for working gold quartz. The frame is of pine timber securely braced and held by tie-rods. One end of the iron mortar is supposed to be removed so as to show the interior. The hopper-shaped box, C, is the self-feeding arrangement. It is shaken at each blow of the stamp by means of an upper tappet which strikes upon one arm of a lever, by which motion is communicated to the forward end of the feed-box, C. It will be observed that the cam-shaft is driven by a belt running from a counter pulley below. The double cam is shown, and the movable arm or bar used to hold or "hang up" the stamp when the battery is not in action. The scale of this drawing is about one-quarter of an inch to one foot.

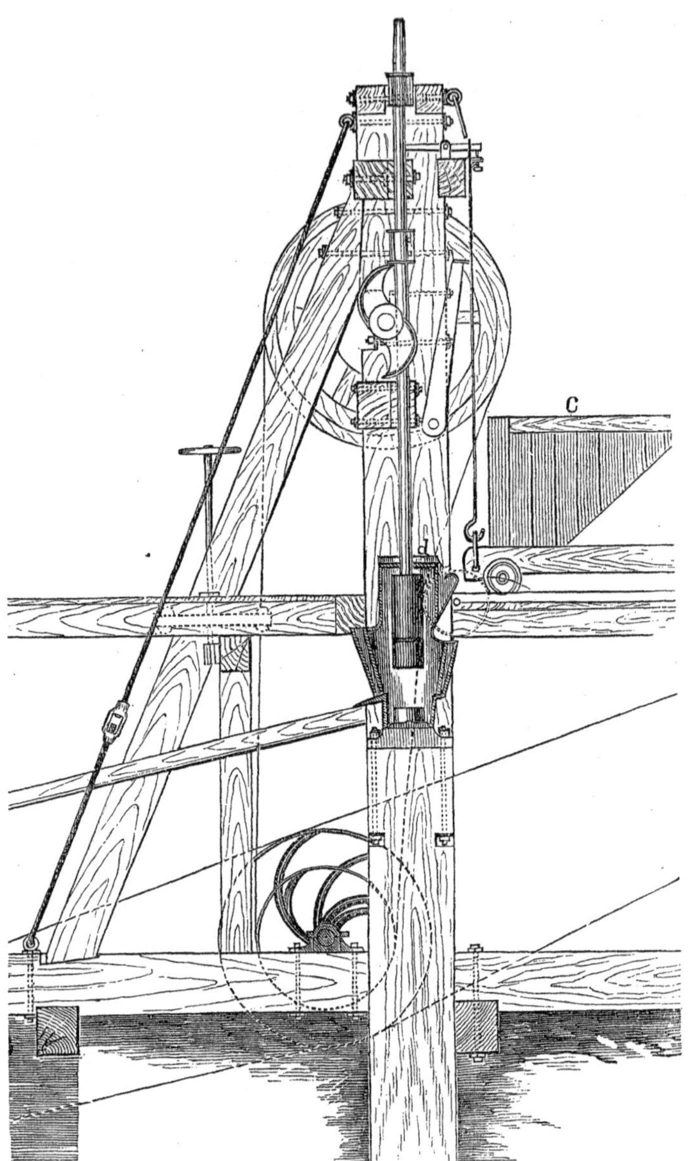

Battery for working gold quartz.

The next figure shows the construction of a battery and its frame for a wet-crushing silver mill. The ore, after passing through a Blake's rock-breaker, is received in the feeding box mounted upon rollers. From this it drops into the mortar. This mortar is made with grates upon each side. The stamped ore, after settling in vats, is worked by charges in pans. The framework of this battery is different from the preceding, but the arrangements for feeding, hanging up stamps, &c., are similar.

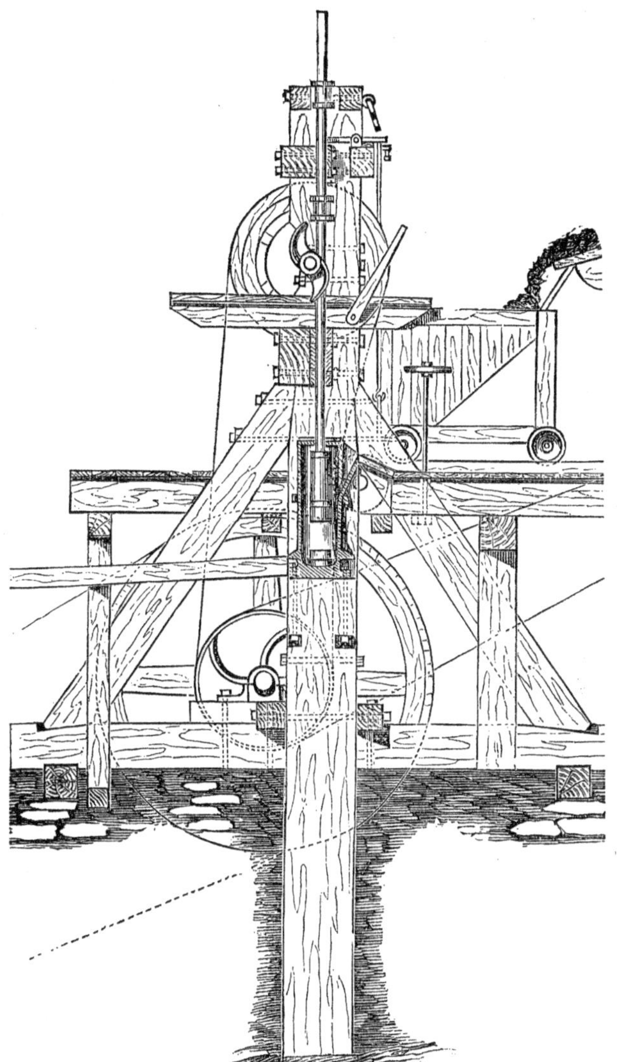

Wet-crushing Silver Battery.

HOWLAND'S ROTARY BATTERY.

This is a compact and portable form of battery, designed and patented by W. H. Howland. It was introduced to the notice of the mill-men of California and Nevada several years ago, and was at first used to a considerable extent, but was gradually replaced in nearly all the mills by the ordinary straight battery. These batteries were early adopted by Mr. A. B. Paul, in the mills erected by him below Gold Hill, and he has recently given his opinion of their merits as follows: "No act of mine in mining has been more criticised than the adopting of these batteries in my Washoe operations. Their adoption was no blind work, as I had used them for three successive years previous, and in no test with other mills was I beat in returns. I had then, and have now, great faith in their principle. It certainly is in the right direction. They will, in time, I am confident, become popular, especially when introduced with the *later improvements*, on account of their simplicity, efficient working, and cheapness."

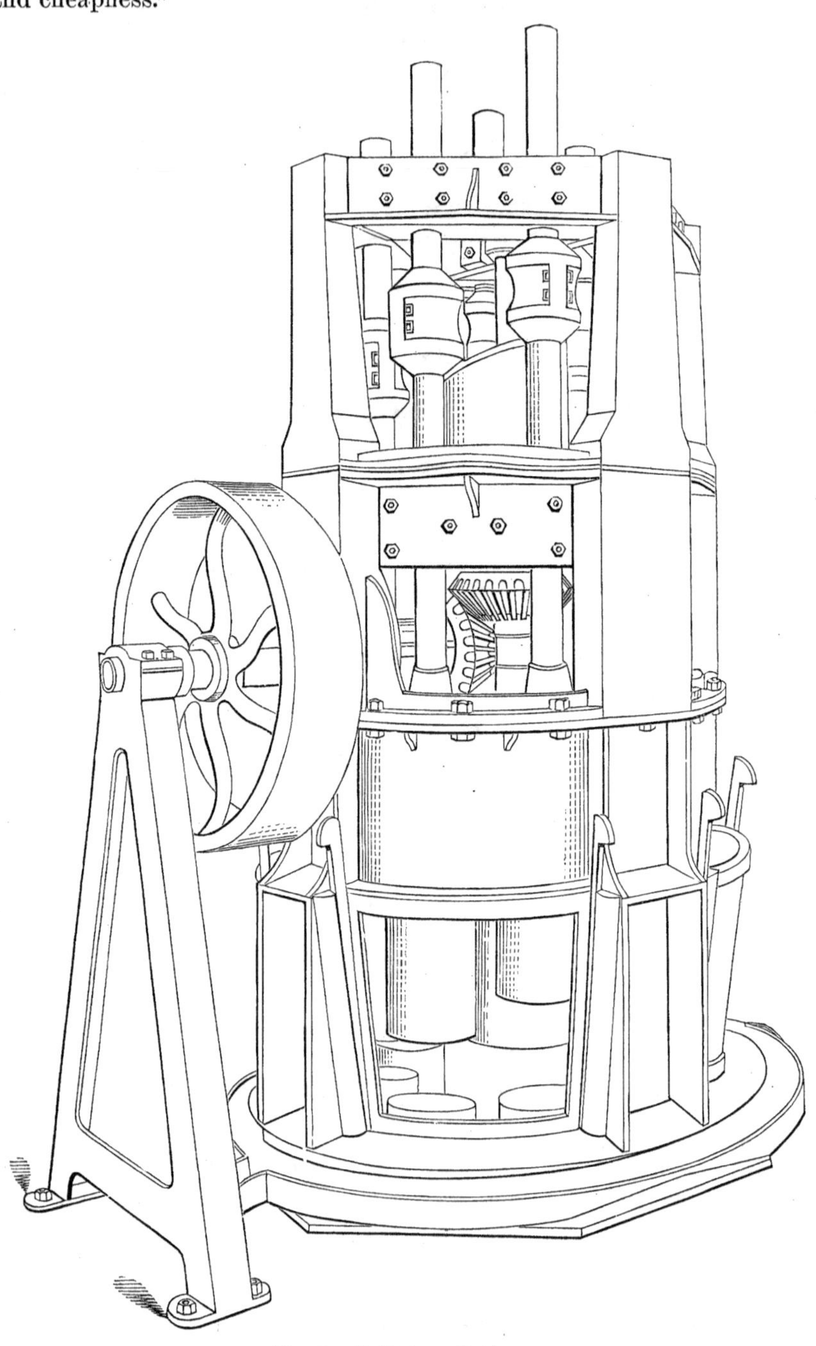

Howland's Rotary Battery.

It is claimed by the inventor that very great improvements in the construction have recently been made, based upon the experience of seven years of constant working of the old style of the rotary iron battery. It is now offered by the Miners' Foundry to miners as a "new and highly improved rotary quartz mill," of less cost than the straight batteries, and requiring less power.

The construction is shown by the figure, page 196. The whole battery is of iron; the stamps are set in a circle around a central vertical shaft carrying the cams. Motion is imparted to this shaft by means of bevel-gearing. The cams are thus carried round horizontally, and lift each stamp in succession. These rotary batteries are cast in three sections. The first section has the mortar or base, screen frames and feed openings in one piece; the second section contains the lower guide boxes, (which are of wood,) driving gears, and cam-wheel; the upper section contains the upper guide-boxes. These three sections are bolted together, with thin pieces of wood-packing between each. The stems, tappets, stamps, shoes, and dies are the same as in the ordinary cast straight batteries.

The openings for delivery through screens of the ordinary construction are seen at the base. The stamped stuff collects in the annular trough, cast in one piece with the mortar, so that there is no leakage, and is discharged by a chute at one side. It is claimed as one of the advantages of this improved form that there is more metal in the mortar or base than in the old form of rotary battery, and that the leakage at the base of the column, the jar and loosening of bolts, and the wear of guide-boxes, formerly complained of, are now entirely obviated.

Its compactness and lightness as compared with the ordinary straight battery, and its being complete in itself, not requiring timber framing and supports, commend it specially to those who wish to work their ores in districts remote from supplies of timber. Mr. W. D. Gray, the superintendent of the mill of the Imperial Company, at Gold Hill, Nevada, writes to Mr. Howland, February, 1869, as follows respecting the rotary battery:

> Yours of 10th instant is at hand, in which you speak of having just finished and shipped for White Pine an 8-stamp rotary battery, made from a new and improved set of patterns. For a new country, where lumber is scarce and labor necessarily high, there is no battery now in use that will equal yours. The little time required to set it up ready to run is an important consideration. The greatest objection urged against the rotary battery has been the cost of keeping them in repair, compared with the straight battery. But my experience for the last eight years proves this a mistake. The annual report of the Imperial Silver Mining Company shows quite a percentage in favor of the Gold Hill mill (five 8-stamp rotary batteries) over the Rock Point mill, both in cost of repairs, expense of running, and yield per ton of ore worked—the first of which I have had charge of for the last five years. The Rock Point mill, run by water, has straight batteries. I think this comparison can be fully substantiated, as far as expense of repairs is concerned; also as compared with any other mill run in Storey County for the last five years.

The mill above referred to was designed for the Grant District, and weighed, when complete, less than six tons. The stamps weighed 600 pounds each, and were designed to make 100 drops per minute. When working up to its full capacity it will crush from twelve to sixteen tons, *dry*, in twenty-four hours. The total height of the machine is about eight feet, and the weight of the mortar is 3,000 pounds.

WILSON'S STEAM STAMPS.

One of the most successful of the attempts to apply steam direct to the stems of stamps has been made by Mr. T. R. Wilson, of Philadelphia, Pennsylvania, whose mills have been in practical operation at several of our western mines. The general appearance and arrangement of the battery is shown by the figure. Steam is taken directly by a two-inch pipe to a short cylinder around the stem of each stamp above the frame and by suitable valves is made to act under or above a piston upon the prolongation of the stem, so as to either raise or throw down the stanp at will. The force of the steam can thus be added to the weight and momentum of the stamp in falling, in order to increase the rapidity and force of the blows, and thus to give an increased product of stamped ore in a given time. Two stamps are placed in each battery. The mortar is made in the usual form for double grates, one on each side, but is heavier than those intended for ordinary stamps. The two stamps are intended to strike about 400 blows per minute, or 200 blows to each stamp; and it is claimed by the manufacturers that they will stamp fine one ton or more of hard rock in one hour.

Wilson's Steam Stamps.

It is automatic in its action, cams being adjusted upon the upper ends of the stems and operating the valves as the stems move up and down. The following data will show the force with which the stamps may be made to strike:

	Inches.
Diameter of cylinder, 5⅝ inches, area in square inches.........	24. 8
Diameter of upper piston rod 2 inches, area in square inches....	3. 1
Total area of piston for down pressure of steam................	21. 7
	Pounds.
Multiply by pressure of steam in the boiler, (70 pounds)........	1, 519
Add weight of stamp and stem..................................	492
Whole force of blow..	2, 011

This shows a force of about one ton, and it is so considered by the inventor. The steam-pressure at the battery is usually less than stated, say 65 pounds. The length of the cylinders is 7½ inches, and the thickness of the piston is 3 inches; there is therefore room for an extreme stroke of 14½ inches, but an allowance must be made for the wear of shoes and dies. In setting up the machine an allowance of five inches is made for this, a space being left of this length under the piston, when the shoes and dies are new. This leaves a space of 9½ inches for the movement of the piston; but in practice it is not run over 6 inches, this stroke or fall of the stamp being found to be quite sufficient. To vary the length of the stroke, the position of the cam is varied upon the top of the stem, being screwed down for long strokes and upward for short strokes. The screw thread is not cut so low as to make it possible for the piston to strike the cylinder-head.

The dies are made in the usual way, and are recessed to a depth of an inch in the bottom of the mortar, which must be bedded upon a firm foundation.

ADAPTATION OF STAMP BATTERIES TO QUARTZ CRUSHING.

The action of stamps is peculiarly favorable to the extraction of free gold. The metal, except in rare cases, is best liberated by simply breaking up the quartz without any grinding or rubbing. Trituration rapidly cuts up and disseminates the gold in such an extreme state of division that it passes off in the water and cannot be recovered. These observations apply in general to all ores. The product from stamps is more granular and contains less fine powder and dust than that of a grinding mill. This is due not only to the manner in which the stuff is acted upon, but also to the manner in which it is delivered. The constant swash of the material and the dash of the stamps carry the finer portion away, and only those portions remain which are too coarse to pass through the screens. Another advantage in respect to gold or any other malleable metal is that a direct blow merely flattens the particles without wearing them away, while trituration cuts and wears them away. Gold, also, when in coarse grains, by its great specific gravity settles in the lower part of the mortar under the sand around and between the dies. The swash of the sand serves to keep the amalgamated copper plates clean and bright, and thus in the best condition to seize and hold the freshly liberated gold particles thrown into contact with them.

Another reason of the great practical efficiency of stamps over other forms of apparatus for fine crushing is the fact that a wide range in the size of material fed is admissible. They act upon either fine or coarse material. Grinding machines require rock to be first broken up so that their surfaces may act upon as many fragments as possible at the same time; but with stamps, the rock fed may vary from mere sand to pieces three or four inches in diameter. All are crushed together, without clogging or causing an increased strain upon the driving-gear, however rapidly or irregularly they are fed. The constant flow of water through the mortar carries out the fine material and leaves the coarse to be further acted upon.

DETAILS OF SEVERAL STAMP MILLS.

In further illustration of the construction and working of stamp mills, the following details regarding some of the principal mills of California may have some value. They are drawn from the manuscript notes of the writer, made at different times during visits to the mines and mills.

The 40-stamp mill at the Hayward Mine, Sutter Creek, Amador County, had in June, 1866:

Stamps in batteries of five stamps each. Battery boxes of wood. Low trough mortars of cast iron. Weight of stamps, 450 pounds each; eleven inches lift; 80 blows per minute. Dies seven inches across face; both dies and shoes are used until they are completely worn out, (from four to six weeks.) Height of discharge-opening eleven inches above dies; different heights from nine to fourteen inches have been tried, but the height of eleven inches has been found to give the best results. Screens on one side of the battery only and made of the best Russia iron, No. 11, punched with vertical slits a little over half an inch in length. These screens are narrow, the delivery being through a vertical height of two inches only. As the openings in the screens wear most rapidly upon the lower ends, the screens are reversed after each run.

The amalgamation is effected in battery, the gold collecting chiefly upon an amalgamated copper-plate at the delivery, directly back of the screens. This plate is four inches wide and is slightly inclined inward. The amalgamated particles of gold accumulate upon this plate in a thick even coat which can be removed in heavy cakes by the aid of chisels. This plate must be placed at the proper angle with due regard to the velocity of the movement of the stamps and the quantity of water used. The pitch must be just sufficient to keep it clear and no more. The apron, outside, is not made of copper, as is usual, since the progress of the amalgamation can be judged of better without it.

It is found that the quartz crushes faster when there is not an over-supply of water. Eighty drops of the stamps per minute are necessary to keep the materials properly in motion.

When the amalgam is collected, the stamps are "hung up," the screens are removed, and the whole of the interior of the battery and mortar is accessible. The amalgam found upon the copper plate is chiseled off, and the fragments are collected in iron vessels. It is then broken up and softened by the addition of a little quicksilver. By this means any fragments of iron and admixed grains of pyrites are floated out to the surface and are washed away. It is then strained through a piece of coarse unbleached cotton cloth, sufficient of the liquid amalgam being taken to give a ball of hard, dry amalgam weighing about fifteen pounds. At the clean-up witnessed by the writer, about 185 pounds of dry amalgam were obtained in 15-pound balls.* It was then retorted in an ordinary pot retort with a long beak or tube of wrought-iron pipe. The retort being luted and closed is placed in a rude furnace in the open air, and a wood fire built on the top and increased gradually. It is estimated that the amalgam will yield about one-third of its weight of bullion, or about $95 in value, to each pound of amalgam.

At the Eureka Mill, Grass Valley, in 1866, there were 20 stamps, 815 pounds each, 10 inches fall; screens raised three inches above die-face, and five inches in front. Worked well; did not cut. No amalgamation in battery; the sands collected on blankets and copper plates amalgamated below the blankets. Twenty tons crushed in eleven hours.

Allison Ranch in 1865 worked 12 stamps of 1,000 pounds each, 10 to 12 inches lift, crushing about 40 tons a day. These stamps were made upon the old-fashioned pattern, with wooden stems and square heads. No quicksilver was used in the battery; the pulp flowed over blankets, and the sands deposited were worked in Attwood's concentrator, and the waste passed through the Lawton pan. Fourteen Lawton bowls were used, and were said to save from $1,000 to $1,200 a month. Sulphurets were concentrated in a long rocker, a square box-trough, giving from five to seven tons a week of concentrated sulphurets.

At the Merrimac Mill, of 10 stamps, the amalgamation was effected in battery. The copper plates are one-eighth of an inch thick and about

* The yield in this case was from about 780 tons of the quartz, or a two-weeks run.

four feet long. Stamps weigh 740 pounds each; 3-inch stems, 16 inches long; 11 inches to 12 inches lift; delivery four inches above the top of dies.

At Rocky Bar Mill, 16 stamps, weighing 1,025 pounds, or an average of 1,000 pounds, each.

Jefferson Mill, Brown's Valley, 12 stamps, four in each battery; 750 pounds each stamp; not lifted high but run fast, (72 to 75 drops per minute,) the quartz being soft. Blankets and a long sluice below them. No. 4 screen; four inches from top of die to discharge.

Sierra Buttes Mills, near Downieville, two mills, 12 stamps each; four stamps in each battery; round stems and heads; weight 600 pounds in upper mill, 640 pounds in lower. Strike 60 to 67 blows per minute, and from nine to twelve inches fall, depending upon the wear of the dies. Delivery five inches to five and a half inches above die. No copper plates in battery. No. 4 screens, 144 holes to the inch, Russia iron. They clean up once in 60 days, and 66 per cent. of the whole yield is obtained in the battery, including the front plate attached to mortar. Blankets were used for some time below battery, but were replaced by amalgamated copper plates, extending for 40 feet below the battery, and having a slope of one in twelve.

Table showing work done by mills on the Mariposas estate, California, during six months ending January 1, 1864.

Mills.	Average No. of stamps.	Working days.	Maximum crushing capacity—Tons per stamp.	No. of tons reduced.	Tons reduced per stamp.		Total of gold per ton.
					Per month.	Per day.	
Benton	$60\frac{1}{3}$	58.16	$1\frac{1}{3}$	3,688	$10\frac{1}{2}$	$1\frac{1}{15}$	$5 59
Mount Ophir	28	24.22	$1\frac{1}{4}$	798	$9\frac{1}{2}$	$1\frac{1}{8}$	11 03
Green Gulch	40	113.20	$1\frac{1}{2}$	6,924	$17\frac{34}{40}$	$1\frac{1}{2}$	9 61
Princeton	24	147.19$\frac{1}{2}$	$1\frac{7}{8}$	6,651	$46\frac{1}{2}$	$1\frac{5}{6}$	13 67
Total and average	$152\frac{1}{3}$	345 $\frac{5}{24}$ $\frac{1}{2}$	$1\frac{1}{2}$	18,061	20	$1\frac{1}{4}$	10 35

The data of measurement of tons are from estimates by the bookkeepers or the mill superintendents, and may not be accurate within 12 per cent.

At the Bigler Mill, Clear Creek district, June, 1866, there were ten stamps; two Hunter's concentrators; one of Hendy's or Prater's concentrators. The order of succession of the fall of stamps was 1, 4, 2, 5, 3. The amalgamation was effected in battery as much as possible. Two amalgamated copper plates were used, one six inches wide between the top of the dies and the screens, the other six or seven inches wide, placed at the back of the mortar under the feeding chute; both plates being inclined inward so as to be washed clean by the swash of the water.

At the celebrated Gould and Curry Mill, as first arranged for dry crushing, the stamps were placed in batteries of five each, and a belt 32 inches wide drove two batteries, (or ten stamps.)

As appropriate to this part of the report I insert interesting details concerning the Mettacom Mill stamp batteries at Austin, Nevada. These particulars were obtained by Mr. Raymond, and I extract them from his chapter upon metallurgical processes :

The weight of the stamps is nearly 900 pounds each. There is not so much difference of opinion now as formerly among good mill-men as to the proper weight for stamps. As the amount of horse-power (and hence of fuel) required to run a battery depends directly upon this weight, it has been necessary to find out by experience whether heavy blows do as much work in proportion as lighter ones, and where the proper medium lies. The question has quite as much to do with the discharge as with the crushing. The blow of the stamp not only pulverizes the rock, but drives it outward through the screens. In dry-stamping this is the only force which effects the discharge. Hence the weight of the stamp should not be so great as to necessitate slow running. Probably 750 to 800 pounds is the best weight for general use; though if all mills were run as skillfully as the Mettacom, even 900 pounds would not be too heavy.

The stems are 3⅛ inches in diameter. The usual size is 2⅞, and these stems are, therefore, nearly 20 per cent. stronger and heavier than ordinary; the proportion being as the squares of the diameters. The advantage of putting a larger proportion of the total weight into the stem is the diminished vibration from the blow on the tappet. The stems should always be fitted as closely as possible to the guides; but light stems spring or bend, and wear the guide in rising. There is no wear of this kind in falling, so long as the stem is true. The stems are set 8½ inches apart, the bosses and shoes work within about two inches of each other, and the distance between the tappets is about three-fourths of an inch. The whole length of each battery-mortar is therefore about 5 feet 6 inches.

The cam-shaft is rigged with single cams. The old fashion of triple cams is now about obsolete; but the usual form is the double cam, which many mill-men still prefer, claiming, that as it gives two drops of the stamp for each revolution, it saves friction in gearing, and enables the battery to be run at high speeds without running the engine as fast. These and other arguments for the double cam only prove that it suits the machinery which has been calculated for it. As a matter of fact, however, I have never seen double-cam batteries equal the single cams in speed; and I think Mr. Howell is right in claiming the advantage for single cams, that the shoulder can be brought directly under the tappet, so as to prevent catching. With the ordinary double cam, the shaft must be set further back from the stems, and the cams are easily caught and broken.

This subject is directly related to the speed of the battery. The Mettacom mill has vindicated triumphantly the wisdom of its peculiar features by the most extraordinary running on record. For months together the batteries have been kept at from 98 to 100 drops per minute, rising to 102, or even 105, and never falling below 94; yet there has never been a cam broken in the mill. The Manhattan, an excellent mill, with double cams and stamps weighing only 750 pounds, cannot safely run on the same ore at higher speed than 85 to the minute, and Mr. Curtis, the able superintendent, with the performances of the Mettacom before his eyes, naturally declares himself in favor of the single cam, which would enable him to run his batteries up to 110 per minute. The Mettacom stamps fall 10 inches. The original drop was 9½ inches; but it was increased to ease the cams and give less jar. The rebound of the stamps amounts sometimes to 1½ inches. Strange to say, the high speed maintained has not caused excessive necessity of repairs. On the contrary, the battery has stood the strain better than any other within my knowledge. Even the shoes and dies, which were not supposed to be unusually good, being bought for ordinary hard iron, lasted for five months of continuous running without being replaced. This fact cannot be adequately explained. Probably that particular set was a lucky cast. Ordinarily, it would have worn out in about six weeks; but I do not doubt that the heavy charges put through the batteries at high speed protected the shoes and dies from pounding on one another, which they are quite likely to do in ordinary mills, especially when the feeder is careless. A mill running at 100 to the minute keeps the feeder busy; and he does not wait for a stamp to thunder out, by pounding on its anvil, that it has finished its last mouthful and wants another.

A fact not to be overlooked in this connection is the great solidity of the battery frame and foundations. Nine-tenths of the stamp-mills ordinarily erected would rack themselves to pieces if run as the Mettacom has been, without breaking so much as a bolt.

The gain in quantity of ore crushed is more than proportionate to the increase of speed. As I have remarked, this quantity depends, in dry-crushing especially, on the discharge. I shall speak of that presently, as it regards the arrangement of screens; but I now refer to the frequency of the drops which supply the direct impulse and the air shock, by which the dry "pulp" is driven through the screens. Mr. Howell found by experiment that with 60 drops per minute he could put through in twenty-four hours only about 4½ tons; 90 drops gave a little over 10 tons; and 102 drops *more than*

$15\frac{1}{2}$ *tons*. If we assume that the increase in consumption of fuel would be the same as that in the power generated by the falling stamps per minute, we shall have—

No. of drops per minute.	Horse-power, per stamp.	Increase of power.	Yield.	Increase of yield.
60	1.36	....	$4\frac{1}{2}$	....
90	2.04	50 per cent..	10	122 per cent.
102	2.22	10 per cent..	$15\frac{1}{2}$	55 per cent.

The increase of speed from 60 to 102, or 70 per cent., increased the yield from $4\frac{1}{2}$ to $15\frac{1}{2}$, or 244 per cent. To this should be added the gain in wages, interest on capital, &c., secured by rapid running. This comparison does not fairly apply to wet-crushing, though I am satisfied that in that process also high speeds are the best. But the difference is not so startling. Most wet-crushing mills come pretty near the average of $1\frac{1}{4}$ tons crushed in twenty-four hours per horse-power developed by each stamp. But the above table shows a variation from 0.33 tons at 60 to 0.70 at 102. The performance of the Manhattan mill is about 0.45 ton crushed in twenty-four hours per horse-power developed by each stamp; and this is a fair, perhaps a high, average for such mills.

When the throat of the battery is open, the pulp will be thrown both ways, and some of it comes back on the feeding-floor. This indicates a fact too often ignored in the construction of mortars, namely, that since the impulse given by the stamp is radial in all directions, the greater the surface of discharge the higher will be the duty performed. The Mettacom batteries are not perfect in this respect. They have only a single front discharge, but this is 18 inches high, instead of 12, as is usual. It is noticed that the fine pulp comes mostly through the upper six inches, and hence, in most batteries, would be thrown back into the mortar until it found exit below. Various forms of mortar with increased discharge have been recommended. The maximum discharge per stamp is attained by Clayton's circular mortar, containing only one stamp. There are also mortars with universal discharge, in which the screens go all the way round, being curved at the ends. The most common are the double dischargers, having screens in front and behind, and the feed over the rear screen. The objection hitherto made to all arrangements involving curved screens is the difficulty of properly stretching and keying them, while in dry-crushing, even a rear screen is found to be inconvenient on account of breakage from coarse ore. Mr. Curtis, of the Manhattan, however, prefers a double discharge, while Mr. Howell cares more for end-dischargers. The Mettacom end-stamps are hung with three-eighths of an inch more fall than the others, and still do less work. The order in which the stamps fall varies in different mills, and for wet and dry crushing. The two extremes to be avoided are a simultaneous drop of all the stamps, which would rack the frame, strain the engine, destroy the continuity of discharge, and probably break the screens; and a drop in regular succession, (1, 2, 3, 4, 5,) which would shove the ore to one end of the mortar, and give the stamps at one end too much, and at the other end too little, to do. Some mill-men prefer to arrange the succession so that no stamp shall immediately follow its next neighbor. The orders 1, 4, 2, 5, 3; 1, 3, 5, 2, 4; 4, 2, 5, 1, 3, would satisfy this condition. Others prefer dropping the two-end stamps first, as 1, 5, 2, 4, 3, or 1, 5, 4, 2, 3. The wave of discharge or splash of the water through the screens in wet-crushing is to be taken into consideration. In dry-crushing, the objects to be secured are an equal distribution of ore under the stamps, giving an equal work per stamp, and a maximum discharge of pulp through the screens. The latter seems to be best secured by letting the middle stamp drop last. The outer stamps should then have slightly longer cams, to increase their fall. It will be found that the central stamps take and distribute nearly all the feed. Much depends on the skill and fidelity of the feeder, in both kinds of crushing. Hence the automatic self-feeding batteries used in Cornwall have found little favor in this country. They do not "humor" the stamps; and the difference in regularity of running and in duty performed is more than equivalent to the wages of a good feeder.

The screens of this mill are No. 40 brass wire, (1,600 meshes to the square inch,) which is preferred for dry-crushing to the "Russia-punched." The latter are frequently preferred by mill-men in wet-crushing, on account of alleged greater durability, or in the belief that slits are better adapted to discharge liquid pulp than meshes. I take leave to doubt, however, whether these advantages in any case counterbalance the greater proportional discharge-area offered by wire screens. The Mettacom screens are not vertical, but lean outward about 10 degrees. The pulp generally goes through obliquely, and is as fine as the siftings of a horizontal No. 60 sieve. The angle given has been established as the best for dry-crushing. The gain in amount of discharge, wet or dry, from inclined screens, is universally recognized; but mill-men do not so generally bear in mind that the screen so set should be a little coarser than the fineness required for the pulp, if the best results are to be obtained. Mr. Howell's observation is that stamps ordinarily crush faster than the batteries discharge. He has often put the pulp back through his battery, and found that it took about as long to go through a sfresh rock. Running slow gives the fine dust a chance to fall back under the stamps; running fast keeps it constantly in motion, and much of it gets out. I venture to suggest some considerations based upon the foregoing facts, and calculated, I think, to put mill-men upon the right track in increasing the efficiency of dry batteries. It seems to me that dropping 900-pound stamps is a costly way of making currents of air to promote discharge. The object of the mill-man should be to get the highest practicable speed from his stamps, and then to give them such facilities for discharge as that every drop shall do its full work in crushing. The increase of the discharge-area is the first and most obvious means, and a useful auxiliary will, I think, be found in producing a current of air with a fan, which shall suck or drive the fine dust through the sieve. I have seen exhausting fans applied in this way in several mills. There was one in the Sheba, at Star City, Humboldt County, and there were several in the early Austin mills, which were finally condemned. Mill-men are too ready to reject such appliances as soon as they cause a little trouble, whether through faulty construction or careless management. But this point will be found too important to be dismissed so easily. I do not remember ever in my life seeing a stamp mill in which the difficulty of discharge did not really delay the work of crushing. The extreme of excessive discharge, which would do no harm, is carefully avoided, and no one can tell to this day how much the stamp now in use could be made to do by simply improving batteries in this respect. The tide of invention is, it appears to me, running the wrong way. We have innumerable devices to increase the force and efficiency of the blow of the stamp, which is already in advance of the rest of the machinery, while the inventions for improving the mortars and discharges are few, generally imperfect, and regarded with too little favor by those practical mill-men who are alone competent to take hold of them and perfect them.

The screens at this mill last nearly four weeks. When the threads wear thin they begin to shift, and the screens must be removed. They are turned to prolong the wear. The middle of the screen lasts longest. The dies, when new, come up to within about one inch of the lowest portion of the discharge. It is very important to make this interval, called the "height of issue," as small as the screens will bear. The dies used for five months wore away about 1½ inches, and the introduction of new ones raised the capacity of the battery nearly two tons per day. Much trouble was experienced in keeping the dies in their places in the bottom of the mortar. Finally, 150 pounds of melted lead was poured in, filling the mortar-bed about one inch. This is found to work well. I think that for dry-crushing a single die, filling the whole bed, would be better yet. When it wears on one side it can be turned, and so used till it is worn out. This is a German plan, and used successfully in some dry-crushing mills managed by Germans in this country.

The foundation of a battery is the most important part of its construction, and it is the feature most neglected in this country. Few mill-owners like to put so much money "out of sight;" the work of preparing foundations is parsimoniously, ignorantly, or carelessly managed; and the result is that the batteries cannot be run at high speed, and even at low speed they are continually settling, or getting out of line. The great efficiency and stability of the Mettacom mill is due to its carefully-prepared foundation. The mortar-blocks are set on end, upon solid bed-rock. They are nine feet deep. Before placing them the rock was thoroughly smoothed and leveled, and the bottom of each block was planed true. The upper ends of the blocks being (as is the case with all large timbers) sun-cracked, melted sulphur was poured into the cracks. The mortars are set on the blocks and screwed down tight. If screwed (as is frequently the case) directly to the blocks, they will in a few months get loose, and rock and sand will work between, putting the machinery out of plumb and endangering the mortar. To prevent this, two thicknesses of blanket soaked in tar were put between the mortars and the blocks. An arrangement was made by which the settling of the mortars could be measured. It is found that after more than a year of steady running they have sunk uniformly less than one-fourth inch—doubtless due to the compression of the blankets. The freedom from jar in the mill, while the batteries were running at tremendous speed, impressed me as decisive proof of the utility of the arrangements described. There is, however, some vibration in the cam-shaft, which should have been five inches instead of four in diameter. Mr. Howell recommends also heavier bearings. The latter are now eight inches, and should be ten. No Babbitt metal is used in the upper box; it cannot be kept in, and smooth iron is therefore preferred. The battery, running at 98 to 100 per minute, requires about twenty-two horse-power, which is perhaps a little more than half the power employed in the mill, and crushes easily seven tons in twelve hours. This being about the usual duty for twenty-four hours, the rest of the mill, especially the reverberatories for roasting, calculated on that basis, cannot come up to the capacity of the battery; and this great defect in the original plans has never yet been remedied. I have frequently found mills in which the capacity of the roasting or amalgamating apparatus is quite unsuited to that of the batteries. In such cases the extra machinery is practically good for nothing, since the capacity of a mill is determined by its least adequate part. The Mettacom batteries must either run but twelve hours daily, or they must run for a longer period at full capacity, and then stand still until the surplus of the pulp has been roasted.

AUSTRALIAN MACHINERY AND STAMPS.

Next to California and Nevada, Australia is the country in which the greatest number of stamp mills have been erected, and where experience more nearly equals our own. It is thus important to glance at the extent and character of Australian mechanical appliances, and, as far as possible, to compare them with similar machines in this country.

The mineral statistics of Victoria for 1868 give some very interesting particulars concerning the weight and cost of stamp-heads and shanks and lifters, the quantities of quartz crushed per diem, the number of holes per square inch in the gratings, the quantity of water used and the quantity of quicksilver used and lost. They have reference only to the principal gold mines in the several districts; but they will not on that account be less useful.

In the Ballarat mining district the stamp-heads and shanks or lifters vary in weight from 4 hundred weight to 8 hundred weight 2 quarters, and the cost is from £3 17*s*. 6*d*. to £15 10*s*. The height the stamp-head falls ranges from 7 to 10 inches. The number of strokes made by stamp heads per minute is from 50 to 85. The quantity of quartz crushed per head per diem of 24 hours varies from 1 ton to 4 tons. The number of holes per square inch in the gratings used is from 40 to 200.—(The latter number is made use of by the Victoria company at Clunes; the grating is fixed at the back of the stamper-box.) The horse-power required to work each stamp is from 1 to 2. The quantity of water used per stamp-head in crushing varies from 950 gallons to 8,640 gallons per diem of 24 hours. The quantity of mercury used in the ripples per stamper is from 5 to 75 pounds. The quantity of mercury lost per stamp-head per week varies from 1 ounce to 8 ounces.

In the Beechworth mining district the stamp-heads and shanks or lifters vary in weight from 4 hundred weight 1 quarter 17 pounds to 7 hundred weight 3 quarters, and the cost from £5 3*s*. 6*d*. to £13 per head. The height the stamp-heads fall varies from 5 inches to 14 inches. The number of strokes made by the stamp-heads per minute is from 40 to 90. The quantity crushed per head per diem of 14 hours ranges from 16 hundred weight to 4 tons. The number of holes per square inch in the gratings used is from 60 to 140. The horse-power required to work each stamp-head is from 0.75 to 1.50. The quantity of water used per stamp-head in crushing varies from 720 gallons to 11,520 gallons per diem of 24 hours. The quantity of mercury used in the ripples per stamper is from 5 to 70 pounds. The quantity of mercury lost per stamp-head per week varies from ½ ounce to 8 ounces.

In the Sandhurst mining district the stamp-heads and shanks or lifters vary in weight from 5 hundred weight to 8 hundred weight, and the cost from £4 5*s*. to £8 11*s*. The height the stamp-heads fall varies from 6 to 18 inches. The number of strokes made by stamp-heads per minute is from 25 to 75. The quantity of quartz crushed per head per diem of 24 hours ranges from 18 hundred weight to 3 tons 3 quarters. The number of holes per square inch in the gratings used is from 64 to 140. The horse-power required to work each stamp-head is from 0.66 to 2. The quantity of water used per stamp-head in crushing varies from 4,000 gallons to 8,640 gallons per diem of 24 hours. The quantity of mercury used in the ripples per stamper is from 10 to 40 pounds. The quantity of mercury lost per stamp-head per week varies from $\frac{1}{2}$ ounce to $5\frac{1}{2}$ ounces.

In the Maryborough mining district the stamp-heads and shanks or lifters vary in weight from 4 hundred weight 2 quarters to 8 hundred weight, and the cost from £4 18*s.* 6*d.* to £8 14*s.* 6*d.* The height the stamp-heads fall varies from 6 to 22 inches. The number of strokes made by stamp-heads per minute is from 50 to 75. The quantity of quartz crushed per head per diem of 24 hours ranges from 1 ton to 3 tons. The number of holes per square inch in the gratings used is from 70 to 144. The horse-power required to work each stamp-head is from 0.50 to 2.50. The quantity of water used per stamp-head in crushing varies from 900 to 8,640 gallons per diem of 24 hours. The quantity of mercury used in the ripples per stamper is from 3 to 30 pounds. The quantity of mercury lost per stamp-head per week varies from $1\frac{3}{4}$ ounces to 8 ounces.

In the Castlemaine mining district the stamp-heads and shanks or lifters vary in weight from 4 hundred weight 2 quarters to 8 hundred weight, and the cost from £4 2*s.* 6*d.* to £21 11*s.* 6*d.* The height the stamp-heads fall varies from 6 to 15 inches. The number of strokes made by stamp-heads per minute is from 35 to 75. The quantity of quartz crushed per head per diem of 24 hours, ranges from 1 ton to 3 tons 5 hundred weight. The number of holes per square inch in the gratings used is from 40 to 144. The horse-power required to work each stamp-head is from 0.50 to 2. The quantity of water used per stamp-head in crushing varies from 4,800 to 12,960 gallons per diem of 24 hours. The quantity of mercury used in the ripples per stamp is from 6 to 40 pounds. The quantity of mercury lost per stamp-head per week varies from $\frac{1}{4}$ ounce to 24 ounces.

In the Ararat mining district the stamp-heads and shanks or lifters vary in weight from 5 hundred to 6 hundred weight 3 quarters, and the cost from £7 to £8 8*s.* The height the stamp-heads fall varies from $7\frac{1}{2}$ to 10 inches. The number of strokes made by stamp-heads per minute is from 60 to 72. The quantity of quartz crushed per head per diem of 24 hours ranges from 1 ton 5 hundred weight to 1 ton 10 hundred weight. The number of holes per square inch in the gratings used is from 90 to 120. The horse-power required to work each stamp-head is 0.75. The quantity of water used per stamp-head in crushing varies from 4,320 gallons to 12,960 gallons per diem of 24 hours. The quantity of mercury used in the ripples per stamp is from 6 to 47 pounds. The quantity of mercury lost per stamp-head per week varies from $\frac{1}{2}$ ounce to 7 ounces.

In the Gipp's Land mining district the stamp-heads and shanks or lifters vary in weight from 6 hundred weight to 7 hundred weight 2 quarters, and the cost from £5 5*s.* to £40. The height of the stamp-heads fall varies from 7 to 10 inches. The number of strokes made by stamp-heads per minute is from 60 to 80. The quantity of quartz crushed per head per diem of 24 hours ranges from 1 ton 10 hundred weight to 2 tons 1 hundred weight. The number of holes per square inch in the gratings used is from 70 to 250. The horse-power required to work each stamp-head is from 0.75 to 1.50. The quantity of water used per stamp-head in crushing varies from 1,600 gallons to 25,000 gallons* per diem of 24 hours. The quantity of mercury used in the ripples per stamp is from 10 to 37 pounds. The quantity of mercury lost per stamp-head per week varies from $_5$ ounce to 32 ounces.

* This is excessive.

It will be interesting, also, for comparison with our own statistics, to note the present number of machines in use in Victoria, Australia, for different mining purposes. The following statement shows, approximately, the number of miners employed, the machinery in use, and its value in the several gold fields in the colony, &c., compiled from the mining surveyor's and register's reports for the quarter ending September, 1869.

The number of miners (including 16,393 Chinese) engaged in alluvial and quartz mining was 68,684.

Machinery for alluvial mining.—Steam engines used in pumping and winding, 422; horse-puddling machines, 1,797; whims, 292; whips or pulleys, 310; sluices, toms, and sluice-boxes, 18,740; hydraulic hose, 13; pumps, 992; water-wheels, 303; quicksilver and compound cradles, 281; stamp-heads crushing cement, 652; boring machines, 21.

In quartz mining.—Steam engines used in winding, pumping, and crushing, 656, with an aggregate of 12,308 horse-power; crushing machines, driven by other power than steam, 67; stamp-heads crushing quartz or other vein stuff, 6,200; winding, washing, pumping, or other machines, moved by water-power, 6; whims, 544; whips or pulleys, 440.

Approximate value of mining plant, £2,219,658. Number of square miles of auriferous ground actually worked upon, 892½. Number of distinct quartz reefs actually proved to be auriferous, 2,808.

Weight and cost of stamps, the quantity of quartz crushed per stamp, &c., at some of the principal gold mines in Australia. Compiled from the "Mineral Statistics of Victoria" for 1867.

Name of district.	Weight of stamps.	Cost of stamps.	Fall.	Blows per minute.	Quantity crushed per stamp in 24 hours.
	Pounds.	£ *s.* *d.* £ *s.* *d.*	*Inches.*		*Tons.*
Ballarat	400 to 850	3 17 6 to 15 10 0	7 to 10	50 to 85	1.0 to 4.0
Beechworth	442 to 775	5 3 6 to 13 00 0	5 to 14	40 to 90	0.8 to 4.0
Sandhurst	500 to 800	4 5 8 to 8 11 0	6 to 18	25 to 75	0.9 to 3+
Maryborough	450 to 800	4 18 6 to 8 14 6	6 to 22	50 to 75	1.0 to 3.0
Castlemaine	450 to 800	4 2 6 to 21 11 6	6 to 15	35 to 75	1.0 to 3¼
Ararat	500 to 675	7 00 0 to 8 0 0	7½ to 10	60 to 72	1.25 to 1.50
Gipps Land	600 to 750	5 5 0 to 40 00. 0	7 to 10	60 to 80	1.50 to 2.05

Name of district.	Fineness of grates. (Holes per sq're inch.)	Horse-power expended per stamp.	Gallons of water per stamp.	Quantity of mercury per stamp.	Loss of mercury p'r stamp.
				Pounds.	*Ounces.*
Ballarat	40 to 200	1.00 to 2.00	950 to 8,640	5 to 75	1 to 8
Beechworth	60 to 140	0.75 to 1.50	720 to 11.520	5 to 70	½ to 8
Sandhurst	64 to 140	0.66 to 2.00	4,000 to 8,640	10 to 40	¼ to 5½
Maryborough	70 to 144	0.50 to 2.50	900 to 8,640	3 to 30	1¾ to 8
Castlemaine	40 to 144	0.50 to 2.00	4,800 to 12,960	6 to 40	¼ to 24
Ararat	90 to 120	0.75	4,320 to 12,960	6 to 47	½ to 7
Gipps Land	70 to 250	0.75 to 1.50	1,600 to 25,000*	10 to 37	1-5 to 32

* This excessive.

STAMP-BATTERIES OF PORT PHILLIP.

For the purpose of comparing our methods in California with those in Australia, the following notice of the Port Phillip Company's mines and mill, at Clunes, Australia, is added to the foregoing descriptions. This company mines upon five veins, with an aggregate drivage of 25,590 feet, equal to 4⅞ miles. The depth of the main shaft is 464 feet; length of tramways on the surface for the conveyance of quartz and refuse, 2,500 feet, single-track; engine for hoisting and pumping at the two shafts, about 85 horse-power. The costs of mining and raising the quartz average about 13*s.* per ton. The large masses of quartz are passed through rock breakers, of which there are two. The number of stamps at work is 80; of these 56 weigh about 600 pounds each, including the lifter. They give about 75 blows per minute, require about 1 horse-power per stamp, and crush an average of about 2 tons 4 hundred weight per head per 24 hours. The remaining 24 stamps weigh about 800 pounds each, including the lifter, give 75 blows per minute, require in the aggregate about 30 horse-power, and crush about 4 tons per head per diem. These stamps have the larger portion of the small quartz delivered to them. The quantity of water required to work the stamps efficiently is about eight gallons per head per minute, being 921,600 gallons per diem.

The construction of the batteries and the method of saving the gold in troughs is shown in the accompanying illustration, giving a section through the battery.

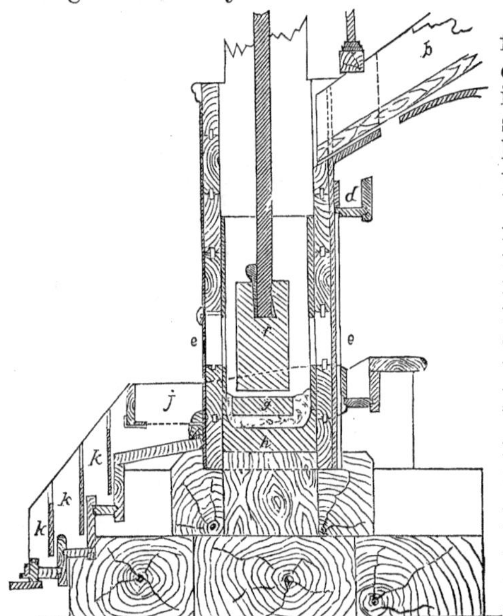

Section of the Battery of the Phillip Company, Clunes.

b is the lower end of the self-feeding hopper, with a spring, *c*, below it. Just below this is the water-trough *d*. The stamp-lifter or stem is made largest at the lower end, so as to be wedged into the head *f* by a key at the side, in this respect being very different from the method of attachment in California. The head is cast also in one piece, without a shoe, and is renewed when too much worn. The die *g* is placed loosely in the bottom box or bed *h*. The delivery is through grates upon both sides of the battery, at *e*, *e*. A perforated plate, *j*, serves to retain any coarse particles thrown out, and the stamped material, passing through this plate, falls into the mercury boxes *k*, *k*, *k*, and thence upon a long line of blanket strakes, the extreme upper end of which only is shown in the cut. These strakes are each several inches broad, and there are nine in succession, one below another, with a mercury-box at the lower end, through which the material passes before entering the waste-trough. This mercury-box serves to catch any fine particles of gold that may have passed the blankets and any stray globules of quicksilver from the upper boxes.*

* The amalgam which slowly accumulates in these boxes has been found to be in a crystalline condition, and, according to Mr. George F. Ulrich, the mineralogist, contains only a small percentage of quicksilver, with a relatively fixed percentage of gold, and forms true crystals, which, under the action of nitric acid, do not become loose and spongy, but take the appearance and lustre of solid gold crystals. They are usually in modified and distorted octahedra, and are sometimes prismatic.

STAMP-MILLS IN BRAZIL.

The stamp-mills, carrying in the aggregate 135 stamps, in use at the Morro Velho mines in Brazil are constructed upon the Cornish pattern, except that each lifter has four iron guides to keep it in position. When new, one of these stamp-heads weighs 230 pounds, and when worn out only 59 pounds. The average weight may be considered to be 150 pounds, and the duration about four months. The total weight of the stamp, with lifter, shank, &c., is about 640 pounds. The battery-box is made of wood and lined with sheet-iron. The distance between the heads and the sides of the coffer is about three inches. The batteries are self-feeding. The grates are nineteen inches long and nine inches wide, and are made of sheet-copper, pierced with conical holes one-twelfth of an inch in diameter outside and tapering to one-forty-eighth of an inch on the inside. These copper plates are found to be, on the whole, more durable than iron. Further particulars of practical value may be obtained from the following tabular statement, given by Mr. J. Arthur Phillips, from the manuscript notes of Mr. F. Dietzsch, the superintendent of the reduction works:

Number and dimensions of stamp mills at the Morro Velho Mines, Brazil.

Names of stamp mills.	Number of heads.	Blows per minute.	Lift of stamp heads.	Number of cams.	Dimension of stamp coffers.						Dimension of wheels.				Ore stamped.		
					Length.		Width.		Depth.		Diameter.		Width.		Tons per day.	Tons per head per day.	Pounds per head per day.
					Ft.	*In.*	*Ft.*	*In.*	*Ft.*	*In.*	*Ft.*	*In.*	*Ft.*	*In.*			
Lyon	30	63	10	....	2	2	1	3	2	0	40	6	3	3	36.73	1.22	2,733
Cotesworth	12	61	11	4	2	2	1	1	1	6	31	0	3	0	10.92	1.41	3,158
Susannah	9	65	12	6	2	3	1	3	2	0	19	2	4	4	10.94	1.21	2,710
Herring	24	78	12	...	2	6	1	6	2	0	42	6	6	0	34.56	1.44	3,225
Powles	36	67	12	4	2	2	1	3	1	10	51	0	5	0	66.10	1.83	4,100
Addison	24	73	12	4	2	2	1	3	1	10	42	0	6	0	35.54	1.48	3,315

The product of stamping issuing from the grates in front is diluted with clean water as it runs, and is conducted over inclined tables or strakes about eighteen inches wide and from twenty-seven to thirty-five feet in length, with a fall of one inch per foot. Bullocks' hides, tanned with the hair on, are spread over the first sixteen feet of these strakes, and baize cloths are placed below, followed again by another series of overlapping skins. These skins and strips of baize are washed at regular intervals in separate tanks. The deposit on the first three skins is known as head-sand, and amounts to 0.42 of a cubic foot per ton of ore stamped. This sand goes to the amalgamating house. The "middle sand," from skins Nos. 4 and 5, contains some six ounces of gold per ton, and is further enriched by being washed over another system of strakes. The products below the fifth skin are known as "tail-sand," and are subjected to further concentration. "Mr. Dietzsch remarks that straking may, on the whole, be considered a cheap, simple, and economical process, by which 67 per cent. of the gold originally present in the ore is obtained in a highly concentrated state, while the 33 per cent. which escapes is in two distinct forms—first, light free gold; second, gold inclosed in the coarser particles of pyrites."

The dimensions and products of the strakes are given in the annexed table:

Dimensions and products of strakes at the Morro Velho Mines, Brazil.

Names of stamp mills.	Number of heads.	Number of strakes.	Length of strakes.		Width of strakes.		Area of strakes.	Square feet per ton of ore stamped.	Tons of ore passing per 24 hours.	Number of skins on strakes.	Number of baizes on strakes.	Quantity of head-sand per day.
			Ft.	*In.*	*Ft.*	*In.*	*Sq. ft.*					
Lyon	30	36	31	10	1	6	1, 719	46. 83	36. 73	288	210	20. 00
Cotesworth	12	13	30	6	1	4½	545	32. 21	16. 92	104	65	5. 50
Susannah	9	8	27	0	1	6	324	29. 61	10. 94	48	48	2. 75
Herring	24	29	35	0	1	6	1, 232	35. 64	34. 56	228	174	18. 00
Powles	36	42	33	7	1	3½	1, 821	27. 55	66. 10	336	252	28. 47
Addison	24	30	31	10	1	5	1, 352	38. 04	35, 54	240	170	17. 00
Total	135	158	....		....		6, 993	....	200. 79	1, 244	919	91. 72

THE GERMAN STAMP BATTERIES.

In Germany the round stem revolving stamp has not been introduced. Square stems of timber with square heads are the most common, and the cams are usually short projections from a large cylindrical wooden shaft, lifting the stamp by catching under a projecting tongue. The stamp stems are also made of rectangular iron rods, either single or bolted together, and secured to the square shank of the stamp-head and shoe (all in one piece) by means of bolts. The head is about six inches square and nine inches high, ranging with the weight desired for the stamp.

The mortar-box or coffer is made of planks lined with sheet-iron,* and the bed usually consists of stamped quartz pounded in by the stamps or solid stone, or, better, of heavy cast-iron dies or anvils as long as the bottom of the mortar. These dies are simply rectangular masses with plane surfaces, and the upper die is four inches thick. As a very firm and even foundation for it is necessary, it is found best to place it on another mass of similar form but heavier, from six inches to twelve inches high. In the cross-sections of batteries given beyond, these iron dies are seen at *g* and *g*. The lower of the two masses rests directly upon the ends of blocks of wood or upon heavy timber, which is supported upon cross-sills still lower, and these in turn upon masonry. When it is intended that the battery shall stand independently of the frame of the building, the foundations are carried to a greater depth. The upper iron block or die of course is subjected to rapid wearing, and it is generally allowed to wear off for one and a half inch before it is turned over. When it has been worn out to this extent on both sides it is reduced to a plate only an inch thick, and is then broken up. These dies do not fit tightly between the sides of the mortar; a little space is left, which is filled by wedges, and when these are removed the die can be easily turned. For convenience of handling they are made with short projections at the ends.

Iron is beginning to be used to some extent for battery frames and mortars, and Rittinger gives figures of end-posts, intended to receive wooden sides, being cast with vertical grooves for the purpose. Into these grooves the planks designed to form the mortar boxes can be fitted and then secured by drawing up the posts by bolts. The posts rise high

* The reader, inclined to wonder that batteries so ingenious and well-constructed in some other respects, still retain the wooden mortar, should remember that they are not built for crushing gold ore, and hence perfectly tight mortars are not required.

enough to receive cross-pieces above, and at the base are expanded into three horizontal branches or feet so as to form a firm base by which the whole is bolted down to a massive foundation of masonry. It does not appear that the California system of anchoring the battery frame to masonry or heavy cross-sills is in use abroad. On the other hand, the timber frames of stamp batteries are frequently united with the framework of the building in which they are placed.

In the Revue de l'Exposition 4, page 154, mention is made of stamps constructed entirely of metal at Silberau near Ems, and shown by a working model at Kalk. A figure is also given which represents the stem as round and very light, with a screw-thread cut at the top, upon which the iron tappet is screwed like a nut. This method of attaching the tappets was formerly used in California, but it has been abandoned since the introduction of the "gib-tappet" already described.

OVERFLOW BATTERIES.

The overflow or float battery is the simplest form, and is made with numerous modifications intended to insure the best working results. The overflow may be along the whole front of the mortar-box, or at the ends alone, or at the front and ends; but in practice it is generally confined to the front and to two forms of the float battery: 1. That with the unobstructed overflow, the stamped stuff with the water being carried over the edge of the front wall of the mortar; 2. The partition overflow battery, or *Schubersatz*, in which the overflow is obstructed by a partition descending below the surface of the water in the battery, leaving only a narrow slit or space through which the water and materials can flow out.

Batteries of the first form are made with the overflow from 8 to 15 or 18 inches above the bed, according to the fineness of the stuff required, being from 15 inches to 18 inches when particles of one millimetre in diameter are to be produced. For coarser materials, the height may be diminished to 8 inches, and with this height particles five millimetres in diameter will be delivered. The amount of water required for each stamp varies from four-tenths to eight-tenths of a cubic foot per minute. The swash in an open overflow battery will always carry over more or less of the coarse uncrushed fragments, particularly when the height of the discharge is not great, and it is to obviate this difficulty that the partition float battery has been devised.

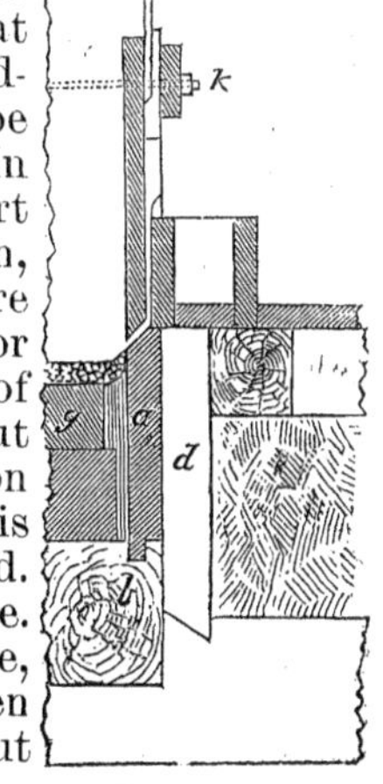

In this form of battery the discharge takes place through a long and narrow slit, opening in the mortar at a height of four or five inches above the die, and extending outward and upward to the height which would be required for the discharge edge of an open battery. In the annexed figure, which is a section of the front part of a mortar made of wood, this opening may be seen, extending from just above the surface of the broken ore upon *g* upward to the top of the trough. The wall or partition between this narrow space and the interior of the mortar-box is so fitted in that it can be taken out in order to clean the mortar or remove any obstruction that may have lodged in the opening. If the slit is placed too low in the mortar it is liable to be choked. It should not be less than three inches above the die. It is also important not to have the opening too large, as the velocity of the upward flow of water would then be diminished, and would not be sufficient to carry out the pulp without the use of a much greater quantity of water than is desirable. It is evident that the quantity and fineness of the stuff delivered by this outward flow of water may be regulated by the supply admitted to the battery. The consumption of water for such stamp, with a three-quarter inch slit, varies from two to three-tenths of a cubic foot per minute.

GERMAN SCREEN BATTERIES.

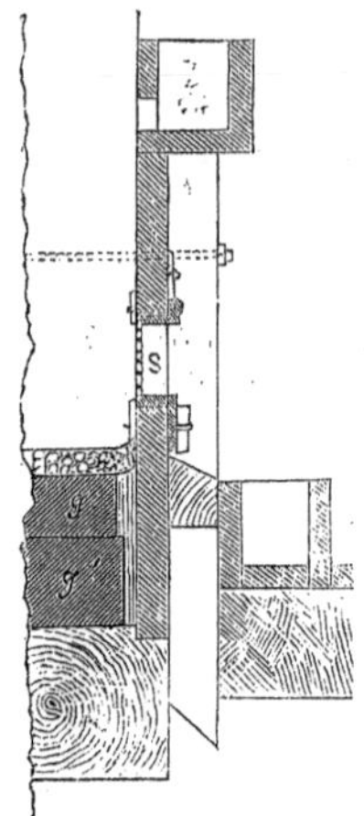

In the German screen batteries, the screens are placed in the front, generally at a height of six inches above the die, and rarely at three inches when the quantity of water is great.

The figure is a section of the front of such a battery, showing a method of holding the screen S in place by means of a frame. An opening of the length and breadth of the screen, is cut out of the planking of the front of the mortar-box, and a rectangular iron frame is bolted or screwed on to the inside of the box and projects so as to form a shoulder three-quarters of an inch wide all around the opening. The screen being placed in the opening fits against this projection, and is then held tightly by another frame or follower which is movable and swings from hinges above, and is provided on its lower edge with a projecting ear that fits over a staple through which a wedge is driven to hold the frame securely in its place. With this construction it is practicable to place the trough for supplying water in the front instead of at the back as is usual. In this figure the two anvils or blocks of cast-iron are seen at g and g'.

The impurities of water flowing through the battery, especially floating objects such as sticks, grass, and the like, tend to gradually close up the meshes or holes of the screens, and thus, by preventing the free exit of the crushed stuff, to diminish the product. In order to prevent this, the form known as the *Stausatz*, or stay-battery, has been devised by Rittinger. It consists essentially in backing water up against the front of the screen, so that both faces are kept washed, and the impurities dislodged by the swash, and not held fast in the holes by the constant pressure of the outward current. This is accomplished by putting on an outer water-box or a plate in front, thus holding the water against the face of the grate. The discharge is at the bottom, through one hole or escape-pipe, made conical in its form, so that by slipping on caps of different sizes the aperture may be varied at will, in order to increase or diminish the flow.

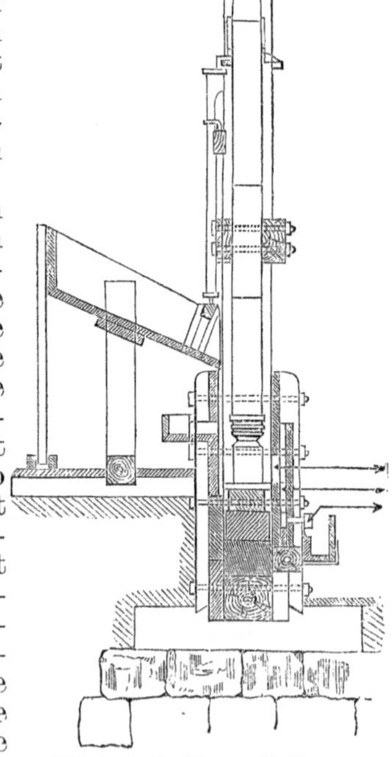

Rittinger's Stamp Battery.

The construction of this battery may be understood from the engraving, which is a section through the center of the battery, showing the stamps; the bed, with the two iron dies; the water-box in front; the escape-pipe; and in the rear of the battery the chute for automatic feeding, which is a common attachment to the German batteries, and usually delivers the ore to the central stamp.

Rittinger* has compared the fineness of the product of the two kinds of battery, the Stausatz and the Schubersatz, each furnished with screens punched with holes one millimetre in diameter, and finds that the Stausatz or stay-battery gives much less slime than the partition float-battery. The following are the figures which he gives in support of his statement:

Size of particles. *mill.*	Stausatz, per cent.	Schubersatz, per cent.
0.00071	12	2
0.00051	31	28
0.00035	10	10
0.00025	47	60
	100	100

CHAPTER XVII.

PANS FOR GRINDING AND AMALGAMATING.

Every period of excitement and enthusiasm in mining brings with it a great demand for machinery, and stimulates the production of numerous contrivances for extracting the precious metals. At such times it is not unusual that men who have had little or no experience in mining, design and manufacture for sale machines for crushing, grinding, and concentrating, and other men of even less experience buy the machines and pay transportation upon them to the real or fancied mine. Such machines, although they may be well constructed and perhaps adapted to some special condition of things when made, are rarely found to answer the intended purpose in practice, and are soon thrown out of the mill, and ranged along the outer wall as relics. These are the machines of which it has been most aptly said, "They are more advertised than used."

But each futile effort has accomplished one useful result. It has instructed by experience, and in more than one case has led gradually to the perfection of machines, and apparatus especially adapted to the peculiar necessities of our mining regions.

THE GREAT NUMBER AND VARIETY OF PANS.

The same necessities which led the metallurgists of the Pacific coast to adopt iron mortar batteries led them also to the construction of iron pans for grinding and amalgamating. The old methods of grinding in arrastras or by Chilian mills were cumbrous and slow, difficult to clean up rapidly, and wasteful of quicksilver and amalgam. The manufacture of pans also received a great impulse from the fact that the ore of the Comstock lode was peculiarly well adapted to working in such

* Lehrbuch der Aufbereitungskunde, 1867, p. 75.

vessels. Its chemical composition is such that the iron of the pans assists its decomposition. It not only contains free gold and silver, but a large part of the undecomposed compounds of silver consists of the sulphide, which, under proper treatment, is readily decomposed in the pan, the particles of iron worn off in the grinding facilitating the process. The ease with which this ore could be reduced in pans, naturally led the mill-men and miners to believe that the same apparatus and processes would work equally well upon other ores—an error which experience soon rectified.

The demand for pans for Washoe and for new mills in the new districts caused them to be made in great numbers and in a great variety of forms, each inventor urging some peculiar excellence attaching to his mode of construction. Some were made for grinding; some for grinding and separating; others were intended simply for amalgamating. This diversity was still further increased by the modifications in the form of each made from time to time by the inventors, so that when we look back for a few years we find a long list of the different forms of pans and amalgamators which have been made for the use of miners and metallurgists, and all of which have been more or less used for the purposes intended. Among these may be cited Knox's, Wheeler's, Varney's, and Hepburn's pans; Wheeler and Randall's tractory conoidal, or excelsior grinder and amalgamator; Wheeler's amalgamator; Excelsior continuous grinder and amalgamator; Belden's pan; Belden's separator; Wheeler and Randall's conoidal separator; Bartola pan; Gaston's pan; Baux and Guiod's grinder and amalgamator; Moore's grinder; Hinkle and Capp's centrifugal ore-grinder; Farrand's amalgamator and separator; Coleman's little giant amalgamator. To these may be added some of the principal pans now in use, as well as some of those mentioned. These pans, which will be described last, are Patton's, Wheeler's, with wooden rim, Booth & Company's, Stevenson's, and Horn's.

The attempt will not be made to describe all of these pans and amalgamators; they are all similar in their action. The grinding in all is effected between two opposing plates of iron, and the chief differences between them consist in the modification of the form of these plates and the extent of their surface. They all combine the qualities of a mill with the capacity to hold a certain amount of ore-pulp, for it is not simply grinding that is required; the operation of amalgamation and chemical reduction of the ores is connected with it. Inasmuch as the constant grinding would soon cut through the thin bottoms of the pans if unprotected, and destroy the mullers, false bottoms or dies are cast for the pans, and face-plates (shoes) of hard white iron for the mullers. These are so made as to be easily taken out, and are renewed when worn out.

In general, the pans are not intended to receive and grind coarse materials, though in some of them ore as large as kernels of corn, or even larger, can be ground to a fine powder without much injury to the pan. In practice it is the battery-pulp and sand which are fed, and this is generally done in charges, (or "batches,") the weight of which depends upon the capacity of the pan. They are first ground, and then, with the addition of quicksilver, and at a lower rate of speed, the amalgamation is effected. The charge is then drawn off into a larger pan, fitted with stirrers, called the separator. In this the pulp is much diluted with water, and the quicksilver and amalgam fall to the bottom and are collected. The principal pans and amalgamators may be grouped in two chief divisions: 1. Those with flat bottoms. 2. Those with curved or conoidal bottoms.

KNOX'S PAN.

One of the oldest and simplest forms of the iron grinding and amalgamating pans is that invented and introduced by Mr. Israel W. Knox, of California, soon after the opening of the mines upon the Comstock lode, and since then extensively used in the reduction mills of the Pacific coast.

This pan is usually made about four feet in diameter for working gold ores, and fourteen inches deep. The pan used for working silver ores is five feet in diameter. The construction may be seen by reference to the figure. The bottom is flat, but rises in the centre in the form of a truncated cone, as high as the rim of the pan. This cone is hollow, and gives room for the bearings of a vertical shaft, geared by bevel spur-wheels to a horizontal shaft under the pan, and intended to give motion to the mullers. These mullers are four in number, thin and flat, and are bolted to an annular collar or centre-piece, surrounding the bottom of the cone, and upon which two upright bars or standards are cast, which lock into the ends of the yoke on the top of the vertical shaft. C C is a board frame, fitting the inside of the pan, and reaching downward to within half an inch of the mullers. B B are amalgamated copper plates, fastened to the board frame for the purpose of catching the lighter particles of gold as they float through the pulp when stirred by the rotation of the mullers. The discharge of this pan is central, through an opening in the cone near the top, D, and controlled by a gate, at the pleasure of the operator. The pulp and waste discharged are received in a sluice, E, below.

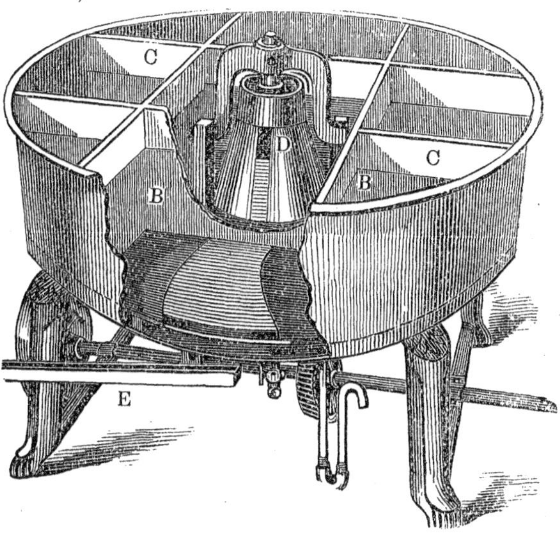

Knox's Improved Amalgamator and Separator.

The bottom of this pan was at first made single; but it was subsequently improved by Mr. Palmer by making it double, thus giving a space or chamber into which steam may be introduced for the purpose of heating the charge, when it is required to promote the decomposition and amalgamation of the ore. This chamber is seen in the figure. The steam is introduced by a pipe. The steam-chamber is formed by means of a false bottom, cast with two concentric annular projections which fit upon the bottom of the pan.

The usual charge of the four-foot pan is 250 to 300 pounds of dry ore, and of the five-foot pan 400 to 500 pounds. The former are most used for amalgamating and separating, and the latter for grinding and amalgamating.

The muller, being made to revolve about twelve times in a minute, carries the pulp and causes it to "swash" against the amalgamated plates, thereby collecting most of the fine float gold and quicksilver. The discharge being near the surface of the liquid pulp, and where there is the least motion, there is little chance of the loss of quicksilver or the precious metals.

It is common to work the pans continuously, but much better results are obtained, at least in some cases, by crushing the ore dry and fine, and then introducing it into the pan by charges, and working until amalgamation is complete.

The simplicity, cheapness, and convenience of this pan, the ease with which it can be charged and cleaned up, together with its effectiveness, have caused it to be largely used, even to this time, by the mill-men of the Pacific slope.

KNOX'S EUREKA GRINDER.

Mr. Knox also makes a pan specially designed for grinding. The central cone is made larger, so that it fills nearly one-half of the diameter of the pan, the object being to have as little difference of velocity between the inner and outer edges of the grinding surface of the muller as possible. The grinding is thus confined as much as possible to the bottom of the annular trough between the sides of the pan and the cone in the center. A die, or false bottom, is placed in this annular trough, and can be renewed when worn out. Its upper surface is grooved, and the shoes, four in number, are made pointed, and curved in such a way that, as they revolve over the grooves of the die, they cut or grind with a shearing action, thus moving with more ease and regularity, and, as is claimed, grinding the pulp with more rapidity.

VARNEY'S PAN.

This is also one of the most extensively used pans. The grinding surface at the bottom is formed by four dies of hard white iron, and there are twelve shoes riveted or bolted to the mullers. The dies have radial grooves which facilitate the grinding. The charge is from 600 to 800 pounds of ore. It will take coarse stuff that passes screens with four meshes to the inch. Curved plates, or guides, serve to throw the pulp back from the circumference to the center, so as to again pass under the mullers. The muller should make about eighty revolutions a minute, and requires to drive it from three to five horse-power. The shoes and dies will last from forty to sixty days, each of twenty-four hours working.

The invention of Varney is declared in his patent to consist "in the employment or use of a rotary and stationary muller placed within a suitable pan or tub, provided with a cover, and arranged in such a manner that when the device is in operation the ore will pass in a current or stream outward from the center, and between the mullers to the circumference of the same, and thence inward over the upper and rotating muller to the center of the same, and down through said muller between it and the stationary one, to be again thrown to the periphery of the mullers, thereby causing all the particles of the ore to be brought in contact with the quicksilver in the pan or tub, or with the amalgamated plates to be attached to the muller or mullers."

"This invention also consists in the employment or use of curved or spiral scrapers placed within the pan or tub, and arranged relatively with the upper surface of the rotating muller in such a manner as to insure the passage or movement of all heavy substances in the pulp, thereby preventing the same from lodging on the rotary muller."

MOORE'S QUARTZ GRINDER AND AMALGAMATOR.

This pan has a flat bottom, with an acute cone rising in the center. The muller is made to fit both the bottom and the cone, and is provided with shoes opposing crushing plates on the cone, so that the stuff which is fed by means of an annular hopper at the top of the muller will be subjected to crushing or coarse grinding before it reaches the broad and horizontal grinding surface at the bottom. This pan is usually made six feet in diameter and with vertical sides. The pulp entering in this manner at the center must traverse the whole distance to the outer margin of the solid muller before it can ascend above it into the body of the pan.

WHEELER AND RANDALL'S EXCELSIOR GRINDER AND AMALGAMATOR.

The excelsior grinder and amalgamator of Wheeler & Randall is a deep pan, with a large conoidal center rising as high as the rim and molded so that its vertical section forms a tractory curve from the top to the bottom. This forms the grinding surface, to which the muller is fitted and revolved by locking on a vertical shaft, to which motion is given by bevel gearing below the pan. Four sizes are made; largest, 4½ feet in diameter, weight 5,000 pounds; medium, 4 feet in diameter, weight 4,000 pounds; prospecting size, 2 feet in diameter, 900 pounds; assayer's pan, 1 foot in diameter.

The advantages claimed by the inventors for this construction are:

1. That perfect uniformity of wear in the grinding surface is obtained by the use of the curved face.
2. That it reduces the ore far more rapidly and at a less expense of power than any other pan of practical form and proportion.
3. That it possesses superior amalgamating qualities.
4. That its mechanical construction as to simplicity, weight, strength, convenience of working, cleaning up, and cheapness, is unequaled by any other grinder and amalgamator.

This is probably claiming too much for this form of pan. That it is an excellent grinder is well known to the writer from observation and personal experience. For amalgamation there are other forms of the pan that are quite as effective. The large space occupied by the cone and muller renders it necessary to make the pan very deep, in order to hold even moderate charges, and it is not as conveniently cleaned as a pan of less depth.

Wheeler's amalgamator has much more space around the muller. The cone is smaller, and the muller broader and flatter. The construction is otherwise nearly the same as in the excelsior grinder, and both are provided with a lever, connected with a hand-wheel, working on a screw at the side, by which the height of the muller above the bottom may be easily varied so as to regulate the rate of grinding.

Both of these pans are also made in sections, so that they can be taken apart and transported on animals into places difficult of access.

Another modification is the continuously working pan, made substantially like the preceding, but with a cover bolted on to the rim and rising to the top of the muller. The pulp, being fed in at one side, escapes at the top, around the narrow neck of the muller, and flows off through a covered chute or rectangular tube, cast upon the cover.

BELDEN'S GRINDING AND AMALGAMATING PAN.

This is an effective and convenient form, and has the advantage of giving plenty of space for the pulp. The grinding surfaces are confined to an annular curved zone, between the sides and a slim central cone. It thus differs materially from the excelsior grinder and amalgamator, in which much of the grinding is effected upon the sides of the cone. Lightness, simplicity, ease of cleaning up, superior grinding and amalgamating qualities, have been aimed at in this machine.

HEPBURN AND PETERSON'S PAN.

This is a deep pan, with the bottom in the form of a section of an inverted cone; the reverse of the pans with conical centers, rising to the height of the rim. In this pan the inclination is towards the center, at an angle of about 28 degrees from the horizontal. A vertical cylinder or tube rises from the bottom in the center, through which the shaft for driving the muller is carried. It is fitted with four dies, which cover the grinding surface of the bottom, and the muller is fitted with fluted shoes, shaped to conform to the curvature of the dies. The charge for this pan is about 1,000 pounds. In grinding, the pulp is thrown from the center under the shoes, and rises highest upon the outer rim, and then falls over toward the center, to be again carried under the muller.

The new Hepburn pan.—Another pan has been introduced by Mr. Hepburn, in which the grinding is not effected by the rubbing of two opposing rigid plates of iron, but by a number of rolling disks, pressing with their flat sides upon the dies, and rolling by friction upon each other. This pan has been experimented with, and noticed by, Mr. Louis Blanding, a metallurgical engineer of large theoretical and practical experience. He says, in June, 1869:

Four months ago I became convinced of its great value, after thorough investigation, and have almost daily since that time worked on it silver ores from Nevada, both chloride and sulphuret ores, and gold-bearing quartz from California. The essential difference between it and pans of the ordinary style consists in this: the former acts by a rolling motion, the disks or rollers being loose in the pan, but crushing and pulverizing strongly against the dies by centrifugal force; the latter by a grinding friction of rigid iron surfaces in contact under great weight. This difference of action explains the difference in power required to operate the respective pans; the Hepburn, other things being equal, consuming not more than 40 per cent. of the power ordinarily required, as shown by tests in the Rock Point mill on the Carson River, and other mills. The disks or rollers, rotating on their own axes upon the dies of the muller plate, also serve to reduce the ore at these lines of contact by a cutting and wearing action, the crushing and wearing operation of the revolving circumference of every two of the rollers on each other effectively aiding the reducing action. These rollers have a peculiar action; they operate to crush the coarse ore on the side dies, and pulverize on the muller dies as well as by the action of their rotating sides on each other. The next point worthy of notice is the fact that this pan will take ore through a screen of half an inch mesh, and reduce it as rapidly and finely as the ordinary pan reduces the sands taken from the fifty-screen of a battery. The rollers, being free and not rigidly fixed, adjust themselves to the size of the material fed to the pan. This avoids the necessity of a battery, (dry or wet,) as the ore will be prepared for the pan by a breaker, or a pair of Cornish rollers, which can be furnished at considerable less cost, and for the work accomplished requires much less power. All drying of the ores and the consequent expense and loss of time are also saved by this mode of work. A third point of particular interest is the fact that amalgamation can be effected by proper management in the bottom of the pan, separate and distinct from the pulverization at the same time proceeding in the upper or working part of the pan, in which point it is essentially different from the pan of ordinary form, and whereby the loss of quicksilver, by excessive grinding and consequent flouring, is greatly prevented. The result of practical work, both in silver and gold ores, shows the loss of quicksilver to be not more than one-third to one-half that usually experienced on charges of ore of equal quantity treated equal lengths of time. There are other minor differences that an inspection of the small 50-pound pan, now working, and of the large 4,000-pound pans, now being constructed at the Vulcan Foundry, in this city, will at once suggest. It was at first difficult to perceive the cause of such rapid action on such coarse and hard stuff in a pan running so easily and lightly; but the solution was readily found by a calculation of the surfaces brought into action in a given time, and which it would be out of place to state here. Theory and practice seem to concur in this matter, at least, and I can only hope that the promise of this really original invention will be realized in large work.

FARRAND'S AMALGAMATOR AND SEPARATOR.

This is a machine which attracted some attention in 1864, but was never extensively used. The motion is not rotary, but reciprocating. The machine consists of a semi-cylindrical, trough-shaped vessel, the interior of which is furnished with movable concave dies, to be replaced when worn out, as in ordinary pans. The mullers are convex, and attached to a substantial shaft, by which they are moved back and forward by crank or eccentric motion. The mullers are held to their places by springs of moderate strength, the pressure of which may be easily regulated. The oscillating motion of the mullers serves to keep the pulp in a constant state of agitation, thoroughly mixing it, and passing it under the mullers without resort to any of the various expedients employed in pans where a circular motion is maintained. In working this amalgamator no quicksilver is placed in the pulp until the trituration is completed. That done, the mullers are raised, so as to completely break contact with the dies, the quicksilver sprinkled into the mass, and the machine set in motion again, the mullers simply acting as stirrers.

PANS NOW MOST IN USE.

The experience with the great variety of pans that have been made has led at last to the adoption of the more simple forms, in which the grinding is effected beween horizontal flat surfaces instead of the curved and conical bottoms. In the pans now most in use, these flat grinding surfaces form an annular floor around the central cone, through which the vertical shaft passes. This central cone is no longer used for grinding, and is made much smaller than formerly. Wood is now also substituted for the sides of the pan, as will be seen by the inspection of the annexed figure of Patton's pan.

PATTON'S PAN.

It will be noted that the wooden sides are vertical and that the staves are held by a strong iron hoop upon an iron flange or shoulder of the bed-plate, which rises in the inside of the pan as high as the top of the muller, this being as high as there is much friction or exposure to the leakage of quicksilver. The bottom is cast in one piece and has a chamber below it for the admission of steam to heat the pulp and

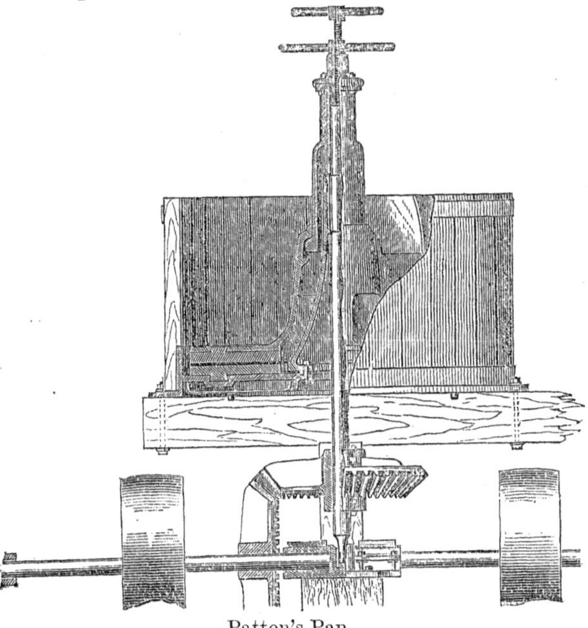

Patton's Pan.

promote amalgamation. The pan or tub is five feet in diameter and two feet deep. The motion of the muller is given by bevel-gearing below. The distance between the grinding surfaces is controlled by raising or lowering the muller by means of a screw working in the top of the vertical shaft.

Wheeler's pan, as now made with vertical wood sides, is shown by the next figure.

WHEELER'S PAN.

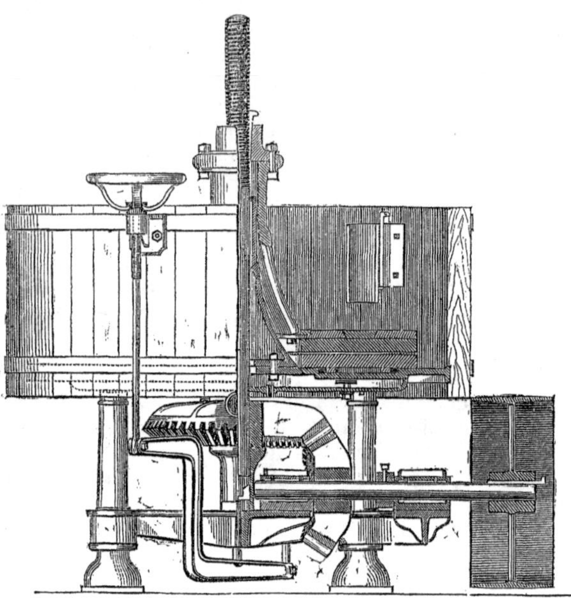

Wheeler's Pan.

It is five feet in diameter, but not quite so deep as Patton's, and the attachment of the staves to the bottom plate is different. There is also a wider annular space between the dies and muller and the sides. The distance between the muller and the dies is regulated by a screw with a hand-wheel upon the outside of the pan, which, by means of a bent lever at the bottom, raises the vertical shaft and so lifts the muller. This arrangement is the same as used in the older forms of Wheeler's apparatus.

Messrs. Booth & Co. make a similar pan with sheet-iron sides. The annular space between the dies and the sides is not so great, but the cast bottom plate rises higher, and is thus more secure against leakage. The sheet-iron rim or side is not only light, but it has this advantage, that when left dry for a time it will not shrink and crack as the wooden tubs must inevitably do.

COX'S PAN.

This is a large, heavy pan, in which the hard gravel cement of the deep placers is broken by revolving arms. Since the pebbles and boulders of this material are usually barren, while the cement between them carries the gold, it is desirable to relieve the stamp-mills from the necessity of crushing the former. The pan is provided with a grating below, through which the finer and auriferous material falls when freed from the boulders, and can be conveyed to the mill, while the boulders remain in the pan, and are removed as they accumulate, and thrown away. It is claimed that this device effects a great saving in the cost of cement-crushing. It was introduced in 1868, I believe, and I have no reports of actual results, though several machines are said to be in use in Nevada County, California, and elsewhere. It resembles the grinding and amalgamating pans only in name and external form.

H. J. BOOTH & CO.'S PAN.

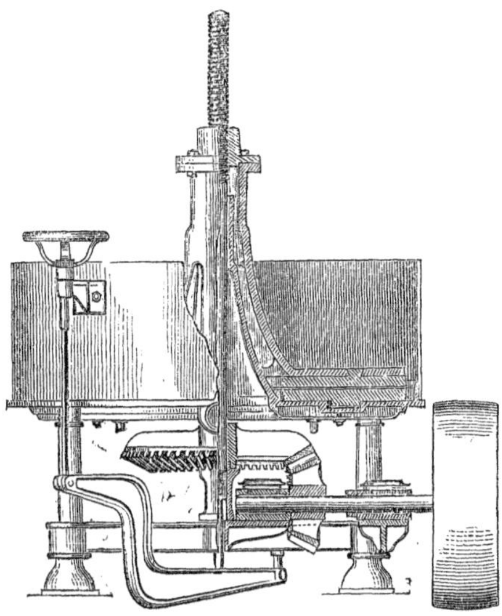

Booth & Co.'s Pan.

Horn's pan, as shown by the last figure of this series, is cast in one piece and is slightly flaring. A depressed annular space three inches wide is left around the dies and is traversed, as the muller rotates, by an arm, which extend to the bottom. The muller is raised by a screw at the top similar to that used for Patton's pan.

HORN'S PAN.

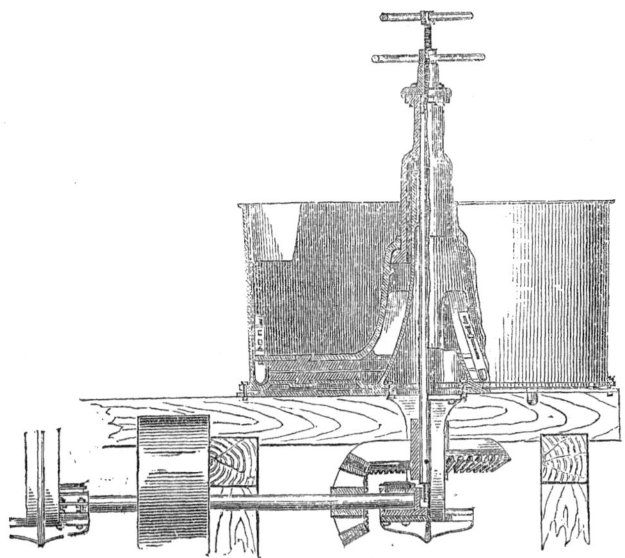

Horn's Pan.

This pan, like all the others here figured, is made with a double bottom, thus giving an annular steam-chest for heating the charge.

SECTION V.—SEPARATION AND CONCENTRATION.

CHAPTER XVIII.

THE CONCENTRATION OF AURIFEROUS ALLUVIUM.

As generally used in mining "concentration" refers to the enrichment by mechanical means of the ores that have been raised from veins. So restricted, it may be said that in the mining regions of the West it is confined chiefly to the separation of gold and sulphurets from quartz. But the grand washing operations of the placer gold miner are properly classed with those of concentration. With the aid of water he sweeps away the earth and gravel, and collects the grains of gold, which, by reason of their greater weight, remain behind.

The simplest and most common implements used for concentration are the miner's pan and the horn-spoon. The pan, so much used in California, not only for prospecting but in cleaning up sluices and mills, is at present stamped out of one piece of the best quality of Russia iron, and is a far better article than was formerly in use. It resembles an ordinary tin milk-pan in form, but its sides are more sloping and it is strengthened by a stout wire in the rim. In the gold region of the Carolinas and Georgia, the pan formerly employed was either the ordinary iron frying pan or a light steel pan, a little deeper, and elliptical in form.

The horn-spoon is a very convenient instrument for washing out samples of crushed vein stuff, or any soft material supposed to contain gold. It has one great advantage over a metallic surface, that it does not become enfilmed with air or grease, so as to prevent the perfect contact of the water on its surface. It is made from the large end of the horn of an ox, cut obliquely, and then scraped down to a suitable thickness. A horn that is black at one end makes the best spoon. Its lightness and durability, as well as many other good qualities, make it a favorite implement with gold prospectors.

The *batea* is another form of washing implement for prospecting and testing. It is a shallow circular plate, made from a single piece of wood, usually by turning in a lathe, and is about twenty inches in diameter and two and a half inches deep at the centre, from which the slope is regular and unbroken to the outer edge. It is much used at the gold mines and washings in Brazil; but in California it is not much known, its use being confined, I believe, to one or two experts who have attained the peculiar skilled manipulation it requires.

The cradle, the tom, and various rockers, are forms of concentrating apparatus familiar to most miners, which need not be here described.

SLUICING.

Sluicing is the simplest form of concentration upon a large scale. It is simply the employment of a current of water upon an inclined plane, which sweeps onward the finer and lighter substances more rapidly than the heavier, and thus effects a separation.

The ordinary board sluice is made of rough pine boards, in sections twelve feet in length, so that they can be fitted one into the other and thus form a continuous trough, from twelve to twenty inches wide and from ten to twelve inches deep. In order that one section may fit into the next, they are made a few inches wider at one end than at the other. The usual grade or inclination is about twelve inches or from ten to eighteen inches, according to the nature of the materials to be washed. Cleats or riffles are placed across the bottom to arrest the flow of the heavier particles, and thus make a favorable point for the lodgment of the gold and quicksilver. In order to protect the bottom from the action of the larger stones and the violence of the current, a set of false riffles is put in. These are usually placed lengthwise of the box, and consist of slats, nailed to cross-bars of wood, so that the whole may be lifted out when the sluice is cleaned up or the bars need repairs. Both bars and sluice-boards wear out rapidly during active washing by the constant attrition of the stones; and when the boxes are no longer fit to be used, or if for any cause they are no longer to be used, they are dried and burned, and the careful washing of the ashes gives a very remunerative return of gold, often enough to buy a new set of sluice boxes.

Some details regarding the construction and working of the larger sluices have already been given in the chapter upon breaking down rock; and it is only necessary here to revert to the fact that the operations of breaking up and crushing, and of washing and concentrating, are inseparably connected in placer mining, as well as in the extraction of gold from quartz taken out of veins. There is one form of sluicing which, however, has not yet been considered. It is the under-current sluice, an improvement introduced in California, and the outgrowth of the gigantic sluicing operations in that State.

UNDER-CURRENT SLUICES.

These are designed to separate the current in the main sluices into two portions, permitting the great bulk of the muddy current and coarse materials to pass on, while the heavier and lower portions are allowed to drop through a grating on the bottom of the sluice into shallower and broader sluice boxes, having a lower grade, and receiving a fresh supply of clean water. The design is to distribute the materials over a greater surface than could be given in the main sluice, and thus allow the gold to settle.

These boxes are made of various widths, from three to nine feet, and from twelve to fourteen inches deep. The grade is usually one in twelve. The grating, through which the stuff is admitted, is made of hard cast iron, with openings an inch wide and eight inches long. The stuff flowing in the under-currents is sometimes divided, a part being dropped into a second system of low-grade boxes, or secondaries, with a width of about thirty inches, and a grade of fourteen or fifteen inches to the box. They receive about one-fifteenth of the water in the under-current. The grating is much finer than that in the main sluice, the spaces being only three-eighths of an inch wide and five inches long. They are very useful for catching quicksilver.

CHAPTER XIX.

THE CONCENTRATION OF VEIN-STUFF.

As has already been remarked, concentration, in ordinary mining parlance, is confined in California chiefly to the separation of gold and sulphurets from quartz. Quicksilver ores and copper ores have, to a small extent at one or two localities, been subjected to concentration, but with these exceptions very little attention has yet been given there to a subject of great importance to the mining interest. The quantity of sulphurets contained in the quartz veins of California rarely exceeds two per cent., and its separation is not attended with any great difficulty, inasmuch as the difference between the specific gravity of the sulphurets and quartz is so great, that, when agitated in water, the particles of sulphuret first find their way to the bottom and form a layer nearly free from the quartz, which settles in an upper stratum. It is upon this difference in gravity of substances, and their consequent different degrees of velocity in passing through water or air, that the operations of concentration are based.

For example, a sphere of gold eight lines in diameter will fall 100 Prussian inches through water in one second of time, while a sphere of quartz of the same size will fall only about 30 inches in the same time. Thus, a mixture of particles of gold and of particles of quartz could be very easily separated one from the other; and also many other substances could be separated where the difference in the velocity of falling is not so great. But the bulk of particles is also an important element, as will be seen from the inspection of the annexed table, in which the relative velocities with which particles of gold, galena, blende, and quartz of different sizes will fall through water is shown:

Table showing the distance in Prussian inches that spheres of various sizes of different substances will fall through water in one second of time.

Diameter in lines.	Gold. Spec. grav. 19. 2.	Galena. Spec. grav. 7. 5.	Blende. Spec. grav. 4.	Quartz. Spec. grav. 2. 6.
8	100	60. 093	40. 825	29. 814
5. 657	84. 090	50. 532	34. 329	25. 071
4	70. 711	42. 492	28. 868	21. 082
2. 828	59. 460	35. 731	24. 275	17. 728
2	50	30. 046	20. 412	14. 907
1. 414	42. 045	25. 266	17. 165	12. 535
1	35. 355	21. 246	14. 434	10. 541
0. 707	29. 730	17. 866	12. 137	8. 864
0. 5	25	15. 023	10. 206	7. 454
0. 354	21. 022	12. 633	8. 582	6. 268
0. 25	17. 678	10. 623	7. 217	5. 270

Thus, while a sphere of gold eight lines in diameter is falling 100 inches, galena of the same size will fall 60 inches; blende, 40. 8 inches; and quartz, 29. 8 inches. But while the sphere of gold eight lines in diameter is falling 100 inches, one of two lines in diameter will fall only 50 inches, or half as fast as the sphere of the same substance with four times the diameter. Further, a sphere of gold 0.707 lines in diameter will fall about as fast as one of quartz with a diameter of eight lines, or one of galena two lines in diameter, and so on. It thus becomes evident that the velocity of fall of substances in water depends not only upon their specific gravity, but upon their bulk and gravity combined, and that for a perfect separation of substances according to their gravity, it is essential that the particles should either be of the same size or that the variation must be confined within certain well-defined limits.

SIZING OF FRAGMENTS—TROMMELS.

From what has already been remarked, it will be seen that a proper sizing of the fragments and particles of crushed ores is an essential prerequisite to successful concentration.

For separating the coarser fragments, such as are suitable for jigging, for example, screens or riddles are used, and for the finer, sieves or perforated plates; while for the separation of the very finest portions resort is had to the action of flowing water.

Screens or riddles are made in a great variety of ways, but are usually flat surfaces of coarse wire or of parallel iron rods, and caused to swing or to jar by rising and falling at one end, so that the stuff may move over the surface by gravity, while the smaller fragments drop through. The product of one riddle may be received upon a second of finer mesh, and the product of the second upon a third, and so on.

For still smaller fragments, sieves in a cylindrical form or trommels are used. They are made to revolve, and are set at an inclination, so that stuff fed into the upper end will gradually descend to the lower, while a portion drops through the mesh and is received either in a suitable box or into an outer concentric cylinder of gauze. This is a form of trommel which was recently exhibited in Paris by Messrs. Huet and Geyler, and which has some novel features. It is not supported upon a shaft passing through from end to end, but is sustained by, and revolves on, trunnions cast upon each of the cast-iron heads or ends, as indicated in the annexed longitudinal section, which represents one of this style of trommels, constructed so as to supply a system of four twin sieves. The crushed stuff is introduced at the hollow trunnion A, and falls upon a grate or perforated iron plate, B, in which the holes are large. The stuff which falls through the plate B, drops upon a second plate, C, perforated with smaller holes, where it is again divided into two sizes, the finer particles dropping through to the outermost plate of all. Each space between the plates has suitable openings at intervals in the cast-iron heads for the discharge of fragments too coarse to fall through the plate below them. This trommel is very compact and will give four sizes of product.

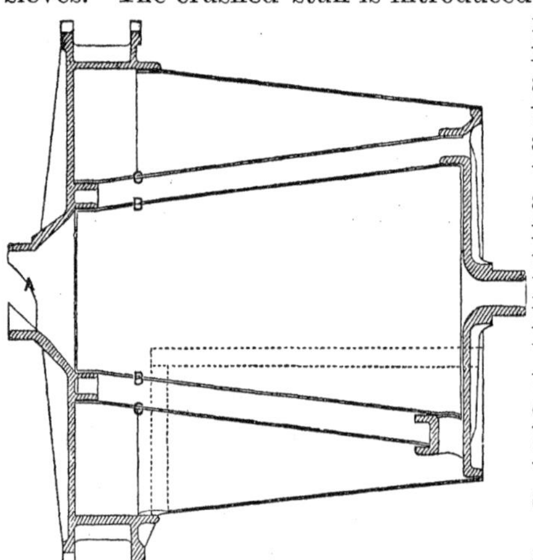

Section of a Distributing Trommel.

In Europe perforated iron or steel plates are now generally used instead of wire-cloth screens, which wear out faster. The Exposition of 1867 was rich in samples of perforated plates of all descriptions and very accurately punched. It is essential to the best working effect that the thickness of the plates should always be less than the diameter of the holes punched in them. The space also between the holes in the finer plates should not be greater than the diameter of the holes—in the medium plates half a diameter, and in the coarser plates one-third of the diameter of the holes. In France perforations less than $0^{m}.002$ in diameter are considered as fine; those between $0^{m}.002$ and $0^{m}.005$ are medium. The fine numbers begin at $0^m.0005$. The finely-perforated plates for trommels are generally made of copper, and the other sizes of steel, iron, or zinc.

Rittinger adopts one millimetre in diameter as the unit of holes for sizing ores for concentration, and the progression beyond this is geometric, as 1, 2, 4, 8, 16 millimetres, giving for the volumes of the grains that will pass the holes respectively 1, 8, 64, 512, 4,096 cubic millimetres. He divides each of these sizes into four classes, each with four grades, thus:

	Diameter in millimetres.	In inches, nearly.	
No. 1, (Stufen)	64.0	= 2.51	coarse.
	45.2	= 1.79	middling coarse.
	32.0	= 1.26	middling fine.
	22.6	= 0.89	fine.
No. 2, (Graupen)	16.0	= 0.64	coarse.
	11.3	= 0.45	middling coarse.
	08.0	= 0.319	middling fine.
	05.6	= 0.220	fine.
No. 3, (Gries)	4.0	= 0.160	coarse.
	2.8	= 0.109	middling coarse.
	2.0	= 0.078	middling fine.
	1.4	= 0.055	fine.
No. 4, (Mehl)	1.00	= 0.0400	coarse.
	0.71	= 0.0282	middling coarse.
	0.50	= 0.0200	middling fine.
	0.35	= 0.0137	fine.

BLANKET CONCENTRATION.

Blanket concentration is only a modification of sluicing; a rough surface being substituted for the smooth flat bottom, with riffles and other obstructions, of the sluice. Blankets are in very common use, being at once the simplest and most effective means of arresting the fine particles of gold that escape amalgamation in battery. The blanketing used for this purpose is made specially for it at the woolen mills of the coast, and is very strong, thick, and hairy. It is woven about thirty inches wide, just wide enough to cover the bottom of the strakes or shallow inclined troughs, and to hang over their edges. The troughs are from twelve to sixteen inches wide, with sides from one and a half to three inches high, and are inclined, according to the desired velocity of the current, from five to fifteen degrees. There are usually two or three blanket troughs abreast, receiving the sands as they flow from the battery; but four would be better. While the blankets of one are being washed, the current is turned upon the others, and the greater the surface provided for the flow the less disturbance is caused by the addition of the flow from the first while the blankets are washing.

The upper blankets, where the heaviest of the sands, with the included sulphurets, are deposited, are washed most frequently, sometimes as often as once in every fifteen minutes, but generally once every hour. The second row is taken off only half as often, and the third once in three or four hours; but the time they should be allowed to remain depends upon the amount of stuff which lodges upon them. The rough surface must not be permitted to become completely filled with heavy sands.

There is a very extraordinary example of blanket concentration in the ravines extending from the mills at Virginia City and Gold Hill. The tailings from these mills, estimated to be not less than 600 tons a day, are allowed to run into Gold Cañon and Six-mile Cañon, where they are passed over a great length of blankets, from five to six miles in each cañon. The surveyor general of Nevada gives the following details of blanket washings in Six-mile Cañon for 1866 and 1867:

Number of mills discharging tailings into cañon	12
Probable number of tons worked during the year 1866	100,000
Estimated value of the tailings saved and worked	$72,000
Saving per ton of ore worked	72 cents.
Length of sluices	22,000 feet.
Cost of sluices	$20,000
Estimated value of tailings saved and worked in 1867	$164,000
Saving per ton of ore worked in 1867	$1 64
Average value of tailings saved per ton	$20

USE OF CAST-IRON FOR CONCENTRATING MACHINES.

Numerous concentrating machines, in a great variety of forms, have been made upon the western coast in the last ten years, and many of them, like the pans and amalgamators, have been more advertised than used. They have all been characterized by the use of iron rather than wood, and by their moderate size and compact proportions, suited to the difficulties and expense of transportation. It has been usual in Europe to construct concentrating machines almost wholly of wood to the exclusion of cast iron; but at the late Exposition some French constructors exhibited machines made of iron to the exclusion of wood, and have written a memoir,* setting forth the superiority of iron for such purposes.

They urge that although wooden machines may be made with the greatest accuracy and care, they are no sooner put into place for work than they begin to swell and warp, and in the case of a circular buddle, for example, the whole surface must be made anew. Then, if for any cause the operation of such machines is suspended for a time, the wood dries and shrinks, and when they are again set in operation they are always found to be out of order, and to require extensive repairs. Another important objection to wood is the great bulk of the machines made of it as compared with those made of iron of equal strength. Again, wooden machines do not bear transportation to distant regions, neither are they so durable or so exact and regular in their operation as machines made of iron.

With cast iron the most favorable forms can be given to those parts with which the stuff to be worked comes in contact. All unfavorable angles and joints can be avoided. With iron and cast iron the forms of machines, and of their various parts, recognized in practice as the most favorable to the end in view, can be adopted. The joints being perfectly tight, the loss of earth, water, or ore is prevented. No change of form in the machines, or any injury to them, need be feared by their exposure to either dryness or moisture. If they are required to remain unused for a greater or less time, or if they have to be transported to a great distance, they are not injured. Changes of season or climate do not affect such machines. During the severity of winter, the taps being

* Mémoire sur l'outillage nouveau et les modifications apportées dans les procédés d'enrichissement des minerais. Par Messrs. Huet et Geyler, ingénieurs, anciens élèves de l'École Centrale. Paris, 1866.

opened and the tubs and pipes being drained of water, the hardest frosts will not injuriously affect them.

These advantages, and the necessity for machines that can be transported to distant regions unchanged, have been recognized in the United States, as already stated. Iron has for several years past been extensively substituted for wood in the construction of stamps, batteries, and concentrating machines in California and Nevada. Most of the concentrating machines and batteries now in use in California, Nevada, Idaho, and Northern and Western Mexico are made of cast iron. When such machines (made in San Francisco) arrive at their destination, they can be set up and put in operation at once, without requiring alteration or repairs.

HENDY'S CONCENTRATOR.

Hendy's improved continuously discharging concentrator, now most in use, is the result of long experience with the pan concentrators, and of their successive modifications and improvements. It consists of a shallow iron pan, five or six feet in diameter, supported by a vertical shaft in the centre, and made to oscillate back and forth by means of cranks on a shaft at one side, and joined by connecting rods to the periphery of the pan. The pan turns upon its vertical axis back and forth, for a short distance, at every revolution of the crank-shaft.

The figure gives an elevation of the machine, with the vertical shaft and one-half of the pan, shown in sections.

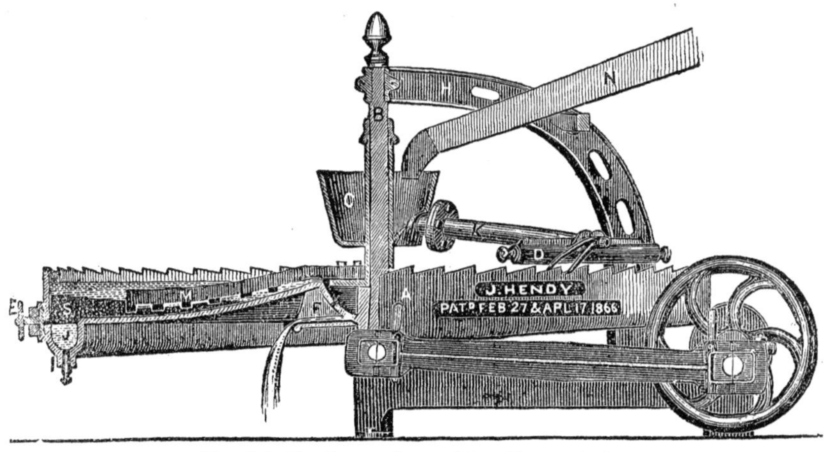

Hendy's Continuously-working Concentrator.

It is made wholly of iron, and thus there is no framing of timbers to be done when it is set up, and no shrinking and leaking after the machine has been allowed to stand idle for a time. A bed-plate, or frame, gives support to the central pin and the crank-shaft, and also to arched arms, H, that rise over the pan and sustain the upper end of the vertical shaft B. The bottom of the pan is not flat, but is raised in the centre around the shaft nearly to the height of the rim, and from this it descends toward the periphery in a cycloidal curve, an approximation to the brachystochrone, by which the movement of the particles from the centre toward the circumference is facilitated, and their passage in the other direction obstructed. This form is especially necessary, inasmuch as the motion and the centrifugal force diminish rapidly toward the centre. It constitutes one of the chief points of difference between this concentrator and others which have preceded it.

When the machine is placed for operation, it must be carefully leveled, so that water will stand at the same height at all points upon the outer rim of the pan. The stuff to be concentrated (usually the tailings from the amalgamated copper plates and blanket-strakes) is delivered, together with the water, by the trough N to the hopper C, from which it is fed through the pipe K and distributor D into the pan near its outer edge. This feeding is not confined to one point, but is made to extend around all parts of the circumference by causing the distributor D to rotate around the vertical shaft. This is accomplished by the movement of the pan. The upper edge of the rim is a continuous ratchet, into which two pawls, connected with D, drop during the motion of the pan *from* the distributor, and in the return motion the distributor is thrown back a distance equal to the arc passed over by the pan. Rake-like arms are bolted to the shaft of the distributor, and are also carried around the circle at the same time, and serve to stir up the compact mass of sand and sulphurets which settles upon the bottom. The crank-shaft makes from 200 to 220 revolutions per minute, thus throwing the pan back and forth an equal number of times, and keeping the materials in a constant state of agitation. The heavier substances, such as the sulphurets and any stray particles of quicksilver or amalgam, settle to the bottom, and accumulate in the lowest part of the pan, gradually displacing the sand and lighter materials, which, with the excess of water, flow over the raised bottom at the centre and out of the pan by a central discharge. The accumulated sulphurets discharge at the gate E, the opening of which must be regulated to correspond in its delivery with the rapidity of the accumulation. If opened too wide, sand from the layer above the sulphurets will be discharged; and if the opening is too small, the sulphurets will accumulate, and begin to flow over the annular bridge at the centre. For the accumulation of amalgam and quicksilver, a depression, J, is provided. This is deepest at the point of discharge I, closed by a plug. The sulphurets are usually allowed to accumulate until the pan is half full, as shown at S, before the gate E is opened. The sulphurets may be received into boxes or into troughs placed under the outlets.

These concentrators weigh 1,000 pounds each. They are run with a belt, and usually set in pairs, for which a single crank shaft is sufficient. Two pairs can be so arranged as to require a driving shaft only six feet in length. The amount of water required is not large; not more than flows away from the batteries with the sands to be concentrated. Each machine will receive and concentrate five tons of stuff every twenty-four hours. Eight tons have, however, been put through in that time; but the product is not entirely freed from sand, the presence of which is not objectionable in some processes of working, and if clean sulphurets are desired the discharge from four machines is delivered into a fifth, and this gives a complete, clean concentration.

At the North Star mine, Grass Valley, the performance of these concentrators has been highly satisfactory in saving not only sulphurets, but amalgam. One machine receiving the product of six, fed with the pulp from the batteries, gave a product containing ninety-five per cent. of sulphurets. Like all the quick concentrators, however, they obtain a clean product at the cost of some loss of valuable material. Their tailings may, with advantage, be buddled.

This form of concentrator may be traced back, through various modifications, to the original Prater or Hungerford concentrator, known generally in 1864 as the Hungerford and Prater's concentrator,* when it was much used in California and Nevada. This machine received its motion in the same way, but was supported in a wooden frame, and the distribution of the pulp was effected by letting it descend from the center outward upon a fixed sheet-iron cover which extended nearly to the outer edge of the pan. It did not discharge the sulphurets; and when they had accumulated sufficiently the machine was stopped and they were dug out. The bottom was not curved downward from the bridge near the center, but had a gradual slope, as also in a later modification of the concentrator by Mr. Hungerford. This modification was patented in 1866, and consisted chiefly in doing away with the wooden frame by substituting one of iron. The distribution was effected as before, over a sheet-iron cap or cover, but a second or outer rim was added all around the pan, forming an annular trough, the only opening to which from the inside of the pan was a series of holes pierced at intervals near the bottom of the pan, with the object of allowing only the sulphurets, or concentrated stuff, to pass through into the outer space and to be kept there, out of contact with the sands and pulp undergoing concentration in the pan. Two openings in the rim of the outer compartment gave the means of drawing off the sulphurets. The discharge of the sand, water, &c., was at the center, and it was claimed to be a continuously working machine, but the delivery of the sulphurets was not satisfactory. The motion was given by two eccentrics acting upon wooden guide-blocks or bearings below the pan. Hungerford's latest machines are preferred by some mill-men to Hendy's, on account of their more solid construction and smoother running. I am informed that these particulars have been improved recently in the Hendy. The principal defect of that machine, whereon I have watched its operation, has been its too slight construction, support, and gearing. These features were the result of a desire to make the apparatus cheap and portable—a motive which has led more than one California manufacturer of mining machinery to sacrifice solidity and due proportion of parts.

All of these oscillating pan-concentrators may be regarded as modifications of the Borlase concentrator, which is an oscillating pan with a level bottom and a central discharge, the height of which can be varied by adding rings as the concentrated ore accumulates in the pan.

CONCENTRATION BY JIGGING.

The simple hand-sieve is the most ancient form of apparatus for sorting and concentrating ores in water by the direct fall of the particles, and it is still in use. Numerous modifications have been made from time to time, with the object of increasing the product by increasing the size of the sieve and supporting it in a frame, as in the hand-jig or brake-sieve, the construction of which is familiar, and by substituting machine power for that of the hand. Much attention has also been directed to the construction of automatic, or continuously working, jigs, by which the stuff to be washed enters in a constant stream, and, after being washed and concentrated, is delivered in two separate portions, without stopping or requiring manipulation.

In such machines the sieves, instead of being alternately plunged into and raised out of a vessel of water, are made stationary—are fixed firmly in a tub—and the water is made to alternately rise and fall, so as to pass

* The Prater concentrator was invented at Washoe in the year 1863, and patented December 5, 1864. Hendy added a self-discharging gate for the sulphurets in 1865, and a contrivance for tipping the pan to one side.

in a strong current through the meshes of the sieve and the layer of ore above it. This motion of the water is produced by means of plungers or pistons acting below the sieve, either vertically or horizontally, or by elastic diaphragms, (as in Petherick's separator at Fowey Consols, 1831,)* which are alternately pushed out and in, as, for example, also in Edwards and Beacher's patent mineral and coal-washing machine.

WIMMER'S CONTINUOUSLY-WORKING JIG.

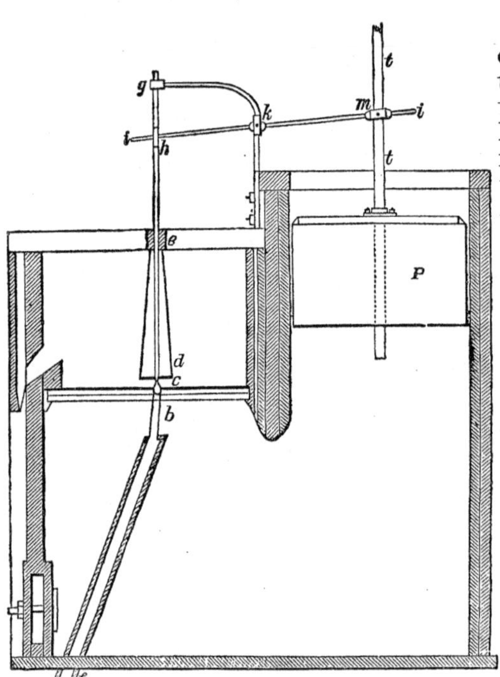

Wimmer's Continuously-working Jig.

One of the simplest forms of the piston jig is shown in the figure. It is made of wood with a piston or plunger P at one side, which, on being forced downward upon the water in the box, causes an upward flow through the grate in the direction *b* to *c*. The peculiarity of this construction, due to Mr. Vogel of Joachimsthal, and Mr. Wimmer of Clausthal, is a valve in the center of the sieve through which the concentrated stuff is delivered as it accumulates, while the refuse passes off over the partition in front. But it was found that the downward current of water when this valve was opened was sufficient to carry down some of the waste stuff from the top; and it became necessary to devise some means of preventing this flow. This was effected by covering the outlet with a conical tube, *d*, supported from a bar of wood above and reaching down through the layer of poor stuff so low that only the heavy and richer portions resting directly upon or near the sieve can pass downward into the discharge pipe *b f*. This pipe is alternately opened and closed at the top by an iron stopper placed at the end of a vertical rod the upper part of which slides through a supporting ring, *g*. By means of an arm, *i*, supported on a pivot at *k*, the stopper is alternately raised and lowered as the piston P rises and falls. The opening in the discharge pipe is thus opened when the piston descends, and is closed when it ascends.† It has been found in practice, however, that this arrangement for opening and closing the discharge pipe does not give satisfactory results.

A somewhat similar machine, in use in the Harz, is shown in section by the next figures. The outlet in the sieve is surrounded by a perforated cylinder *d*, so as to prevent the refuse from entering, while the ore escapes through the tube and is delivered at the side. From five to six

* Ure's Dictionary, supplement, p. 852.

† *Vide* La Préparation Mécanique des Minerais au Harz en 1857. Rapport par M. Aug. Gillon: Paris, 1858.

cubic metres of stamp stuff can be passed through this apparatus in twelve hours.

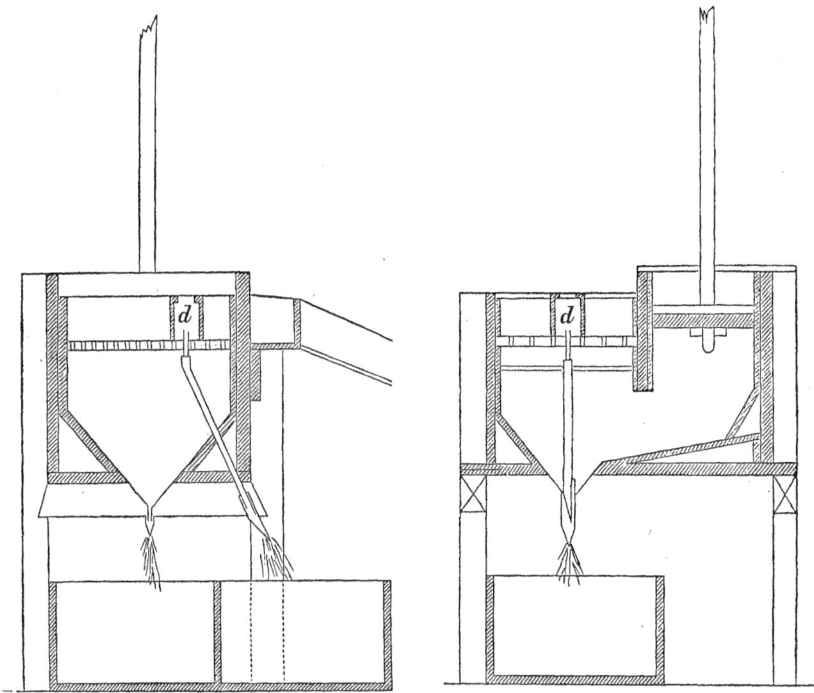

Self-discharging Jig—Harz.

RITTINGER'S SELF-ACTING JIG.

One of the best jigs of the continuously-working class is the invention of Rittinger, and was exhibited at the great Exposition in Paris in 1867.

It is represented in the annexed figure and is characterized by the inclination of the grates and the lowness of the front partition, over which the poor and lighter stuff falls continuously, and with very little water, while the heavier and richer portions fall through the opening or slit *o*, at the base of the partition. This partition is the segment of a cylinder, and is supported upon the lever or arm *d*, so as to be movable back

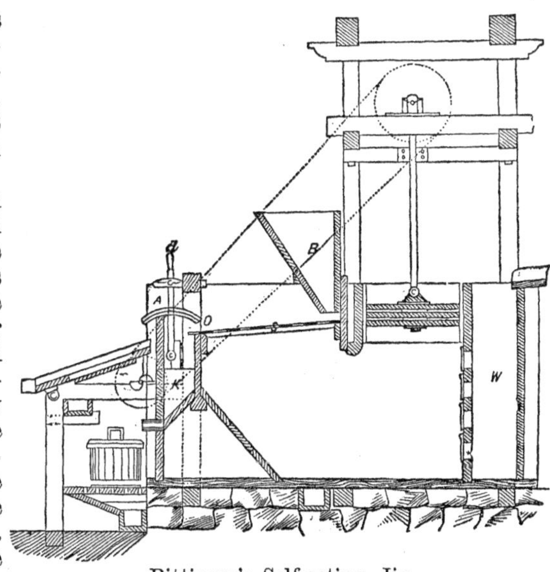

Rittinger's Self-acting Jig.

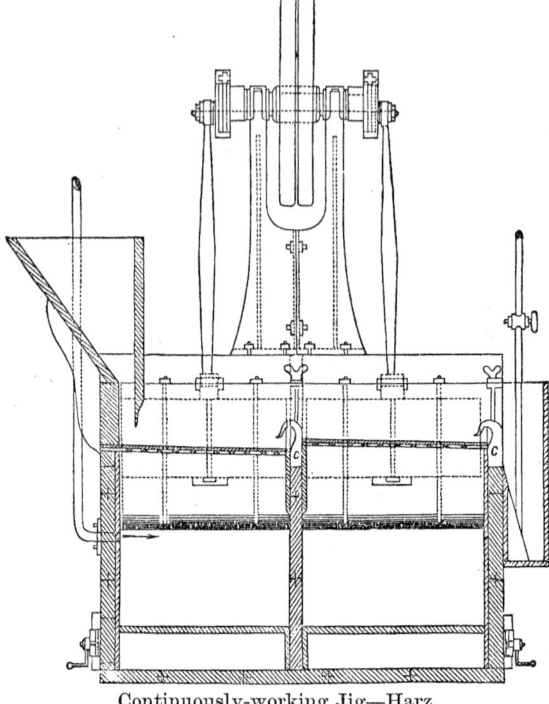

Continuously-working Jig—Harz.

and forth in such a manner that the opening or slit *o* may be increased or diminished at pleasure. The heavy stuff, passing through the opening, falls into the box K, from which it is removed as required. The inclination of the grate in this machine is from five to eight degrees. It is fed through the hopper B, which plunges below the surface of the stuff accumulated on the grate. The loss of water which occurs at each stroke of the piston is replaced from a reservoir, W, at the back of the apparatus. According to Rittinger, experience has shown that the duty of self-acting machines of this kind is generally three times as great as that from the ordinary intermittent working apparatus.

CONTINUOUSLY-WORKING JIG—HARZ.

In 1863 Mr. Geyer, an engineer from Baden, introduced continuously-working jigs into the great ore-dressing establishment erected by him on the banks of the Lahn. In the construction of these machines both wood and metal were employed. The arrangement of the parts is represented by the accompanying figures. It is a double machine, composed of two grates and two pistons, actuated simultaneously by means of cranks on a shaft above, the motion being communicated by two connecting rods. The grates are inclined forward, and are provided

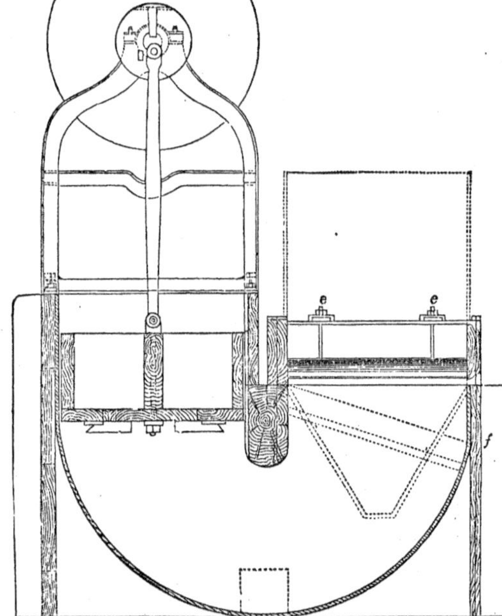

Continuously-working Jig—section through piston.

with a crevice or gutter at the lower edge, through which the concentrated ore falls into inclined troughs *c*. The stuff passes from one grate to another, and thus two different grades of fineness may be secured. Iron plates or partitions are placed so as to govern the discharge, and these may be raised or lowered at pleasure by the thumb-screws *e e*. These machines, worked at seventy strokes per minute, will wash about nine cubic metres of stamp stuff, diameter of $0^{m}.005$, in a day, and they require about 300 litres of water.

HUET AND GEYLER'S SELF-ACTING JIG.

Messrs. Huet & Geyler exhibited this form of jig at the Paris Exposition in 1867, and its satisfactory operation upon lead ore was witnessed by the writer. It is constructed of cast iron, and is very compact.

Most self-acting jigs require a large quantity of water, and this in many localities is a great objection to their use; but this jig is designed to work with but little loss of water, and, at the same time, by the aid of an automatic scraper, to increase the product.

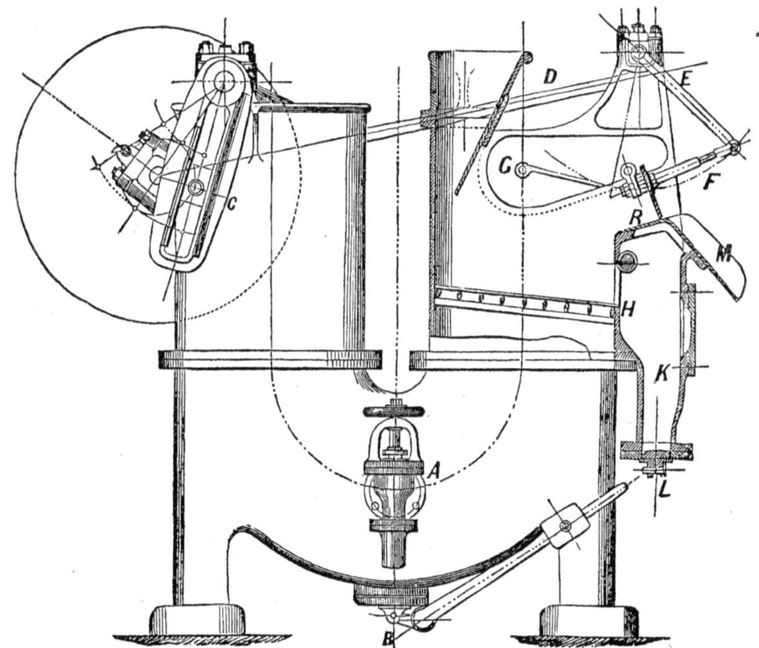

Automatic Jig of Huet & Geyler.

The tub is shaped like the letter U, and is divided into two compartments, one for the piston and the other for the working grate. Water is supplied through the valve A, at the side, and the fine stuff or slime which falls through the sieve settles upon the botton, and is discharged through an opening, B, controlled by a lever reaching out to the front of the apparatus. The piston is operated by means of a shaft and crank, which works in an inclined slide, C, connected with a lever carrying the piston, so as to give a rapid descending stroke with a period of rest at the bottom, and then a slow upward movement; thus giving the most favorable conditions for the rapid and perfect separation of the stuff upon the grate.

The motion of the piston may be varied at will, in order to secure the best flow or motion of the water for different grades of ore. This adjustment is effected by shifting the position of the head of the piston along the lever or arm, and by this means increasing or diminishing the amplitude of its motion. The construction of this slide is shown in the figure. By turning the fixed screw *s s*, the head of the piston may be moved forward or backward.

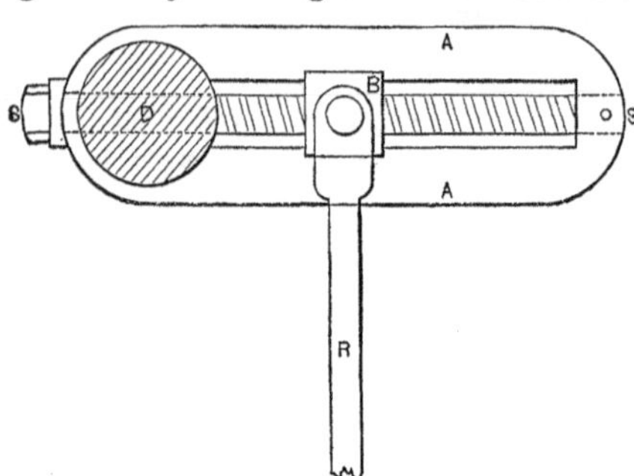

The machine is provided with a scraper R, actuated by the long rod D, which is attached to an eccentric on the main shaft and moves the levers E and F, giving to the scraper a forward and backward motion over the top of the stuff upon the grate, and throwing out a portion of it at each movement. The path of the scraper is determined by the guides G, attached to each side of the tub. It can be varied by means of screws upon the lever or arm F. In passing backward, the roller or projection on the scraper, which follows the guides, rises upon the movable inclined plane G, and on its return passes below this plane, following the double-dotted line in the figure. The poor stuff from the top, which is constantly thrown forward and off by this scraper, falls over the front of the tub at R, along the chute M. The grate is inclined as in the machine of Rittinger, and the opening for the escape of the heavier and rich portion is similarly placed at the foot of the incline and just below the bridge over which the poor stuff is scraped. The opening is shown at H. It is closed by a valve which extends along the whole front edge of the sieve, and can be opened and closed at pleasure by a lever. The stuff passing through this valve falls into a receptacle K, from which it may be removed at pleasure through the opening L. The scraper is so made of perforated sheet-iron that it does not throw the water out together with the waste. These jigs are made with great care and accuracy, and work in a satisfactory manner, as the writer assured himself by personal inspection of the machine in operation near the Champ de Mars, in 1867.

KROM'S DRY ORE CONCENTRATOR.

This machine may be called an *air jig*. Dry ore in powder or coarse grains is subjected to sudden puffs of air from below, through a grate, precisely as water is forced up through a grate in the pump jigs. In this machine the dry ore is supplied automatically upon a horizontal sieve, and the concentrated portion is discharged upon one side and the refuse upon another. It consists of a receiver, to hold the crushed ore; an ore-bed, on which the ore is acted upon; gates, to regulate the flow of ore from the receiver and the depth of ore on the ore-bed; bellows, to give the puffs of air; a trip-wheel and spring, to operate the bellows; and a ratchet-wheel and pawl, to operate the discharge roller. There are six projections on the trip-wheel, and therefore the moderate speed of 50 to 70 revolutions per minute of the trip-wheel shaft gives 300 to 400 movements to the bellows, and a corresponding number of puffs of air. This rapidity is a great advantage. The use of water in concentration admits only from 50 to 80 lifts per minute, while in air from 300 to 400 are obtained. This is due to the fact that bodies fall much more rapidly in air than in water.

The sieve or ore-bed is made of wire gauze tubes, placed from one-quarter to one-half of an inch apart, according to the kind or grade of ore to be treated. The concentrated ore settles down in openings between these tubes, and accumulates in a reservoir from which the discharge is regulated by a roller, so as to keep it filled and thus form a support for the upper layer of ore to be acted upon.

The experimental working of this machine is certainly very satisfactory; and it is claimed for it that it will accurately separate zinc-blende from galena—a severe test. The machine measures five feet by two feet, is three feet ten inches high, and weighs about 800 pounds.

SEPARATION OF ORES BY FALLING THROUGH A COLUMN OF WATER.

Various forms of apparatus have been devised to effect the separation of the grains of either coarse or fine stamp stuff having nearly the same volume, but differing in density, by allowing them to fall through a column of water either at rest or in motion. Such machines may be regarded as modifications of the jig; a greater length of fall of the materials in water being substituted for a succession of short falls, the result of the repeated shocks or jerks given to the sieve. Apparatus of this kind forms a connecting link between jigs and the slime separators.

These machines depend for their operation upon the difference in the time required for particles to fall through a given height of column of water, which, for particles of equal size, is in the order of their specific gravities. As the time required is modified by the bulk of the particles, a careful sizing is an essential prerequisite to the success of this form of concentrating apparatus.

One of the simplest forms is a stationary cylinder, designed by Messrs. Huet & Geyler, and exhibited at the Exposition in Paris, 1867. It consists of two stationary concentric cylinders, E and I, kept full of water by means of a supply pipe T, while a portion of the water escapes through the opening in the conical bottom C, and the excess overflows at G, around the top.

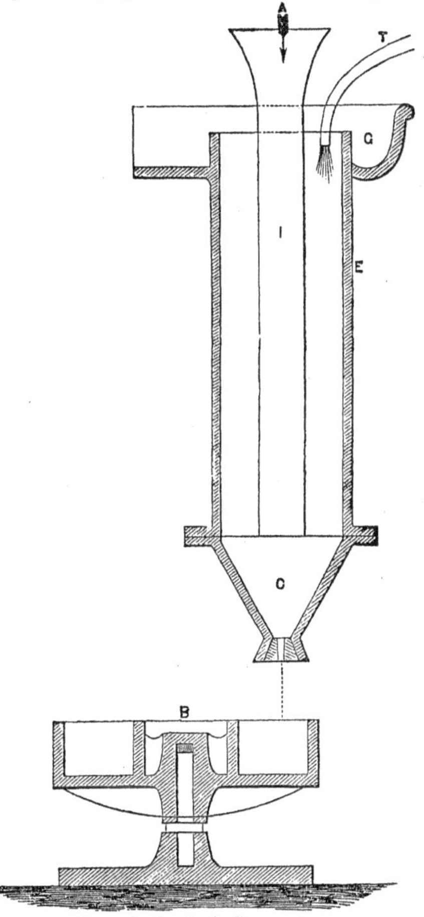

Huet & Geyler's Separator.

Directly below the aperture in

the bottom of this cylindrical vessel, a receiving tub B is placed, so as to receive the water and ore that fall through. This tub is divided into compartments and rotates around a central vertical axis. The stuff to be concentrated is supplied *at intervals* at the top of the cylinder I, at A, and falls in the direction of the arrow. In falling through the three feet of water, the particles separate according to their specific gravity, and the heaviest arrive first at the outlet and are caught in one of the compartments of B. As the next grade of ore reaches the outlet, the tub B has turned so as to bring another compartment under the orifice, and the stuff is thus classified. The revolution of B must be carefully timed to the rate of descent of the particles and the interval of the periodic changes.

The following tabular statement shows the time required for the fall of stamp stuff of different minerals, and of different diameters:

Size of the gravel in millimetres.		Galena, gravity 7.56.	Pyrites, gravity 4.60 to 5.00.	Barytes, gravity 4.50.	Blende, gravity 4.15.	Quartz, gravity 2.70.	Carbonate of lime, gravity 2.60.
From	to	*Seconds.*	*Seconds.*	*Seconds.*	*Seconds.*	*Seconds.*	*Seconds.*
30.00	18.00	0.90	....	....	....	2.36	....
18.00	7.00	1.11	....	....	....	3.67	....
7.00	5.50	1.50	....	....	....	4.61	....
5.50	4.44	1.84	....	....	....	6.10	....
4.44	4.17	2.03	2.54	2.81	2.88	7.27	3.86
3.94	3.67	2.48	3.43	3.73	4.61	7.61	5.56
2.77	2.50	3.11	4.41	5.55	6.53	....	6.83
1.77	1.50	4.14	6.21	8.30	9.78	....	10.17
	1.00	5.27	10.36	11.33	11.67	14.64	17.21

This table shows that the velocity of the receiving tub must be proportioned to the size of the particles of the stuff to be separated and to the height of the fall. For a height of $1^m.00$, the number of revolutions of the tub per minute must be, for particles of $0^m.016$ in diameter, 21 revolutions; $0^m.004$, 11 revolutions; $0^m.001$, 6 revolutions; $0^m.00025$, 2.7 revolutions.

This apparatus has not yet been long enough in practical operation to prove its value, and it requires to be studied and experimented with further before the results will be satisfactory, yet it has already been found that a thorough classification of the stuff is essential; that the feeding and the motion of the rotating tub must be regular; that the grains which separate best are those between $0^m.004$ and $0^m.01$ in diameter; and that with fine stuff the results are incomplete. When the particles are $0^m.014$ in diameter, and have a density of 3.15, they will precipitate from compartment to compartment, in the following order:

First compartment, density, 4.2; 7 per cent.
Second compartment, density, 3.2; 52 per cent.
Third compartment, density, 2.9; 24 per cent.
Fourth compartment, density, 2.9; 12 per cent.
Fifth compartment, density, 2.9; 3 per cent.
Sixth compartment, density, 2.8; 2 per cent.

For the particles of $0^m.014$ in diameter, the proper number of turns is three and a half, and for particles of $0^m.004$, five turns. One of these contrivances will deliver about 750 quarts of gravel per hour.

HUNDT'S SETTLING TUB.

Hundt's settling tub operates similarly, but differs in this, that the receiving tub is *fixed*, and the water column is made to rotate. The ore is not supplied in the center of a column of water, but into an annular or cylindrical column in a continuous stream, differing in this respect also from the first described apparatus. It is a continuous working machine, designed to separate or sort the particles according to their velocity of fall through the column of water. The particles of stuff entering this machine are subjected to two motions, the direct fall due to gravity, and the movement of translation due to the motion of the water. It follows that they take a diagonal course and reach the bottom at different distances from the point at which they entered the column.

This apparatus was first used at the Landerkrone mines, near Wilnsdorf, in 1854. It consists of a circular tub, within which an open cylinder is supported and made to revolve by a vertical shaft. This cylinder is partly closed by means of a cone, so adjusted that only an annular opening is left, 5 centimetres wide at the bottom, and 13 centimetres at the top. The outer tub is $1^{m}.75$ in diameter, and is 2 metres high. The inner cylinder is $1^{m}.60$ in diameter. Small partitions, *s s*, between the cone and the cylinder serve to carry the water filling the space around with the cone and cylinder during their rotation.

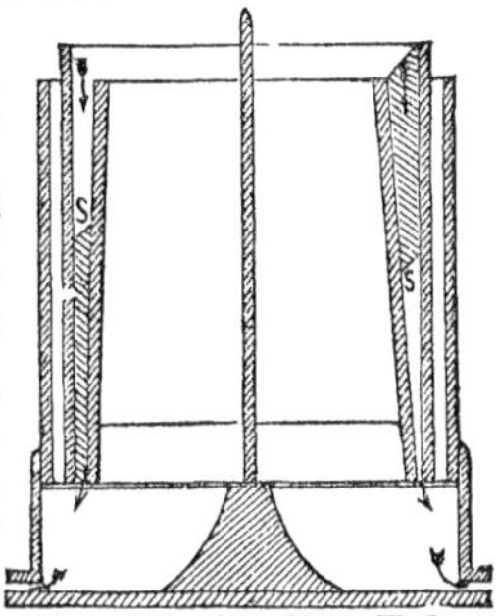

Hundt's Settling Tub.

The stuff to be treated is introduced in a continuous stream at the top, and in falling through this height of two metres of water, and being at the same time carried around by the revolution, is classified according to the rapidity of the fall of the particles. It may be withdrawn from the vessel by suitable openings around the bottom. By careful management of these openings, very little water is lost; and this economy of water, and the very small quantity required for the proper working of the apparatus, renders it especially worthy of the attention of mill-men and metallurgists, in such regions in New Mexico, Arizona, Nevada, and Sonora, where water is scarce. The number of revolutions of the drum should range between 2 and 6 per minute, the diameter being 4 feet, and the size of the grain from $\frac{1}{32}$ to $\frac{1}{2}$ of an inch. Used with ore-stuff particles of which differ in size, the machine sorts these particles according to their rate of fall. As the product in such a case would consist of small and dense particles mingled with larger ones of less specific gravity, the separation can readily be effected by the simple operation of sifting.

RITTINGER'S SETZ-RAD.

The apparatus of Rittinger is upon the same principle as Hundt's, and it is not clear which was suggestive of the other. It is a self-feeding continuous working machine, and consists of a stationary wooden tub *a a*, the bottom of which is divided into eight conical compartments connecting with pipes *c*, which, after descending for a short distance into the foundation, turn upward and outward, and are curved at the end so as to deliver the water from the tub into an annular trough *d*. A double cylinder, *f f*, supported by a shaft, *g*, is made to turn in the tub *a*. The stuff to be separated is delivered in a constant stream through the hopper and distributor *k* into the revolving cylinder, and falling through the water in this space is sorted and collected in the conical reservoirs and tubes *b*. A branch tube, closed by valves *s s*, permits the removal of this concentrated stuff from time to time. The waste stuff, delivered through the tubes *b* into the annular trough *d*, flows into another trough or conduit *m*, whence it is lifted by the wheel *n*, and returned to the tub *a*.

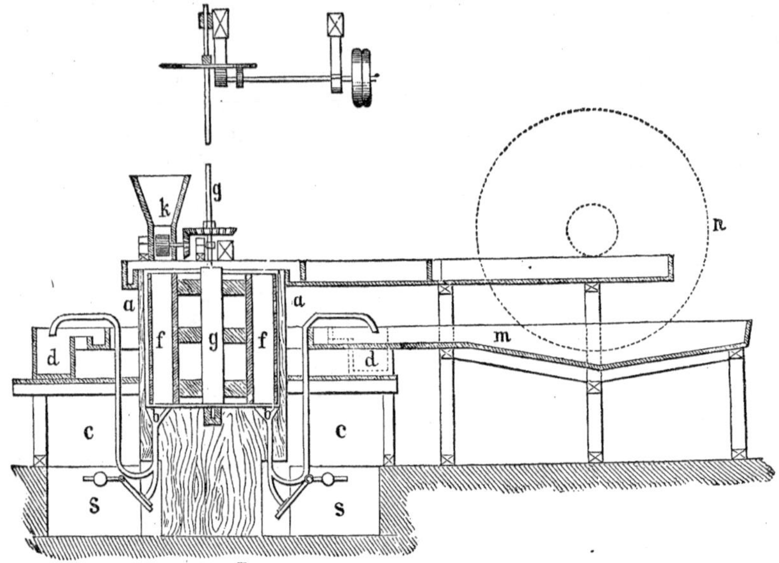

Settling apparatus of Mr. de Rittinger.

Rittinger in his *Aufbereitung* describes a machine of similar construction, in which the stuff is not received into an annular column of water, but into an ordinary tub in which the water is made to revolve by a wing-wheel, the wings of which would correspond in position to the sections of the cylinder *ff* in the last figure. The bottom is divided into eight radial compartments ending in funnel-like cavities, as shown. With grains of lead ore $\frac{5}{32}$ of an inch in diameter, 91 per cent. of all the lead-ore contained in the stuff will be delivered into the second compartment at the bottom, and 8 per cent. in the next. But with grains $\frac{2}{32}$ of an inch in diameter, only 75 per cent. will be found in the second, and 20 per cent. in the third compartment.

SLIME SEPARATORS AND SORTING BOXES.

A convenient and effective form of the cone apparatus is here shown on a scale of $\frac{1}{25}$, the upper cone in section. A complete series is usually composed of five or six, arranged in succession, one below another, as shown. The construction is very simple; and they can be made of cast-iron, so as to be very durable, and at the same time exact in form. Each part consists of two cones, one inserted in the other, so as to leave an annular space in which water flows upward from a reservoir or chamber at the lower, or pointed end. The stuff to be concentrated is conveyed by a launder into the upper cone, and, passing through holes, encounters the upward current. The largest of the stuff so fed should not exceed three-quarters of a millimetre in diameter. The lighter portions are at once carried upward and over the upper edge of the inner cone, and fall with the escape-water into an annular trough, by which they are conducted away to the next lower cone, while the particles of sufficient weight to resist the current fall through it, and accumulate in a small

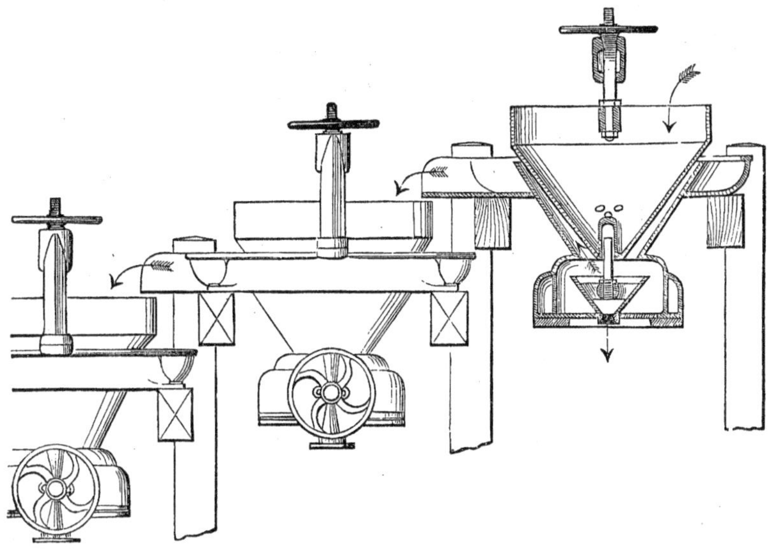

Conical Separators.

inverted cone, in the chamber below, from which they are allowed to drop by the small aperture at the apex in the direction indicated by the arrow. This orifice is controlled by a valve, and can be regulated at will, according to the rapidity of the accumulation. So, also, by means of a screw above the upper cone, the distance between the cones can be regulated according to the necessities of each case. The apparatus requires considerable water, and the overflow from one cone is carried to the next, and so on in succession.

RITTINGER'S SEPARATING TUBS WITH ASCENDING CURRENTS.

This is another modification of the conical tubs or pointed boxes, but the shape is rectangular, and the water current is not confined to a narrow zone or space between partitions. This form consists of a succession of deep trough-like depressions placed edge to edge, and gradually increasing in size and depth. But as the ends and sides are the highest, the series forms, in reality, but one vessel, the water covering all of the intermediate edges, and thus permitting a continuous flow from one end to the other. This will be seen from the inspection of the figure. Seven compartments, B B, are shown, and the direction of the flow from C to W is indicated. The whole series is supported upon a frame at such a height that the attendant can pass under it, and reach the openings at the apex of the pyramidal tubs, at A A, where the concentrated stuff flows out. A supply-pipe, P P, delivers clear water into each compartment through a branch pipe reaching nearly to the bottom. The stuff entering at C deposits the heaviest particles, and, aided by the ascending flow of water from the pipe, the lighter portions pass over into the next tub, and so on. The flow of water into each compartment must be carefully regulated. As the size of the compartments increases, the ascending current has less and less force, and finally only the very lightest and poorest portions are carried away.

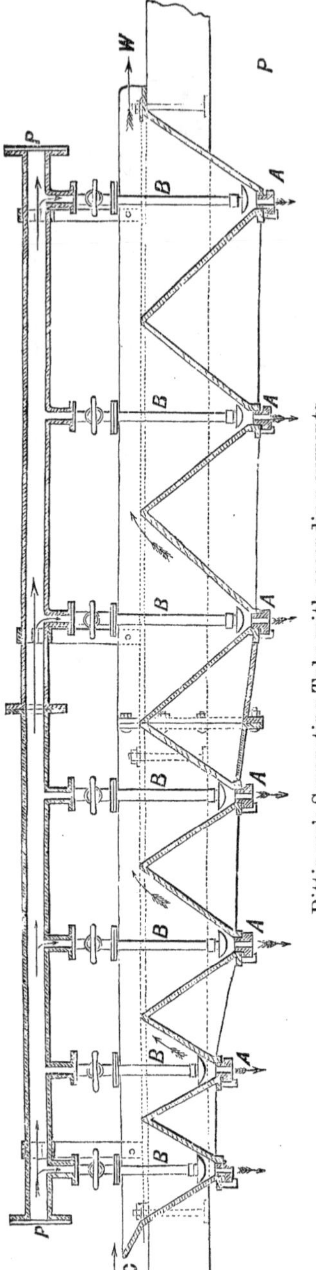

Rittinger's Separating Tubs with ascending currents.

The arrangement gives very satisfactory results. It requires from 120 to 150 quarts of water a minute, and will separate about a ton of battery pulp in each hour. It may be constructed either of wood or of iron. The apparatus shown in the figure is made of iron.

RITTINGER'S CONTINUOUSLY-WORKING STOSSHEERD.

This is another and important machine for concentrating by the flow of the stuff over a plane inclined surface. It has, in addition, a percussive shock, given laterally at right angles to the flow, and not parallel with it, as in many of the inclined tables, and, for example, in Hunter's concentrator.

It consists of a wooden table or platform, about eight feet long and four wide, suspended at the four corners, and inclined forward so that water and fine stuff poured upon the upper part will flow evenly down to the front edge. A lateral throw and percussion is given to the whole table by means of cams, *c*, upon a shaft at the side, and the reacting wooden spring S upon the opposite side of the table. Two tables are usually combined in one, and they are separated by a narrow strip of wood extending the whole length; similar strips are placed on each side of the table, and serve to keep the water and stuff from flowing off. The stuff to be washed is delivered upon the tables at the upper left-hand corner, at A. The distributors P P P furnish clear water. While the table is at rest, the tendency of the stuff is to flow down the slope in a direct line from A to A′. By means of the lateral percussion, however, the path of the heavier particles is changed, and they are gradually thrown from left to right, along the surface of the table, at right angles to the direction of the current of clear water. This current tends at the same time to sweep the particles downward, and it acts upon the light sterile matters more rapidly than upon the heavy ore. The result is, that the heavier and richer particles are gradually separated from the poor stuff and describe the path upon the table indicated by the dotted lines. By the time the particles have reached the foot of the table, the richest portions have been transferred to the corner of the table diagonally opposite to that upon which the stuff entered, and they flow off into the compartment E. The "middlings" are dropped into the next compartment D, and the poor falls into C.

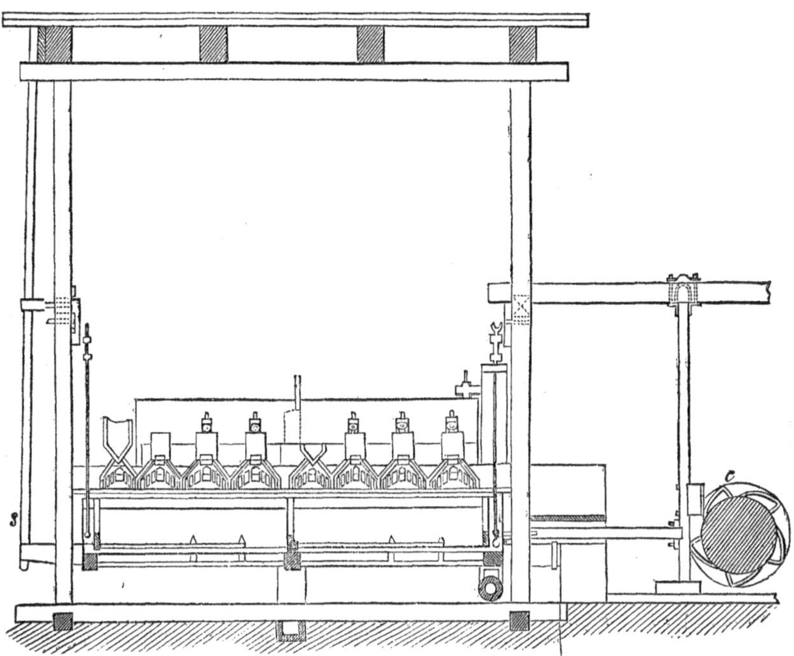

Rittinger's Continuously-working Stossheerd—front view.

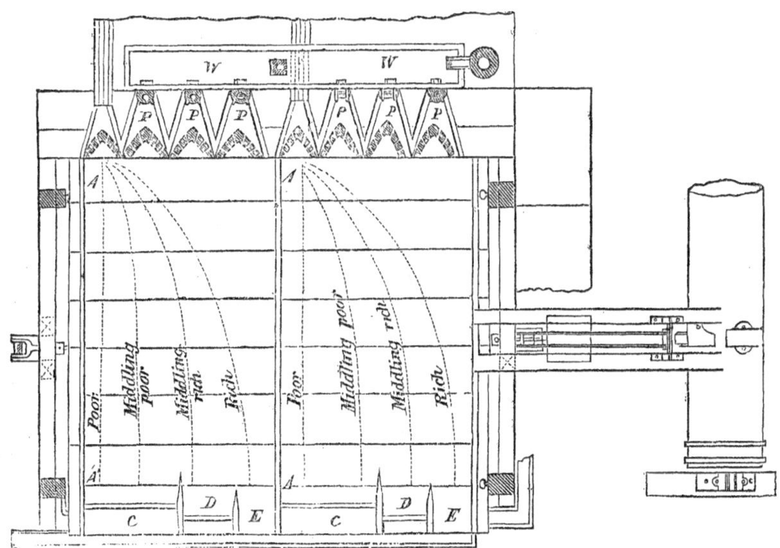

Rittinger's Continuously-working Stossheerd—view from above.

In order that good results may be obtained with this apparatus, the following conditions must be observed:

1. The surface of the table must be very smooth.

2. The length must be about $2^m.50$, and the width from $1^m.25$ to $1^m.50$. The width of space over which the stuff is delivered must be from $0^m.20$ to $0^m.30$.

3. The inclination of the table must be in direct ratio to the size of the stuff to be washed. For sand, it requires to be about six degrees, and for fine powders about three degrees.

4. The amount of clear water to be admitted at the top of the table, and to be spread over a width of from $0^m.30$ to $0^m.35$, will be nearly constant. For sand, about six quarts a minute is necessary; and for dust, or fine stuff, from three to three and a half quarts. If the slope of the table is diminished, and the size of the stuff remains the same, the quantity of water should be increased. It is necessary to distribute this supply of water quite near to the stuff to be washed, so as to facilitate the separation of the light and poor stuff from the rich.

5. The number of shocks per minute should be, for sand, from 70 to 80; for dust, 90 to 100; for poor and fine slime and dust it is sometimes advantageous to carry the number of shocks or jerks as high as 120, and sometimes 140 per minute.

6. The tension of the spring is equal to 100 or 112 kilogrammes. The amount of movement necessary to produce the requisite vibrations is, for sand, $0^m.065$; and for dust, $0^m.020$ to $0^m.013$.

7. The velocity of the current upon the table should be from $0^m.25$ to $0^m.15$ per second, according to the nature of the stuff.

8. The greatest regularity must be observed in the number of jerks or shocks; in the quantity of stuff admitted upon the table, including water; in the nature of the stuff to be treated; in the slope of the table, which must be diminished as the stuff to be washed grows poorer and lighter. Careful attention to all these points is essential to success.

The apparatus gives three products. The mixed or middlings can be passed over the table a second time. Stuff of which the particles are $0^m.004$ in diameter can be treated as successfully as the finest slime. It saves much labor. One man can attend two twin-tables. The power required for ten twin-tables is about one-quarter of one horse-power.

ROTATING BUDDLES.

Two forms of rotating buddles were shown at the Exposition by Messrs. Huet & Geyler, one being concave and the other convex, and both

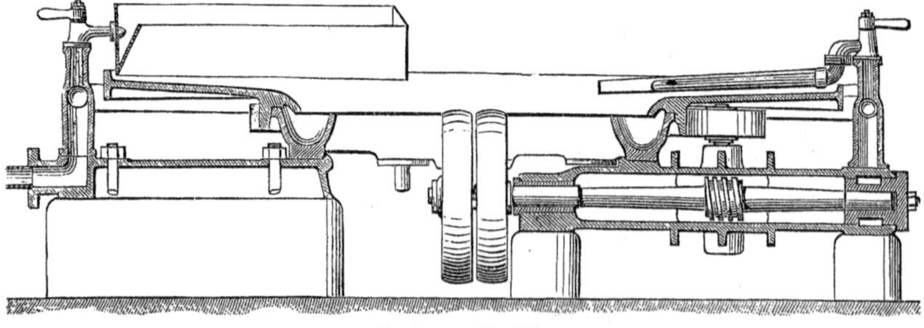

Concave Buddle.

made entirely of iron and accurately finished. The construction of the concave buddle is shown by the figure. The stuff to be crushed is supplied at the circumference of the circular or annular table, and is discharged into different compartments at the centre.

The foundation plate sustains the distributing pipe, the water pipe, the waste gutter, and the driving shaft. An endless screw upon this shaft gives motion to the concave table. Experience in using this buddle has shown that it is desirable to have a greater number of sprinkling pipes than are generally used in the Harz. It is said that the washing of the stuff is completed in one operation, while with the German construction it sometimes happens that the stuff must be passed twice over the machine to obtain an equal result.

The convex buddle is also an annular table, but instead of sloping inward toward the center, it slopes from the center outward, being the reverse of the concave buddle. The stuff is supplied on the inner margin and flows outward to the lower edge, and is delivered into a succession of annular troughs.

The construction is similar to that of the concave buddle. A cast-iron frame supports the table, the driving shaft, the water pipes, and all the fixtures. The tangent screw and the driving shaft work in a hollow case of cast-iron.

ARRANGEMENT OF A COMPLETE SILVER MILL.

In conclusion I present, by an engraving annexed, a general view of the construction and arrangement of the parts of a complete dry-crushing silver mill, as constructed January, 1870. It hardly needs explanation. The ore received at the highest point falls from one machine to another, and is handled as little as possible. It passes from the dump pile under the car *a* to the rock breaker *b*; thence over a sheet-iron drying platform at *e* to the feed-box *d*. After stamping it is roasted in the furnace *g*, and is worked in successive charges in the pan *i*, from which it is drawn off into the settler *j*, and finally passes through the concentrator K. The amalgam is retorted in a cast-iron retort set in a small furnace outside the building.

www.ingramcontent.com/pod-product-compliance
Lightning Source LLC
LaVergne TN
LVHW010250110826
845151LV00004B/1438

* 9 7 8 1 4 2 5 5 2 2 8 4 1 *